CRIMINAL JUSTICE

CRIMINAL JUSTICE

A New Zealand Introduction

Edited by Jarrod Gilbert and Greg Newbold

AUCKLAND
UNIVERSITY
PRESS

First published 2017

Auckland University Press
University of Auckland
Private Bag 92019
Auckland 1142
New Zealand
www.press.auckland.ac.nz

ISBN 978 1 86940 876 3

© Jarrod Gilbert and Greg Newbold

A catalogue record for this book is available
from the National Library of New Zealand

This book is copyright. Apart from fair dealing for the purpose of private
study, research, criticism or review, as permitted under the Copyright Act,
no part may be reproduced by any process without prior permission of
the publisher. The moral rights of the author have been asserted.

Book design by Katrina Duncan
Cover design by Gideon Keith

Printed by 1010 Printing International Ltd

Contents

Introduction *Jarrod Gilbert and Greg Newbold*   1

Origins and History   3

CHAPTER 1 Explaining Crime through the Ages *Trevor Bradley*   5
CHAPTER 2 Crime Rates *Greg Newbold*   46
CHAPTER 3 The History of Policing *Heather Wolffram*   70
CHAPTER 4 Contemporary Policing *John Price, Mike Webb and Simone Bull*   91
CHAPTER 5 Corrections *Greg Newbold*   115

Current Practice   139

CHAPTER 6 Evidence and Human Rights *Chris Gallavin*   141
CHAPTER 7 Where Cases Are Tried, and How *Jeremy Finn*   163
CHAPTER 8 Sentencing *Debra Wilson*   183

Key Issues   207

CHAPTER 9 Psychology and Criminal Justice *Randolph C. Grace, Anthony McLean and Sarah Beggs Christofferson*   209
CHAPTER 10 Māori and Justice *Sacha McMeeking*   225
CHAPTER 11 Youth Justice *Andrew Becroft and Sacha Norrie*   250
CHAPTER 12 Justice and Injustice *Jarrod Gilbert*   279
CHAPTER 13 Crime and News Media *Tara Ross and David Fisher*   296
CHAPTER 14 Gangs and Underworld Justice *Jarrod Gilbert*   316

Contributors   331
Index   335

Introduction

The New Zealand criminal justice system is made up of a number of complex and important pillars that support the principles of Western democratic societies. In many ways, the health of these societies depends upon the smooth and systematic functioning of judicial procedures, and this is as true in New Zealand as anywhere around the globe.

The contributors to this book have sought to introduce the key ideas, principles and frameworks that define criminal justice in New Zealand. Although many of the issues are complex and challenging, we have striven to create an interesting, readable book which will be useful to students and practitioners alike.

Criminal Justice: A New Zealand Introduction provides answers to many of the questions that people frequently find confusing about the way the justice system functions, such as: How can crime be explained? Is crime rising or falling and if so, why? How do the police operate? How do the courts work? What is the meaning of a 'life' sentence? What is the link between crime and mental instability? Why are Māori over-represented in the criminal justice system? How do we deal with youth offenders? How do judicial miscarriages arise? Do the stories we read about crime in the media reflect reality? How does justice operate in the criminal underworld?

We have aimed to produce a book that will not only serve as a key resource for students, but will also be of value to practitioners in the criminal justice field, as well as others interested in the area. In particular we are thinking of members of the public who seek greater understanding of issues that may seem familiar but are at the same time unclear, and to students of legal studies in the nation's secondary schools.

With that in mind, a number of experts in relevant areas around New Zealand were invited to offer chapters. Contributors to the book include not only a

INTRODUCTION

number of professorial leaders and national experts in fields like corrections, policing, gangs, court procedure and sentencing, but also non-academic experts such as Canterbury District Police Commander John Price, National Manager of the New Zealand Police's Assurance Group Mike Webb, Principal Adviser to the New Zealand Police Executive Simone Bull, Chief Youth Court Judge Andrew Becroft, criminal and youth lawyer Sacha Norrie, and award-winning journalist David Fisher. The result is a collection of fourteen chapters written by eighteen contributors with recognised expertise in specialised fields, covering a range of topics which will be of critical interest to those in the criminal justice domain.

Jarrod Gilbert and Greg Newbold
June 2017

Origins and History

This first section of the book has a focus on history. Trevor Bradley begins with a historical look at criminological theory from its onset in ancient Greece, following its development up to the current day. Greg Newbold then describes rises and falls in crime rates that have occurred over the last five decades and interrogates the many reasons for the changes. The subject of policing is dealt with in two chapters, with Heather Wolffram focusing on the origins and development of formal policing and John Price, Mike Webb and Simone Bull describing the organisation and practice of policing in modern times. Finally, Greg Newbold outlines how various forms of correctional sanction have evolved in New Zealand, and what the current system looks like.

1.

Explaining Crime through the Ages

TREVOR BRADLEY

Introduction

Explaining the causes of crime is often thought to be a uniquely modern endeavour. It's a perception often encouraged by introductory-style books that claim the first real theories of crime appeared in the eighteenth century. The standard narrative, then, has it that crime theory progressed in the nineteenth century in tandem with science and scientific ways of thinking.

However, while the earliest *criminological* theories were developed in the late eighteenth century, attempts to explain crime can, in fact, be traced to antiquity. Ancient Greek philosophers had something to say about crime and how it should be punished. Indeed, some of those antiquarian ideas, like those on deterrence, continue to inform criminal justice today. The essential questions of modern criminology – what crime is, why people commit crime, and what our response should be – have been asked for more than two millennia. Attempts to explain crime, in other words, are almost as old as crime itself.

While there is disagreement about the precise chronology, there is near universal agreement that theories of crime are informed by the wider social, political and/or cultural contexts. Viewed from this perspective, New Zealand's especially punitive approach to law and order and our 'exploding' prison population (*Dominion Post*, 18 February 2016), is best understood as an ongoing legacy of political promises to 'get tough' on crime (Pratt and Clark, 2005). Just as our responses to crime change with the times so too do our explanations of it. Crime, then, has been explained in very different ways at different points in history. As Vold, Bernard and Snipes (1998: 3) suggest, the history of crime theory may tell us more about the changing values of politics and society than it does about improved knowledge of crime.

This chapter outlines the attempts to explain crime and criminality across the ages. After a brief introduction to the nature of theory, the chapter traverses five chronological periods. First, the explanations prevalent in Ancient Greece are outlined, the earliest to have survived in written form. Next we move to the Middle Ages and the dominant theological perspective. The first recognisably modern theory of crime, the late eighteenth-century school of Classicism known contemporarily as 'rational choice', is considered next. This is followed by a survey of the positivist criminology of the nineteenth and twentieth centuries with its focus on biological, psychological and later sociological causes. Finally, we arrive at the contemporary era and those theories that have developed since challenges to positivist criminology first emerged. The radical theories of the 1960s and 1970s are outlined before a range of more recently developed critical perspectives on crime and criminality are presented.

What Is Theory?

According to Akers and Sellers (2004: 1–2), theory has an undeserved reputation, being often regarded as fanciful and bearing little connection to the real world; an attitude summed up by 'that's all very well in theory, but what about the facts?' If properly developed, however, theory *is* all about the real world, real situations and real human experiences and behaviour (Akers and Sellers, 2004). Such theory can help us make sense of the facts and therefore we should not be intimidated by it. After all, most of us theorise about crime on a daily basis and instinctively react to lurid accounts of crime with our own explanations. If young people are involved, some theorise that parents are to blame for not raising their children the 'right way' or for not adequately controlling them. Such ideas may be more common sense than criminology, but they provide a base from which more sophisticated theories develop.

At its most basic level, theory tries to explain the things we observe or experience. William and McShane (1988: 2) define theories as 'generalisations . . . they help explain how two or more events or factors are related to each other'. A theory of crime tries to explain how and why a certain thing or things are related to criminal behaviour. As Bohm (2001: 1–2) points out, theories proposed by biological positivists assume that crime is caused by biological things like neurological disorders. A recently proposed biological explanation for the apparent drop in violent crime over the past decade suggests that before paint and petrol became lead-free, some adolescents affected by high doses developed a disposition for aggression and violence (see Monbiot, 2013). Lead poisoning and its deleterious effects is the 'thing' that explains crime in this theory (see Nevin, 2007). Still other theories assume that crime is explained by psychological things (abnormal personalities), sociological things (economic strain) or some combination of all of these. Critical or radical theories, in contrast, question the very meaning of crime and how the label 'criminal' is conferred, and seek to illustrate how crime is not merely an act but also a reflection of a political process. Finally, theory refers to the relationships between actual events and attempts to explain *what is* or *what will be* rather than answering questions about *what should* or *ought to be*.

Crime and Criminality in Ancient Greece: Crime as Vice

Arrigo and Williams (2006: 5) argue that the earliest attempts to understand crime are weaved into Plato's general moral philosophy. Plato explained crime in two main ways: as a form of ignorance and as a form of psychological conflict. Both assumed that a hallmark of criminality was a flawed or deficient character. In that sense not much has changed! In the first explanation, 'ignorance' doesn't refer to ignorance of the law but ignorance of, and an inability to distinguish between, just and unjust, moral and immoral. Those with knowledge, or wisdom, could make this distinction and were regarded as virtuous. Those that couldn't were regarded as vicious and in a state of vice. For the ancient Greeks, virtue and morality were complementary, while vice equalled immorality. Crime was therefore regarded as a form of immoral behaviour.

Plato argued that the virtuous have knowledge of what is right, good and just. Being in possession of this knowledge means virtuous people will *necessarily* pursue what is right, good and just. Herein lies Plato's first explanation: all people aim at that which they think is good but some are *mistaken* about what is actually good and therefore exist in a state of ignorance and vice. All failure is due to a mistake and the only reliable road to a good and happy life is through knowledge.

For Plato, 'if a man fails, it is because he is ignorant; and if he is ignorant he is bound to fail. Failure, therefore, is always a matter of mistake' (McKenzie, 1981: 137). Plato transforms 'no-one fails willingly' into 'all wicked men are, in all respects, unwillingly wicked' (Arrigo and Williams, 2006: 5). Accordingly, if criminals were able to understand the unjust nature of their crimes, they would abstain and lead good lives.

In his second explanation Plato draws a connection between vice (crime) and the appetitive or desiring part of the soul. He speculated the soul (or psyche) consisted of three parts or aspects: reason, or the rational part; the spirited, or hot-blooded, part; and the appetitive part. Plato tell us the three parts of the vicious soul exist in a state of conflict. The criminal is thus affected by what might today be described as a psychological disorder. Just as knowledge is essential for virtue and happiness, order among the three aspects is equally essential. In the virtuous person (non-criminal) the rational part of the soul controls the desiring part and all three parts are in harmony. In the vicious soul (criminal) the rational part has 'lost mastery' and our appetites or desires become so 'inflated' they can 'compel vile action' (McKenzie, 1981: 174). In other words, the disordered soul is overcome by uncontrollable appetites and there is no mastery over those vicious impulses that lead to crime.

Because criminals are unwillingly wicked, they are pitied though not excused from punishment. In arguing for humane punishment, Plato suggested three forms and justifications. The first, *restitution*, involved offenders righting their wrongs by compensating the victim. In the second, *reform*, punishment acts as a psychic health service that when combined with moral education can rid patients (criminals) of their moral disease. Punishment is thus a form of therapy for the soul equipping criminals to exert control over vicious impulses. Some criminals were, however, beyond reform. Thus the third form of punishment, *deterrence*, was applied to those regarded as incurable. For these, the only 'humane' option was execution or exile; those beyond reform had to be eliminated. This benefited others in society by *deterring* them from crime and by removing a potentially evil influence. Clearly, while execution will deter, it's not quite what later deterrence theorists had in mind.

While Greek philosophy developed sophisticated explanations, its ideals were rarely matched in reality. In contrast to therapy for the soul, serious offenders could face a 'bloodless crucifixion' in which they were slowly strangled to death. Moreover, while some of their ideas, like deterrence, seem familiar today, they are historically specific and need to be understood in the context of that particular time and place. And, as Arrigo and Williams (2006) suggest, the historically specific nature of crime theory is particularly apparent in the dramatic changes that characterised Europe during the Middle Ages.

Crime as Sin: Explaining Crime and Criminality in the Middle Ages

Between the end of antiquity and the arrival of modern age, supernatural explanations reigned supreme. The dominance of theology was a defining feature of this period and should be understood in the context of the overwhelming influence of spiritual forces on all cultural and political life (Schild, 1981: 31). Crime was thus caused by a supernatural force that compelled harm against others, against the natural order and against God himself. Crime was a transgression against God and equated with sin (Vold, Bernard and Snipes, 1998: 4).

Humans were conceived as engaged in spiritual warfare and the earth as a battleground occupied by the competing forces of good and evil. When one succumbed to evil the result was criminal and other deviant behaviour and was explained as the outcome of either temptation or demonic possession (Pfohl, 1994: 22–24). While these represent different, though related, causes, both imply that the devil lurked behind every criminal act. Adam and Eve provide the original temptation template. Seduced by the promise of Godlike knowledge, they ate the forbidden fruit. After being cast out from the Garden of Eden, their original sin rendered them forever weakened and vulnerable to the forces of evil. When faced with temptation humans are afforded some choice and can, in theory, reject the devil's overtures. However, because we inherited the weakness and susceptibility of the original sinners, only the truly faithful have the resolve to resist. The evil (crime) to which humans are susceptible took various forms but typically included the seven deadly sins of sloth, anger, lust, pride, envy, gluttony and greed (Solomon, 2001). Crime, then, occurred because our appetites for worldly pleasures were 'enticed by the devil' and were sufficiently powerful to overcome our God-given conscience and will to resist (Einstadter and Henry, 2006: 37). Following Barnes and Teeters (1943: 2), 'the criminal was a man [sic] who succumbed to diabolical temptation'.

The second process, demonic possession, was clearly more deterministic because a possessed person has been literally invaded or taken over. Possession is thus involuntary. Some notable exceptions, however, include witches and warlocks who, because of their *desire* to do evil, actively pursued a pact with the devil. Whatever the source, procedures were required to identify evil's presence, remove it, determine guilt or innocence and punish the wrongdoer (Pfhol, 1994). 'Trial by ordeal' is the most familiar of these processes of identification, diagnosis and punishment, and was, in effect, trial by torture. The first stage was to determine if the crime indicated the devil's work. It was overseen by diviners, witch-finders and other experts able to detect the presence of evil and effect its removal (Einstadter and Henry, 2006). If the devil's work was discovered, this was followed by the ordeal itself and the infliction of various agonies.

Common ordeals included trial by fire during which the accused was forced to hold a red-hot iron bar, walk over red-hot coals or lick a red-hot iron with the tongue. If no burns appeared, or if after three days there was evidence of healing, then the accused was declared innocent. If not, he or she was hanged. Often the reaction of the accused to the agonising pain was interpreted as a sign of guilt or innocence. It was assumed the guilty would eventually cry out whereas the innocent, fortified by God, would endure their pain in silence (Pfohl, 1994). There were also various devices used to elicit confessions. These included the rack, upon which the body was stretched until 'the bones and joints were plucked asunder' (Pfohl, 1994: 25). Another was the 'Scavenger's Daughter', which instead of stretching, crushed the body of the accused until the pressure was such that blood squirted from the nostrils and finger tips (Hibbert, 1963).

Finally, there were various 'sacred punishments' that served an apotropaic function, which means they were designed to ward off evil. Perhaps the most infamous was 'breaking on the wheel', where each major bone was fractured in order to break the evil spirit's hold on the body (Einstadter and Henry, 2006). In another example, it was not until relatively modern times that hanged criminals were cut down and buried because of fears their inner demons might 'seep into the earth and endanger its fertility' (Pfohl 1994: 30).

In cases of demonic possession, exorcisms were employed to purge offenders. While evil could never be completely eradicated, it could be chased out. If exorcism failed, the possessed person would be executed by state authorities. Death was not intended to punish the possessed but to frustrate the devil and remove his earthly medium (Masters and Robinson, 1990: 54). Witches, on the other hand, were almost always burned because it was both a method of total destruction and represented the image of hell as the 'final resting place for unpurged sinners' (Einstadter and Henry, 2006: 41). The principle of *lex talionis* – 'an eye for an eye, a tooth for a tooth' – provided yet another religious justification for the physical mutilation of offenders: thieves could lose their hands, rapists their genitals and traitors their hearts.

In today's largely secularised world such explanations are rejected as simple superstition. However, given what Gray (2016: 7) calls the 'fading belief' in politics combined with a 'renascent religion' that contends with 'faith in science', it would be foolish to write off this perspective entirely. In the United States, a 2013 YouGuv poll found that 57 per cent of respondents still believed in the devil. While fewer New Zealanders hold such beliefs, a 2011 survey of over 2000 people found that 35 per cent agreed with the statement 'I am a spiritual person interested in the supernatural' (Vaccarino, Kavan and Gendall, 2011: 1). Similarly, while the Scavenger's Daughter is obviously unacceptable in today's world, other medieval practices are still evident. In April 2016 an Auckland nurse complained to police about a bizarre 'community exorcism' during which a pastor repeatedly punched her face to exorcise her demons. The exorcism was led by a pastor advertised as a 'Prophet of God able to deliver people from spiritual attacks and demons'. The pastor claimed that all but three of a crowd of 40 were possessed. At least twenty were punched but most didn't complain to police because they believed they were being healed (*New Zealand Herald*, 20 April 2016).

Demonology provided the dominant explanation for crime for a thousand years and formed the basis of European criminal justice policies. Claiming to be acting in the name of God gave both Church and state the moral authority to inflict agonising tortures (Vold, Bernard and Snipes, 1998: 14). However, Enlightenment thinkers provided a successful alternative to this perspective. At the same time, there were also growing demands for political reform and an end to the arbitrary, oppressive power of the Church and aristocracy. One significant outcome was the emergence of the first modern theory of crime and justice, namely Classicism.

Classicism and the Rise of Modern Criminology: Crime as Rational Choice

Associated with the work of Enlightenment philosophers Cesare Beccaria and Jeremy Bentham, Classicism is an eighteenth-century school of thought that revolves around due process, the social contract, free will, proportionality and deterrence. Classicists were more concerned with a fair and rational justice system than with understanding the causes of crime *per se* and focused on the act, not the actor, and on the law and process of justice.

Criminal justice, to the extent it existed in the late 1700s, was notable for its exceptional severity and barbaric punishments. In late sixteenth-century Britain, 50 separate offences carried the death penalty. By the early 1800s this had risen to 225 (McLynn, 2013). Capital offences included murder and highway robbery but also sheep stealing, cutting down trees and thefts worth more than 5 shillings. An illustration of the irrationality of the system was that while pickpocketing was a capital crime, child-stealing was not defined as an offence, despite its high incidence (McLynn, 2013: xiii). Less serious crimes were met with corporal punishments: whipping, lopping off ears and branding foreheads and cheeks (Sharp, 2001). For obvious reasons the system was known as the 'bloody code'.

Depending on the offence, and the offender's status, the mode of death was typically hanging or beheading, and in extreme cases quartering and burning. Beheading was reserved for higher-status individuals because of its 'nobility'. Hanging was thought more appropriate for those, like the poor, that were 'held in disdain' (Newman, 1978: 35). The more serious the offence, the more bizarre and barbarous the execution. Regardless of its mode, punishment was always a public spectacle. A 1757 *Gazette d'Amsterdam* report of a traitor's execution is re-presented by Foucault (1977: 3–5) as an especially horrific example:

> the flesh will be torn from his breasts, arms, thighs and calves with red-hot pincers ... and, on those places where the flesh will be torn away, poured molten lead, boiling oil, burning resin, wax and sulphur ... and then his body drawn and quartered by four horses and his limbs and body consumed by fire.

Criminal trials were accompanied by much pomp and theatricality. They were a symbolic display of the power, majesty and authority of judges. The importance of symbolism meant justice had to be seen to be done, hence there was no secrecy and cases were always heard in public. No exemptions were made for children or the insane and even animals were occasionally prosecuted. Beirne (1994) recounts the story of how a French sow was tried and convicted of killing a child, dressed in human clothes and hanged in the town square. The rhetoric proclaimed that all were subject to the law but it was the poor that made up the vast majority of defendants (Hay, 1975).

The system inherited by Classicism was grossly inefficient and plagued by corruption. During public executions riots frequently erupted when, if sympathetic to the prisoner, the crowd 'shape-shifted into the mob' (Arnold, 2012: 99). Public executions were often more macabre carnival than sombre display and often attracted huge crowds (Laquer, 1989: 307–8). It's estimated that celebrity executions, like that of the notorious English jail-breaker Jack Sheppard, could be attended by over 100,000 (Arnold, 2012).

Classicism emerged as a protest against such irrational practices and in response to a series of momentous social, political and intellectual changes. These helped sow the seeds of Classicism and informed many of its key features. They included significant increases in Europe's population; the rise of the modern nation-state and an improved law-making and enforcement capacity; and the development of capitalism and the early phases of the industrial revolution. The most important intellectual inspiration, however, was the Enlightenment. Characterised by the motto *desiderium ad cognitionis*, loosely translated as 'the desire to know' (see Nowotny, 2016: 2), this was the great age of ideas. Enlightenment thinkers emphasised individual rights, the primacy of human reason, and the importance of the social contract. From this point on, individuals were seen as rational and hedonistic creatures capable of freely choosing between right and wrong. The prevailing system of justice, then, simply didn't fit the new intellectual and cultural environment (Bradley and Walters, 2001: 83–84).

In 1764 Cesare Beccaria campaigned for a legal and justice system that was rational, certain, swift and effective. In reaction to the barbarity of punishment its central concept was that *the punishment should fit the crime*. This 'fit' between crime and punishment is known as the principle of proportionality. Over the centuries it has become almost cliché, but in the 1800s this idea was a radical departure from prevailing thought. Beccaria's highly influential book *An Essay on Crimes and Punishments* (1764) presented a series of reform propositions. It argued that everyone can commit crime so the law must be applicable to everyone regardless of wealth or status. There should be as little law as possible and it should be clear, simple and impartial. Laws should be published to educate the public. In reaction to the unpredictability and corruption created by judicial discretion, Beccaria insisted that the law should be fixed and certain and that a predictable and consistent due process be introduced.

Classicism also advocated for legal and political reforms to protect the rights of individuals. It proposed a system based on the idea of a free and legal contract between free and equal individuals. At that time contracts were a practical necessity. Contracting was the method by which people hired labour, sold goods and acquired property, all of which were becoming dominant features of the nascent capitalist economy. Beccaria argued for a similar method to bind together society's diverse interests. Drawing on the work of English philosopher Thomas

Hobbes, Beccaria's preferred method was a social contract that represented those values considered beneficial to the common good. This contract is an imaginary agreement entered into by freely consenting adults, supported and enforced by the nation-state. For Classicists, the social contract was necessary to avoid what Hobbes described as a 'war of all against all'. Thus it was rational for individuals to sacrifice a degree of freedom to the state in order to enjoy a much greater freedom from threats to life and property. We all have a contract with society about things we must do, like pay tax, and things that we must not do, like kill one another. For the common good we're all bound or 'contracted' to obey the law.

Free will is another fundamental concept in Classicism. Every individual was regarded as rational, free-thinking and governed by self-interest. Because everyone was equal before the law, everyone had an equal social and legal responsibility. People who committed crime did so out of a rational and calculated choice. For Classicists, then, it was this ability to choose, based upon a calculation of costs and benefits, that caused crime. Offenders weighed up the chances of detection and likely punishment against rewards and then chose to commit or refrain from crime (Bradley and Walters, 2011).

The belief in rationality and free will lay behind the creation of a just and equally rational legal system. If individuals were to make informed decisions (Walklate, 1998), they must first have reliable information about those costs and benefits. The unpredictability of the system meant it was not possible to make informed and calculated choices, which brings us to the final key feature of Classicism: deterrence (Burke, 2009). Beccaria maintained that it is better to prevent crime than punish it, that inflicting punishment as retribution is irrational and that punishment should serve a more logical and productive end. If it is to achieve the goal of deterrence, punishment must fit the crime: too severe and it's unjust; too lenient and it won't supply a disincentive. There can be no defence to criminality because all have consented to a binding social contract. Crime is thus regarded as a deliberate and wilful deviation. Deterrence theory is focused on individual offenders and wider society. Individual, or specific, deterrence is achieved via punishments that are proportionate to the harm caused but sufficiently severe to deter further offending. General deterrence uses punishment as an example to society by sending a message to those who have not offended (Akers and Sellers, 2004). If punishment is to achieve its deterrent effect, then, it must be certain and predictable, proportionate, and be delivered swiftly. Offenders must know what to expect and to learn the desired lesson they must psychologically associate their sentence with their offending.

From the early 1800s, Classicism's key principles were slowly adopted. The number of capital offences was reduced and corporal punishments were replaced by proportionate prison sentences (McLynn, 2013: xxi). Judicial discretion was significantly curtailed through introducing a consistent and predictable due process and the use of uniform punishments based on a fixed scale of seriousness. All offenders were regarded as essentially the same and similar offences received similar penalties without regard to the individuals or the circumstances involved (Vold, Bernard and Snipes, 1998). Ultimately, the era of the bloody code gave way to the era of the penal code.

However, the practical application of the penal code soon revealed its weaknesses (Pfohl, 1994). The uniformity of punishment attracted criticism for its rigidity and the inflexibility. Critics pointed out that no exceptions were made for those with impaired rationality. Mitigating factors were also ignored, as were the differences between first-timers and recidivists, and between spontaneous and premeditated offenders. Given the differences between offenders, the issue of who should be held responsible, and to what degree, became a major problem (Bradley and Walters, 2011).

Other problems became apparent when analyses of French crime statistics for 1827 showed that in contrast to expectations, crime was going up, not down. More distressing still, recidivism was also increasing. This suggested that Beccaria was mistaken in thinking that changes to process and punishment alone could prevent and deter crime. Classicism was judged to have gone too far in creating an objective, impersonal and predictable system; a system so blind to the differences between people and cases that it simply couldn't deliver justice in a world where people were not identical. If offenders received prompt, proportionate sentences following a fair and consistent process but continued to offend, then perhaps factors other than free will were involved? Perhaps criminals are somehow different to non-criminals and, compared to the law-abiding, are deficient in some way?

In response, a series of modifications known as the 'Neo-classical compromise' was introduced (Burke, 2009). Exceptions were made to the notion of 'equally rational, equally responsible' and included children and the feeble-minded. In Britain the 1843 murder case of Daniel McNaughtan successfully introduced the insanity defence and the issue of guilty intent, or *mens rea*. Recognition of mitigating circumstances, like provocation, reduced the degree of responsibility and it was recognised that similar punishments could have very different effects on different people (Burke, 2009). Much more attention thus began to be paid to the actor and the often significant differences between offenders and their circumstances. Neo-classicism presented a more flexible framework while creating the necessary space for scientific theories that argued criminals *were* different to non-criminals and that different offenders were affected by different causes. Neo-classicism laid the foundations for a full-blown positivist perspective.

The Appliance of Science: Criminological Positivism and the Search for Causes

When criminological positivism appeared in the late 1800s the industrial revolution had generated new forms of mass production (the factory system) and a more powerful source of energy (steam). Industrial production extended to agriculture and while it increased efficiency it also stripped entire villages of secure employment. Agricultural workers migrated to the cities and a huge growth of urban populations was accompanied by a growth in anonymity. The presence of large numbers of urban poor and unemployed in London and Paris intensified existing social problems, including crime. There was no welfare system for the poor and unemployed and in 1800 it was estimated that 30,000 Parisians relied on robbery as their only income. Twenty years later it was estimated there were 20,000 professional criminals and 120,000 'rogues' in the city (Chevalier, 1973). Concentrations of urban poor and the emergence of the working class in early nineteenth-century Britain were accompanied not only by rises in crime, but also by major industrial and political conflicts. This, in turn, led to growing governmental concern about these dangerous classes and the threat they posed to law and order. It was assumed that crime and revolution were symptoms of the same disease (Beirne and Messerschmidt, 2006).

This was also a time of profound scientific discovery. The evolutionary biologist Charles Darwin's *On the Origin of Species* (1859) was especially important and marked the end of pre-scientific thinking about the causes of behaviour. Such questions became the preserve of science, first in biology, then psychology and later sociology (Burke, 2009). Darwin showed that humans are not a species distinct from the animal world and are equally subject to the laws of nature that govern all behaviour. The theory of evolution led to claims that certain individuals are less evolved, which proved to be especially important for biological positivism. As a contributor to scientific progress, the medical profession supplied another source for understanding behaviour. This period also witnessed the development of the social sciences and their adoption of the scientific method. Auguste Comte, known as the inventor of sociology, argued that only scientific methods can produce reliable knowledge about human behaviour and society. Into the nineteenth century, then, science was well established as the 'language of intellectual life' (Jones, 2016: 4).

Criminological positivism offers a fundamentally different approach to explaining crime. The early positivists lauded their own scientific methods while caricaturing the unscientific philosophising of Classicism. They rejected the 'foolishness of free-will' (Rafter, 1997: 112), arguing instead that crime is determined, hence the doctrine of determinism. Positivism's fundamental truth was that individuals are driven by forces beyond their control (Barnes and Teeters, 1943: 174). Whereas Classicism is referred to as the 'rational actor model', criminological positivism is referred to as the 'predestined actor model'. Positivism thus focuses on the actor and not the act and insists that punishment must *fit the criminal*, not the crime. Because criminality is determined, treatment designed to reform, rehabilitate or cure was emphasised over punishment and tailored for individual needs. It was informed by the logic that if crime is determined by factors beyond our control, then could punishment really have any effect?

Biological Positivism

Biological theories of crime assume that criminals are physically different from non-criminals and criminality became associated in particular with abnormality, defectiveness or inferiority. Cesare Lombroso (1835–1909), often referred to as the father of modern criminology, performed autopsies on 66 criminals and claimed to have detected similarities between their skulls and those of primitive humans. He also compared the physical features of male and female criminals, soldiers and lunatics. The results were published in his book *The Criminal Man* (1876), in which he stated: 'I seemed to see all of a sudden . . . the problem of the nature of the criminal . . . an atavistic being who reproduces the instincts of primitive humanity. . . . Characteristics found in savages . . . are also to be found in habitual criminals' (cited in Beirne and Messerschmidt, 2006: 2).

Lombroso also discovered other common criminal stigmata including prognathous jaws, abnormal teeth, long arms and enormous brow ridges (Bradley and Walters, 2011). Criminals, he concluded, could be identified on the basis of these physical stigmata. Lombroso, then, was the first to discover the secret of criminality in the biological make-up of individuals. This born criminal was an atavist, a genetic throwback to an earlier stage of human evolution. Because such physical features are passed down through the generations, Lombroso's was the first theory based on heredity (see Burke, 2009).

Lombroso's work has often been lampooned for its naiveté and lack of scientific credibility. Nevertheless, it left an important legacy and inspired a broad range of other biological explanations. In 1913 the English medical officer Charles Goring published *The English Convict*. His comparison of inmates, undergraduates and patients found no differences between these groups across 37 different physical traits used for comparison. He concluded that Lombroso was wrong; there was no such thing as a physical criminal type (Bohm, 2001). While Goring's findings dampened enthusiasm for Lombrosian theories, they did support two of his major themes: the idea of degeneracy and the inheritance of criminality. Goring argued that criminals are born with a mental inferiority that had disposed them to crime (Vold, Bernard and Snipes, 1998: 42–44). Criminals are not merely different, then, but also biologically deficient, abnormal or inferior (Beirne and Messerschmidt, 2006).

My Body Made Me Do It: Body Types and Criminality

Lombroso's essential ideas next found expression in the theory of somatotypes or body shapes. The notional link between body shape and criminality was developed by German psychiatrist Ernst Kretschmer in the 1920s, but it was American psychologist William Sheldon (1949) who gave new life to the idea that body structure could be associated with crime. Sheldon identified three distinct body shapes – *endomorphic* (soft, round), *mesomorphic* (muscular, athletic) and *ectomorphic* (skinny, fragile) – and associated each with a particular personality. Mesomorphs were said to be more active and assertive while ectomorphs were introverted and timid. Unsurprisingly, Sheldon categorised most offenders as mesomorphic. Similar research by Glueck and Glueck (1956) and Cortes and Gatti (1972: 345) came to a similar conclusion.

Ultimately, rigorous, peer-reviewed assessments, including the Cambridge Study in Delinquent Development (1961–81), found no evidence that offenders are physically different to non-offenders. This did not, however, deter researchers like Raine et al. (2000) who have argued that three year olds who are taller than their peers are more likely to become bullies. This in turn has led to the ambitious suggestion that such children have a higher chance of becoming violent criminals. Despite contrary evidence, the belief that appearance reveals inner character is still prevalent in some circles.

My Genes Made Me Do It: XYY and the Super Males

A biological explanation that maintained the idea of inherited criminality is based on genetic and chromosomal abnormalities. The normal chromosomal pattern for men is XY; for females it is XX. Thus it is the Y chromosome that confers maleness upon a developing embryo. However, in the mid-1960s, Patricia Jacobs's study of male patients in a Scottish psychiatric hospital discovered an extra male chromosome in some of them. This XYY pattern, with its extra dose of maleness, was soon labelled the 'super male syndrome' and was linked with abnormal inclinations toward violence (Bohm, 2011). Later inmate testing in a hospital for the criminally insane found that just 3 per cent were XYY. The super male syndrome nonetheless captured the popular imagination and this breakthrough led to a 1970 meta-analysis of all existing research. It found just one in every 1500 to 3000 males is XYY and no evidence linking it to higher rates of violence. The only physical characteristic consistently linked to XYY is above-average height (Burke, 2009).

Twin studies supply another, more sophisticated method of assessing the association between genetic inheritance and crime. Being the product of a single egg, the heredity of identical twins is the same. Logically, then, if there's a greater similarity of behaviour between identical than fraternal twins, this must be due to genetic inheritance. A significant problem common to all genetic theories, however, is the difficulty in separating out environmental and genetic influences. Identical twins spend more time together, are treated alike and can share a sense of mutual identity. These are environmental and not genetic influences. While empirical research has indeed revealed differences between the criminality of identical as opposed to fraternal twins, the difficulty is separating out the role of genetics from that of the environment remains (Bohm, 2001: 36).

Contemporary research on crime and genetics adopts a less deterministic position (Ainsworth, 2000). What is inherited is not the tendency to commit crime *per se* but inheritance of certain personality traits, like aggression or impulsivity. More generally, criminologists interested in genetics now suggest it's the combination of, and interaction between, genetic inheritance and the environment that is most important. Hence, contemporary bio-social theories suggest it's possible that genetic make-up may provide predispositions but that these become manifest only when triggered by the environment. Thus some argue that poor heredity may simply magnify the problems created by poor social circumstances. The notion of and search for bad or criminal genes has been largely abandoned today and the bio-social paradigm proposes that biological, psychological and sociological characteristics interact together to produce criminal behaviour. More generally, suggestions that genetics play a direct role is problematic because crime is comprised of such a huge variety of different behaviours, the only shared characteristic being legal prohibition (Newburn, 2013: 136–7). Moreover, if genes are a primary cause of crime then why do so many of us simply grow out of it, and why do crime rates rise and fall?

My Brain Made Me Do It: Dysfunction and Neurotransmitters

A range of other biological explanations, offspring of the genetic inheritance and faulty genes theses, are variations on the theme of abnormal brain function. Focused on young people in particular, one such controversial idea is 'minimal brain dysfunction'. Associated with genetic predispositions and neurological immaturity, it's commonly referred to as attention deficit hyperactivity disorder (ADHD), a syndrome characterised by impulsivity, hyperactivity and inattentiveness. Around half of those presenting with ADHD are also likely to experience learning difficulties like dyslexia and the associated frustrations can lead to disruptive, aggressive and even violent behaviour. According to New Zealand's ADHD Association, ADHD affects around 3–5 per cent of all children, has roughly equal gender distribution, and its incidence is largely the same across all countries and ethnicities. Counter-intuitively, ADHD is typically treated with highly stimulant drugs like Ritalin and dexamphetamine. Ironically, Ritalin generates its own crime problems and exists on the black market as a cheap substitute for methamphetamine. A 2008 independent study of drug use in Christchurch found that for 6 per cent of survey respondents, Ritalin was the drug of choice (Wilkins, Sweetsur and Girling, 2008: 20). This may simply reflect significant increases in supply. In 2013, 144,000 prescriptions for ADHD medication were issued, an increase of 47 per cent since 2005 and a 10 per cent increase since 2012 (Edmunds, 2014).

A more recent manifestation of the abnormal or faulty brain thesis suggests that an under-/over-supply of the neurotransmitters serotonin and dopamine may be linked with crime. Neurotransmitters are biochemical messengers that, because of their association with mood changes and levels of arousal, can play a role in criminality. Research also suggests that biochemical activity changes with age and this may help explain changes in criminal offending over the life-course. Under normal circumstances these chemicals are in equilibrium but when this is disturbed it can lead to unpredictable and aggressive behaviour (Wortley, 2011: 74–75). One needs to be aware, however, that the influence of neurotransmitters is often significantly affected by other external factors such as consumption of alcohol or other drugs, and by diet and nutrition (Marsh, 2006). Questions have also been raised about how aggression, violence or the ambiguous anti-social behaviour is measured, and whether such measures are used consistently (Marsh, 2006).

Psychological Positivism: Searching for Causes in the Mind and Personality

There are parallels in the respective histories of criminology and psychology on the one hand and of biological and psychological positivism on the other. Both originated in the nineteenth century and both rapidly expanded in the twentieth century (McGuire, 2004: 19). Psychological explanations also emerged in the spaces opened up by Neo-classicism and the new-found focus on the actor (Bradley and Walters, 2001). The introduction of intelligence and other mental tests at the turn of the twentieth century fixed attention on the specific mental aspects of criminal behaviour and thus began studies in and explorations of the criminal mind (Newburn, 2011: 864). In contrast to biological positivism, psychological positivism involves the scientific study of mental processes and behaviour (Wortley, 2011). While determinism played a role in the early perspectives, more recent theories have rejected the hard determinist tradition by incorporating elements of choice (Shoemaker, 2005: 51). In contrast to the biological perspectives, then, according to psychological positivism criminals are largely made and not born. Moreover, contemporary psychological approaches pay considerable attention to the social and environmental context of crime. As McGuire (2004: 15) points out, 'most current theorising . . . adopts a broader psycho-social orientation'. Nonetheless, it is the individual who has the problem and so it is the individual that is the focus of analysis and intervention.

Much of psychological positivism developed within criminal justice institutions where researchers had ready access to offenders (Garland, 1988). Psychology was also heavily influenced by the medical profession, and as knowledge of physical disease grew, so too did knowledge of mental disease. The medical influence encouraged a view of criminality as a symptom of individual pathology or sickness. If offenders are sick, the solution is to diagnose the condition and devise appropriate treatments (White and Haines, 2004). Various perspectives are grouped under psychological positivism including those focused on low intelligence quotient (IQ) and mental deficiency, childhood development, behavioural and learning theories, and personality and cognition (Hunter and Danztker, 2012: 98). More recently, psychology had also made important contributions to our understanding of evolution, genetics and neuroscience (Durrant, 2013).

Learning to Be Criminal

Behavioural or learning theories propose that all behaviour, including criminal behaviour, is learned (Hunter and Danztker, 2012: 97). Behavioural theory is one of the few approaches that does not suggest there are inherent differences between criminals and non-criminals and is one 'that places the environment at the centre of analysis' (Wortley, 2011: 161). Indeed, environmental influences and the process of learning criminal behaviour also inform Sutherland's differential association theory, a sociological perspective discussed later in the chapter. The behavioural approach suggests that as we develop and interact with others we learn how to behave in different ways. Hence, behavioural or learning theories examine the learning processes that lead to crime and the environmental stimuli that shape behaviour. As Wortley (2011: 139) points out, for behaviourists there is nothing special about crime, it is just another behaviour that must be learned. One prominent and contemporary example is social learning theory. Developed in the 1970s from a combination of behaviourism and cognitive psychology, it is comprised of three core concepts. First, many of the things that humans do are learned. Second, learning occurs in a social context. The third concept highlights the complex nature of our brain; the basis of our consciousness and perceptions, understanding and imagination. These processes are known as cognition or simply as thinking. Social learning theory, then, maintains that we learn cognitively through observing the behaviour of models (Wortley, 2011).

To Be a Criminal You Have to Think Like One

Cognitive theories, in contrast, examine how thought processes affect one's behaviour (Hunter and Danztker, 2012: 98). An early example is Yochelson and Samenow's 1976 work on the criminal personality, which claims to have identified the thinking patterns of all criminals (cited in Blackburn, 1994). At its core is the suggestion that criminals share flawed ways of thinking. Where most people make rational choices, criminal personalities are characterised by thinking errors (Putwain and Sammons, 2002). Criminal behaviour, then, is the result of poor and ineffective thinking styles that are at odds with social conventions and laws. Criminal thinking patterns are characterised by lack of empathy, poor perspective on time, a perception of self as victim and a general steadfastness in beliefs. In short, some criminals see nothing wrong with their behaviour and often fail to understand the consequences of their actions. Criminals have internalised different ways of thinking about the world and fail to understand why their behaviour is unacceptable (see Newburn, 2013).

Historically, the relationship between criminology and psychology has, at times, been openly antagonistic. McGuire (2004) suggests this is partly due to a perception of psychology's over-emphasis on individualised explanations and of being overly deterministic. Since the 1980s and 1990s, however, there has been a 'return to cordiality' (Hollin, 2007: 43–47), in part because contemporary psychological approaches seek understanding of the ways in which social and environmental factors influence crime. It is to those social explanations, or sociological positivism, that we now turn.

Sociological Positivism: Society Made Me Do It

Where individual positivism argues that explanations for crime are located within the individual, sociological positivism stresses the importance of external factors. Both are concerned with identifying the causes of crime but sociological positivism searches for causes in society and in social or environmental conditions. While the notions of deficiency or abnormality are retained, the emphasis is on social pathologies, deficiencies or abnormalities. However, both individual and sociological positivists agree that crime and criminality are largely determined by causes beyond our control and reject Classicism's emphasis on free will (Bradley and Walters, 2001).

Sociological positivism is an extremely diverse collection of theories which date from the early nineteenth century but rose to particular prominence following World War II (White and Haines, 2004). Until the arrival of Neo-liberalism in the late 1970s, with its critiques of big government, welfarism and intention to roll back the state (Kelsey, 1995), sociological positivism provided the main intellectual framework for crime prevention (Garland, 2001). Its origins lie with the aforementioned French philosopher Auguste Comte, who rejected the metaphysical philosophy of the Classicists and embraced instead an approach based on experience, observation and objective facts (Swingewood, 1991). When it first emerged, sociology was conceptualised as a kind of social physics or social mechanics. Comte regarded sociology as the last science to develop but also the most complex and significant. A generation later Emile Durkheim (1964) carried Comte's interest in the collection and analysis of social facts into the twentieth century.

Anomie and Crime: The Collective Conscious Rules

Emile Durkheim, a French sociologist writing in the late nineteenth and twentieth centuries, supplied important and original insights that anchored many later sociological theories. He analysed how order could be restored in France as it transitioned from a pre-industrial society to a more complex modern one. The issue of method was particularly important and Durkheim believed only the scientific method could be relied upon. Following in the footsteps of Comte (Swingewood, 1991), Durkheim searched for law-like regularities in social behaviour (Bierne and Messerschmidt, 2006), what he termed 'social facts' and what Comte before him had termed 'social physics'. Durkheim argued that society has its own unique reality and was more than the sum of its individual parts. Crime was a social fact, a feature and product of society, and Durkheim therefore rejected suggestions that crime could be explained via individual biology or psychology (Bohm, 2001). Moreover, because crime exists in all societies it's both a normal and an inevitable feature; indeed, a society without crime would be abnormal. As crime is a normal social component, Durkheim argued that it also serves a positive social function. It encourages innovation in the way society responds by marking the boundaries of public toleration and morality, indicating what is and is not acceptable. New forms of criminal or deviant behaviour force consideration of these important questions and generate a collective understanding about what we wish to defend. Crime, in other words, reveals the collective sentiments of society precisely by offending them. For Durkheim, an action doesn't shock the common conscience because it's criminal, it's criminal because it shocks the common conscience. Moreover, as an expression of individual freedom, and as a necessary and desirable precursor of social change, crime helps society to evolve. Durkheim (1933: 81) reminds us that many of today's heroes and history-makers – such as Socrates and the heretics of the Middle Ages – who paved the way for the ideas of the future were defined as criminals in their time.

For Durkheim, then, crime is a normal fact of society and as such its existence needs no explanation. However, when crime rates are fluctuating crime can no longer be regarded as normal but becomes instead pathological because it indicates social disorder. Such a society becomes characterised by anomie, or normlessness, and anomic conditions. According to Durkheim, crime results from anomie, which is the product of rapid social change or transformation due to urbanisation, industrialisation, war or financial crisis (Newburn, 2013). Everyone aspires to certain goals in life but if these cannot be reached or become confused because of such changes then individuals may reach a state of anomie in which nobody knows the rules. Similarly, society places limits upon the goals and aspirations of its members but in anomic conditions society can no longer impose or maintain these limits: the members of society can no longer be regulated and integrated via the collective conscience (Burke, 2009). Furthermore, through a process of excessive individualism people become so self-centred and egoistic they no longer care about the welfare of the collective. Anomie, in other words, undermines social control and as the norms that bind society lose their force, individuals adapt in their own sometimes deviant or criminal ways. A society beset by anomie, then, 'lacks the regulatory constraints necessary for the adequate social control of its members' (Pfhol, 1994: 253).

Merton's Anomie: Blocked Opportunities Made Me Do It

An adapted version of Durkheim's anomie was developed in the 1940s by Harvard University sociologist Robert King Merton. Like Durkheim, Merton sought a sociological explanation of crime to counter the still dominant individualised positivist explanations. According to Marsh (2006: 101), Merton argued that crime 'came from individuals or groups of people responding in an expected and normal manner to the social situation they found themselves in'. Where Durkheim focused on the destructive effects of social and economic change,

Merton focused on what he saw as the contradiction between the great American dream of financial success and the available opportunities to realise that success. Merton identified, in other words, a major disparity between this widely held cultural goal, which continues today as the hallmark of consumer culture, and the social structure through which it could be achieved (Bradley and Walters, 2011).

For so many people, acquiring financial success represents the ultimate achievement, particularly in the developed world. Monbiot (2016: 10) cites a recent survey of British children that found very few aspired to be train drivers or nurses while over a fifth said they 'just wanted to be rich'. Wealth and fame was the sole ambition of 40 per cent of those surveyed. Merton's primary insight was that the means, or the structures, for achieving success – the labour market and education system – are not equally accessible to all. His strain theory is thus often referred to as 'blocked opportunities' and argues that individuals adapt to the strain of this experience in various ways. Among these, conformity refers to people playing by the rules and chasing legitimate success. Retreatism refers to people dropping out of the race including alcoholics, drug users, or other outcasts or outsiders. Innovation, however, is the adaptation at the root of crime and, having been blocked from achieving legitimately, innovators pursue dominant cultural goals by illegitimate means. In adapting to their circumstances, those who cannot envision legitimate success strain or deviate from accepted behaviour and try to achieve success illegally through force or fraud (Einstadter and Henry, 2006: 164–6).

Anomie Modified: Doomed to Fail

Merton's theory inspired a range of later modifications including Albert Cohen's (1955: 13) work on sub-cultures. Writing in the 1950s, Cohen suggested that much youth crime was non-utilitarian in nature and when young people aren't involved in criminal behaviour 'just for the hell of it', they are searching for status rather than material success. For Cohen, Merton's use of the term culture implied a dominant culture. Cohen suggested that if there is a dominant culture, then by implication there must be others, which he termed sub-cultures. Cohen focused on juvenile gangs and sought understanding on why they exist and why some but not other juveniles joined them. He argued that sub-cultures, like gangs, exist because they provide solutions to problems of adjustment among the working class, a product of the difficulties experienced in measuring up to dominant middle-class standards (see Hunter and Dantzker, 2012: 127). Because working-class boys especially are constantly assessed against what Cohen called the 'middle-class measuring rod' they are doomed to fail, particularly in the education system. As a consequence, they find themselves at the bottom of the hierarchy where they experience 'status frustration'. Their reaction is to create or join delinquent sub-cultures, which have their own cultural norms and values, and where they seek the status, success and respect otherwise denied to them (Bierne and Messerschmidt, 2006: 345–9).

The Chicago School and the Ecology of Crime

After Durkheim developed his theory of anomie in Europe, in the 1920s and 1930s sociologists at the University of Chicago began developing a rather different, though related, approach. The Chicago School, as it become known, soon gained a reputation for its innovative, multi-faceted approaches to research and for its ecological and ethnographic studies in particular (Marsh, 2006). It emphasised a pragmatic approach to research, the whole point of which was to better understand the social world. In believing that 'the social world is itself manufactured by the practical experience of those who live in it' (Downes and Rock, 1998: 65–66), Chicago school sociologists conducted their work 'not in faculty offices or libraries but in the open . . . in the field, on the streets, in opium dens and in brothels' (Beirne and Messerschmidt, 2006: 317). For Robert Park, an early and influential figure in the development of the Chicago School, the most effective research required 'sociologists to participate personally in the world which they would analyse' (Downes and Rock, 1998: 66). Beyond such methodological innovation, their pioneering work on crime and deviance was also significant because it marked the beginning of a distinctly American criminology.

The twin processes of industrialisation and urbanisation resulted in Chicago's population growing from just a few hundred in the 1820s to over 3 million in the 1930s. Just a hundred years after its founding Chicago had become America's second-largest city. Mass immigration from Ireland, Poland, Germany, Sweden and Italy, along with large-scale internal migration of African Americans from the South, hugely increased the city's cultural and ethnic diversity. Each group had to adapt to, and find a place for themselves in, a city characterised by constant change (Downes and Rock, 1998). For the Chicago School such remarkable growth and diversity had led to pathological levels of social disorganisation characterised by poverty, residential transience and ethnic heterogeneity (Newburn, 2013). Indeed, social disorganisation was thought to be at the root of all social problems, of which crime was just one (Bohm, 2001).

In common with Durkheim, members of the Chicago School were among the first to 'consider the social origins of criminality as opposed to the individual roots of crime' (Walklate, 1998: 21), and more specifically the relationship between the crime rates of particular neighbourhoods and their social, economic and cultural characteristics. The Chicago School was especially focused on understanding the patterns and impacts of social change and, in turn, the links between crime and the social environment. Underpinning their approach was a belief that cities were ecological systems, the development of which was not entirely random but naturally patterned in the sense that they were never entirely planned but developed organically (Marsh, 2006). As Downes and Rock (1998, 68) point out, 'just as plants, insects and animals translate a physical terrain into a mosaic of distinct communities, so people become separated into a network of unlike communities'. Robert Park was the first to propose this organic or biological analogy; that is, the similarity between the organisation of nature and human beings in societies (Bradley and Walters, 2011). The Chicago School is therefore associated with human ecology as it too studied people in their natural environment and linked crime with the way that American cities grew and developed.

Drawing on the zonal hypothesis of Park and Burgess (1928), Shaw and McKay (1942) deployed the concept of social disorganisation to describe the criminogenic conditions of certain parts of the city. Zonal theory suggests that cities expand from the centre so that typical American cities like Chicago consisted of concentric circles marked by five zones. The central business district at the centre was encircled by a zone of transition, which was encircled by a zone of workers' homes, a residential zone and finally a commuter or suburban zone (Newburn, 2013). Shaw and McKay (1942) found that even over long periods of time the highest rates of crime and delinquency occurred in the zone of transition, despite a consistently high turnover of its residential population. This led to the conclusion that the criminogenic factors must be located in the environment and not in the residents inhabiting the environment, because as residents moved out and were replaced by others, offending rates within the zone remained stable.

The key question, then, was what is it about this zone that produces so much crime when compared to surrounding areas and how is it culturally transmitted from one generation of occupants to the next? The answer lay with the constant turnover and transience of residents. The zone of transition typically offered the cheapest accommodation and was close to workplaces, and so it attracted newcomers to the city. As their financial positions improved, residents moved further out from the centre to the more stable and established areas and were, in turn, replaced by successive waves of newcomers. The constant movement of residents meant that the types of social controls evident in more stable communities were absent precisely because of continual residential turnover. Such transience led to social fragmentation, impersonality, and the breakdown of traditional norms and values (Walklate, 1998). The predictable consequence was crime, and as Beirne and Messerschmidt (2006: 319) point out, offenders were not regarded as 'malicious miscreants' but as essentially normal people adapting to abnormal environments. Social disorganisation, then, highlights the roles of cultural diversity and constant population movement as processes that weaken those family and community ties that bind people together.

Differential Association: Learning Crime Sociologically

In the 1940s Shaw and McKay's work on social disorganisation was adopted and adapted by another significant name in criminology: Edwin Sutherland. Sutherland had already built a reputation from his pioneering work on white-collar crime, a term he in fact coined. His theory of differential association argued that criminal behaviour, like any other behaviour, is learned through interaction with others and can be passed on to other groups and other generations. Crime, then, is a product of the associations we have others and from whom we learn 'motives, drives, rationalisations and attitudes' (Sutherland, 1947: 6). As Newburn (2013: 193–4) points out, at its core differential association suggests that when individuals are exposed to more ideas or messages that promote criminal activity than ideas or messages that discourage it, then crime becomes more likely. As Sutherland (1947: 6) himself stated, 'a person becomes delinquent because of an excess of definitions favorable to violation of law over definitions unfavorable to violation of law'. Differential association therefore emphasises the role of peers and acquaintances in the process of learning to be criminal. This process includes learning the techniques of crime. Newburn (2013: 194) informs us that differential association can vary in intensity, frequency and duration and that it is those associations that occur earlier in life, are the most intense, and endure the longest that are likely to be the most influential on whether or not we become involved in crime.

Sociology Goes to the Dark Side: Social Bonding

Travis Hirschi's (1969) more contemporary sociological theory approaches the problem of crime from an entirely different perspective. The central question of his social control theory is not why people commit crime but why more do not. Hirschi argued that sociological theory had failed to produce convincing evidence that crime is actually caused by things like strain or status frustration. He therefore suggested that searching for the causes of conformity might be more productive. Social control theory, then, reflects a darker vision of human nature because it assumes people will commit crime unless they are specifically prevented from doing so (Bohm, 2011). For Hirschi (1969), crime and anti-social behaviour is more likely when the bonds that connect individuals to society, and which provide them with a stake in conformity, are absent or weak. In other words, the controls that prevent crime are created from a bond with society; when the bond vanishes, so do the controls (Bradley and Walters, 2011).

Hirschi's (1969) explanation is that we form bonds with those people and institutions that are important in our life. The stronger the bonds, the less likely we will engage in crime (Vold, Bernard and Snipes, 1998: 207–8). There are four elements to the social bond. *Attachment* refers to the care for others and their values and beliefs. It's regarded as the most significant bond due to its importance for internalising norms and values. *Commitment* refers to our investment or stake in society and the time and effort invested in conformity; having something means having something to lose. *Involvement* refers to the extent to which people are preoccupied with conventional activities and which thereby reduce opportunities to engage in crime. *Belief* refers to a belief in the value of conformity and the extent to which the law is viewed as legitimate and worthy of obedience (see Rock, 2002: 57). As Bohm (2011: 90) explains, criminality is more likely when there is inadequate attachment, especially to parents and school; inadequate commitment to educational/occupational success; inadequate involvement in conventional social activities; and inadequate belief in the legitimacy of the law and its institutions.

Criminology Diversifies: The Rise of Critical Criminology

The importance of the wider social and political context within which theories develop is nowhere better illustrated than in the emergence of the critical, or radical, criminological perspectives of the 1960s and 1970s. In rejecting the assumptions underpinning positivist criminology, and in challenging the political status quo, they have inspired more recent, ongoing critical perspectives that have together extended the boundaries of criminology and the range of issues it confronts. In focusing attention on a wider array of non-conventional crimes and other harms, critical perspectives marked the beginnings of the theoretical diversity that now characterises criminology. As White and Haines (2004) suggest, the significant changes affecting developed countries in the 1960s and 1970s gave much impetus to the rise of this new way of understanding and deconstructing crime. The assumption that society was characterised by consensus and that everyone had a stake began to disintegrate under the pressure of mass social movements, each of which demanded fundamental reform.

During the 1960s and 1970s young people increasingly rejected dominant cultural conventions and expectations and simply 'dropped out'. For example, the second wave of feminism, which began in the 1960s, contested existing notions of the role and place of women. Conventional attitudes to sexuality and sexual preference were condemned. The civil rights movement in the United States politicised millions of black Americans who demanded economic and political equality and actively encouraged the similarly focused indigenous rights movement and a rising political consciousness among colonised peoples the world over (Bradley and Walters, 2011). In New Zealand in the 1970s, a new generation of Māori radicals demanded recognition of the Treaty of Waitangi and restitution for historical grievances (Walker, 1990). Other significant cultural changes included new lifestyles that rejected materialism, and the popularisation of recreational drug use. The term counter-culture was coined to describe the values of a wide range of groups united in their opposition to the dominant culture and political authority (Yinger, 1982).

These various movements collectively represented a process of demystification. The Vietnam War, political and racial assassinations, the destruction wrought by urban renewal, environmental degradation and widespread corporate offending all opened the eyes of the public to 'the true nature of current events' and how the 'elites' benefited from such activities (Bohm, 2001: 103–5). This led to an increasingly sceptical attitude towards political and other authorities. Racism, sexism, homophobia, imperialism, exploitation and oppression were all used to describe the prevailing social and political landscape. The new critical theories revealed society as pluralistic and fundamentally conflict-ridden (Burke, 2009).

Criminologists thus opened a Pandora's box by using a key provided by Robert S. Lynd's (1939) famous question "Knowledge for what?" (see Beirne and Messerschmidt, 2006: 378). For many social scientists a 'naive acceptance' of the status quo and 'belief in the purely benevolent actions of government' ended as critical scholars began questioning the uses and applications of their research and knowledge and their support for a potentially biased and oppressive justice system (Bohm, 2001: 104). Critical criminology argued the research agenda was not value-free or apolitical and that scientifically objective research is often appropriated to serve political purposes. It advocated instead for a deliberately politicised research agenda favouring disadvantaged and oppressed people; an attitude encapsulated in Becker's (1967) rallying call: 'Whose side are we on?' Highlighting social, economic, racial and gender inequalities, and justice system bias, became a key objective.

Critical, or radical, criminology is a collection of theories that claim crime is the product of conflict, domination and oppression. These theories maintain that economic and political elites get to define what counts as crime; definitions that criminalise the actions of the powerless while ignoring the harmful behaviours of the powerful. They are critical because they refuse to confine themselves to state-defined crimes and contest the very meaning of crime. Attention was focused instead on a much wider array of social, economic, political and environmental harms. Positivist analyses of causes were rejected because of their failure to account for how offenders are often themselves victimised, first by society via inequality or marginalisation, and then by a biased system of justice. The justice system was opposed because it was often the instrument of injustice. These theories are also deemed radical because they demand a fundamental transformation of dominant political and economic institutions (Einstadter and Henry, 2006: 235); a radical agenda indeed.

Two prominent critical perspectives that inspired more recent developments in critical criminology are labelling theory and the feminist perspectives. Labelling theory, the earliest, supplied a series of original insights that underpin most of the later critical perspectives. Feminist perspectives also supply original insights and reject much of positivist criminology; they were also instrumental in identifying criminology's most glaring historical omission: it's almost total neglect of gender.

Labelling Theory, Social Reaction and the Power to Criminalise

Labelling perspectives first emerged in the United States in the early 1950s when sociologists began to question the almost exclusive focus on crimes of the poor and powerless while neglecting crimes of the powerful. However, labelling theory came into its own in the 1960s, in the wake of the mass arrests that took place during protests against racial inequality and American involvement in the Vietnam War. Labelling theorists point out that crime is committed in every stratum of society and by people from all backgrounds, and question why the poor and powerless are the primary victims of criminal justice. Who defines behaviour as criminal and who gets to attribute the label 'criminal' are the most important questions. Labelling theory, then, is primarily concerned with the *process* of criminalisation and the selective application of the label 'criminal'. It argues that 'power elites' attribute criminal labels by performing the role of 'moral entrepreneur' (Becker, 1963). In contrast to positivism, labelling theorists are more interested in the social reaction to offenders than in individual or environmental causes (Burke, 2009).

A core assumption of labelling theory is that crime is not an inherent quality of the behaviour itself. According to Becker (1963: 9), whose early work was on marijuana use, 'social groups create deviance by making the rules whose infraction constitutes deviance'. For Becker, then, crime is not 'a quality of the act' but a consequence of the successful application of the label 'criminal', hence the focus upon the process of labelling. This process takes the form of 'status degradation ceremonies' (Garfinkel, 1956: 421) – formal criminal trials, the explicit purpose of which is to shame, stigmatise and exclude. The labelling process can, however, become a 'self-fulfilling prophecy' (Burke, 2009: 172) in that over time individuals may come to accept and internalise the meaning inherent in that label and behave in conformity to it. Therein lies labelling theory's explanation of why people commit crime and conceive of themselves as criminals (White and Haines, 2004).

Another labelling theorist, Edwin Lemert (1969), divided offending into two main categories: primary and secondary deviance. Primary deviance refers to the initial acts of law-breaking most of us engage in because of any number of social, cultural or psychological reasons. The important point is that primary deviance does not fundamentally transform our sense of identity. Secondary deviance, however, is the main concern of labelling theory and occurs *because* of an official negative reaction to primary deviance. It is this negative reaction, the ritualised degradation, the application of a stigmatic label and the resulting shame and loss of status that leads to secondary deviance and the embrace of a criminal identity. Thus secondary deviance is said to occur when, because of the negative social reaction, individuals experience a fundamental re-orientation of their identity and in turn their behaviour (Bohm, 2001). Labelling people as criminal is purposely designed to mark them out and change the way society reacts and responds to them. Being shunned by society can, in turn, encourage those so labelled to view themselves as criminal and act accordingly, in what's described as a process of 'deviancy amplification' (Wilkins, 1964). Ironically, then, the very outcome we're trying to avoid, further crime, is actually promoted by our negative social reaction.

If negative reaction and stigmatisation creates the very thing to be avoided, then don't react, at least not in ways that purposely stigmatise and degrade. Labelling theory recommends informal responses that don't stereotype on the basis of typically minor offences committed while young. It advocates instead for a 'radical non-intervention' (Schur, 1973) or 'hands-off' approach that suggests 'the best control systems are those that control the least' (Akers and Sellers, 2004: 142). This is especially important for youth offenders who are more vulnerable to the negative effects of stigmatic labels (White and Haines, 2004: 85).

In New Zealand, labelling theory underpins Family Group Conferences (FGCs), a restorative justice approach regarded as the lynchpin of youth justice (Becroft, 2009: 27). FGCs provide a forum for mediation and reconciliation between victims, offenders and their families. By avoiding the stigmatic shaming and other adverse effects of formal trials, FGCs lower the likelihood of re-offending by re-integrating offenders back into society (Watt, 2003). Similarly, diversion aims to minimise contact between youth and adult offenders and the formal criminal justice system. Labelling theorists also believe that far too many behaviours are defined as crimes simply because they 'offend' the state or morality. Thus behaviours that are voluntarily engaged in and are victimless should be decriminalised. The case of illegal drugs is especially relevant. The belated realisation that the global war on drugs has been nothing short of a disaster has led to a growing number of countries, including the principal prosecutor of that war, the United States, to decriminalise and even legalise cannabis and other drugs (Hall, 2015). The decarceration movement is also closely associated with labelling theory. Since imprisonment has *the* most stigmatising and criminogenic effect, it makes sense to decrease its use wherever possible. Unfortunately for New Zealand, the prison population reached an all-time high of 9400 in April

2016 and is predicted to reach 10,000 by 2017 (Ellingham, 2016). It appears that any commitment to decarceration is a step too far for politicians desperate to avoid the tag of being 'soft on crime'. Finally, another programme informed by labelling theory is tattoo removal. Tattoos, especially gang-related tattoos on the face, neck and fingers, are a self-inflicted barrier to employment and reintegration; a literal physical stigmata that reinforces the metaphorical stigma of a criminal conviction.

Feminist Criminologies

There is no universal brand of feminism and there is no one feminist perspective on criminology but rather a collection of perspectives or criminologies (Gelsthorpe, 2002). These different perspectives do, however, share important features and objectives. They agree that traditional criminology has been gender-blind and has failed to understand the significance of gender and sex-role socialisation. They highlight the patriarchal organisation of society, the subordination of women's rights and privileges, and that male–female power differentials are at least as important as the power differentials by race, class and age (Akers and Sellers, 2004). They demand recognition of the historical and contemporary oppression and abuse of women, and of the fact that most victims of unreported crime are female victims of male violence. They also emphasise that law and criminal justice are gender-biased (Einstadter and Henry, 2006: 263). More generally, feminist perspectives, including liberal, radical, Marxist, and socialist feminism (see Tong, 1989), are united in their desire to 'make the invisible visible' by focusing on society's gender structure and in their 'commitment to revealing and attempting to negate the subordination of women by men' (Gelsthorpe, 2002: 115).

Feminist perspectives first appeared in the 1970s coincident with the developing women's liberation movement. The early perspectives focused on developing 'a comprehensive critique' of criminology for its neglect of women (Gelsthorpe, 2002: 18). An undisputed fact of crime is that, despite recent increases in female crime, 80 per cent of known offenders are men (Lynch, 2014). Despite the existence of this 'gender ratio problem', it had been all but ignored (Chesney-Lind, 2006). 'Malestream' criminology, then, was described as a gender-blind and gender-biased discipline (Menzies and Chunn, 1991: 7) dominated by men studying other men (Gelsthorpe, 2002).

Traditional criminology employed one of two equally unreliable approaches to explain female crime. In the first, 'special theories' depicted female offenders in distorted, often sexualised, terms based on stereotypical assumptions of their biological and psychological nature (Morris, 1987: 75). While criminology had reduced its 'slavish adherence' to biological positivism, this didn't extend to female offending (Burke, 2009: 195), which remained rooted in biological determinism and stereotypes of women as essentially passive, domestic and maternal (Smart, 1976). Because crime was regarded as masculine, female criminals contradicted the ideal of femininity and were therefore 'doubly deviant'; they broke the law and expected gender norms/sex roles (White and Haines, 2004: 125). The second traditional approach naively assumed that theories developed for men could be equally applied to women. Feminist scholars rightly questioned whether these could be generalised or applied to women *and* explain the significant gender differences in offending (Daly and Chesney-Lind, 1988: 518). In response, feminist scholars formulated explanations to specifically account for both women's criminality and conformity. For some it involved little more than adding women to extant theories. Others suggested that existing theories could be adapted to explain female crime and the gender ratio problem (Morris, 1987). Still others paid much closer attention to the 'dimensions of gender and sex roles' and how these affect the treatment of men and women in criminal justice (Akers and Sellers (2004: 245).

Female Emancipation Causes Crime

Following increases in female crime in the 1970s, the first attempt to address the generalisability and gender ratio problems was based on women's liberation. It argued that the changing role of women had brought about a greater involvement in crime, especially crimes normally associated with men (Adler, 1975). As women transitioned into the workplace they had taken on masculine qualities and in becoming more competitive and aggressive were behaving more like men. Women's liberation had therefore created 'a new female criminal'. Rita Simon (1975), on the other hand, argued that women's greater involvement in crime was due to increased opportunities. As women moved into the workplace they encountered, and took advantage of, a greater variety of previously unavailable criminal opportunities (Vold, Bernard and Snipes, 1998).

Freedom and Control

An alternative explanation, and an extension of social control theory, is Hagan's (1989) power-control theory. This explains gender differences in crime by linking male and female involvement to the type of family structure (patriarchal or egalitarian) and the degree of parental control exerted over boys relative to girls. In patriarchal families, parents exert greater control over their daughters than their sons, which can then influence their respective perceptions of and different orientations to risky behaviour. Because they're afforded more freedom, sons are more likely to pursue risky activities such as crime without fear of consequences. The greater control of daughters, however, renders them more risk averse and more likely to experience stronger emotional bonds that constrain criminal behaviour (Akers and Sellers, 2004: 255).

Masculinities and Crime

More recently, various feminist writers have shifted focus by asking what is it about maleness that produces so many male criminals (Cain, 1990). This perspective recognises 'multiple and contested' masculinities and argues that the types of crime committed by young men are based on their interpretation of masculinity and that crime provides a way of 'doing masculinity' (Messerschmidt, 1993). The actual form of offending varies depending on how different class and ethnic groups define masculinity and on the available resources or opportunities to demonstrate masculinity. Adapting Merton's theory, Messerschmidt argues that in modern societies masculinity is based around financial independence and success. When these are unavailable, through poverty or unemployment, boys and men may turn to crime to accomplish their masculine identity: male crime is thus 'a form of social practice invoked as a resource . . . for accomplishing masculinity'. As Einstadter and Henry (2006: 276–7) note, different contexts require different constructions and demonstrations of masculinity. We therefore 'do gender' and crime differently depending on the social situation and circumstances we encounter (Messerscmidt, 2005: 218). Cunneen and White (2007: 216), for example, argue that marginalised working-class boys have a higher involvement in violent crime because they must rely on physical rather than financial domination to express their masculinity.

The feminist perspectives have had a threefold influence on criminology. First is the development of alternative explanations for both female criminality and conformity. Second, in gendering crime, they focus attention on criminology's hitherto gender blindness. Third, they have forced recognition of the different female experience of crime, victimisation and criminal justice. Related to the last, feminist perspectives have also been particularly influential in raising awareness of female victimisation and those crimes disproportionately committed against women by men. Women have successfully campaigned for police and the courts to respond to cases of rape and sexual violence with greater sensitivity and sympathy. They have also raised awareness of the previously invisible issue of domestic violence, with the effect that victims are reporting their experiences more frequently. However, both domestic and sexual violence continue to be significantly under-reported and clearly remain very significant problems in New Zealand, where between 2009 and 2012 an average of 35 people a year were victims of domestic violence and related homicides (Newbold, 2016; Vance, 2015).

More Recent Critical Perspectives

In moving beyond positivism and its search for causes, the critical theories of the 1960s and 1970s, including the labelling and feminist perspectives, marked the beginning of the theoretical diversity that is a characteristic feature of contemporary criminology. By highlighting the selective process of criminalisation, social and political conflict, and economic and gender inequality, these approaches inspired a range of more recent critical perspectives. Like the labelling and feminist theories before them, their attention is not confined to those acts defined as crimes by the state. These theories maintain that a much wider range of harms should be the object of analysis and in turn that harm reduction should be a guiding principle and the sought-after outcome. The recently developed critical perspectives are therefore closer in orientation to zemiology, or the study of social harm, than criminology and its traditionally narrow focus on conventional crime (Burke, 2009). Contemporary critical perspectives, then, extend the boundaries of criminology and broaden its focus of inquiry by looking beyond crime to consider threats posed by environmental degradation, corporate crime, workplace health and safety breaches and human rights violations; all of which are responsible for 'more widespread and damaging consequences' than all of those behaviours currently labelled criminal by the state (Newburn, 2013: 254). More generally, contemporary critical perspectives aim to 'integrate rather than exclude; to reduce or abolish deliberately inflicted pain and to seek restoration rather than retribution' (Burke, 2009: 215).

Peacemaking Criminology

Peacemaking criminology does not attempt to explain crime and criminality *per se*; it assumes that social and political conflict is the root cause. Far more important for peacemaking criminology is the failure of criminal justice at every level and the often significant harms it creates in the process. The primary justification for inflicting pain via the justice system is that it deters offending and reduces crime. And yet, as White and Haines (2004: 189) suggest, imposing punishment and humiliating offenders cannot and never will solve social problems like crime. Trying to reduce violence and suffering through the imposition of yet more violence and suffering makes little sense and the various wars on crime or drugs or terrorism only make matters worse. Criminal justice practice, then, is often iatrogenic; that is, it produces more harm that it resolves (Liebling and Maruna, 2005). Building on the insights of labelling theory, feminist perspectives, socialist humanism, pacifism and various religious traditions, peacemaking criminology argues that when dealing with offenders, and wider social and political conflict, we need to adopt humanistic, restorative and participatory approaches to conflict resolution. Fuller (2003) has developed a 'peacemaking paradigm', the main features of which are used to inform practical programmes for dealing with crime and other conflicts. It advocates for non-violent responses and emphasises the importance of social justice and the elimination of all forms of discrimination whether based on age, social class, ethnicity or gender. It seeks inclusive approaches to the justice process, that everyone involved is aware of the procedures, rules and regulations, and that all individuals regardless of background are treated with respect and dignity. In this respect peacemaking has much in common with restorative justice; an inclusive, reconciliatory process that seeks to heal the victim and right the wrongs of criminal offending. It is also a way of 'doing' justice that was to a large extent pioneered in New Zealand.

Green Criminology

Until recently, plundering the earth's natural resources was not regarded particularly seriously. However, it is now widely recognised that the very means to our collective survival is slowly being destroyed and that all manner of crimes and violations are routinely perpetrated against the environment (South, 1998). The green perspective is an emergent development in criminology. It first appeared in the 1990s as a critical and activist approach to the study of environmental harm, laws and regulations (South, 1998). Much of its work has involved exposing widespread environmental and ecological destruction and injustice whilst critiquing governments for failing to address this destruction and adequately regulate the behaviour of corporations (White, 2011). Its key focus is environmental crime, but in common with other critical perspectives it also incorporates the study of harmful activities regardless of their legal status (White and Heckenberg, 2014: 7–9).

Carrabine et al. (2004) divide their subject matter into primary and secondary environmental crime. The first involves direct destruction or degradation of the environment and the earth's resources, while the second involves violations of environmental regulations. Green criminology casts a wide net in terms of the types of harms and activities studied. These include illegal trades in endangered species; illegal harvesting of natural resources; illegal disposal of toxic waste and the accompanying air, land and water pollution; and negative ecological consequences of new technology like genetically modified organisms. Unsurprisingly, green criminology has more recently turned its attention to climate change and global warming (White and Heckenberg, 2014: 9).

Just a cursory glance at the extent of the environmental destruction already sustained, along with projections of future losses, explains why criminology has adopted, albeit belatedly, a green perspective. Carrabine et al. (2004: 317) inform us that 10 million hectares of forest, an area the size of South Korea, is lost every year. Between 1960 and 1990 around 20 per cent of the world's tropical forests was lost – forests that provide the habitat for between 70 per cent and 95 per cent of the earth's species. Carrabine and associates estimate that 50 different species are lost every day; that 46 per cent of all mammal and 11 per cent of all bird species are at risk; and that by 2020, 10 million species are likely to have become extinct. Despite such dire predictions, there is still major trafficking of animals and animal parts across the world. Freshwater ecosystems are everywhere in decline and water contaminated with pollutants kills around 25 million people every year. While around 58 per cent of the world's reefs and 34 per cent of all fish may be at risk, extensive water pollution and overfishing continues unabated. Recent research by the World Wildlife Fund and the Zoological Society of London has confirmed that the fastest decline among animal populations is found in freshwater ecosystems, where numbers have plummeted 75 per cent since 1970 (Carrington, 2014).

In spite of its 'clean, green' image and '100% Pure' marketing slogan, New Zealand has its own growing problem of environmental degradation. According to Mike Joy, a New Zealand ecological scientist, New Zealand is 'slipping badly on environmental performance and it's hard to know how much longer we can keep up the clean-green pretence' (Joy, 2013). Joy points out that a University of Adelaide study ranked New Zealand 120th in the world due its biodiversity loss and poor water quality. According to 2013 Ministry for the Environment figures, more than 60 per cent of the rivers it monitors are unsafe for swimming (Kirk, 2013). Figures supplied by 'Kiwis for Kiwis', a charity raising funds for predator removal, show that 27 kiwi die each week, a fatality rate that could see them disappear in the wild in just 50 years. Being the nation's icon has done little for the kiwi, given that their numbers have dropped from 100,000 in the early 1990s, when protection programmes first began, to 70,000 in 2014.

Conclusion

This chapter has presented a broad overview of different ways of thinking about crime and changes to that thinking over time. The diverse range of explanations considered reflects the inter-disciplinary nature of criminology and the diverse backgrounds of those involved in theory construction. Different theories developed at different points in time often try to explain different things and focus on different offences and offenders. In this sense, and in recognition of the huge diversity of behaviours labelled criminal, there simply can't be one all-encompassing explanation. Crime is a much contested concept and the same goes for the ways in which it's explained.

It will also be clear that each explanation for crime is more readily understood, and makes much more sense, when located within its wider historical, social and political context. In interpreting and understanding theories of crime one must always be aware of the influence and impact of time and place. This chapter has employed a broadly chronological approach and briefly traced the major shifts in thinking associated with different time periods. It's important to note, however, that the emergence of new theories or explanations does not necessarily eradicate or replace existing forms of explanation. This is especially true of the modern era, where there is rarely, if ever, any clean break marking the rejection of one theory or way of thinking and the adoption of another. In practice, different theories, and especially parts of theories, often exist alongside one another and compete for recognition and funding.

In New Zealand two of the justifications for punishment are based on contradictory theories. In the first, informed by a theory of deterrence, offenders are punished to deter future offending. In the other, offenders are 'treated' through an array of rehabilitation programmes to 'cure' them of their criminality. Thus one views crime as a result of free will while in the other crime is determined by factors beyond free will. Each is now over a century old but both continue to shape how and why we punish. Moreover, while some theories emerged long ago, and are in that sense historical, they should not be considered dead or of purely historical interest. On the contrary, Lombroso's theory of degeneracy and inherited criminality emerged in the 1870s but continues to inspire more recent work on genetic inheritance. The Human Genome Project, which recently mapped all of our 20,000 genes, has and will continue to encourage ongoing, and well-funded, investigations into genetic influences on crime. Biological stigmata and degeneracy are still with us, not as Lombroso envisaged, but as serotonin depletion or genetic markers. The bio-social perspective, first developed in the 1970s, continues to examine the interactive effects of biological and environmental factors. Similarly, the rational choice perspective of Classicism continues to inform contemporary theories that argue offenders exploit available criminal opportunities by weighing costs and benefits, and it forms the basis of more recently developed theoretical frameworks such as routine activities theory and situational crime prevention, both of which aim to reduce the available opportunities for crime. Criminological theory, in other words, evolves over time as it accumulates ever more theories and explanations.

In the twenty-first century, given the pace of social and political change and the numerous threats to our collective well-being, debates about crime and criminality are likely to intensify. It is, then, more important than ever to think critically about how crime is explained because almost every crime-related policy or intervention is informed, however loosely, by one or more underlying theories of crime. Without these theoretical guides officials would be intervening in people's lives, often to their detriment, with only a vague sense of why. Understanding theory, and the contexts in which it's developed, is thus important because of its many implications for our responses to crime. Equally important, citizens of liberal democracies like New Zealand need some understanding of crime theory in order to spot the ways in which it's often manipulated for political advantage, bureaucratic expedience or sensationalist media headlines.

REFERENCES

Adler, F. 1975. *Sisters in Crime*. New York: McGraw-Hill.
Ainsworth, P. 2000. *Psychology and Crime: Myths and Reality*. Harlow, UK: Longman.
Akers, R., and Sellers, C. 2004. *Criminological Theories: Introduction, Evaluation and Application*. Los Angeles: Roxbury.
Arnold, C. 2012. *Undercover London: Crime and Punishment in the Capital City*. London: Simon and Schuster.
Arrigo, B., and Williams, C. 2006. *Critical Perspectives in Criminology: Philosophy, Crime, and Criminology*. Urbana: University of Illinois Press.
Barnes, H., and Teeters, N. 1943. *New Horizons in Criminology: The American Crime Problem*. New York: Prentice Hall.
Becroft, A. 2009. 'Are There Lessons to Be Learned from the Youth Justice System?', in G. Maxwell (Ed.), *Addressing the Causes of Offending: What Is the Evidence*. Wellington: Institute of Policy Studies, Victoria University of Wellington.
Beirne, P. 1994. 'The Law Is an Ass', *Society and Animals* 2(1): 27–46.
Beirne, P., and Messerschmidt, J. 2006. *Criminology*. Los Angeles: Roxbury.
Bohm, R. 2001. *A Primer on Crime and Delinquency Theory*. London: Wadsworth.
Bradley, T., and Walters, R. 2011. *Introduction to Criminological Thought* (2nd ed.). Auckland: Pearson.
Burke, R. 2009. *An Introduction to Criminological Theory* (3rd ed.). Abingdon, UK: Taylor and Francis.
Cain, M. 1990. 'Towards Transgression: New Directions of Feminist Criminology', *International Journal of the Sociology of Law* 18: 1–18.
Carrabine, E, Cox, P., Lee, M., Plummer, K., and South, N. 2004. *Criminology: A Sociological Introduction* (2nd ed.). London: Routledge.
Carrington, D. 2014. 'Earth Lost 50% of Wildlife in Past 40 Years Says WWF', *Guardian*, 29 September.
Chesney-Lind, M. 2006. 'Patriarchy, Crime, and Justice: Feminist Criminology in an Era of Backlash', *Feminist Criminology* 1(1): 6–26.
Chevalier, L. 1973. *Labouring Classes and Dangerous Classes in Paris during the First Half of the Nineteenth Century*. Princeton, NJ: Princeton University Press.
Cohen, A. 1955. *Delinquent Boys: The Culture of the Gang*. New York: Free Press.
Cortes, J., and Gatti, F. 1972. *Delinquency and Crime: A Bio-Social Approach*. New York: Seminar Press.
Cunneen, C., and, White, R. 2007. *Juvenile Justice: Youth and Crime in Australia* (3rd ed.). South Melbourne: Oxford University Press.
Daly, K., and Chesney-Lind, M. 1988. 'Feminism and Criminology', *Justice Quarterly* 5(4): 498–538.
Darwin, C. 1859. *On the Origin of Species by Means of Natural Selection*. London: John Murray.
Durkheim, E. 1933. *The Division of Labour in Society*. Glencoe, IL: Free Press.
Durkheim, E. 1964. *The Elementary Forms of Religious Life*. Glencoe, IL: Free Press.
Durrant, R. 2013. *An Introduction to Criminal Psychology*. Abingdon, UK: Routledge.
Edmunds, S. 2014. 'ADHD: Living with a 1000 Distractions', *New Zealand Herald*, 6 July. Accessed 10 February 2016. http://www.nzherald.co.nz/susan-edmunds/news/article.cfm?a_id=772&objectid=11288304
Einstadter, W., and Henry, S. 2006. *Criminological Theory: An Analysis of Its Underlying Assumptions*. Lanham, MD: Rowman and Littlefield.
Ellingham, J. 2016. 'New Zealand Prison Population Rising', *New Zealand Herald*, 18 May. Accessed 1 June 2016. http://www.nzherald.co.nz/nz/news/article.cfm?c_id=1&objectid=11640707
Foucault, M. 1977. *Discipline and Punish: The Birth of the Prison*. London: Allen-Lane.
Fuller, J. 2003. 'Peacemaking Criminology', in M. Schwartz and S. Hatty (Eds), *Controversies in Critical Criminology*. Cincinnati, OH: Anderson.
Garfinkel, H. 1956. 'Conditions of Successful Degradation Ceremonies', *American Journal of Sociology*, 61(5): 420–4.
Garland, D. 2001. *Culture of Control*. Oxford: Oxford University Press.
Gelsthorpe, L. 2002. 'Feminism and Criminology', in M. Maguire, R. Morgan and R. Reiner (Eds), *The Oxford Handbook of Criminology* (3rd ed.). Oxford: Oxford University Press.
Glueck, S., and Glueck, E. 1956. *Physique and Delinquency*. New York: Harper.
Gray, J. 2016. *The Soul of the Marionette: A Short Enquiry into Human Freedom*. St Ives, UK: Penguin.
Hagan, J. 1989. *Structural Criminology*. New Brunswick, NJ: Rutgers University Press.
Hall, W. 2015. 'Legal in the USA: Consequences of Cannabis Law', *Policy Forum*, 14 December. Accessed 15 June 2016. http://www.policyforum.net/legal-in-the-usa-the-consequences-of-cannabis-laws

Hay, D. 1975. *Albion's Fatal Tree: Crime and Society in Eighteenth-century England*. New York: Pantheon Books.
Hibbert, C. 1963. *The Roots of Evil: A Social History of Crime and Punishment*. London: Weidenfield and Nicolson.
Hirschi, T. 1969. *Causes of Delinquency*. Berkeley: University of California Press.
Hollin, C. 2007. 'Criminological Psychology', in M. Maguire, R. Morgan and R. Reiner (Eds), *The Oxford Handbook of Criminology* (4th ed.). Oxford: Oxford University Press.
Hunter, R., and Danztker, M. 2012. *Crime and Criminality: Causes and Consequences* (2nd ed.). Boulder, CO: Lynn Rienner.
Jones, S. 2016. *No Need for Geniuses: Revolutionary Science in the Age of the Guillotine*. London: Little, Brown.
Joy, M. 2013. 'Reputation Dragged through the Muck', *Stuff.co.nz*, 21 August. Accessed 10 February 2014. http://www.stuff.co.nz/dominion-post/comment/columnists/9067550/Reputation-dragged-through-the-muck
Kelsey, J. 1995. *The New Zealand Experiment: A World Model for Structural Adjustment?* Auckland: Auckland University Press.
Kirk, S. 2013. 'Many NZ Rivers Unsafe for Swimming', *Stuff.co.nz*, 27 July. Accessed 30 July 2013. http://www.stuff.co.nz/national/8978223/Many-NZ-rivers-unsafe-for-swimming
Laquer, T. 1989. 'Crowds, Carnival and the State of English Executions 1604–1868', in A. Beir, D. Cannadine and J. Rosenheim (Eds), *Modern Society: Essays in English History in Honour of Lawrence Stone*. Cambridge: Cambridge University Press.
Lemert, E. 1969. 'Primary and Secondary Deviation', in D. Cressy and D. Ward (Eds), *Delinquency, Crime and Social Process*. New York: Harper and Row.
Liebling, A., and Maruna, S. 2005. 'Introduction: The Effects of Imprisonment Revisited', in A. Liebling and S. Maruna (Eds), *The Effects of Imprisonment*. Devon, UK: Willan.
Lynch, N. 2014. 'Girls Behaving Badly? Young Female Violence in New Zealand', *Victoria University Law Review* 45: 509–24.
Lynd, R. S. 1939. *Knowledge for What? The Place of Social Science in American Culture*. Princeton, NJ: Princeton University Press.
Marsh, I. 2006. *Theories of Crime*. Abingdon, UK: Routledge.
McGuire, J. 2004. *Understanding Psychology and Crime*. London: Sage.
McKenzie, M. 1981. *Plato on Punishment*. Berkeley: University of California Press.
McLynn, F. 2013. *Crime and Punishment in Eighteenth-century England*. London: Routledge.
Menzies, R., and Chunn, D. 1991. '"Kicking against the Pricks": The Dilemmas of Feminist Teaching in Criminology', *Critical Criminologist* 3(1): 7–15.
Messerschmidt, J. 1993. *Masculinities and Crime: Critique and Reconceptualisation of Theory*. Lanham, MD: Rowman and Littlefield.
Messerschmidt, J. 2005. 'Masculinities and Theoretical Criminology', in S. Henry and M. Lanier (Eds), *The Essential Criminology Reader*. Boulder, CO: Westview Press.
Monbiot, G. 2013. 'The Crime Behind the Grime', *George Monbiot*, 7 January. Accessed 28 May 2015. http://www.monbiot.com/2013/01/07/the-grime-behind-the-crime/
Monbiot, G. 2016. 'Falling Apart', in G. Monbiot (Ed.), *How Did We Get into This Mess?* London: Verso.
Morris, A. 1987. *Women, Crime and Criminal Justice*. Oxford: Blackwell.
Nevin, R. 2007. 'Understanding International Crime Trends: The Legacy of Preschool Lead Exposure', *Environmental Research* 104: 315–36.
Newbold, G. 2016. *Crime, Law and Justice in New Zealand*. New York: Routledge.
Newburn, T. 2013. *Criminology* (2nd ed.). London: Routledge.
Newman, G. 1978. *The Punishment Response*. London: Transaction.
Nowotny, H. 2016. *The Cunning of Uncertainty*. Cambridge: Polity Press.
Pfohl, S. 1994. *Images of Deviance and Social Control: A Sociological History*. New York: McGraw-Hill.
Pratt, J., and Clark, M. 2005. 'Penal Populism in New Zealand', *Punishment and Society* 7: 303–21.
Putwain, D., and Sammons, A. 2002. *Psychology and Crime*. London: Routledge.
Rafter, N. 1997. *Creating Born Criminals*. Urbana: University of Illinois Press.
Raine, A., Lencz, T., Bihrle, S., LaCasse, L., and Colletti, P. 2000. 'Reduced Prefrontal Graymatter Volume and Reduced Autonomic Activity in Antisocial Personality Disorder', *Archives of General Psychiatry* 57: 119–27.
Rock, P. 2002. 'Sociological Theories of Crime', in M. Maguire, R. Morgan and R. Reiner (Eds), *The Oxford Handbook of Criminology* (3rd ed.). Oxford: Oxford University Press.

Sharp, J. 2001. 'Crime, Order and Historical Change', in J. Muncie and E. McLaughlin (Eds.), *The Problem of Crime*. London: Sage.

Schild, W. 1981. 'History of Criminal Law and Procedure', in C. Hinkeldey (Ed.), *Criminal Justice through the Ages*. Rothenberg, Germany: Mittelalterliches Kriminalmuseum.

Schur, E. 1973. *Radical Nonintervention*. Englewood Cliffs: Prentice Hall.

Shoemaker, D. 2005. *Theories of Delinquency* (5th ed.). Oxford: Oxford University Press.

Simon, R. 1975. *The Contemporary Woman and Crime*. Washington, DC: Government Printing Office.

Smart, C. 1976. *Women, Crime and Criminology*. London: Routledge and Keegan Paul.

Solomon, R. 2001. *Wicked Pleasures: Meditations on the Seven Deadly Sins*. Boston: Rowman and Littlefield.

South, N. 1998. 'A Green Field for Criminology? A Proposal for a Perspective', *Theoretical Criminology* 2(2): 211–33.

Swingewood, A. 1991. *A Short History of Sociological Thought*. London: Macmillan.

Vaccarino, F., Kavan, H., and Gendall, P. 2011. 'Spirituality and Religion in the Lives of New Zealanders', *International Journal of Religion and Spirituality in Society* 1(2): 85–96.

Vance, A. 2015. 'Government Aims to Tackle High Domestic Violence Rates', *Stuff.co.nz*, 2 August. Accessed 10 September 2015. http://www.stuff.co.nz/national/politics/70752097/Government-aims-to-tackle-high-domestic-violence-rates

Vold, G. B., Bernard, T. J., and Snipes, J. B. 1998. *Theoretical Criminology* (4th ed.). New York: Oxford University Press.

Walklate, S. 1998. *Understanding Criminology: Current Theoretical Debates*. Buckingham, UK: Open University Press.

Walker, R. 1990. *Ka Whawhai Tonu Matou – Struggle without End*. Auckland: Penguin.

Watt, E. 2003. *A History of Youth Justice in New Zealand*. Unpublished research commissioned by Principal Youth Court Judge. Wellington: Department for Courts.

White, R. 2011. *Transnational Environmental Crime: Toward an Eco-global Criminology*. London: Routledge.

White, R., and Haines, F. 2004. *Crime and Criminology: An Introduction* (3rd ed.). South Melbourne: Oxford University Press.

White, R., and Heckenberg, D. 2014. *Green Criminology: An Introduction to the Study of Environmental Harm*. London: Routledge.

Wilkins, L. T. *Social Deviance: Social Policy, Action, and Research*. London: Tavistock.

Wilkins, C., Sweetsur, P., and Girling, M. 2008. *Trends in Drug Use in Auckland, Wellington and Christchurch*. Palmerston North: Centre for Social and Health Outcomes Research and Evaluation and Te Ropu Whariki, Massey University.

Williams, F., and McShane, M. 1988. *Criminological Theory*. Englewood Cliffs, NJ: Prentice Hall.

Wortley, R. 2011. *Psychological Criminology: An Integrative Approach*. London: Routledge.

Yinger, J. 1982. *Countercultures: The Promise and Peril of a World Turned Upside Down*. New York: Free Press.

2.

Crime Rates

GREG NEWBOLD

Introduction

One of the most important tasks for any policy-active criminologist is to understand crime rates. Understanding crime rates involves not only comprehending why crime rates sometimes rise and fall, but also knowing about how crime data are gathered and the advantages and disadvantages of various crime collection methods. It's important also, when comparing crime frequencies over space or time, to be sure that the data are comparable; that is, to be sure that you are comparing 'apples with apples'. Definitions of what constitutes murder, for example, can vary from one data set to another. The definitions of rape and incest vary greatly also and figures are highly sensitive to differences in reporting conventions and legal classification. The purpose of this chapter is to examine some of the principal means by which crime figures are gathered, before considering the reasons for rises and falls in selected areas of criminal activity.

Calculating Crime Rates

Police Data

A primary source of crime data is the police. When a crime is reported to the police the information is submitted to a national database. Since 1978 the system used by the whole justice sector has been the national Law Enforcement System (LES), which produces electronically coded figures drawn from paper files. Where the police are concerned, the system also records information about arrests and resolution rates. Police crime statistics, therefore, give us a pretty good picture of what crimes are being reported and where they occur. But there are problems with total reliance on police figures:

1. *Not all crimes get notified to the police.* Drug crimes, traffic crimes, sexual violence and domestic violence offences, for example, are often not reported, whereas others like robberies and serious assaults usually are. So the number of crimes reported is dependent on things like levels of policing activity, as in the case of traffic and drug crimes, and public consciousness in the cases of sex crimes and domestic violence. Where traffic crimes are concerned, a police 'blitz' on traffic safety or drink driving can have the effect of boosting reported levels of traffic crime and creating the impression of a crime wave. In the cases of sexual and domestic violence, public consciousness-raising campaigns increase the likelihood of a crime being reported, with the same effect. Levels of sexual or domestic violence may thus appear to be rising even though actual levels are steady or in decline.
2. *Not all reported offences end up as crimes.* Police are often called to domestic violence incidents which turn out to be loud verbal arguments or just rowdy parties, and some reported sexual violence turns out to be false. On the other hand, much sexual and domestic violence is never reported at all, so trying to determine actual levels from police data can be difficult.
3. *Inconsistency in reporting methods.* The police are frustratingly inconsistent in the way they report crimes. In the 1960s and 1970s, for instance, they broke down the categories of reported crime and listed them in great detail in their annual reports. Nowadays they only report broad categories such as 'Homicide' or 'Robbery'. Categories like 'Homicide' have to be treated with special caution, because these data sometimes include accidental killings and attempted murders which did not result in death, thus skewing the figures upwards. The police often change their categorisation of crimes too and sometimes they decide not to report any crime figures. Between 1956 and 1959 police annual reports carry no useful crime data at all and a researcher is forced to seek alternative sources. A problem

with police statistics today is that the police have recently decided to completely change their method of gathering offending data. Whereas in the past police counted annual reported offences and apprehensions, from 2015 onwards they have instead counted instances of victimisation, victims, and instances of police proceeding against an offender. What this means for the criminologist is that published police data collected from 2015 are not comparable with data collected before this date. This represents yet another frustration for analysts wishing to look at historic crime patterns in order to compare them with what is happening now (see Brook, 2016).
4. *Uncertainty about the perpetrators.* Because many crimes are unresolved, police are often unable to tell us much about the perpetrators. If we want to know who commits various types of crime in terms of gender, race or age, for example, published police figures are of little use. For this type of information we need to go to other sources, such as the Ministry of Justice.

Justice Data

I have noted that police figures give us little information about perpetrators. If we wish to know about the characteristics of offenders, our best source is justice data coming from the courts. The sex, age and ethnicity of offenders and the types of sentence they got are available from a number of agencies, including the Department of Statistics and various publications and reports published by the Ministry of Justice. Justice data are not comparable with police figures because not all crimes get prosecuted, not all prosecutions are successful, and crimes logged by the police in one year may be dealt with by the courts months or even years after they are notified. So the figures have to be looked at separately. It is important too, when looking at conviction data, that notice is taken of whether the figures refer to convictions recorded or persons convicted. Some crimes, such as the killing of Bradley Haora in 1975, result in the arrests of several offenders. In the Haora case twelve defendants were charged with murder but all were acquitted of the charge at trial. However nine were convicted of manslaughter. The case was investigated as a single murder by the police and logged as such, whereas nine manslaughter convictions would have been entered into the justice data set. By the same token, sometimes a single offender can be convicted of a number of crimes, and sometimes those crimes vary greatly from possession of drugs and/or firearms, to burglary, robbery, assault and theft. These offences will usually appear independently in the police data sets, but only once in justice sets. In the latter case, normally only the offender's 'primary offence' is listed.

Self-reported Crime and Victimisations

Another way of determining crime rates is to randomly survey a population and ask people to report confidentially how many times they have been victimised and in which ways they have been victimised over a given period, or to ask them about the crimes they have committed over a certain period – say in the last 5 years. These figures give us a good indication of who the victims or perpetrators of crimes are and of the circumstances that characterise victims or perpetration.

Although subject to the risk of sampling error and false reporting, when properly conducted, self-report of surveys have a high level of reliability and replicability. Victimisation data are regularly published by the Ministry of Justice (see, e.g., Cunningham, Triggs and Faisandier, 2007; Ministry of Justice, 2014; Morris et al., 2003). Self-reported offending studies, however, are normally conducted by private individuals. One such survey (unpublished) conducted by American criminology professor Chris Eskridge at the University of Canterbury in 1992, for example, found surprisingly high rates of self-reported crime among Canterbury university students, including offences such as class A and B drug use, serious property crime and even rape. This raised quite a fuss at the time but the figures weren't really surprising; in fact, the results were remarkably similar to results Eskridge had obtained previously in a survey of students at the University of Nebraska. The fact is, as the great criminologist Bill Chambliss (1973) discovered in his study of two groups of youths in a small American community, police-reported crime rates have a lot to do with where the police concentrate their attention. They tend to focus on areas where they think crime is a problem: in the lower-class areas where the gangs and 'troublemakers' hang out. They tend to ignore the middle- and upper-class districts and thus they discover less crime there than they would if they policed those areas with equal vigour.

Rises and Falls in Crime Rates

As everyone knows, rates of crime are not constant. Every year when the police release their reported crime statistics there is a flurry of publicity and comment about why rates of certain crimes may have risen or fallen. In actual fact, policing is only a small part of the explanation for rising and falling crime and, as we've seen, rates can be artificially inflated or deflated by public attitudes and policing policy.

That said, we cannot deny that real changes have taken place in crime since World War II, and the most important general reason for the changes is shifting social conditions. After the war ended in 1945, crime rates remained pretty flat, with the total reported crimes of 33,110 in 1945 rising to just 35,390 in 1950. Today there are ten times as many crimes reported as there were in 1950, even though the national population has only increased by 140 per cent. So what is going on?

Part of the explanation lies in the types of crime being committed. Dishonesty crime, for example, such as burglary, theft and fraud, represents more than half of all reported offending, whereas more serious crimes like violence and sexual violation only represent 12 per cent. So a jump in property offending inevitably forces crime levels up, even though serious crime may be falling. Moreover, some of the reasons for changes in property offending patterns can be different from the drivers of change in violent crime or drug crime. So if we want to understand these changes we really need to look at them individually. There is a good online data set published by the Department of Statistics going back to 1993 which relates to reported crime, so I'll rely mostly on this for recent figures. Reported crime for early years will be drawn from data available in the annual police reports.

Dishonesty Crime

In 1950 there were about 12,000 dishonesty crimes reported to the police, which rose to 50,000 in 1960. The big jumps in reported offending started in the 1950s, and had much to do with a range of social factors associated with adolescent youth. The post-war era spawned a rebellious youth culture, with rock 'n' roll music arriving in the United States in 1954, and the first American 'bikie' gangs emerging in the late 1940s and in New Zealand in the early 1950s. These were the days of the 'bodgies' and their female counterparts the 'widgies', who shocked their parents by listening to loud music, drinking lots of beer, riding fast

FIGURE 2.1 **Reported dishonesty crime 1956–2014**

motorbikes and driving noisy cars, and engaging in premarital sex (see Gilbert, 2013; Newbold, 2016; Yska, 1993). The term 'teenager' first became popular after World War II to describe the problem group and in 1954 the New Zealand government appointed a conservative Christian barrister called Dr Oswald Chettle Mazengarb to chair the Special Committee on Moral Delinquency in Children and Adolescents in order to find solutions to the problem (see Mazengarb et al., 1954). This was augmented in 1958 with a small book called *The Bodgie: A Study in Abnormal Psychology*, by psychologist A. E. Manning.

It was in this atmosphere of youthful rebellion and social change that crime rates, boosted by youth offending, began to change. Other factors, too, contributed to rising dishonesty crime:

1. *Urbanisation.* After the war there was a move towards the cities, with the urban population of New Zealand growing from 74 per cent in 1945 to 85 per cent in 1991. Māori were a significant component of this drift. Before the war Māori were primarily a rural people, with only 26 per cent living in cities. After the war they moved steadily into the cities and by 1990 80 per cent of Māori were urban. Māori offence rates are higher than non-Māori in nearly all areas and by the late 1950s a 'Māori crime problem' had been officially identified. Urbanisation is associated

with higher crime because the anonymity of cities negates the informal controls of small communities, and victims of crimes in cities are more likely to involve the police. Small communities tend to solve social problems themselves.
2. *Demographics.* As young soldiers returned from the battlefields of Europe and the Pacific after the war, there was a surge of marriages and child births, creating what was known as a 'baby boom'. The boom started in 1945 and by 1955 many of these 'baby boomers' were nearing adolescence and the age of high-risk offending. Accelerating dishonesty crime rates commenced in 1956 and continued until 1984, when there was a brief respite. Dishonesty crime peaked in 1997, when there were 28 times as many dishonesty crimes as there were in 1950.
3. *The economy.* The 1950s was a time of affluence and high expectations among youth, with young people wanting to own cars, motorbikes and record players, which because of strict import controls were relatively expensive. Although there was full employment, people had to work hard to afford these things and some found it more convenient to steal. Unsophisticated security systems at the time made theft, burglary and fraud relatively easy. Later, after the 'long boom' of post-war economic prosperity ended at the end of the 1960s and permanent unemployment commenced, pressure to steal increased. The oil shocks of 1973 and 1979, when revolutions in the Organization of the Petroleum Exporting Countries (OPEC) caused petrol prices to explode and boosted inflation, also impacted on unemployment. Unemployment was worsened after the Third Labour Government began introducing free-market principles to New Zealand in 1985. Many businesses collapsed during this period and thousands of people were put out of work. This was added to by the catastrophic global share-market crash of October 1987, during the course of which New Zealand shares lost 60 per cent of their value.

As a result of these factors, unemployment in New Zealand grew from 0.1 per cent in 1970 to 11.77 per cent in 1989 (Thorns and Sedgwick, 1997: 91). Unemployment is a correlate of crime because unemployed people become frustrated, alienated and bored. Crimes involving theft, burglary, fraud, robbery and drug dealing are seen as effective ways of easing the pains of poverty and bringing some excitement to life.

But just as dishonesty crime peaked in 1997 and seemed destined to continue rising, a strange thing happened: it began to fall again. After 1998 there was a sudden and sharp decline in reported dishonesty crime. In fact, recorded dishonesty crime in 2014 was 45 per cent lower than 1997, even though the New Zealand population was 31 per cent higher. These drops were recorded in all the major areas of dishonesty: thefts were down 35 per cent, burglaries were down 33 per cent and frauds were down 71 per cent.

Why has dishonesty crime fallen? As is usually the case with crime rates, there is no single answer. In fact there are a number of explanations for why dishonesty crime fell from the late 1990s:

1. *Unemployment has dropped.* High unemployment of around 11 per cent continued from 1989 through to 1993. After that it began to drop, stabilising at around 6 per cent from the late 1990s. More people in work reduces frustration, boredom and the perceived need to supplement an unemployment benefit through crime. People with jobs have hope and a sense of purpose in their lives.
2. *The age structure has changed.* The ages 15–24 are when the greatest risk of offending occurs. Youthful offenders are not only more likely to commit crimes; they are also more likely to get caught. The percentage of people within this age cohort fell from 17 per cent in 1991 to 14.1 per cent in 2013.
3. *Profits are lower.* Electronic transfer and credit systems and a reduction in cash transactions means there is less cash lying around to be stolen than there was before the 1990s. Additionally, the removal of import duties on electronic and other items such as televisions and stereos after 1984 made these commodities cheap to buy and reduced their value on the black market. Moreover, the passage of the Proceeds of Crime Act in 1991, replaced and strengthened by the Criminal Proceeds Recovery Act 2009, allows a court to seize any assets that an owner cannot prove were legally obtained, even without a criminal conviction. So illegal profits are vulnerable to confiscation.
4. *Security systems are better.* Silent alarms, movement detectors, private security patrols, security tags in shops, electronic car registration, GPS systems, cell phone cameras, computer monitoring technology, CCTV and DNA profiling have all made property crimes harder to commit and easier to get caught for. So not only is there less to steal, but the chances of being caught are much higher.

5. *The profitability of drug dealing.* A major explanation for the drop in dishonesty crime is simply that there are easier ways of making money. Growing marijuana requires relatively little capital outlay and kilos of good head sell for between $5,000 and $10,000. Methamphetamine, or 'P', although more difficult to produce, is even more profitable and sells for between $600 and $1,000 a gram. Dealing in drugs is by far the most lucrative form of criminal activity, and is easy to get away with because individual crimes are seldom detected.

So there are a number of different and unrelated factors that have caused the drops in dishonesty offending over the past two decades. Some of these influences have been responsible for falls in other crimes, but there are other influences as well.

Violent Crime

As we have seen with dishonesty crime, levels of violent crime were very low in the early 1950s, but they soon shot upwards. Where violent crime is concerned the big jumps occurred in the 1960s, as the first baby boomers entered their mid-teens. In 1950 there were only 1341 violent crimes reported. By the time violence peaked in 2009, there were 66,464 offences – nearly 50 times the 1950 figure. This rise is truly astronomical.

Explaining changes of such magnitude is a difficult task for the criminologist. Certainly the arrival of youth culture and the emergence of gangs in the 1950s is one explanation. There are a number of other factors as well:

1. *The post-war drift of Māori into the cities.* Māori rates of all forms of violent crime are many times higher than non-Māori (Newbold, 2016) and when young Māori moved into the cities they shifted from an environment where behaviour was to a large extent controlled by local kaumātua and tribal leaders, to one where the police took over. Many urban migrants were under-skilled and lived in impoverished areas where crime levels were high. When the gangs began forming in these areas in the late 1950s and early 1960s, a lot of young Māori joined them. Working-class Māori were accompanied by hundreds of thousands of Pacific Island (Pasifika) migrants, mostly from Samoa, who came to New Zealand in

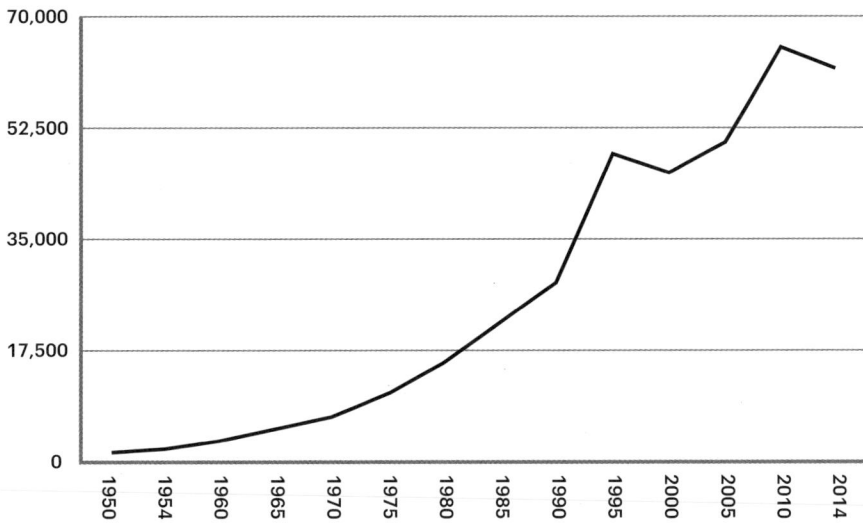

FIGURE 2.2 **Reported violent crime 1950–2014**

increasing numbers after 1962. Like the Māori, Pasifika migrants tended to settle in the poorer areas of the cities where high levels of violent crime and gang membership are recorded. One of the earliest Pasifika gangs is the King Cobras, which formed in central Auckland in the 1960s.

2. *Rising unemployment.* When large numbers of people are out of work they not only commit more property crimes, they are also more likely to find solace in gangs and to become frustrated and violent. Violence, when it occurs, is more often perpetrated upon people one knows than upon strangers, and this is particularly so among families. When children witness or are themselves exposed to high levels of violence at home or in the community, they tend to imitate the same patterns as they grow up. Thus the problem of family violence and more general violence within the community is inter-generational and self-perpetuating. Violent crime reached a peak in 1995, just after the peak in unemployment. It then dropped back a bit before rising again after 2000 and stabilising from 2009.

3. *Alcohol consumption.* Where violence is concerned, alcohol is a big contributor. Figures vary according to sources, but the bulk of studies show that in about 50 per cent of all violent incidents, at least one of the parties had been drinking prior to the incident. So alcohol consumption may be a component in violence statistics. Data since 1945 show that after

World War II per capita alcohol consumption increased steadily. During the 50 years before 1967, pubs had to close at 6:00 p.m. but in that year this ended and alcohol consumption increased further. Consumption continued to rise until 1978, after which it began to fall, largely as a result of drink-drive campaigns (Newbold, 2016). We have seen that rates of violence continued to climb after this so we can say that although alcohol is a factor in violence and may have contributed to the post-war rises, other factors were of greater significance.

After peaking in 2009, reported violent crime fell only slightly and then stabilised. The figure for 2014 is just 7 per cent below the 2009 figure. But more than half of violent crime takes the form of assaults, and more serious but less-often reported crime like homicide, robbery and sexual assaults have responded to different factors. So we need to look at them individually in order to understand them.

Assaults

Assault is a category of offending which is difficult to get a timeline on in police figures because some data sets divide assaults into 'serious' and 'minor', while others do not, and some sets use categories such as 'Acts intended to cause injury' (1994–2014) or 'Serious assaults resulting in injury' (1996–2014). The sets are not comparable and can make things confusing. But accepting what we do have, we can see that assaults generally grew exponentially after 1950, peaked in 2009, then reduced and stabilised. If we look at serious assaults causing injury we also see a peak around 2007–10, followed by a drop of 17 per cent. The big jumps in assaults after the 1950s have been explained above in the discussion about violence generally. Serious assaults increased nine-fold between 1975 and 2007, when the data series stops. The 2007 figure represents an 86 per cent jump on 10 years before. What we can adduce, then, is that since the onset of permanent unemployment there have been huge jumps in the number of recorded assaults, but these continued to rise even after unemployment and alcohol consumption levels dropped. In recent years they have fallen only slightly. It's very difficult to figure out what is going on here, and explaining the trends fully would require a comprehensive study of what types of assaults are being committed, when, where, by whom, and how they are being recorded by the police.

CRIME RATES

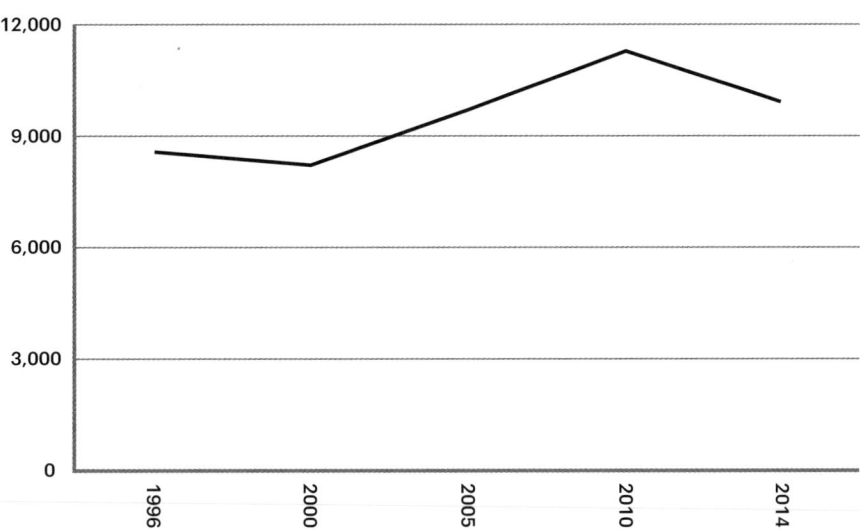

FIGURE 2.3 Reported serious assaults resulting in injury 1996–2014

FIGURE 2.4 Reported murders 1950–2014

Homicide

Homicides give a clearer picture. Like other forms of violent crime, homicides increased sharply during and after the 1950s. In the present discussion I will refer to reported murders, since homicide data are contaminated by attempted murders, assisted suicides, infanticides and so on. Reported murders averaged only 8.6 a year between 1950 and 1956 but then grew somewhat erratically to peak at over 70 in 1991 and 1992. The problem with this is that between 1990 and 1997 there were six mass murders involving between five and thirteen victims, thus affecting reported levels for the years of 1990, 1992 (two incidents), 1994, 1995 and 1997. Strangely, there have been no mass murders since 1997 and the last one before 1990 was in 1941. So mass murder seems to have been a fad of the 1990s. Since then, however, murders have definitely fallen and have averaged just 43 a year since 2010.

The rise in murders after the 1950s can be explained in the same way as other forms of violent crime. But the reasons for the falls are more interesting. We see that murders summited in the years when unemployment peaked, but there are other factors too:

1. *Medical care.* Medical care, especially in emergency response situations, is constantly improving and lives can now be saved which in the past would have been lost. So this is one certain reason why fewer people have died.
2. *Women's refuges.* Women's refuges first appeared in Christchurch in 1974 and now exist in more than 30 locations up and down the country. Women's refuges have impacted on domestic murders because women have been able to extricate themselves from potentially fatal abuse and get help from qualified personnel. In addition to this, pro-active police involvement in domestic violence cases and policies of presumptive arrest in evidential cases of domestic assault since 1987 have removed violent perpetrators from situations which can end in a fatality if not acted upon.
3. *Gun control.* Strict gun control is a factor which limits use of, and access to, firearms. After the 1990 massacre at Aramoana when thirteen people were killed, the 1992 Arms Amendment Act made acquiring an arms licence far more difficult than before. Licence applicants are now heavily screened for emotional and mental stability and arms are automatically confiscated if there is a record of domestic conflict. Risk-averse firearms policies mean that fewer guns end up in unsafe hands and firearms killings, which account for about a quarter of all murders, are reduced.

The Mass Murders of the 1990s

1990   At Aramoana on the Otago Peninsula, David Malcolm Gray, a 33-year-old unemployed recluse, killed thirteen people including a policeman and wounded another three people, while armed with a variety of semi-automatic and repeating firearms. He was shot dead by police.

1992   At Paerata, South Auckland, farmer Brian Schlaepfer (64) killed six family members using a range of weapons including a knife and a double-barrelled shotgun. He committed suicide.

1992   At Masterton in the Wairarapa, unemployed shearer Raymond Wahia Ratima (25) clubbed and stabbed seven family members to death including his three children, his brother-in-law and his sister-in-law, who was 8 months pregnant. He was jailed for life.

1994   In Dunedin, Otago University music student David Cullen Bain (22) was charged with killing five family members with a .22 rifle fitted with a silencer. He was convicted and sentenced to life imprisonment with a 16-year minimum but was acquitted on retrial in 2009. Nobody else has been charged.

1995   In Hamilton, six people died in the arson of the New Empire Hotel. Unemployed man Alan Lory (41) was convicted of arson and manslaughter. He was sentenced to 12 years for arson and life for manslaughter.

1997   At Raurimu in the central North Island, unemployed schizophrenic Stephen Anderson (22) used a 12-gauge shotgun to kill six and wound another six at a family gathering. He was acquitted by reason of insanity and detained in hospital as a special patient.

Robbery

Robbery is an area where violence levels have risen steeply. In the early 1950s robberies were almost unheard of – between 1951 and 1954 there was an average of only 26 robberies each year. Numbers increased but remained below 100 until 1966. Twenty years later they had exceeded 1000, 10 years after that they passed 2000, and they peaked at almost 3000 in 2006. The 2006 figure was 111 times higher than those of the early 1950s. Again, the increase is astronomical and difficult to explain. We can consider the usual factors: alcohol, unemployment, poverty and violent gang culture, but none of them seem sufficient. For one thing, robberies continued to climb after unemployment peaked in the early 1990s and after alcohol usage levels dropped. It seems that in certain sectors of society, robbery became the 'in' thing to do from the mid-1980s onward. It was also an easy way of getting fast money for those who knew what they were doing. In the 1980s professional robbers were able to steal lots of money with a high chance of getting away with it. Banks and businesses still carried lots of cash and security systems were relatively primitive. In March 1983, for example, a group of at least five well-known Auckland criminals robbed an Armourguard van of $285,000, but only two were ever caught. In 1988 the introduction of the

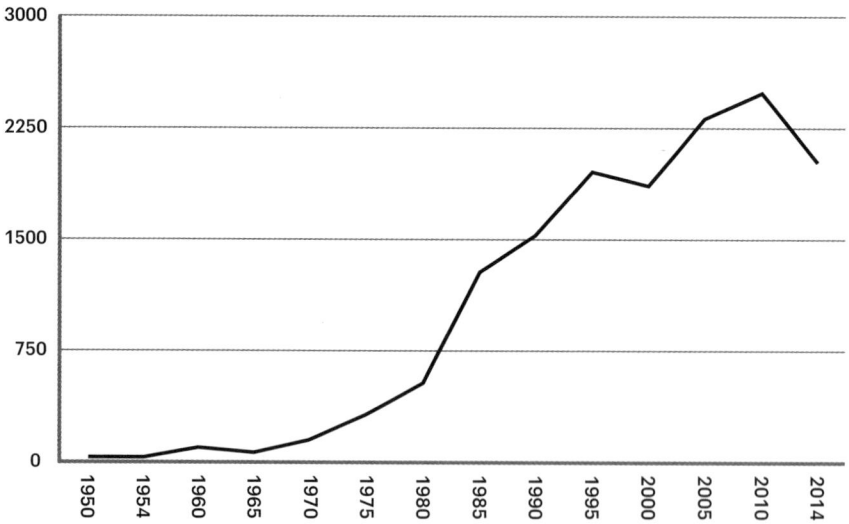

FIGURE 2.5 **Reported robberies 1950–2014**

police 'Eagle' helicopter halted the rise briefly, but the machine hit another aircraft and crashed in 1993, after which its threat disappeared.

After 2006, however, robberies fell sharply, and are now 31 per cent lower than 20 years ago and back to the levels they were at in the late 1990s. There are a number of clear explanations for why robberies have fallen:

1. *Declining profits.* Potential profits now are much lower now than they were last century, with greater reliance on electronic transfer and pay systems resulting in less cash sitting in vaults, tills and security vehicles.
2. *Better security.* Security is tighter now and robberies are harder to get away with. CCTV, DNA profiling and private security guards standing outside financial institutions all make it much harder these days to get away with robberies. One friend of mine, who I know got away with dozens of robberies in the 1980s, says that the presence of security guards is the greatest single deterrent to robbery and is one of the main reasons he gave them up.
3. *Drug dealing.* As we have seen with burglary, there is much more money to be made today from drug dealing. Professional robbery is a thing of the past. After the turn of the century, professional robbers gradually began retiring from their trade as they aged, and either pulled out of crime altogether or, as in the case of my friend mentioned above, began dealing in methamphetamine. So who is committing the 2000 or so robberies that are currently reported every year? These jobs are mainly being pulled by hapless young amateurs and bunglers who rob individuals, bottle stores and dairies of small amounts of cash, cigarettes or booze, and who almost always are quickly identified, caught and sent to prison.

Sexual Assaults

Sexual assault is a crime that has become highly politicised since the feminist movement began profiling it in the 1970s. But crimes of this type are difficult to compare over long periods because the way the police record them is inconsistent. This is complicated by the fact that in 1985 the Rape Law Reform Bill changed the law to introduce the term 'Sexual Violation' to refer to all forms of illegal sexual assault. Sexual Violation has two main categories: Rape, which involves non-consensual penile penetration of a woman's vagina; and Unlawful

Sexual Connection, which covers all other forms of sexual or anal assault. For this reason it is easiest just to consider reported rape figures, because the definition of rape has remained fairly constant.

Figures for rape show a similar pattern to robbery and assaults, except that there has been no recent reduction in incidence. Between 1950 and 1954 reported rape was rare, with an average of just under sixteen rapes reported each year. There are no data for 1955–58 but in 1959, 70 rapes were recorded and 126 the following year. Rapes stabilised at about this level until the early 1970s, before steadily rising to the 2014 level of 775 rapes – the largest number ever recorded and about 47 times greater than that of the early 1950s. In the last 10 years alone, reported rapes have grown by more than half.

Explaining the rises is difficult, but some of the reasons are no doubt the same as with other forms of violent crime. Where rape is concerned, however, there is another factor: higher reporting. Prior to the 1970s women were reluctant to report rapes for a number of reasons which included unsympathetic treatment from the police, intrusive and embarrassing questioning by defence counsel about their sexual histories at trial, and high levels of cynicism from juries if a woman was portrayed as having encouraged an accused in any way or as being a woman of low character. As a result, many legitimate rape complaints ended up with the perpetrator walking free and the victim looking like a tart. To make

FIGURE 2.6 **Reported rapes 1950–2014**

things worse, until the law changed in 1985, it was not illegal for a man to rape his wife. Sex on demand was seen as a married man's right, irrespective of the wishes of his wife. This was known as the 'marital exemption'.

Today these attitudes look outrageous but at the time they were internationally accepted. The reason attitudes changed had much to do with the feminist movement, which started in the United States in the first half of the 1960s, and reached New Zealand soon after. By the early 1970s rape had become identified as a feminist issue, with Women Against Rape (WAR) formed in Wellington in 1973. From 1974, articles about rape became a common feature of the New Zealand feminist magazine *Broadsheet*, and even of the traditionally conservative *New Zealand Woman's Weekly*. Feminist conferences and public demonstrations focused on rape, as did a large number of books. Consciousness about the problem grew rapidly. Parliament followed public sentiment, with restrictions on the cross-examination of women in rape trials first appearing in 1977, followed by further changes to law in the 1980s regarding such things as prohibiting the publication of the names of rape victims, the dropping of the marital exemption, and changing the law in relation to matters of consent, corroboration and historic complaints so that victims would be more likely to come forward and complaints would be more likely to be believed (see Newbold, 2016, for more detail). In 1993 the maximum term for rape increased from 14 to 20 years and the open-ended sentence of preventive detention became available on a first offence of sexual violation.

It was changes of this type which encouraged more women to lay complaints of rape, including historic events that had occurred years before. Between 1980 and 2014, the number of recorded rape complaints grew 300 per cent. A large proportion of these were historic. For example, in 1997, 57 per cent of all rape convictions related to offences that had taken place at least 2 years before (see Newbold, 2016). Higher reporting levels appear to be at least partially responsible for the continuing rises in rape figures, and tougher sentences have had no apparent impact on rape incidence. It is to the question of tougher penalties that I now turn.

Penalties for Violence

In the 1980s, in an attempt to stem the exponential rises in violent crime, penalties for violent offences began to increase. In 1985 imprisonment became almost mandatory for violent crimes punishable by at least 7 years imprisonment, which was reduced to crimes punishable by at least 2 years in 1987. In 1987 non-parole periods for life imprisonment were increased from 7 to 10 years, and in 1993 courts became empowered to give non-parole minimums longer than the statutory minimum. In 2002 a standard 17-year minimum was introduced for murders committed with certain aggravating features, and remission for all sentences over 2 years was removed and replaced by parole. Preventive detention was widened, average sentences grew longer, and parole became harder to get. As noted, in 1993 the maximum penalty for rape was increased to 20 years (see Newbold, 2007). Finally, in 2010, a 'three strikes and you're out' law was created, with enhanced penalties and removal of parole for repeat violent offenders. By June 2015, 5630 violent offenders had received first strike warnings.

The impact of these legislative changes has been burgeoning prison populations (which grew from 2769 in 1985 to 9300 in early 2016) and an increased percentage of prisoners doing very long sentences for crimes of violence. As we have seen, however, violent crime has been unaffected by the heavier penalties. The explanation for the rises in violent crime lies in social and cultural circumstances, not in the absence of a tough deterrent.

Drug Crime

Drug crime is an area which has only been problematic since the late 1960s, although reported offending is an unreliable indicator of drug crime because most of these crimes are unreported. However, police figures do give us a broad picture of what is happening where illicit drug use is concerned.

Before the 1960s drug offending was not a major issue in New Zealand. Youth in the 1950s and early 1960s knew little about illegal drugs and it wasn't until the late 1960s that use of marijuana and LSD became noticeable. Between 1960 and 1963 an average of only 73 drug offences was reported each year, but in 1964 the number began steadily to rise, reaching over 400 offences in 1970, 3000 in 1977, and almost 18,000 in 1987. Drug crime stabilised at about 20,000 per year between 1991 and 2012 and fell to about 16,000 in 2013 and 2014.

The reason for what was part of a worldwide explosion in drug crime is the changes in youth culture that started in America in the mid-1960s. From 1960 onwards young middle-class Americans became increasingly politically aware, protesting and often getting beaten up and arrested for publicly challenging racist laws and discrimination in the American South and, from the mid-1960s,

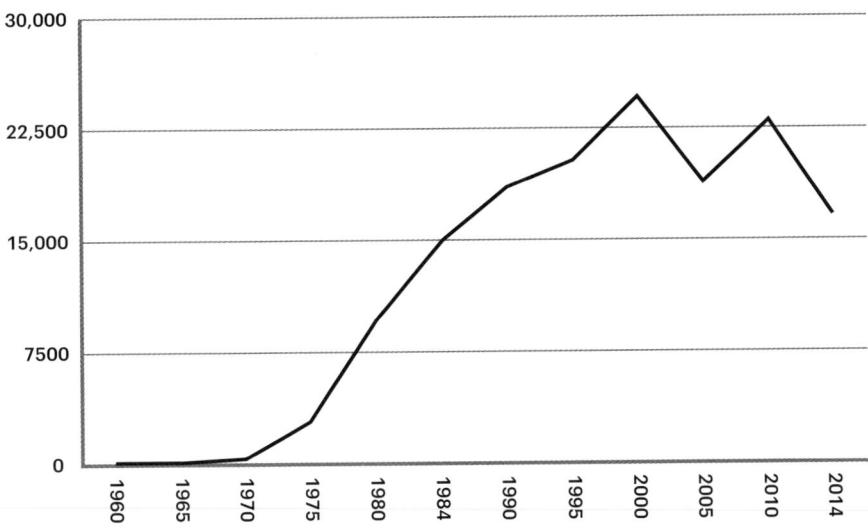

FIGURE 2.7 **Reported drug crime 1960–2014**

for protesting against American involvement in the civil war in Vietnam. Out of this youthful rebellion came a new culture known commonly as 'hippie' culture and with it new forms of music, dress and drug use appeared (see Haskins and Benson, 1988). Peace, love, justice and social harmony were the themes of hippiedom, and the hippie drugs of choice, marijuana and LSD, were both psychotropic substances capable of invoking feelings of tranquillity, empathy and personal introspection in the user.

Hippie subculture and its values were transmitted rapidly around the Western world through music, film and television – which had arrived in New Zealand in 1960. In 1966 private pirate radio started in Auckland, transmitting all-hit music 24 hours a day, thus giving the country's youth full exposure to the musical and drug-use trends of the world's largest and most influential economy. By 1970 marijuana (or 'weed') and a few years later LSD (known as 'acid') were easily available and being widely used by New Zealand middle-class youth in all of the major urban centres. By 1974, Māori and the working classes were beginning to smoke weed and were dropping acid as well. Although marijuana remained the most commonly-used drug, others soon entered the scene. Heroin and morphine, initially stolen in pharmaceutical burglaries but later imported, became widely used and imported Thai heroin began commonly appearing from about 1974, followed by home-grown 'New Zealand Green'. Later, in the 1990s, ecstasy and methamphetamine grew increasingly popular, the latter largely displacing heroin as the drug of choice for harder users.

Because of the popularity of illegal drugs and the considerable profits available for producing or marketing them, long sentences – of up to life imprisonment in the case of class A drugs such as heroin, LSD, cocaine and methamphetamine – have had little impact on drug availability. Studies I have cited elsewhere (Newbold, 2016) show that illegal drug use is as popular now as it has ever been. In fact, as noted previously, drug dealing has supplanted other forms of illegal activity as the primary source of income for the professional and organised criminal. The recent 25 per cent drop in reported drug offences is not due to less drug use, but to the police shifting their attention from low-level marijuana cropping and use to the more serious job of busting methamphetamine labs and blocking the importation of meth and its precursors.

Women and Crime

Before closing this chapter, it is appropriate to take a quick look at gender differentials in crime. I have noted earlier that the ages 15–24 are when a person is most at risk of offending and that Māori are disproportionately represented in crime figures, particularly regarding violent and property crime. But what about women?

Internationally, figures indicate that as a rule women offend less seriously and less often than men. In New Zealand, women are only represented in 23 per cent of all convictions and only constitute about 6 per cent of the prison population. Where women come closest to men is in dishonesty crime; here they commit about a third of all offences. They are least represented in offences of violence, sex crimes and crimes against good order such as rioting.

This will come as no surprise, although self-report studies do show that the gap between male and female offending may not be as great as statistics indicate. However, self-report studies confirm that female offending is still less frequent and less serious, on average, than men's (Heidensohn and Silvestri, 2012; Morris, 1987: 24–25).

Another factor in lower female crime rates is that courts, in general, are more tolerant when dealing with women offenders than they are with men. A comprehensive study by Jeffries in the early 2000s confirmed that even when relevant sentencing variables are held constant, women get lighter sentences than men for crimes of equal gravity (see Jeffries, Fletcher and Newbold, 2003).

An interesting fact about women's offending internationally is that its frequency and seriousness have increased over the past few years, relative to men's. In 1963, women only accounted for about 7.7 per cent of all convictions in New Zealand but by 1972 this had grown to 11 per cent. In 1989 women constituted 16 per cent of convictions and in 2014 the figure was 23 per cent: about triple the ratio of 50 years earlier. In the early 1960s women were almost absent from serious crime figures, but by 1989 they were appearing more often in court facing serious charges such as violence (8 per cent of all offenders in 1989, which grew to 16 per cent in 2014). Other crimes featuring a major increase in female representation between 1989 and 2014 are drugs (from 16 per cent of offenders to 22 per cent), property (from 24 per cent to 33 per cent) and traffic (from 15 per cent to 26 per cent) (Newbold, 2016).

The reasons why women are appearing more often in crime statistics have to do with the changes that have taken place in women's social position since the 1960s. During the 1950s the life expectations of women were largely restricted to getting married, having children and looking after the home. At home, a woman's accepted role was subservience to her husband, who was head of the household and the principal breadwinner. The feminist movement, commencing in the United States in the first half of the 1960s and soon spreading around the Western world, challenged these notions and over the next 40 years a revolution took place which saw increasing numbers of women entering higher education, politics, the professions, the judiciary, and the boards of corporations. More women drove cars, more chose not to get married, or to divorce, or to have children out of wedlock, and more women became financially and personally independent.

This new independence is reflected in rising female crime rates: the greater number of women appearing in traffic-related offences, for example, is a result of more females owning and driving cars, and the greater number of women committing dishonesty crimes – particularly fraud – is related to their financial independence and their access to large amounts of money as directors or financial controllers of businesses.

But how has this new independence affected violent crime? Part of the message that feminism had for the new 'liberated' woman of the 1970s and 1980s was not only that she should be financially independent but also that she should be emotionally strong and capable of standing on her own feet, without male support. Women were encouraged to be aggressive in their pursuit of autonomy and to fight against gender prejudice and male bullying. In the 1970s and 1980s classes in the principles of self-defence and how to repel a male sexual assailant, for example, became very popular among women, particularly in Auckland where Sue Lytollis, a judo black belt, attracted a huge following by teaching self-defence based on 'feminist concepts'. A side effect of this type of thinking was the image of the 'new woman', portrayed in books, video, television and film – a glamorous heroine, capable of defending herself and fighting on an equal standing with the best of male combatants. Images portrayed in TV programmes such as *Cagney and Lacey* (1981–88), *Xena, Warrior Princess* (1995–2001) and the movie *The Girl with the Dragon Tattoo* (2011) created role models which are particularly attractive to young women with weak or dysfunctional family bonds who have frequently witnessed or been subjected to high levels of violence during their lives. These women often identify with, and act out the role of, the arse-kicking female action hero. It is this type of person who is overwhelmingly represented in the growing catalogue of extremely violent offences committed by young women against men or other women, and who is the principal driver of the higher female violent crime figures that we have seen since the early 1990s. Interestingly, however, and unlike male violent offending, which has stabilised, the number of females convicted of violent crimes has actually fallen slightly since peaking in 2010. It is too early at this point to tell whether this is a blip or the commencement of a trend.

Conclusion

This chapter has given a brief introduction to how crime rates are collected and assembled in New Zealand and indicated some of the cautions that should be exercised when analysing crime data, especially those from disparate sources. We have seen that crime rates escalated sharply after the 1950s but that for the most part, they began to decline during or after the 1990s. There is no single or simple explanation for these rises and falls. As has been shown, a combination of factors is responsible for changes in crime rates and different forms of crime respond to different forces. Crime is part of a very complex social dynamic and cannot be separated from it. In order to comprehend the aetiology of crime, therefore, we must look closely at the social, legal, political, cultural, economic and historical contexts in which it takes place. Only after doing this can an effective understanding of fluctuations in reported crime be achieved.

REFERENCES

Brook, E. 2016. 'Where It Counts: How New Zealand's Crime Statistics Have Changed', *Police News* (January–February): 6–9.
Chambliss, W. 1973. 'The Saints and the Roughnecks', *Society* 11(1): 24–31.
Cunningham, C., Triggs, S., and Faisandier, S. 2007. *Analysis of the Māori Experience: Findings from the Crime and Safety Survey, 2006*. Wellington: Ministry of Justice.
Gilbert, J. 2013. *Patched: The History of Gangs in New Zealand*. Auckland: Auckland University Press.
Haskins, J., and Benson, K. 1988. *The 60s Reader*. New York: Viking Kestrel.
Heidensohn, F., and Silvestri, M. 2012. 'Gender and Crime', in M. Maguire, R. Morgan and R. Reiner (Eds), *The Oxford Handbook of Criminology* (5th ed.). Oxford: Oxford University Press, pp. 336–69.
Jeffries, S., Fletcher, G., and Newbold, G. 2003. 'Pathways to Sex-based Differentiation in Criminal Court Sentencing', *Criminology* 41(2): 701–22.
Manning, A. E. 1958. *The Bodgie: A Study in Abnormal Psychology*. Wellington: Reed.
Mazengarb, O. C., et al. 1954. 'Report of the Special Committee on Moral Delinquency in Children and Adolescents'. *Appendices to the Journals of the House of Representatives*, H-47.
Ministry of Justice. 2014. *New Zealand Crime and Safety Survey*. Wellington: Ministry of Justice.
Morris, A. 1987. *Women, Crime and Criminal Justice*. Oxford: Basil Blackwell.
Morris, A., Reilly, J., Berry, S., and Ransom, R. 2003. *New Zealand National Survey of Crime Victims 2001*. Wellington: Ministry of Justice.
Newbold, G. 2007. *The Problem of Prisons: Corrections Reform in New Zealand since 1840*. Wellington: Dunmore.
Newbold, G. 2016. *Crime, Law and Justice in New Zealand*. New York: Routledge.
Thorns, D., and Sedgwick, C. 1997. *Understanding Aotearoa/New Zealand: Historical Statistics*. Palmerston North: Dunmore.
Yska, R. 1993. *All Shook Up: The Flash Bodgie and the Rise of the New Zealand Teenager in the Fifties*. Auckland: Penguin.

3.

The History of Policing

HEATHER WOLFFRAM

Introduction

A quick survey of New Zealand Police (NZP) today reveals a professional law enforcement agency that polices by consent, provides a range of specialist police functions and aims to be representative of the community it serves in terms of gender and ethnicity. How our police service has come to manifest these characteristics and how its current priorities differ from those of its predecessors is only really apparent, however, if we consider New Zealand policing historically. In order to appreciate the unique set of influences that have shaped law enforcement in this country since 1840, this chapter begins by describing the development of English policing, which provided both the first and a number of subsequent models for police in New Zealand. Turning to consider the challenges of policing the colony between the 1840s and 1880s, the chapter will then show how the fractious relationship between Māori and Pākehā and the law-breaking associated with events like the gold rushes forced civil policing to take a back seat to paramilitary policing. In the lead-up to World War I, however, as New Zealand society became more peaceful, the police increasingly focused on the professional skills required to police civil society, rewriting rules around recruitment and training while incorporating a range of new technologies. The impact of the two world wars and the turbulent inter-war period, as this chapter will show, saw the police temporarily engage in coercive political and moral policing, while the second half of the twentieth century witnessed renewed emphasis on professionalism, as represented by specialisation and improved recruitment and training.

Policing before the Nineteenth Century

In many ways, NZP's vision of 'Safer Communities Together', which relies on the cooperation of individuals, families and communities with the police (Policing Act, 2008), is reminiscent of pre-nineteenth-century forms of policing. Before the emergence of a centralised, professional police force in 1829 (the London Metropolitan Police, from which New Zealand took its cue), English law enforcement was reliant on a number of different systems, often using private citizens. From the thirteenth century, for instance, when King Henry III (1207–72) ordained that every village and township should have a constable or two, private individuals were legally obliged to report crimes to the local constabulary or Justice of the Peace, apprehend criminals who they witnessed committing felonies, and assist constables to put up a 'hue and cry' to catch and prosecute offenders (Emsley, 1986: 70; Emsley, Hitchcock and Shoemaker, 2016). Citizens' obligations did not end there, however. In the early modern period (1500–1800) householders within a parish were expected to take turns in performing nightwatch duties, which were unpaid and often onerous. Patrolling the streets of the parish between nine or ten in the evening and dawn, the watchman's role was preventive, his task being to observe those acting suspiciously and to arrest people who disrupted the peace or were caught in the commission of a crime (Emsley, Hitchcock and Shoemaker, 2016). Given that watchmen were armed only with a staff and a lamp, they often became victims of violent offenders and drunks, encouraging many householders to pay deputies to take on their rotation.

Like the role of watchman, that of constable was also unpaid voluntary work carried out by local householders. The constable's duties, however, involved supervision of the night watch, execution of warrants issued by Justices of the Peace and the maintenance of order via periodical sweeps of the street for prostitutes, vagrants, drunks and gamblers (Harris, 2004: 85). While perhaps not as dangerous as the watch, acting as a constable was inconvenient and disruptive for many householders, who, by the eighteenth century, were frequently paying others to take their place (Emsley, 1986: 85). This meant that in some parts of London by 1700 both the night watch and constabulary had become fully-paid forces (Beattie, 2001: 150).

Murder of a Watchman

The potential dangers of the night watch are evident in a 1680 trial for murder at the Old Bailey in London. According to the trial proceedings, Isaack Smith, a Watchman, had been patrolling Paternoster Row at 3 a.m. on 29 May when he encountered an unruly group of men, including the accused, John Watkins and Edward Whittaker. When Smith attempted to stop them to ask their business, they resisted, engaging in a scuffle that soon saw Smith on the ground. Watkins then took up his staff and struck Smith on the left side of his head. According to the physician who testified at the trial, this wound caused Smith's death, although he languished until 22 September. In their defence, Watkins and Whittaker argued that they were fruiters with legitimate business in Newgate Market and that the deceased had first assaulted them. Both men, however, were found guilty of murder on 13 October 1680 and sentenced to death ('Old Bailey Proceedings, 13th October 1680', 2017).

In the late seventeenth century, when London's citizens believed they were experiencing a crime wave, substantial rewards began to be offered for the return of stolen goods and the arrest of highwaymen. Those who responded to these rewards and made their living off them became known as thief-takers and enjoyed a dubious reputation. Successful thief-takers were often criminals or former criminals themselves, using their contacts with the criminal underworld to negotiate the return of stolen goods or to trick naive young people into committing offences that the thief-taker would then claim the reward on (Beattie, 2012: 7). This practice largely came to an end with the first Transportation Act (1718), which outlawed rewards for the return of stolen goods without a prosecution.

From the 1730s the cities of London and Middlesex established 'rotation offices' so that people could find a magistrate at fixed hours in order to report crimes. Henry and John Fielding, who ran the Bow Street office from 1748, created a system of both preventive and detective policing that not only made use of registers of crimes and prosecutions, stolen goods and wanted criminals, but also employed thief-takers on a retainer (Styles, 1983: 127–49). These former thief-takers, who became known as Bow Street Runners, collected and disseminated information about crimes and took part in foot and horse patrols, ultimately forming a formidable crime-fighting force, which, as the Fieldings had intended, prevented crime by convincing criminals they were increasingly likely to be apprehended (Babington, 1969: 176; Beattie, 2012: 9).

English Policing in the Nineteenth Century

In the late eighteenth and early nineteenth centuries, policing in London and elsewhere was still largely organised and paid for at the parish level. This had distinct advantages because communities organised and controlled their own policing, but it also had disadvantages, including the inability of poorer parishes to pay for adequate policing in an era of increasing urbanisation and crime. As has so often happened in the history of policing, a crisis of confidence around the 'fitness for purpose' of the current police system led to calls for reform. In the late eighteenth and early nineteenth centuries, events such as the Gordon (anti-Catholic) Riots of 1780 as well as a number of grisly murders, such as the Ratcliffe Highway murders involving seven victims in 1811, saw reformers push for the establishment of a centralised, professional police force in London (Emsley, 1986: 4).

The series of police and watch bills that resulted between the 1780s and 1820s, however, failed (London and Westminster Police Bill, 1785; Justices' Bill, 1792; Nightly Watch Regulation Bill, 1812). These attempts at reform were largely stymied by a fear that the new police would not police by consent, but would mimic those in France who used arms and subterfuge to suppress the working class and to spy on citizens. In addition, there was strong resistance to a centralised model of policing from wealthy parishes like the Square Mile of the City of London, which feared the loss of control over their own policing systems (Emsley, 1986: 74). The matter was so contentious that it was not until 1829, when the Home Secretary Sir Robert Peel proposed a new bill that excluded the Square Mile of the City of London and guaranteed that the new police would be civilian and unarmed, that a centralised police force was finally established.

This centralised force, named the Metropolitan Police, has often been regarded by historians as a marked improvement upon the watch system that preceded it, but a closer look at the first decades of its life tells a more complex story (Emsley,

The Ratcliffe Highway Murders and Resistance to Police Reform

In 1811, the horrific murders of two families at Ratcliffe Highway, an area then on the fringes of London, led to public outcry about policing in the metropolis. Reformers used this opportunity to claim that a centralised police force would prevent such outrages, but others regarded the proposed changes to policing as illiberal and un-English, mimicking the French system of despotic political policing and use of informers. Among these sceptics was the Earl of Dudley, who wrote to his sister:

> ... these things make people cry out against the laxity of our police. The fact, however, I am inclined to suspect is that it is next to impossible to prevent outrages of this sort from happening in those parts of town that are inhabited exclusively by the lowest and most profligate wretches in the nation, except by entrusting magistrates with powers vastly too extensive to be prudently vested in such hands. They have an admirable police at Paris, but they pay for it dear enough. I had rather half a dozen people's throats should be cut in Ratcliffe Highway every three or four years than be subject to domiciliary visits, spies, and all the rest of Fouche's contrivances. (Ward, 1811, cited in Emsley, 1996: 22)

1986: 75). Community control and involvement in policing, which had been a hallmark of law and order prior to the nineteenth century, was lessened in London as a result of the new centralised system and led to a range of objections. Parishes, particularly on the city's rural fringes, for instance, found that they were paying significantly more for policing than they had in the past, often for little improvement in service. Ealing, for example, in the 20 years leading up to 1830, had paid £100 per annum for its constables and watch, but under the new system helped subsidise urban parishes with an £880 contribution (Paley, 1989: 114). Others objected to the new police officers (known as 'Peelers' after Sir Robert Peel) because they suspected they would act as another branch of the military designed to control the population and enforce middle-class ideas about proper public behaviour.

Claims by some historians that the Metropolitan Police were an immediate improvement on the watch system that had preceded it, particularly in terms of personnel, are also questionable (Paley, 1989: 95–130). Recruits to the new police tended not to be well-educated, to have received minimal training and to be inexperienced and unfamiliar with their beats. Housed in barracks and made to wear uniforms even when off duty, these poorly-paid constables often maintained other jobs, although they were forbidden to do so, or snuck off to get drunk while on duty. Indeed, in the first 2 years of the Metropolitan Police more than 3000 constables left the force, nearly two-thirds being dismissed for infractions such as drunkenness. The efficiency of the new force in its first decade was also questionable. The night watch had patrolled all the streets and alleys of a parish at least every 45 minutes because beats were only 500 to 600 metres long. In comparison, police constables had beats of several kilometres and only patrolled main thoroughfares. Each police division was patrolled by 40 men at one time and while there was an increase in terms of day patrols, there was a major cut to night patrols (Paley, 1989: 115).

Despite these early issues, by 1840 it was clear that the Metropolitan Police was regarded by London's middle classes as an effective preventive force that kept the streets clear of drunkenness, riot and debauchery. Where the public believed the new police remained ineffective in the early 1840s, however, was in the area of detection.

A number of unsolved crimes, particularly murders, led the press to criticise the Metropolitan Police for their lack of a Detective Branch during the early 1840s, coming to a head with the murder case of Daniel Good on 28 April 1842 (Beattie, 2012: 262). Prompted by this case *The Times*, comparing the new police to the efficient detective system offered by the Bow Street Runners, made the following observations:

> The officers, although most useful as a preventive force, are most inefficient as a detective police. That fact has been clearly shown by the results in the cases of murder of the boy Brill, in the wood at Ruislip near Uxbridge; of Eliza Davies, the barmaid in Frederick street, Regent's-park; of Richard Westwood, the watchmaker in Prince's street, Leicester square; and of Eliza Grimwood, in the Waterloo road, the perpetrators of which still remain undiscovered; but want of tact and ability as a detective police displayed on all occasions by the old Bow street officers has been more fully demonstrated in the present case of Daniel Good, the Roehampton murderer ... unless some important alterations are made by the appointment of

a detective police, or an improvement in the system, the perpetrators of crimes, however horrid and revolting their nature, will in nine cases out of ten, escape the hands of justice. ('The Murder at Roehampton', 1842)

In response, Richard Mayne, the joint first Commissioner of Police of the Metropolis, established a Detective Branch in June 1842, consisting of two superintendents and six sergeants. This small group of detectives grew slowly during the 1850s and 1860s and took up residence at New Scotland Yard in 1875 (Shpayer-Makov, 2011: 32–40). Not long afterwards, however, in 1877 a turf fraud scandal, involving detectives who had been paid off by a criminal, led to a Committee of Inquiry that saw the dissolution of the Detective Branch and the establishment of the Criminal Investigation Department (CID), which was comprised of 250 men (Shpayer-Makov, 2011: 38–39). In the remaining decades of the nineteenth century the CID exhibited increasing professionalism in adopting new procedures for investigation, allowing detectives to specialise in specific types of crime and incorporating new technologies.

Policing in New Zealand, c. 1840–1886

The suspicion exhibited by some residents of London in 1829 that the new Metropolitan Police would act as a branch of the military, tasked with keeping the public in line, was not entirely without foundation. The Home Secretary, Robert Peel, who introduced this new force, had experience with armed policing, having helped establish the system of policing that resulted in the paramilitary Irish Constabulary in 1836 (McEldowney, 1991: 19–20). While the Irish model did not get taken up in England, where policing by community consent became the norm, it did become the template for a number of British colonial police forces, including those in New South Wales and early colonial New Zealand.

The emphasis on policing by consent rather than by coercion, which was apparent in the Metropolitan Police Bill (1829), was initially absent in New Zealand, where it was believed that force was required to ensure order (Hill, 2012). Indeed, when the colony was established in 1840, it was the heavily armed New South Wales mounted police, used to dealing with convicts, and police magistrates supported by constables, who provided the new colony's policing. By the mid-1840s, however, this system was proving insufficient to deal with an increasing number of Māori uprisings and Governor George Grey decided that the colony's policing must become more militant (R. S. Hill, 1986: 93–159). With this in mind, the Armed Police Force (APF) was established in 1846, directly modelled on the Irish Constabulary (R. S. Hill, 1986: 235–335). The APF, to which a number of high-born Māori were also recruited, policed both towns and outlying areas that remained under Māori control, in many instances using extreme force to suppress rebellion (R. S. Hill, 1986: 238). As the uprisings of the 1840s came to an end, however, the APF took on a peace-keeping role and in some areas, particularly parts of the South Island, began to move towards civil policing.

Responsibility for policing moved to the provinces, of which there were initially six, on their creation in 1853 (Reid, 1966). In the South Island and other areas where Māori were not perceived as a threat, civil policing developed further and the role of the police constable began to resemble that of the bobby on the beat. Where there was continued anxiety about the rebelliousness of the Māori population, provincial armed police forces continued to engage in paramilitary-style policing. When wars between Māori and the colonial government broke out in the North Island after 1860, some of the provincial forces that had largely abandoned the use of armed police resorted to them again, combining military and police functions (Hill, 2012). On Grey's return to New Zealand as Governor in 1861, he renewed his emphasis on using Māori in policing, establishing a system of rūnanga with their own police forces. These, however, did not prevent further war and were abolished in 1863 (R. S. Hill, 1986: 801–939).

The *Canterbury Police Gazette* published from 1863 until 1877 provides a snapshot of policing in early provincial New Zealand. What is evident from these reports is the kind of crime that police dealt with on a daily basis. Tables of arrests indicate that the most common reasons that people were taken into custody were larceny (theft of personal property), public drunkenness and assault, although forgery, indecent assault and murder make an occasional appearance too. Police were also interested in keeping track of potential recidivist criminals, publishing physical descriptions of those people released from Lyttelton, Christchurch and Timaru jails. In the June 1869 *Gazette*, for example, we find a description of a 26-year-old, 6-foot Englishman named George Duffell, who had served 3 months' hard labour. Apart from brown hair and grey eyes, the *Gazette* noted: 'Scar on first finger of right hand, large feet, slovenly appearance' (Jollie, 1869: 24).

Around the same time, gold rushes developed in the South Island, creating problems for small provincial police forces that were overwhelmed by the influx of miners. The resulting social unrest was dealt with by using the Irish-style police methods tested in the Australian goldfields (R. S. Hill, 1986: 536–632). The latter part of the 1860s also saw seizures of Māori land in the North Island that required protection, but did not justify the maintenance of a permanent colonial army. Instead, the Armed Constabulary (AC) was formed in 1867 to occupy and police conquered regions, with constables acting as both soldiers and sworn police. Between 1876 and 1877, after the provincial governments were abolished, the AC absorbed the provincial police forces and became the New Zealand Constabulary Force (NZCF) (Hill, 2012). While one division of the NZCF carried out civil policing in towns and cities, a reserve division remained to provide military-style surveillance of Māori in some areas.

Sporadic experimentation with Māori police, as we have seen, began early in New Zealand's colonial history and was frequently a response to crises involving conflict between Māori and Pākehā communities. In the South Island during the 1860s, however, the drive to recruit Māori constables was the result of a different kind of crisis, set in motion by the West Coast gold rush. In reminiscences published in the *Star* in 1901, a former member of the AC noted that in Lyttelton about 1860 'the whole police force, except myself and another member, resigned and left for the diggings. As a result I was called upon to discharge the duties of nine officers'. The solution to this predicament turned out to be the recruitment of 'a few able-bodied and qualified Maoris selected from the Wellington district'. Five such 'stalwart fellows' were accordingly sent to Lyttelton by the General Government and subsequently trained by the AC officer in a range of civil policing tasks ('The Armed Constabulary', 1901: 6).

Policing in New Zealand, c. 1886–1914

By the 1880s the need for paramilitary policing had declined to the extent that the civil policing division could be formally separated from the reserve division (by this stage known as the Field Force) and renamed the New Zealand Police Force (NZPF). The Police Force Act of 1886 created a national civil police force that was unarmed and intended to police by consent (Hill, 1995: 5–26). At the same time a detective branch was formed, known as the Criminal Investigation Branch (CIB). The Act specified criteria for entry into and promotion within the force, which included a height of no less than 5 foot 9 inches, at least a year's experience in the permanent militia, good character, energy and ability ('New Police Regulations', 1887: 2).

After the NZPF was formed in 1886, continued use was made of so-called native constables, but it is clear from their declining numbers leading up to World War I that they were largely being phased out. Annual reports on the strength of the NZPF between 1886 and 1914 indicate that the number of these Māori policemen began at 22 in 1886 (from a force of 494) but had fallen to 11 by 1889 ('Annual Report of the NZPF', 1887: 1; 'The New Zealand Police', 1889: 5). It then hovered at between 7 and 9 between 1893 and 1902 and was 8 in 1913 (from a force of 846) ('Police and Crime', 1893: 1; 'The Police', 1896: 5; 'The Police Force of the Colony', 1899: 2; 'The Police Force', 1902: 5; 'Police Force', 1913: 5).

Just over a decade later, however, confidence in the NZPF had been shaken by the widespread perception of its corruption and inefficiency. At the annual convention of the Canterbury Prohibition Leagues in 1897, for example, the delegates resolved that 'in view of the frequent incidents demonstrating the widespread nature of the corruption and inefficiency of the police force of the colony, this convention urges the immediate appointment of a Royal Commission of Inquiry authorised to thoroughly investigate the morality and organisation of the force' ('Police Efficiency', 1897: 2). In response to such complaints a Royal Commission was convened in 1898, headed by a retired Metropolitan Police detective, John Tunbridge (1850–1928), who became the first professional policeman to head the national force (Dunstall, 2006: 158). Tunbridge's role as Commissioner and his recommendations to the Royal Commission, which included training depots for recruits, better pay, a pension scheme, better discipline and freedom from government interference, saw the NZPF become more consciously modelled on the Metropolitan Police than at any time in the past (Dunstall, 2006: 158; 'The Police Force', 1898: 2).

Although another Royal Commission into the NZPF followed in 1909, Tunbridge's reforms were successful in initiating the professionalisation of New Zealand's police. This was particularly evident in the CIB, the reputation and number of which had declined during the 1880s. By 1900, Tunbridge had increased the number of detectives from twelve to twenty and was instigating better systems of selection and training. In addition, the introduction of new investigative technologies like fingerprinting helped improve detection rates, which had been criticised both by members of the police and by the wider public (Dunstall, 2006: 159–60; 'The Detective Force', 1905: 6). By the outbreak of World War I in 1914, it was clear that the NZPF had succeeded in its transition into a professional civil force, which policed by community consent. As a 1912 article argued:

Fingerprints

The first use of fingerprints in an English trial occurred in 1902 shortly after the Metropolitan Police adopted this form of criminal identification. Not long afterwards, in 1905, fingerprints helped secure a conviction for murder at the Old Bailey. The New Zealand Police (NZP) were not far behind in adopting this new technology.

In July 1904, the *Thames Star* reported excitedly on evidence for the value of fingerprints as a system of criminal identification. The paper noted that a man named Otto Herrdigan, alias J. C. Morris, who had been serving two and a half years for breaking and entering, had escaped Dunedin Jail in November 1903 and had not been recaptured by the NZP. The *Star* went on to say that this same man, now calling himself John Pinero, had just been identified in Sydney, where he was awaiting trial on charges of breaking and entering. The Sydney Police had forwarded his fingerprints to the Commissioner of New Zealand, who was able to establish that they were identical with those of the man who had escaped Dunedin Jail ('On Our Outside Pages', 1904: 2).

A year later, in 1905, the *Wairarapa Daily Times* was able to report that the City Police Court in Wellington had held the first New Zealand case 'in which the prosecution depended solely upon fingerprint evidence ... when John Clancy was charged with having broken and entered and robbed'. According to the *Times*,

> a detective found fingerprints on the broken pane of glass near where the breaker had evidently caught hold of the sash to pull the window down. The pieces of glass where the prints showed were cut out and submitted to the Finger-print Branch of the Police Force, and the result was that one of the finger-marks was found to correspond with the imprint of the third finger of the right hand of John Clancy, impressions of whose fingers had been taken a considerable time ago by the police. ('Tracing Criminals', 1905: 6)

The police force is much maligned, and always will be by some members of the community. But when one looks into the inner side of the life one sees that New Zealand has a fine stamp of men to protect the public, to check crime, and to preserve law and order. They are men who are proud of their physique, interested in the well-being of their countrymen, and always courteous and obliging in work which is not always congenial and inviting. ('The Policeman's Life', 1912: 5)

Policing in Times of War and Crisis, c. 1914–1950

The two world wars (1914–18 and 1939–45) and the turbulent inter-war period presented the NZPF with a number of challenges and opportunities, some of which continued to shape New Zealand policing in the second half of the twentieth century. Perhaps foremost among the wartime challenges was the shortage of personnel caused by men leaving the police to join the armed forces. As the 1919 *Annual Report of the Police Force of the Dominion* demonstrated, police became very thin on the ground during World War I, with 240 of the 327 police stations across the country being one-man stations (Plumridge and Carroll, 2015). Short-handed, the NZPF had to relax its recruitment standards in order to fill vacant positions. An article in the *New Zealand Herald* in November 1941 makes clear that this happened during both world wars. The article, titled 'Police Needed. Force to be Increased', stated that 'the engagement of the new men will be for the duration of the war, but if applicants prove suitable there is a likelihood of permanent engagement. Regulations regarding the physique of men applying for positions were relaxed during the last war, and it is expected they will be relaxed in this war' ('Police Needed', 1941: 10). Those who responded to such calls after 1914, however, could not expect rigorous training, as the depots established in Wellington for this purpose (initially in 1898 and expanded in 1909), halted operation not only during the two world wars, but also during the 1930s Depression (Dunstall, 1999: 82, 98; M. Hill, 1986: 62–63). In addition to being short-handed and under-trained, members of the NZPF in the early twentieth century were also faced with extra duties, particularly during wartime, when other government departments felt they could call on the police to fulfil non-police roles. In 1918, for example, of the NZPF's 878 officers, 327 were acting as registration officers, 290 as sub-enumerators for collecting agricultural statistics, 125 as clerks of the court, 133 as bailiffs and 164 as inspectors of factories (Plumridge and Carroll, 2015). Police performed other roles as well. But the extra duty that created the most community resentment in this period was the NZPF's political and moral surveillance of their fellow New Zealanders.

The surveillance and intelligence roles that police were asked to fulfil during World War I remained part of the NZPF's purview until 1957 when these duties were transferred to the Security Intelligence Service (M. Hill, 1986: 20). The year 1914 saw the expansion of New Zealand's sedition laws, which made striking and political agitation criminal offences (Dunstall, 1999: 256). The laws also gave the police the power to covertly observe both the activities of foreign nationals residing in New Zealand and to round up men avoiding war service (Dunstall, 1999: 314–21). From 1916, the police were most engaged in charging those who made 'seditious utterances', which tended to be public statements against wartime measures like conscription (Plumridge and Carroll, 2015). In the inter-war period intelligence efforts were redirected towards unionists in order to pre-empt possible strike action, and towards members of suspect political groups, such as the Communist Party (Dunstall, 1999: 257–8, 259–62). These reactions to the politico-social exigencies of war and crisis should make us question, as Plumridge and Carroll (2015) of the New Zealand Police Museum do, whether the ideal of policing by consent, which arguably had been achieved earlier in the century, was suspended during the early twentieth century.

Beyond focusing on political threats, there was a growing emphasis in this period on behaviours that endangered public health and morality, including prostitution (which was blamed for the spread of venereal diseases), and the illegal sale of alcohol by unlicensed sellers, also known as 'sly-grogging'. During World War II, particularly with the arrival of American servicemen in Auckland and Wellington, both civic and church leaders became concerned about sexual immorality and public inebriation – the two often going hand in hand. Aided by new powers that allowed the NZPF to search premises without a warrant, the police were able to raid brothels or lodging houses where they suspected servicemen and young women were going to have sex. In addition, women suspected of prostitution could be put under surveillance, generally being given warnings by the police if their conduct was considered questionable (Dunstall, 1999: 335–6). The restrictive liquor laws that existed in New Zealand during the 1940s, which included 6 p.m. closing of bars (1917–67), encouraged illegal alcohol sales, particularly to American servicemen on leave. Although many arrests and prosecutions were carried out, the practice remained prevalent because there were good profits to be made (Dunstall, 1999: 336).

One possible solution to the shortage of manpower during the wars and the desire of the government to monitor public behaviour was to recruit women into the NZPF. During World War I in Britain and a number of other countries, women police aided their male colleagues by looking after the welfare of women and children (Levine, 1994: 34). In practice, this often meant the surveillance of women on war pensions in order to ensure they were behaving morally, and of prostitutes around army barracks (Levine, 1994: 42–45). While no such moves were made in New Zealand during World War I, by the inter-war period there were calls from the public for the introduction of women police. The Women's Christian Temperance Union, for instance, began urging the government to establish female police in 1927 ('Women as Police', 1927: 12). While the government declined to pursue this suggestion during the 1920s and 1930s, a more serious consideration came during World War II in the context of growing concerns about prostitution and illegal alcohol sales. In February 1940, when the New Zealand League of Nations Union urged the government to 'take immediate steps to establish a force of women police as a necessary measure in combatting social evils, especially in view of the accentuation of such evils in the disturbed social conditions associated with the war', it appears that planning was already under way ('Women Police Appointment Urged on Government', 1940: 8). Accordingly, in October 1941 ten police women, who had undergone 3 months' training, were posted to the four main centres and given responsibility for the protection of children and the monitoring of young girls' and women's behaviour (M. Hill, 1986: 66; 'Training at End', 1941: 10). These un-uniformed women police proved useful in dealing with both prostitution and sly-grogging, because they often had more success entering night clubs and bars illegally selling alcohol than their male colleagues (Dunstall, 1999: 335–6). By the end of the war their number had increased to 33 and in 1952 they became uniformed (M. Hill, 1986: 66–67; 'More Women Police', 1943: 6; 'Women Police', 1943: 6). While these were remarkable advances from earlier in the century, when women's policing was limited to the role of prison matron or policeman's wife and searcher, the second half of the century, as we will see, brought numerous challenges for women in NZP (M. Hill, 1986: 66).

Developments in the Second Half of the Twentieth Century

The period after 1950 saw significant change for New Zealand's police, including an alteration of name in 1958 from the NZPF to New Zealand Police, which made manifest the new Police Act's philosophy of policing by consent. In addition, the decades following mid-century witnessed increasing specialisation within the police, which necessitated both better training and the creation of specialist sections and squads; the aim being to transform NZP into a modern professional police organisation (M. Hill, 1986: 28). The second half of the century also saw the demography of NZP begin to alter, reflecting not only a growing acceptance of the capacity of women to carry out all policing roles, but an evolving desire to recruit more Māori and Pasifika. The logic behind these developments was to create a police force that more fully represented the constitution of the population it served. To facilitate the move towards more professionalism and diversity, however, NZP needed to rethink its training methods, develop new specialisations and revamp its recruitment strategies.

Training during the wars and the inter-war period, as we have seen, was haphazard, curtailed, in part, by the periodic closure of the training school at Wellington South. While this school reopened in the late 1940s (replaced in 1953 by the Lyttelton naval barracks), it was clear by the late 1950s that police training was insufficient. The 8–10 weeks of training, which put heavy emphasis on law and theory, was replaced, on the basis of recommendations made in a 1955 report known as the Ball Report, with a 13-week training course that stressed practical policing skills (observation and note-taking) and physical fitness. From 1956 this training was conducted at Trentham (Butterworth, 2005: 86–90). Beyond basic training, the Trentham School also provided courses for detective sergeants and senior detectives (Butterworth, 2005: 88). By 1971, however, the need for purpose-built training facilities which could cope with the increasing sophistication of police education had become clear and planning began for a new Police College near Porirua (M. Hill, 1986: 65). This facility, the Royal New Zealand Police College, was officially opened in 1981.

In response to a rapidly-evolving society in which certain types of crime, including drug trafficking and organised crime, were becoming increasingly problematic (see Chapter 2), NZP also began to develop new specialist sections during the 1950s and 1960s (M. Hill, 1986: 29).

The shooting deaths of four police within 4 weeks in 1963 provided the impetus for the formation of the Armed Offenders Squad (AOS) in 1964. Concerned with police safety after the killings which took place at Waitakere (two detectives) and Lower Hutt (two constables), Detective Sergeant Bill O'Brien, who had questioned the Waitakere shooter, provided Police National Headquarters with a report outlining the need for a specialist squad, similar to that used in New South Wales, to deal with armed offenders. The new squad, whose first callout involved an armed escape from Mt Eden Prison in 1965, was hand-picked from among CIB and uniformed officers and underwent 2 weeks of training at the Papakura Military Camp in the use of firearms, tear gas, grenades, radio procedures and the loud hailer. The AOS considered the loud hailer and telephone as perhaps their most important weapons in dealing with armed offenders as they sought to resolve most situations as peacefully as possible, their philosophy being to 'cordon, contain and appeal' (Stringer and Brook, 2012: 290–1). Recent evidence of this philosophy is to be found in deployment statistics for the years 2006–14. At the time that the AOS celebrated its 50th anniversary in 2014, they were being called to attend c. 800 incidents a year, but deployment statistics indicated that on average shots were fired by police only once for every 260 deployments (NZP, 2014: 5–6).

Other new sections included Vice, Drugs, Document Examination, Juvenile Crime Prevention (renamed Youth Aid Section in 1968), Criminal Intelligence, Search and Rescue and Crime Prevention (M. Hill, 1986: 29; Butterworth, 2005: 108–17). Specialist squads and sections naturally required training beyond that required of ordinary sworn officers. In the period from 1968 to 1987, a large number of new training courses were introduced in order to cater to these specialist sections and senior police. These included armed offenders, search and rescue, and prosecutors' courses in 1968; CIB advanced topics and drug law-enforcement courses in 1974, and intelligence analysis, electronic surveillance and community constable courses in 1985. Each of these courses provides an indication of the increasing scope and specialisation of NZP from the mid- to late twentieth century (Butterworth, 2005: 167).

It was in this period of specialisation and training reform that NZP also began to increase opportunities for women. The training of male and female recruits, which had previously occurred separately, began happening together from 1956 ('The New Zealand Police', 1967). Following a debate about pay equity in the early 1960s, equal pay was introduced in 1965 and the Women's Divisions, which had concentrated on the welfare of women and children, were dissolved as NZP embraced the idea of policewomen in general policing roles (Butterworth, 2005: 72). Since this time women have been engaged in all aspects of policing, including CIB, the dog squad and the AOS, and have risen within the police hierarchy to the upper echelons. But, while pay equity might have been achieved in the mid-1960s, discrimination against women remained. The 1976 Human Rights Commission Act, for example, allowed NZP to discriminate against women at the recruitment level in order to keep the total number of policewomen at no more than 4 per cent of the service (NZP, 2016a). In spite of this, the total percentage of women in NZP climbed slowly but steadily over the next few decades, growing from 4.39 per cent in 1977 to 13.2 per cent in 1995 (NZP, 2016a). Growing tolerance within the service for married women and maternity leave (first introduced 1959) ensured that a career in NZP and a family were in theory, at least, not mutually exclusive. But as late as the 1990s there was no provision for women who wanted to work flexibly while their children were young.

The biographies provided by retired police women for the 75th anniversary of women in NZP are perhaps some of the best indicators of the rewards and challenges that women faced in a male-dominated workplace during the second half of the twentieth century. Betty Bennett's work history, for instance, demonstrates the capacity of women police to carry out a wide range of police duties and to ascend the police hierarchy, while still facing pay discrimination. Betty, who began her police career in 1955, was among the first class of women to train with male colleagues at Trentham and was one of three Māori women in her wing. As a member of the Women's Division in Auckland, she was rapidly promoted to Detective in 1959 and then Sergeant in 1961. Betty's promotions coincided with the Government Service Equal Pay Act (1960) and thus provided the impetus for a review of policewomen's pay, which was 80 per cent of that of their male colleagues. In spite of this review, Cabinet did not grant policewomen equal pay until 1965. In the late 1960s, Betty became the first policewoman to become a Commissioned Officer, subsequently using her influence to resist a reinstatement of the Women's Division on the basis that women had proved their capacity to police any situation (NZP, 2016b).

Cushla Watson's work history makes clear that even in the late 1980s very experienced and senior women within the police could not expect flexible working conditions that would enable them to have both a career and a family. Cushla began her career in 1973 and by the mid-1980s was an experienced detective. In 1985, she was heavily involved in the investigation into the sinking of the *Rainbow Warrior* and was sent overseas in order to gather evidence that would ultimately lead to the prosecution of Alain Mafart and Dominique Prieur. Towards the end of the 1980s, Cushla put her career on hold to start a family, but when she tried to return to work, suggesting that she and another female officer with childcare responsibilities job share, her request was denied. Both women ultimately resigned, unable to convince the police administration of the need for workplace flexibility (NZP, 2016b).

While the number of women in NZP over the last three-quarters of a century is relatively easy to ascertain, the number of Māori and other ethnic groups who have served is somewhat harder to establish. In large part, this is a result of a failure to record the ethnic and cultural backgrounds of police recruits and staff until the 1990s; although between 1973 and 1985 the number of Māori and Pasifika recruits in each training wing was noted (Butterworth, 2005: 244). A commitment to involving Māori in policing had, of course, been evident in some of Governor Hobson's policing experiments during the nineteenth century, but in the early twentieth century the number of native constables declined into insignificance. In the mid-1950s, however, new efforts were made to recruit Māori, with 25 of the first 100 places available at the Trentham School being reserved for them; an offer taken up by 14 men and two women in the period 1955–56 (Butterworth, 2005: 243). By the mid-1960s another campaign to recruit Māori got under way and the magazine of the Department of Māori Affairs, *Te Ao Hou*, published a story in 1967 on Māori police. The article noted that Māori men and women were to be found in all branches of the police and at the highest ranks, going on to give short descriptions of the roles of sixteen officers ('The New Zealand Police', 1967).

It was in the late 1960s also that a discussion about Pacific Islanders' suitability for police work took place. While they had previously been turned away as recruits, from the early 1970s a small but growing number of Pasifika now began to enter NZP (Butterworth, 2005: 244). By the late 1990s, however, there were some Pasifika officers clearly frustrated at what they saw as discrimination against them. Former Inspector Tyrone Laurenson, for example, complained that 'Pacific Island officers were rarely promoted and Pacific issues were not given a fair go' (cited in Robertson, 1997: 4). He had been appointed to a committee to establish why fewer Pasifika were joining and staying in the service, but in 1997 the police did not even know how many Pasifika officers there were (Robertson, 1997: 4).

Conclusion

Many of the trends and developments witnessed in the second half of the twentieth century have continued in the new millennium. Among these have been further promotion of and reflection upon women's roles in the police. A 2000 report on 'Women in the CIB', for instance, attempted to consider both the opportunities and barriers to the recruitment, progress and retention of women in the CIB and solutions to these problems (Hyman, 2000: 1–114). The ten recommendations made in this report sought to address issues around recruitment procedures, gender discrimination, childcare, CIB decision-making and lack of knowledge about the gender and ethnic background of CIB members (Hyman, 2000: 1–8). Three years later a 'Women in Policing Plan' was introduced with the intention of recruiting more women and supporting them to fulfil their career aspirations (NZP, 2016a). That this plan was less than successful was evident in a critical report by Dame Margaret Bazley in 2007 that found that women were under-represented at senior levels and that there was a culture of nepotism and discrimination within the police (Talia, 2014: 15). More recently, in 2016, NZP celebrated 75 years of women in the police, pointing to the challenges and discrimination faced by women during that time as well as the remarkable achievements of New Zealand's policewomen (NZP, 2016a). As of 2016, the percentage of women among the constabulary staff was 19.8 per cent (32.19 per cent of all NZP staff). The percentages of women promoted above the level of Constable (Sergeant 11.6 per cent; Senior Sergeant 11.4 per cent; Inspector 12.3 per cent and Superintendent 14 per cent) indicate that there are still hurdles to women's recruitment and career progression; however, there has been marked improvement since the beginning of the millennium (NZP, 2016a).

In a similar fashion, NZP continues to interrogate not only their relationship with Māori and Pasifika in the community, but also the ways in which they might encourage recruitment into the police. In 2001, for example, targets were set as part of the NZP Human Resource Strategy that by 2005, 12.5 per cent of sworn staff would be Māori and 7 per cent would be Pasifika (Wehipeihana et al., 2010: 13). While the number of sworn Māori officers remained fairly static at 11–12 per cent in 2005, there was some upwards movement among new recruits, particularly Pasifika. In the 12 months to June 2007, 11.1 per cent of recruits were Māori and 3.6 per cent were Pasifika. And in the 12 months to June 2008, 12.4 per cent of recruits were Māori and 7 per cent were Pasifika (Wehipeihana et al., 2010: 14). A 2010 report on Māori recruitment found that the main barriers to Māori joining NZP were negative perceptions of the police and lack of knowledge about the nature and extent of policing (Wehipeihana et al., 2010: 26). In addition, a 2014 campaign was launched to recruit more Pasifika into NZP. An article that appeared in the *Dominion Post* in September 2014, for example, called for 'young Pacific Islanders with a penchant for crime-fighting TV shows . . . to consider becoming real-life detectives' (Talia, 2014: 15). It went on to say that there were currently 490 Pasifika in the police, representing a total of 5 per cent of the service (Talia, 2014: 15).

The continuing efforts of NZP in the new millennium to include and support more women, Māori and Pasifika fit with the principle that the police should reflect the gender and ethnic composition of the community. While further work remains to be done in these areas, NZP over the course of the last century has clearly made efforts to become a professional organisation that seeks to police with community support, cooperation and public consent.

REFERENCES

'Annual Report of the New Zealand Police Force'. 1887. In *Appendix to the Journals of the [New Zealand] House of Representatives*, Session 1, H-5.

'Arrests Made. Seven Germans'. 1939. *New Zealand Herald*, 23 December, p. 8.

Babington, A. 1969. *A House in Bow Street: Crime and the Magistracy in London, 1740–1881*. London: MacDonald.

Beattie, J. M. 2001. *Policing and Punishment in London, 1660–1750: Urban Crime and the Limits of Terror*. Oxford: Oxford University Press.

Beattie, J. M. 2012. *The First English Detectives: The Bow Street Runners and the Policing of London, 1750–1840*. Oxford: Oxford University Press.

Butterworth, S. 2005. *More Than Law and Order: Policing a Changing Society, 1945–1992*. Dunedin: University of Otago Press.

Dunstall, G. 1999. *A Policeman's Paradise? Policing a Stable Society, 1918–1945*. Palmerston North: Dunmore Press.

Dunstall, G. 2006. 'Local "Demons" in New Zealand Policing, c. 1900–55', in C. Emsley and H. Shpayer-Makov (Eds.), *Police Detectives in History, 1750–1950*. Aldershot, UK: Ashgate, pp. 157–82.

Emsley, C. 1986. 'Detection and Prevention: The Old English Police and the New, 1750–1900', *Historical Social Research* 37: 69–88.

Emsley, C. 1996. *The English Police: A Political and Social History* (2nd ed.). Harlow, UK: Longman.

Emsley, C., Hitchcock, T., and Shoemaker, R. 2016. 'Crime and Justice: Policing in London', *Old Bailey Proceedings Online*. Accessed 18 February 2016. https://www.oldbaileyonline.org/static/Policing.jsp

Harris, A. T. 2004. *Policing the City: Crime and Legal Authority in London, 1780–1840*. Columbus: Ohio State University Press.

Hill, M. 1986. *In the Line of Duty: 100 Years of the New Zealand Police*. Auckland: Endeavour Press.

Hill, R. S. 1986. *Policing the Colonial Frontier: The Theory and Practice of Coercive Social and Racial Control in New Zealand, 1767–1867*. Wellington: Government Printer.

Hill, R. S. 1995. *The Iron Hand in the Velvet Glove: The Modernisation of Policing in New Zealand, 1886–1917*. Wellington: Dunmore Press.

Hill, R. S. 2012. 'Police', *Te Ara – The Encyclopedia of New Zealand*. Accessed 21 May 2017. http://www.TeAra.govt.nz/en/police/print

Hyman, P. 2000. *Opportunities for and Barriers to the Recruitment, Progress, and Retention of Women in the Criminal Investigation Branch (CIB)*. Accessed 21 May 2017. http://www.police.govt.nz/sites/default/files/publications/women-in-cib.pdf

Jollie, E. 1869. 'Description of Persons Discharged from the Lyttelton, Christchurch and Timaru Gaols: From the 25th April to 25th May 1869', *Canterbury Police Gazette* 7(6): 23–24.

Levine, P. 1994. '"Walking the Streets in a Way No Decent Woman Should": Women Police in World War I', *Journal of Modern History* 66(1): 34–78.

McEldowney, J. F. 1991. 'Policing and the Administration of Justice in Nineteenth-Century Ireland', in C. Emsley and B. Weinberger (Eds), *Policing Western Europe: Politics, Professionalism and Public Order, 1850–1940*. New York: Greenwood Press, pp. 18–35.

'More Women Police'. 1943. *Auckland Star*, 24 July, p. 6.

'New Police Regulations'. 1887. *Grey River Argus*, 18 January, p. 2.

New Zealand Police. 2014. *Armed Offenders Squad 50th Anniversary Media Kit*. Accessed 21 May 2017. http://www.police.govt.nz/about-us/publication/armed-offenders-squad-50th-anniversary-media-kit

New Zealand Police. 2016a. '75 Years of Policewomen Firsts', New Zealand Police. Accessed 21 May 2016. http://www.police.govt.nz/about-us/75-years-women-police/looking-back/75-years-policewomen-firsts

New Zealand Police. 2016b. 'Policewomen over the Decades', New Zealand Police. Accessed 21 May 2016. http://www.police.govt.nz/about-us/75-years-women-police/looking-back/policewomen-over-decades

'Old Bailey Proceedings, 13th October 1680'. 2017. *Old Bailey Proceedings Online*. Accessed 21 May 2017. https://www.oldbaileyonline.org/print.jsp?div=16801013

'On Our Outside Pages'. 1904. *Thames Star*, 28 July, p. 2.

Paley, R. 1989. 'An Imperfect, Inadequate and Wretched System?' Policing in London before Peel', *Criminal Justice History* 10: 95–130.

'Police and Crime'. 1893. *Oamaru Mail*, 26 August, p. 1.

'Police Efficiency'. 1897. *Wanganui Chronicle*, 2 April, p. 2.

'Police Force'. 1913. *New Zealand Times*, 6 August, p. 5.

'Police Needed'. 1941. *New Zealand Herald*, 13 November, p. 10.

Plumbridge, E., and Carroll, R. 2015. 'New Zealand Police during the 1914–18 War', in *Policing the First World War: Slygrogging, Sex and Sedition Exhibition*. Wellington: New Zealand Police. Accessed 21 May 2017. http://www.police.govt.nz/about-us/history-museum/museum/exhibitions/policing-first-world-war-slygrogging-sex-and-sedition

Reid, L. W. 1966. 'Police' [From A. H. McLintock (Ed.), *An Encyclopedia of New Zealand*. Wellington: Government Printer]. *Te Ara – The Encyclopedia of New Zealand*. Accessed 21 May 2017. http://www.teara.govt.nz/en/1966/police

Robertson, C. 1997. 'I Never Got a Fair Go – Samoan Cop', *Dominion Post*, 26 December, p. 4.

'Sale of Sly Grog. Elderly Labourer Fined'. 1944. *Auckland Star*, 23 October, p. 3.

Shpayer-Makov, H. 2011. *The Ascent of the Detective: Police Sleuths in Victorian and Edwardian England*. Oxford: Oxford University Press.

Stringer, D., and Brook, E. 2012. 'To Cordon, Contain and Appeal', *Police News* 45(11): 290–1.

Styles, J. 1983. 'Sir John Fielding and the Problem of Criminal Investigation in Eighteenth-Century England', *Transactions of the Royal Historical Society* 33: 127–49.

Talia, S. 2014. 'Police Seek Greater Pacific Presence', *Dominion Post*, 20 September, p. 15. 'The Armed Constabulary'. 1901. *Star*, 1 June, p. 6.

'The Detective Force'. 1905. *The Press*, 2 February, p. 6.

'The Murder at Roehampton'. 1842. *The Times*, 28 April.

'The New Zealand Police'. 1889. *The Press*, 7 August, p. 5.

'The New Zealand Police'. 1967. *Te Ao Hou*, 1 September.

'The Police'. 1896. *The Press*, 21 August, p. 5.

'The Police Force'. 1902. *The Press*, 10 July, p. 5.

'The Police Force of the Colony'. 1899. *Evening Post*, 5 July, p. 2.

'The Policeman's Life'. 1912. *Nelson Evening Mail*, 30 July, p. 5.

'Tracing Criminals. Effective Modern Methods. How the Finger-Print System Is Working'. 1905. *Wairarapa Daily Times*, 7 March, p. 6.

'Training at End. Valuable Duties to Start End of Next Week'. 1941. *Evening Post*, 2 October, p. 10.

'Under Surveillance. Austrians and Germans in New Zealand'. 1914. *Waikato Argus*, 7 August, p. 3.

Wehipeihana, N., Fisher, E., Spee, K., and Pipi, K. 2010. *Building Diversity: Understanding the Factors That Influence Māori to Join Police*. Accessed 21 May 2017. http://www.police.govt.nz/sites/default/files/publications/building-diversity-evaluation-report.pdf

'Women as Police. Request to Government'. 1927. *New Zealand Herald*, 26 March, p. 12.

'Women Police Appointment Urged on Government'. 1940. *The Press*, 1 February, p. 8.

'Women Police. The Need for More'. 1943. *New Zealand Herald*, 24 July, p. 6.

4.

Contemporary Policing

JOHN PRICE, MIKE WEBB AND SIMONE BULL

Introduction

This chapter presents a snapshot of policing in New Zealand in 2016/17. It describes how New Zealand Police (NZP) is organised, funded and has its independence protected; what it takes to become a police officer, the sorts of activities officers typically deal with, and how these compare to NZP's statutory functions; the ranks and roles, and how to pick them from the uniform officers wear; and typical steps involved in solving a high-volume crime. The chapter also features mini case studies to delve into real-life examples of NZP's four main 'pillars of policing': prevention, response, investigations and resolutions. To give readers a feel for the cultures that exist within NZP, the chapter also scatters throughout the text some terminology commonly used by NZP staff.

Organisation

Unlike Australia, England and Wales, Canada or the United States, New Zealand has a single, centralised, police service. NZP is a large organisation. It has more than 12,000 staff spread across 12 semi-autonomous geographical Districts (encompassing more than 350 communities; see Table 4.1) as well as service centres. Service centres include NZP's three Communications Centres where the bulk of calls for service are handled, the Royal New Zealand Police College

(RNZPC) in Porirua where officers are trained, Police National Headquarters (PNHQ, pejoratively called 'The Castle'), and others.

Of NZP's 12,000-plus staff, just over 9000 are constabulary (the colloquial term is 'sworn'). Included in the 9000 are 300 public-facing Authorised Officers with limited policing powers. They tend to be involved in custodial management at police stations, prisoner transportation, scene guarding duties, and so on. Authorised Officers can be distinguished from police officers by their black version of the traditional blue NZP uniform.

As reflected in Table 4.1, the distribution of NZP's staff (and its bricks-and-mortar stations) is primarily determined by population, with police needing to provide nationwide 24/7 coverage, from the top of the North Island to the bottom of the South, as well as communities on Stewart Island and the Chatham Islands. Heavyweight policing Districts include the three which service the Auckland region, as well as Wellington and Canterbury. The three smallest Districts in human terms are Northland, Eastern and Tasman, but these present some of the most challenging geographies to police, and also have some other challenging features.

TABLE 4.1 Constabulary full-time equivalents (FTEs) per NZP District in 2017

	FTE per 100,000	FTE
Northland	213	347
Waitemata	132	745
Auckland City	179	812
Counties / Manukau	199	1050
Waikato	173	615
Bay Of Plenty	197	671
Central	189	673
Eastern	205	423
Wellington	161	776
Tasman	177	318
Canterbury	153	868
Southern	180	557

NZP is not technically part of the public service, and strictly speaking NZP employees are not *public* servants; they are *state* servants sitting outside of the core public service. Being a non-public-service department is a hallmark of an agency with constitutional separation from the government of the day. Perhaps because of that, NZP has a reputation in the public sector for getting things done. It is one of NZP's greatest strengths, but also one of its potential weaknesses. The agency has a tendency to leap to quick solutions when careful planning is required. Nonetheless, it jealously guards its arm's-length relationship with government, which is entrenched by section 16 of the Policing Act 2008. Although NZP's operational independence is enshrined in statute, the Police Commissioner is still responsible to the Minister of Police for the effective, efficient and economical management of NZP, and for giving effect to lawful ministerial directions. Legally, what differentiates NZP from the core public service is that it is 'an instrument of the Crown' as described in section 7(1) of the Policing Act 2008.

NZP is also not a force. The word 'force' has been defunct since the Police Act 1958. Under section 9 of the Policing Act 2008, NZP exists to ensure the safety of society is preserved by:

- Keeping the peace
- Enforcing the law
- Maintaining public safety
- Supporting and reassuring the community
- Ensuring national security
- Managing emergencies
- Supporting international policing activities.

In line with its law enforcement function, NZP formally administers three statutes: the Arms Act 1983, the Policing Act 2008, and now the Child Protection (Child Sex Offender Government Agency Registration) Act 2016. Over 200 laws and regulations that are not administered by NZP nonetheless rely on police enforcement. The Chief Constable and Chief Executive of NZP is the Police Commissioner. The holder of this position has not always been a constabulary member and has not always been promoted from within the ranks. From 1955 to 1958, for example, Samuel Barnett served in the role under the title of 'Controller General'.

The Police Commissioner is typically appointed for a term of between 3 and 5 years. Supporting the current Commissioner are three Deputy Commissioners, one of whom is a statutory Deputy under section 13(1) of the Policing Act 2008. Alongside the three Deputy Commissioners are five Deputy Chief Executives, only one of whom is sworn. Together, these nine comprise NZP's Executive Leadership Board (ELB). They are a reasonably diverse bunch: currently, one is Māori by descent, two are of Māori ethnicity, three are women. All of the constabulary members of the ELB are ex-Criminal Investigations Branch (CIB) – a pattern that has existed for decades.

The ELB is supported by a hand-picked Senior Leadership Team of 'Tier 3s and Tier 4s' (Assistant Commissioner or National Manager level). Out in the field are twelve District Commanders, all of whom hold the rank of Superintendent. This makes them the highest-ranking officers in Districts (though some Districts have more than one Superintendent). One-third of the twelve District Commanders at present are women, including the first Māori woman (of Ngāti Porou descent) to hold a District Commander position in NZP's history.

Rising to the rank of Inspector, let alone Superintendent, is a big deal in NZP. Inspectors and above are what used to be called commissioned officers, whom you will often hear addressed as 'Sir' or 'Ma'am'. There are only 325 officers at the level of Inspector or above, so they represent the top 4 per cent of NZP's constabulary workforce (the top 3 per cent of the total workforce). Below the rank of Inspector are Senior Sergeants and Sergeants, supervisory ranks that often go by the title 'NCOs', which stands for non-commissioned officers.

The entry-level rank for sworn NZP employees is Constable; after an officer has put in 14 years of 'long service and good conduct' he or she has the right to be referred to as Senior Constable. Variations on a theme come from membership of the CIB, which entitles an officer to carry the title 'Detective'. Because of their roles in fronting often high-profile investigations with media, it is common to see Detective Constables, Detective Sergeants ('DSs'), Detective Senior Sergeants ('DSSs'), Detective Inspectors ('DIs') and occasionally Detective Superintendents ('DSupers') speaking on NZP's behalf in television and newspaper reports. Differences in rank, and role, determine the uniform an NZP employee wears (see Figure 4.1).

Each constable costs approximately $100,000 to recruit, train and deploy, though only $60,000 of that is their base salary upon graduation. As they acquire more experience, try their hands at more specialised roles and climb the ranks, their salaries (and benefits) increase. Annual wage increases contribute to that. This is due, in part, to the fact that NZP staff cannot go on strike (see section 69 of the Policing Act 2008). Instead, every few years, NZP enters into a bargaining process with the main police union groups, which determines whether or not there will be any wage increases over the coming years; and if so, how big an

CONTEMPORARY POLICING

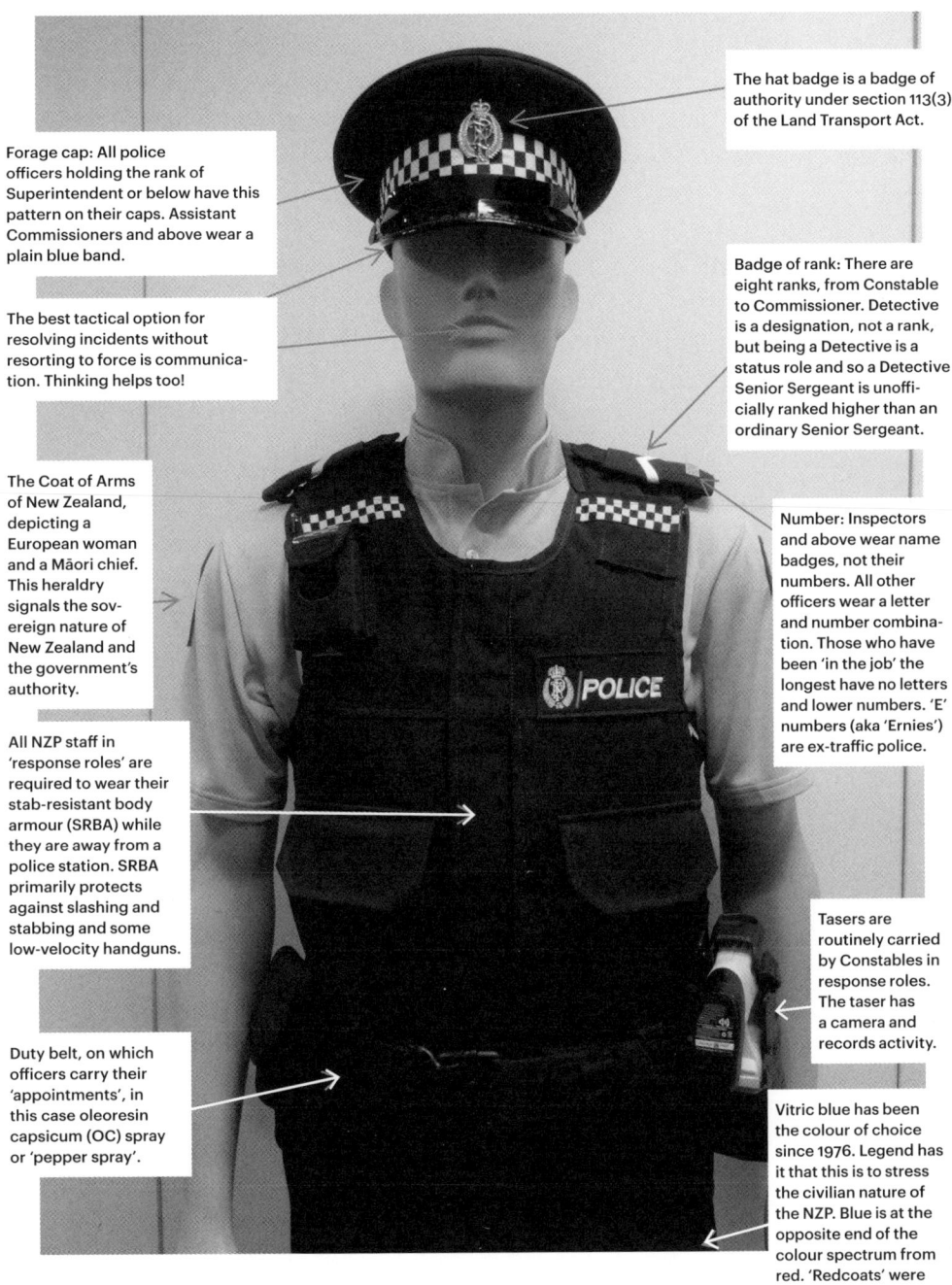

FIGURE 4.1 **Anatomy of a police officer**

increase. General staff are entitled to the same wage increase, though they are typically paid 5 per cent less than their constabulary equivalents, who have to be deployable at any time. The remuneration of some of the most senior people is not determined by NZP but by the Independent Remuneration Authority.

Badges of Rank

All police officers trained in New Zealand start at the rank of recruit. As a matter of policy, lateral entry into higher ranks is not currently permitted. Figure 4.2 shows all of the badges of rank worn in NZP.

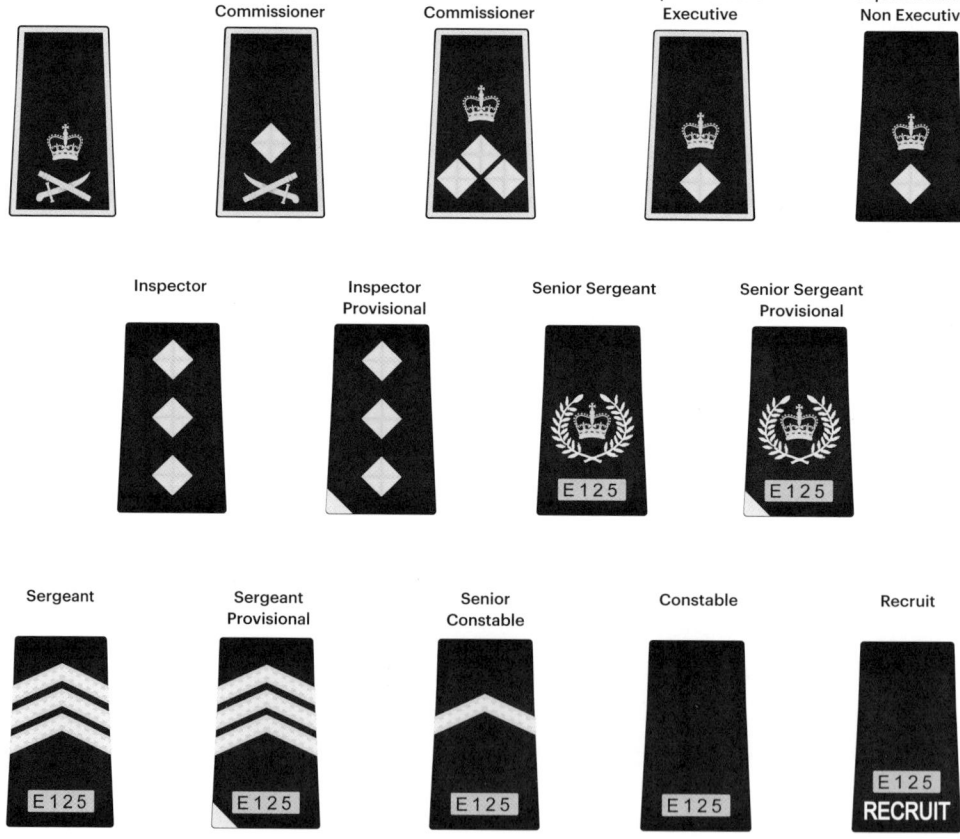

FIGURE 4.2 **NZP badges of rank**

It takes a year, on average, from submitting an application to being accepted into the candidate pool to become a new recruit. About 90 per cent of people who apply don't make it. Applicants' chances are much greater if they:

- Are physically fit, are a confident swimmer, and generally are in excellent health
- Have an education level equivalent to NCEA level 2 or higher
- Have no convictions for drugs, dishonesty, sexual offences, violence or drink driving
- Have a driver's licence, and can obtain a full licence within 12 months of applying
- Can type at least 25 words per minute
- Demonstrate the following qualities: excellent communication skills, empathy, loyalty, commitment, integrity and problem-solving abilities.

Successful candidates are organised into 'wings'. Normally, up to eight wings are trained at the RNZPC in Porirua each year, with a minimum of 40 recruits per wing. Each wing has its own number and patron. Past wing patrons have included public office holders like Governors-General, Human Rights Commissioners and retired members of the judiciary, mayors and other community leaders, and influential figures from the worlds of sports, business and the charitable sector. Members of the 294 Dr Anwar Ghani Wing were the first to enter the RNZPC under a new training regime that consists of 12 weeks of distance learning followed by a 16-week RNZPC course.

As soon as recruits start training at the RNZPC they are given limited policing powers (sufficient to complete training exercises) and start earning a wage. Upon successful completion of this training, recruits participate in an Attestation Parade where they swear the oath under section 22 of the Policing Act 2008 and are assigned to Districts as probationary Constables with full policing powers. Demand for newly-trained 'cops' is greatest in the Auckland region, but they are also sought after in Waikatō, Northland and the Bay of Plenty.

Two years of on-the-job learning and coursework follow. If a recruit meets all of the requirements he or she is awarded a Diploma of Policing and becomes a constable. It used to be the case that the order recruits finished in their wing determined the number they wore on their shoulder. For example, officer 8784 got better results than officer 8785 but not as good as officer 8783. These days the numbering does not reflect standing in the wing – it is purely sequential. Even 're-joins' (people who leave NZP and come back again within a specified number of years) get given a new number in sequence.

Once a recruit achieves the rank of Constable, he or she can then apply for different roles in NZP. There are many to choose from, in units as diverse as Public Safety Teams, Dive Squad, Neighbourhood Policing Teams, Disaster Recovery, Prosecutions, Organised Crime, Cyber Crime, Information and Communications Technology, International Services Group, Highway Patrol, Maritime, School Community Officers, Iwi Liaison Officers, Youth Aid, Intel, Police Infringements Bureau, Traffic Crash Unit, Policy Group, Online Child Exploitation, Adult Sexual Assault and Child Protection, Tactical Crime Squads, Calibrations and Dog Squad (aka 'Delta'). Many roles, such as those in the CIB, Armed Offenders Squad, Special Tactics Group, Diplomatic Protection Service, and others, require additional training and certification.

After 14 years of service, Constables are eligible to receive 'long service and good conduct' medals. Legend has it that 14 years was chosen because NZP was established by the 1886 Police Force Act, which was passed 14 years after the last shot was fired in the New Zealand Wars in 1872. It follows that 14 years was the most any constabulary member could have served without the chance of being able to claim a medal in recognition of service. A large number of those serving prior to February 1872 would have qualified for the New Zealand Medal (Wills, 1990: 17).

In order to be promoted to Sergeant, Sergeant to Senior Sergeant and Senior Sergeant to Inspector, you have to pass Core Police Knowledge (CPK) exams and apply for and be appointed to a vacancy. As at 2016/17, the breakdown of officers in the respective ranks is:

- Recruits (1 per cent)
- Constables (74 per cent)
- Sergeants (16 per cent)
- Senior Sergeants (5 per cent)
- Inspectors (3 per cent)
- Superintendents (0.4 per cent)
- Assistant Commissioner or above (<0.1 per cent; n=9).

The gender and ethnic makeup of the constabulary has changed over the past decade but the pace of change is slow because of NZP's stubbornly low attrition rate. Even if the new recruits each year exactly matched the general population

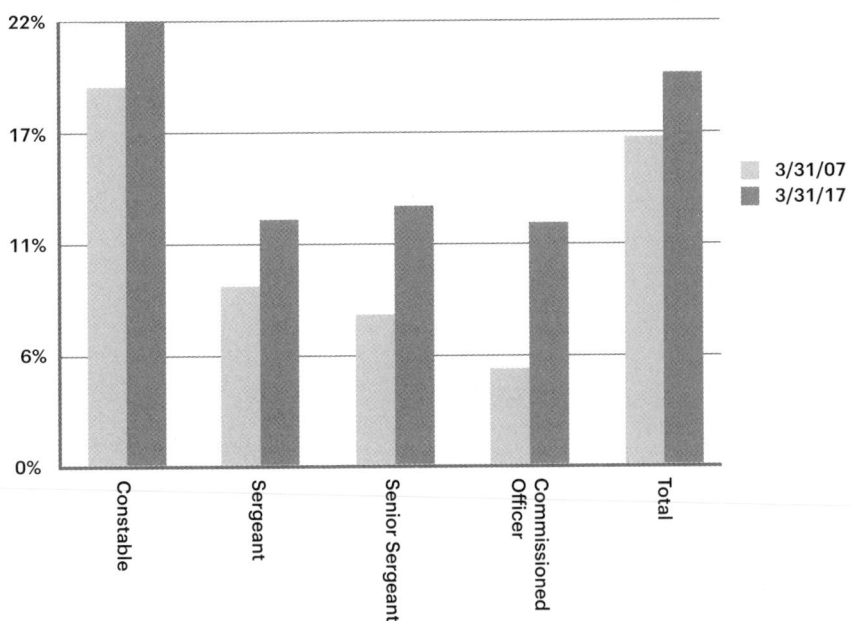

FIGURE 4.3 **Female proportion of constabulary employees by rank in 2007 and 2017**

FIGURE 4.4 **Constabulary full-time equivalents (FTEs) by age in 2007 and 2017**

it would take many years for the total workforce to diversify. Figure 4.3 shows how the female proportion of constabulary employees by rank changed between 2007 and 2017.

NZP's constabulary workforce has also aged considerably, as shown in Figure 4.4. There are a number of reasons for this. The most significant is the removal of compulsory retirement at 55, which happened a little over a decade ago. Low attrition (4 per cent for constabulary, 9 per cent for other NZP staff) and low recruitment (roughly 360, or 4 per cent, per year) have also accelerated the ageing of the constabulary workforce. NZP is trying to minimise the impact of an ageing population on its workforce by targeting 18–25 year olds in its new 'Do You Care Enough?' recruitment campaign.

'Doing God's Work': A Day in the Life

Attendance at family violence incidents and alcohol-fuelled disorder is the staple diet of every Constable. Together they account for as much as half of an officer's workload. Reporting of family violence has more than doubled since 2009, to the point now where police attend one family violence incident every five minutes (spatial and temporal patterns aside).

Around one-third of people taken into custody are under the influence of alcohol to varying degrees. An increasing number of people taken into custody are also affected by other drugs. NZP uses annual New Zealand Arrestee Drug Use Monitoring (NZ-ADUM) surveys and reports to monitor this, as well as the direct observations of staff, including watch-house nurses dotted around a handful of stations. While not comprehensive, Table 4.2 draws on 2016 NZP data to give a snapshot of the types of activities which the organisation and its people are involved in on a daily basis.

Road policing is a key area of service delivery. In theory, up to 20 per cent (the road policing share of NZP's budget) of a general duties officer's time can be spent dealing with crashes, reported traffic offences, the 'fatal five' areas (speed, drink/drug driving, restraints, dangerous/careless driving and high-risk drivers), and denying offenders the use of the roads. For example, on average, NZP receives 141,426 traffic-related calls for service from members of the public annually. Of these, roughly 25 per cent are attended.

NZP is also actively involved with a wide range of initiatives involving schools, community groups and other organisations. Some of it is 'compensatory'; that

TABLE 4.2 **A day in the life of the NZP**

In one day NZP will:		
carry out	371	foot patrols
carry out	906	bail checks
stop	1719	vehicles
check	149	licensed premises
conduct	4036	breath tests
answer	2304	111 calls
answer	1928	general calls
respond to	2542	emergency and non-emergency events (including injury and non-injury vehicle crashes)
finalise	67	investigations into crimes against people
finalise	79	investigations into crimes against property
attend	7	search and rescue events
attend	613	family incident repeat calls for service
issue	41	Police Safety Orders
escort/hold in custody	443	'prisoners' in police cells following arrest, on remand, post-sentence, or awaiting mental health assessment
execute/serve/deliver	163	documents (summonses, breaches, warrants) authorised by a legislated authority
receive	123	mental health and suicide-related calls for service
attend	74	mental health and suicide-related incidents, which can take 2–3 hours to resolve
take into custody	11	people who have not committed an offence who require a mental health assessment
investigate	16	sudden deaths
investigate	53	missing persons reports
answer	81	calls relating to lost property
revoke	1	firearms license
prosecute	276	cases
successfully complete	11	diversions

is, NZP is compensating for perceived shortfalls in other services, such as mental health. More people die each year as a result of suicide than as a result of traffic crashes. NZP receives around $323 million a year from the National Land Transport Fund (hypothecated from road user charges, levies and so on) to police our roads. Conversely, NZP is not directly funded for the growing number of

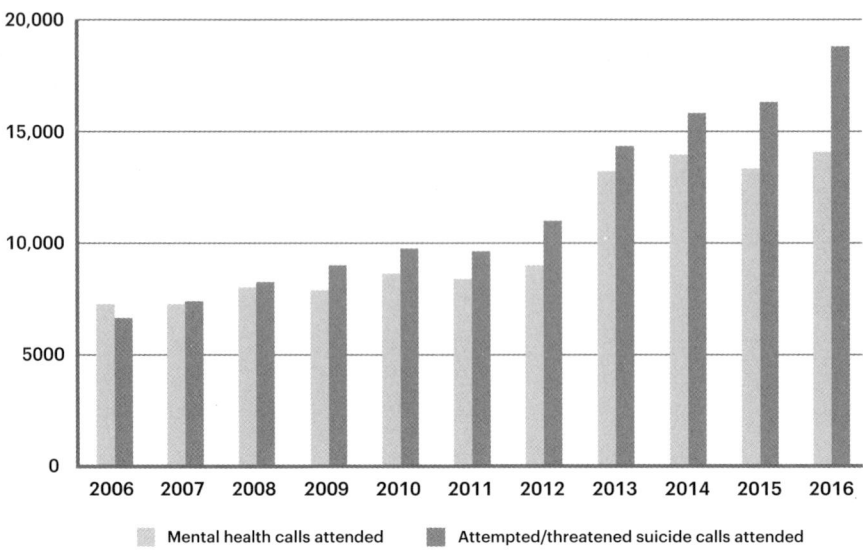

FIGURE 4.5 **Incidents relating to mental health and suicide threats/attempts attended 2006–2016**

recorded mental health and attempted/threatened suicide incidents police attend every year, which are illustrated in Figure 4.5.

Cybercrime could surpass all of these as a source of demand for policing services in the future. Judging from international experience, online reporting for cybercrime and cyber events could lead to hundreds, if not thousands, of new offences per month being formally reported to NZP.

As it is, there has been a 34 per cent increase in calls for service to NZP since 2009. Police are now attending 3.8 million events a year. However, only 24 per cent of events police are dispatched to are crime-related. Of the crime-related events that officers are dispatched to, burglary is all too common. Acquisitive crimes like burglary and drug use often go hand in hand, as people look for ways to 'feed their habit'. Burglaries are also not easy to solve, making re-offending more likely. Even if officers locate the stolen goods and arrest the person in possession of them, often this will not be sufficient evidence to successfully bring a prosecution for burglary. Instead, the statistics will record the burglary is unsolved and create a new 'receiving stolen goods' offence. Figure 4.6 illustrates some of the complexity surrounding the crime of burglary.

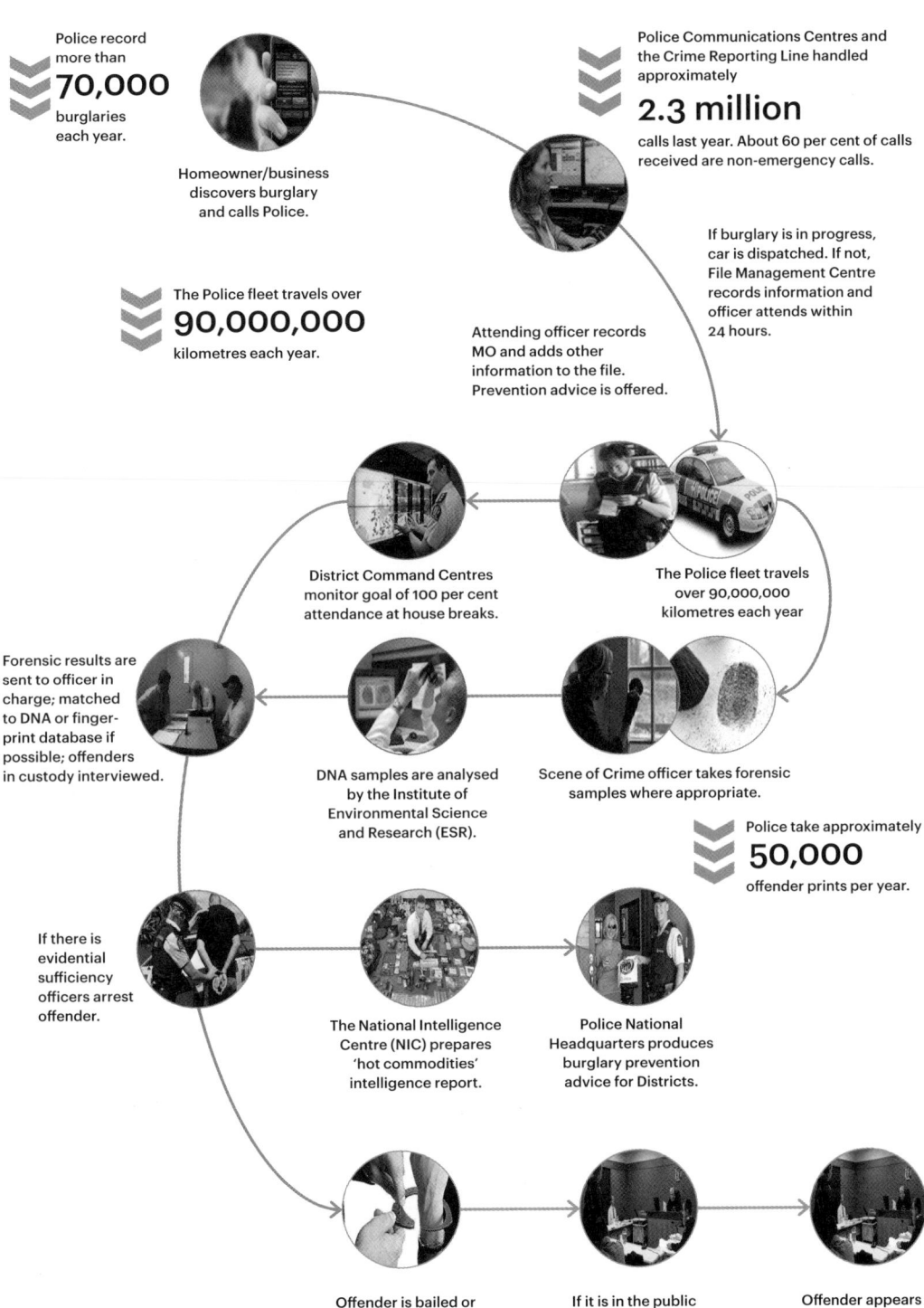

FIGURE 4.6 **Lifecycle of a burglary**

Case Study: Phillipstown – Not in Our Community

The campaign against gangs and drug dealing in the Christchurch community of Phillipstown reduced recorded crime by nearly one-third and helped give local people their community back. When the Neighbourhood Policing Team (CPT) was deployed in 2011, the Phillipstown community was blighted with long-term social deprivation and lack of social cohesion. Driving high crime rates was an overt organised crime presence, an open drug-supply market, and alcohol-fuelled disorder and family violence.

The NPT used several methods to bring about change in the community. First, they collected information from NZP databases, door-to-door surveys and consultation with community groups and government agencies. From this information they came up with a three-pronged response: Enforcement, Prevention and SafeGrowth.

The enforcement phase saw 16 search warrants executed, 15 drug-dealing houses identified and 22 arrests made. Stolen property, cannabis and methamphetamine were recovered. This was made possible with support from informants and specialist NZP units (notably, organised crime and intelligence). They also worked with landlords to evict organised crime elements while engaging with locals to transform the community.

During the prevention phase a neighbourhood safety panel was established. Drug education pamphlets were distributed and neighbourhood support groups were encouraged. Before the NPT started operating there were only four neighbourhood support groups in the community. After, there were more than 40.

A community survey revealed 90 per cent of local residents now felt safe in their community. So the third and final phase, SafeGrowth, focused on sustaining community safety. This included crime prevention through environmental design and a transition strategy.

Overall, crime in the Phillipstown area dropped by 28 per cent, resulting in 215 fewer victims, and $10 was saved for every $1 spent.

Case Studies in the Pillars of Policing

Back in 2008–9, as part of a 'Policing Excellence' package, NZP set out to boost the amount of effort being put into prevention, reduce recorded crime, and hold people to account for their offending without clogging up the courts or increasing the likelihood of re-offending.

Prevention

One way of achieving prevention was the introduction of NPTs – small, highly visible and accessible teams of officers based in communities where people are particularly likely to be victims of crimes and crashes. More than 30 NPTs were established to partner with local communities, using local knowledge and intelligence-collection plans to identify crime and safety issues, target known offenders and prevent problems from escalating.

Response

In May 2016 records showed NZP had attended approximately 115,000 family-violence events in the previous 12 months, but offences were detected in only 39,000 (roughly one-third). That may signal a lower threshold for reporting – potentially a good thing, as long as the only place people have to go is NZP. However, a new model being trialled in Christchurch helps to ensure NZP is not the only agency people can turn to for help.

Increased priority being given to family violence across agencies, and community publicity appear to be leading to increased levels of reporting to NZP. Increased reporting indicates trust and confidence in NZP, but in order to maintain that trust and confidence NZP has to be able to meet demand. The agency is taking a strategic risk by paying closer attention to 'lower-level' incidents involving family members in order to reduce repeat calls for service and escalation in the medium to long term. This is one of the risks involved in increasing the emphasis on prevention – throwing time and money in early, before things get bad, is arguably where the biggest gains are to be made.

Case Study: Christchurch Integrated Safety Response Pilot

Since July 2016, Canterbury Police have been piloting a new multi-agency Integrated Safety Response (ISR) to family violence. ISR brings together a range of agencies to collectively change the way they provide support to victims and their families and better manage support services.

At Christchurch Central Police Station, representatives from NZP, Health (including mental health), Child Youth and Family, Corrections, and others meet Monday to Saturday to assess family safety. On the agenda are medium- and high-risk family-violence incidents as they come to NZP attention, family-violence offenders about to be released from prison, and victims and offenders with existing plans still in place. The agency representatives share relevant information about the people involved (including children) and patterns of behaviour right up to the most recent incident. Together they consider risk and protective factors, agree tasks and assign a lead.

In one case, a victim with 140 previous family-violence episodes was considered to be at high risk of death or serious harm because of a head injury sustained in a prior assault. An Independent Victim Specialist and Perpetrator Outreach Service worker were allocated. During the daily ISR meeting, agency representatives identified a role for the Accident Compensation Corporation (ACC). The victim has now built a trusting relationship with ACC and is no longer isolated from the support she needs. Before ISR, the information would not have been shared with ACC and the opportunity for them to support the victim would not have presented itself.

The Christchurch ISR pilot is being independently evaluated, and a second pilot was launched in Hamilton in December 2016. The results from both will influence decisions about introducing the ISR model in more locations.

Investigations

NZP does not always get it right, though. When things go wrong, NZP can invite the Independent Police Conduct Authority (IPCA) to help understand what went wrong, why, and what changes (if any) need to be made to systems and processes. When police (in)action results in death or serious injury, the IPCA automatically launches an investigation.

Section 27 of the IPCA Act 1988 confirms that the Authority is entitled to 'form an opinion' about whether a NZP decision the IPCA has investigated is 'contrary to law, unreasonable, unjustified, unfair, or undesirable' (section 1). The IPCA can also recommend criminal proceedings against NZP employees (section 2). However, the decision to prosecute rests with the relevant prosecuting agency, free from any outside influence. Section 16 of the Policing Act 2008 is equally clear that the Police Commissioner must act independently regarding prosecution of offences.

Resolutions

The fourth pillar of policing, and key feature of the 'Policing Excellence' package, involves holding offenders accountable for their crimes, ideally in a way that does not clog up the courts or increase the likelihood of re-offending. Within NZP, this area of focus is called Resolutions, and in the public sphere is often associated with the work of the Police Prosecution Service and Youth Aid Officers (who deal with younger-age offenders). One of the learnings which has come out of NZP's work to resolve crime is that you can't prosecute your way out of every situation.

Policing Māori Communities

Problem-solving with Māori is essential to good policing in Aotearoa/New Zealand, and as an instrument of the Crown NZP has obligations to tangata whenua as a partner to the Treaty of Waitangi. This is reflected in a formal sense through one of NZP's organisational values: 'commitment to Māori and the Treaty'. New Zealand is the only police service in the world that has a core value like this, with a dedicated unit at PNHQ to make sure the organisation lives up to it.

Back in 1996, the then new Police Commissioner Peter Doone (1996–2000) expressed his concern that NZP's response to Māori 'over-representation' in the

Case Study: Operation Austin

Although unfamiliar to many younger New Zealanders, trust and confidence in NZP was rocked in the mid-2000s by historic allegations of sexual offending by past and present officers and their associates, sparking a government-ordered Commission of Inquiry by a High Court Judge and retired senior civil servant (Dame Margaret Bazley). Serious claims of rape and other crimes, said to have occurred in the Bay of Plenty during the 1980s, were made even more damaging by suspicions of a cover-up, plus the sense things 'went all the way to the top' – with one of the alleged assailants by then a District Commander, and the Assistant Commissioner responsible for policing the entire Auckland region.

A criminal investigation known as Operation Austin was quickly established, under the command of a senior officer from the opposite end of the country, Southern District Commander Detective Superintendent Nick Perry. The Austin team originally began with thirteen police officers and support staff, but more than doubled in size over the course of a two-and-a-half-year investigation process. A total of 30 sworn and 18 other NZP staff or contractors (brought in for their analytical experience and specialist skills in areas like complex file management) eventually worked on the multiple inquiries.

Given the sensitivity of the allegations, a conscious call was made to recruit inquiry team members from outside the Bay of Plenty – principally the South Island. Moreover, to protect against any suggestions of conflicts of interest, no one on the Operation Austin team had any past connection with the police officers who were suspects in the case.

With fresh allegations being reported on a regular basis, inquiries by the Operation Austin team ultimately led to contact with 50 women, leading to four major investigations and resulting in prosecutions. Despite the challenges and complexities, over the course of a more than 2-year investigation, Operation Austin set new benchmarks for professionalism in areas such as victim care, case management and pre-trial disclosure.

Examples included the appointment of what was at that time a ground-breaking move to establish and maintain a Victim Contact Register, and later assigning each complainant a detective to act as a Victim Liaison Officer throughout the long and gruelling prosecution processes.

Other hallmarks of the investigations included a meticulous approach to recordkeeping and updating formal Investigation Plans (particularly important when new allegations surfaced), ensuring the inquiry team was well versed in contemporary best practice for sexual abuse investigations, and seeking legal opinions on and peer review of key steps or decisions. The team also took the then unprecedented step of commissioning an independent quality assurance review of all pre-trial disclosure to guard against error.

Looking back, there is much to be proud of in how Operation Austin was run; especially in the context of 'investigating your own' at a time when confidence in NZP was so low. Even by today's standards, it stands as a beacon of painstaking investigative practice.

criminal justice system had fallen short of a full commitment to the principles of Te Tiriti o Waitangi. He was firmly of the view that to succeed in producing 'Safer Communities Together', NZP needed to establish, maintain and develop problem-solving partnerships with Māori.

Three dozen Māori police officers gathered at the RNZPC to discuss the development of a strategy to address this shortfall. Also in attendance was the late Ngāti Porou kaumātua and scholar Apirana Mahuika. Mahuika lamented the position of Māori in the criminal justice system and coined a whakataukī (proverb) to inspire courage in the face of adversity, which is reproduced in Figure 4.7.

This whakataukī, and accompanying logo, are widely used within NZP today. The logo is one of several policing articles that can only be worn with permission. A NZP article is 'any crest, badge, emblem, design, logogram, or other distinguishing article used, worn, or carried by any New Zealand Police employee while on duty and described in [the Policing Regulations 2008]'. Within a few years of the 1996 hui at the RNZPC:

Case Study: Pre-charge Warnings

NZP has always had the ability to give informal, verbal warnings. In September 2010, following a trial period, NZP introduced more formal 'pre-charge warnings' (PCWs). PCWs allow officers to hold people to account for their behaviour without criminalising them for minor offences. In order to be eligible for a PCW:

- An offender must be at least 17 years old
- The offence must carry a maximum penalty of 6 months' imprisonment or less
- Victim and reparation considerations must be taken into account (but issuing of a PCW is not contingent on the victim agreeing to such an outcome, or reparation being made).

PCWs are not a 'soft option' aimed at massaging down crime statistics. In order to get a PCW, one has to be arrested, and the offence will get counted in 'the crime stats'. Once arrested, NZP must decide how to proceed against the offender. PCWs are also counted in the official 'proceedings' statistics.

While PCWs are a way of holding offenders to account for their actions, importantly research has shown that such formal warnings also reduce the likelihood of re-offending. Data analysis using propensity score matching shows a 26.9 per cent re-apprehension rate within a year of being given a first PCW, versus a 39.7 per cent re-apprehension rate for those prosecuted for a first and similar offence over the same period.

Between September 2010 and November 2016, NZP issued just over 108,000 PCWs to slightly in excess of 85,000 people. In cases where victim reparation is required or an offender has a bit of 'history', NZP is trialling Community Justice/Iwi Panels. Early results have been promising.

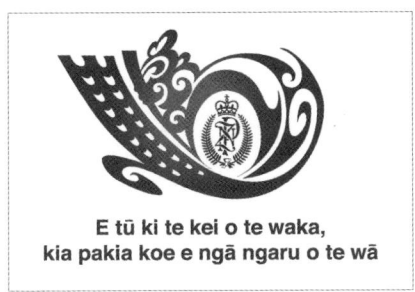

FIGURE 4.7 Whakataukī coined by the late Apirana Mauika and accompanying logo; the English translation is 'Stand at the stern of the waka and feel the spray of the future biting at your face'.

- New Iwi Liaison Officers had been appointed in all twelve policing Districts across the motu (roles now complemented by both Pacific Liaison Officers and Ethnic Liaison Officers)
- Māori Advisory Boards were also established in Districts (and some Districts also now have fono and ethnic councils to turn to for advice about engaging with Pasifika and other ethnic communities)
- A Superintendent had been appointed at PNHQ to provide advice on cultural affairs
- The first version of NZP's Responsiveness to Māori strategy had been developed.

In December 2012, the first Māori-specific criminal justice strategy in New Zealand was launched by members of the Police Commissioner's Māori Focus Forum, alongside the Police Executive. Known as 'The Turning of the Tide', it is one of three key strategies for NZP, alongside 'Prevention First' and the 'Safer Journeys: Road Policing Strategy'. Together, iwi/Māori and NZP set themselves six targets to meet in 6 years. The objectives were to:

- Stop Māori from entering the criminal justice system in the first place
- If Māori do enter, ensure they don't come back (flipping the usual customer service rule)
- Change behaviour rather than 'throw the book' at people for lower-level offending
- Stop unsafe roads and road use from claiming Māori lives, and contributing to Māori experiencing injuries from road crashes.

The Price of Policing

Mirroring trends in the wider justice sector, the cost of policing in New Zealand has more than doubled over the last decade and a half, from $650 million in 1999 to $1.6 billion in 2016/17. Broadly speaking, this overall envelope of funding is split between covering operating costs (20 per cent of the overall total), direct and indirect personnel costs (approximately 71 per cent of the total), and what are essentially accounting expenses (depreciation and capital charge: 9 per cent of the total), which sounds a lot, but is driven by the fact NZP has to own or lease a lot of physical assets (buildings for police stations or service centres; IT and other operational equipment like Tasers; and a large fleet of vehicles).

Breaking down the numbers further, the sizeable amount of money NZP is voted by Parliament every year is split between a number of what are called 'output classes'. Table 4.3 was generated by the Office of the Auditor-General – the public sector watchdog – to help inform members of Parliament about where NZP's money is allocated to be spent.

TABLE 4.3 **NZP 2016/17 output expenses (total = $1.597 billion)**

Output expenses		% of total
General crime-prevention services	$172,115,000	11%
Specific crime-prevention services and maintenance of public order	$164,072,000	10%
Police primary response management	$398,694,000	25%
Investigations	$402,086,000	25%
Case resolution and support to judicial process	$133,029,000	8%
Road safety programme	$323,024,000	20%
MCA OE*: Policy advice and ministerial servicing (0.3%)	$4,233,000	0%
Total	$1,597,253,000	

* MCA OE = multi-category appropriation output expense.

In terms of money in, roughly 80 per cent of the $1.6 billion comes from central government coffers. The remaining 20 per cent comes from the National Land Transport Fund – one of the few remaining hypothecated funds. The basic idea is that any money collected from road user levies (not speeding infringements) must be re-invested back into road-related services. Revenue gathered from NZP-issued traffic infringement notices goes back to the government's Consolidated Fund rather than into NZP's budget.

Although small amounts of NZP money may be made available for one-off contributions or joint operations, NZP is not a funding agency. This can be a problem. It is well known that a lot of people who come to the attention of NZP need help to deal with addictions, anger management, past victimisation, and any number of other underlying issues. Where possible, NZP will refer people to agencies that can give them the help they need, but because NZP does not fund those agencies, the people referred can sometimes be given low priority. Since many services are over-subscribed, this means people referred by NZP can miss out.

Conclusion

There is far more to modern-day policing in New Zealand than meets the eye or is seen on TV. A textbook chapter cannot do it justice. Nonetheless, this chapter has sought to provide some insights into the complexities involved in becoming a cop, running a large state service, and policing our streets, homes and roads. The risks and rewards of prevention and early intervention, as opposed to criminalisation, are evident in the case studies; as is the need for top-notch investigative work, action to hold offenders to account, providing excellent service for victims, and making sure people are safe and feel safe. Some widely-held assumptions and stereotypes about cops and the work of NZP may even have been challenged along the way.

Acknowledgements

This chapter would not have been possible without the assistance of Cassimar Larkin, Sharon Hart, Jane Cairns, Rebecca Wright, Senior Constable Andy Melville, Michael Sutorius, Dr Catherine Alington, Jackie Mulligan and the many others whose work has filtered into our consciousness and the words on these pages. Thanks to you all.

REFERENCES

New Zealand Police. 2016. *Annual Report 2015/16*. Wellington: New Zealand.
Wills, J. D. 1990. *The New Zealand Police Medal*. Auckland: J. D. Wills and New Zealand Police.

Other Resources
New Zealand Police recruiting website: www.newcops.co.nz
New Zealand Police. 2017. 'Crime Statistics'. Accessed 21 May 2017. http://www.police.govt.nz/about-us/publications/statistics
New Zealand Police. 2017. 'Update on The Turning of the Tide – Making a Difference Now and for Future Generations'. Accessed 21 May 2017. http://www.police.govt.nz/about-us/m%C4%81ori-and-police/update-turning-tide-making-difference-now-and-future-generations
Office of the Auditor-General. 2016. *Briefing to the Law and Order Committee, 2016/17 Year*. Accessed 21 May 2017. https://www.parliament.nz/resource/en-NZ/51SCLO_ADV_00DBSCH_EST_69148_1_A517680/af3871c9ad011a3390357694dd5db6b909f80777

5.

Corrections

GREG NEWBOLD

Introduction

The final point in the criminal justice process – after the crime has been committed and the offender identified, tried and sentenced – is the corrections system. When speaking about corrections most people think of prisons but corrections also includes non-custodial sanctions like probation and community-based sentences. This chapter deals with both custodial and non-custodial corrections.

In New Zealand, as in most countries, the great question within corrections is whether the system should be primarily dedicated to punishing offenders or to reforming them. In fact, both goals are usually attempted, but with varying amounts of weight depending on policy at the time, the offence, the type of sentence and, where prisons are concerned, the prison itself and the security classification of the offender. But there is more to the purpose of corrections than punishment and rehabilitation. There is in fact a range of essential functions that prisons perform, some of them quite obvious and others less so.

The Functions of Corrections

There are six important functions that the corrections system addresses:

1. *Control and custody.* The control and/or custody of offenders is one of the key purposes of a corrections system. Where prisons are concerned the

function is clear: prisons are committed to keeping offenders who are a danger to the community in secure confinement and out of harm's way. This is why prisons have walls and razor wire, and why escapes are treated seriously. Minor offenders often get sentences of probation, home detention or sanctions within the community, where they are controlled with monitoring and restrictions on residence, employment, social interaction and behaviour.

2. *Rehabilitation.* Most corrections systems are required, in one way or another, to attempt to 'rehabilitate' or 'reform' offenders. The obvious purpose of rehabilitation is, after identifying offenders' criminogenic patterns and triggers, to turn them away from crime. In prisons this takes place through programmes such as anger management, sex-offender therapy and vocational training initiatives. In the case of community alternatives the function is more obscure but is present nonetheless. The rationale for changing offenders' lives is to divert them from negative or dangerous pastimes and towards activities such as full-time employment which draw them away from criminal activity.

3. *Punishment.* All correctional systems punish to some extent. Since New Zealand abolished capital punishment for all crimes in 1989, loss of liberty remains the most severe sanction on the statute books. Few people like being in prison and most people hate it. It is, therefore, inherently punitive. Community corrections are less punitive, but sanctions such as community work, which require an offender to work for free for a certain number of hours, or home detention which restricts liberty beyond the home, are punitive as well as custodial and are intended to be so.

4. *Deterrence.* A cousin of punishment is deterrence. Sometimes known as general deterrence, deterrence means discouraging people, other than the offenders themselves, from committing crime by way of example. The reason that the early prisons were built with their characteristic imposing dark Gothic architecture, for instance, was to inspire awe and dread in citizens and frighten them away from crime. The reason that criminal offences and punishments are freely reported in the newspapers is to advertise to the general public the consequences of law-breaking.

5. *Retribution.* Apart from being punitive, corrections are also retributive. A lot of people deny the retributive function and argue that the state should not pander to the base instinct of 'paying someone back' for harm

they have done. But most people like to see criminals get their just deserts and only a saint would not feel a twinge of *schadenfreude* when a villain gets what's coming to him. This is retribution; the idea that wrongdoers should face consequences and that irrespective of anything else, a sinner should suffer for his sins. The greater the crime, the more they should suffer. Sentence lengths are influenced by this factor.

6. *Affirming the legitimacy of the state.* This is one of the least obvious functions of corrections, but it is one of the most important. When crimes get committed, the public needs confidence that the police are effective and will pursue the offender, and that, if caught, the culprit will be prosecuted and dealt with fairly and in accordance with the law. The New Zealand judicial oath – to apply the law 'without fear or favour' – has its origins in the Magna Carta of 1215 and is designed to ensure that the law is upheld and impartially applied. If the public loses confidence in the ability of the law to be systematically applied, anomie, anarchy and lawlessness are the inevitable results. So the correct and impartial enforcement of the law, and judicious application of sanctions to law breakers, are fundamental to public acceptance of the country's legal procedures and our system of government.

These are the principles which underlie our criminal justice process. Since it is impossible to understand contemporary corrections without reference to its background, however, before we look at New Zealand corrections today it is necessary to review their historical development.

History of New Zealand Corrections

New Zealand's legal system and its administrative machinery were inherited from Britain when the country became a Crown Colony following the signing of the Treaty of Waitangi in 1840. Having no laws of its own, originally New Zealand was subject to the laws of New South Wales but in 1842 a legislative council was established and thereafter New Zealand became increasingly responsible for the administration of its own laws, guided by the laws of England and overseen by the Colonial Office in London. New Zealand did not become fully self-governing until the Constitution Act of 1852 (Hill, 1986; Missen, 1971; Ringer, 1991; Spiller, Finn and Boast, 1995).

Jails at this time were ramshackle affairs, made mostly of wood, steel and raupō and run by the small settlements within which they were located. New Zealand handled its own executions – the first being the hanging of Wiremu Maketū for killing four settlers in the Bay of Islands in 1841 – but until 1854 New Zealand transported its worst criminals to the convict colonies in Australia. That ended with the Secondary Punishment Act 1854 which introduced the sentence of penal servitude. The number of prisoners in New Zealand at the time was about 70 (Hill, 1986).

The Constitution Act had set up a system of administration through six (later, ten) local provinces and the jails of the time were part of that (Ringer, 1991). Prisoners were mostly sentenced to hard labour and could be seen in local communities chained together and employed in public works. But the provinces were short of money and, of course, the jails bore the brunt of fiscal shortfalls. Thus, jailers were badly paid, food and clothing were poor, and prisons were run-down and unsanitary. There was no national prison system, nor any coherent penal policy.

It was ongoing criticism from judges and visiting justices which eventually changed this. As the colony grew older, larger and more mature, the disgraceful condition of the country's eleven major jails and nineteen lockups received increasingly strident comment and finally, in 1878, a decision was made to centralise prison administration. That year the position of Inspector General of Prisons was advertised in England and 2 years later Captain Arthur Hume, a former career soldier and past deputy governor of several English prisons, arrived in New Zealand to take up the post (Newbold, 1981).

The Hume Years: 1880–1909

Although Irish by birth, Hume had been schooled in the repressive traditions of Victorian England and it was this culture that he brought to New Zealand. In his report of 1892 he wrote, 'The English system is the best system and is, as far as practicable, being carried out in New Zealand prisons'. Hume was a dyed-in-the-wool authoritarian and like his English forebears he thought that the key to convict reformation was discipline and deterrence. He believed that New Zealand prisons weren't tough enough and accordingly when he arrived he advocated solitary confinement for hardened offenders, restrictions on prisoner communication, a reduction in ration scales, a prohibition on smoking, removal of sentence remission for good behaviour and the abolition of inmate education beyond basic literacy.

Although all Hume's recommendations were not followed – his proposal for birching for prison indiscipline, for example, was rejected – and he modified his views as time went on, his basic philosophy remained repressive. However, he introduced a system of graduated privilege for good behaviour, created the first low-security work camps, and in 1886 oversaw the introduction of the world's first national probation system. He had new prisons built at Mt Eden in Auckland, Napier, New Plymouth, Mt Cook in Wellington, Dunedin and Invercargill. A road-building camp in Fiordland failed, but successful tree-planting camps were established at Waipa Valley in the Waikato, Waiotapu near Taupo, Dumgree in Marlborough, and Hanmer in Canterbury. The major piece of prison legislation during Hume's time was the Habitual Offenders and Criminals Act 1906, which provided for repeat offenders of certain types to be declared habitual criminals and detained indefinitely. This remained until 1954 (Newbold, 1981, 2007).

The New Method: 1909–1925

Hume's methods were considered archaic and unduly punitive by the progressive men of the young dominion and it was with a certain sigh of relief that Hume's resignation was accepted in 1909. The government had clear ideas about where it wanted prisons to go and accordingly Hume's role was taken over by the Minister of Justice of the governing Liberal Party, Dr John Findlay.

Findlay was an educated man of strong liberal persuasion who had knowledge of contemporary developments in corrections overseas. Thus, as soon as he took over, Findlay set about reforming the prison system. In 1910, impressed by the experiment in rehabilitating young criminals that had been under way at Elmira Reformatory, New York, since 1876, Findlay sponsored the passage of the Crimes Amendment Act 1910 which established a sentence called reformative detention. Reformative detention was an indeterminate sentence which allowed reformable prisoners to be sent to special training institutions called reformatories for up to 10 years. Although the sentence never worked as intended, it remained on the books until 1954.

Findlay's tenure was short – he lost his seat in 1911 and the Liberals were defeated by the Reform Party the following year – but his legacy was continued by Charles Matthews, who took over as Controller General of Prisons in 1912. Although slightly more conservative than Findlay, Matthews carried on in the tradition of his predecessor, and he and the Reform Government are largely responsible for the establishment of a network of prison farms between 1912 and 1925. New Zealand was developing as a strong agricultural economy at the time and it was felt that, by introducing prisoners to healthy outdoor living and what Matthews called 'the gospel of hard work', they could be trained to become productive citizens. In 1910, Findlay had bought large tracts of undeveloped land for conversion into farms at Invercargill and Waikeria. The Reform Government now added to these with purchases at Paparua in Canterbury, in 1914; Waikune, near Ruapehu, also in 1914; and Tongariro (Hautu/Rangipo), near Taupo, in 1921. These purchases developed into large and successful prison farms so that by 1919, 53 per cent of all inmates were engaged in farming or land development. In 1924 the idea of reformative detention was added to by the Prevention of Crime Act, which introduced a sentence called borstal detention; an indeterminate training sentence of up to 5 years for boys aged between 15 and 21. In addition, in 1917 the parole system, which had initially been set up to deal with habitual criminals, was extended to all prisoners serving more than 2 years. The minimum for life was set at 8 years. In 1920 parole was widened to include all inmates after 6 months and to lifers after a minimum of 5 years (Matthews, 1923; Newbold, 1981, 2007).

The Dallard Era: 1925–1949

These were indeed imaginative times and sentence administration was far more liberal than it is today. But in 1924 Charles Matthews died in office and a period of retrenchment began. The 1920s were a time of economic instability, leading towards the onset of the Great Depression in 1929. Matthews's replacement, Bert Dallard, was a reflection of this, a conservative public service accountant whose principal concern was the fiscal bottom line. Dallard steered the Department of Prisons through difficult times: the depression of the early 1930s followed by World War II. There wasn't much money around and to help balance the books, so Dallard spent a lot of time economising and developing the prison farms in the hope of making them self-sustaining. The First Labour Government (1935–49) abolished capital and corporal punishment in 1941, but that was against Dallard's wishes. The only major capital investment during his time was the building of a new women's prison at Arohata just north of Wellington (Dallard, 1980; Newbold, 1981, 2007).

The Barnett Era: 1949–1960

In 1949, after a splurge of negative publicity from newspaper critics for being overly punitive, Dallard retired at the compulsory age of 60. The end of World War II had ushered in a mood for liberalism in prisons, as soldiers returned from the battlefields or from the Nazi and Japanese prisoner of war camps. Otherwise, the times were conservative. The First National Government had been sworn in in 1949 and one of the first things it did was bring back capital punishment. Between 1950 and 1957 (when Labour again became government and declined to conduct executions), eight men were hanged for murder, all of them at Mt Eden Prison.

Despite reinstating capital punishment, National's corrections policy was highly progressive. There were three Ministers of Justice during the 1950s but the driving force of reform was the Secretary for Justice Sam Barnett, a trained lawyer and career public servant; a powerful personality with a highly developed sense of compassion and reason. It was Barnett who inspired his ministers to make many of the reforms that began under his watch.

The first thing Barnett did was to advise the government of the need for a new Criminal Justice Act, which in 1954 abolished hard labour, reformative detention (which had for years been defunct), and the habitual criminals declaration. This last was replaced by a new indeterminate sentence called preventive detention, with 3–14 years available for certain categories of repeat adult offender and 3 years–life for repeat adult child sex offenders. It continues in modified form today. Borstal detention was modernised as a sentence of 0–3 years and renamed borstal training. A new sentence called corrective training was created, which was similar to borstal training but aimed at young men aged 21–30. Parole was abolished for finite sentences and replaced with an automatic standard remission of 25 per cent of sentence. The probation system was overhauled and professionalised, with compulsory probation for all prisoners sentenced to at least 12 months imprisonment.

Within the prisons themselves, a revolutionary programme of reform was also started, with improved rations, new uniforms for staff and inmates, the appointment of prison psychologists, welfare officers and education officers, the secondment of chaplains to each prison, and the commencement of organised training for prison officers. Classification committees now professionalised the security determination of inmates. Under an initiative called Reformative Recreation, prison life was improved with recreation and welfare committees

The Hangings of the 1950s

1952   William Fiori (30), a borderline mental defective, hanged for shooting his employer and his employer's wife for money, in Otorohanga.

1953   Eruera Te Rongopatahi (23), hanged for the random shooting of a taxi driver in Ashburton, after an argument with his girlfriend.

1953   Harry 'Darkie' Whiteland (56), an Indian-born railwayman, hanged for shooting a female co-worker in Reefton after an argument with her.

1955   Frederick Foster (26), an English immigrant, hanged for shooting his former girlfriend Sharon Skiffington, in a Queen Street milk bar in Auckland.

1955   Edward Te Whiu (20), hanged for strangling an old lady in Whangarei when she discovered him burgling her house.

1955   Harvey Allwood (34), hanged for shooting a friend in Te Anau after a drunken argument while they were out rabbit shooting.

1955   Albert 'Paddy' Black (20), an Irish immigrant, hanged for stabbing a romantic rival in a Queen Street café in Auckland.

1957   James Bolton (68), hanged for poisoning his wife in Wanganui. He had been having an affair with his wife's sister. (Newbold, 1981)

appointed, weekly movies, daily newspapers, and hours of lockup reduced. At the maximum security Mt Eden Prison an inmates' council was formed to advise the superintendent on prisoner affairs, bowling competitions with outside excursions were organised, a competitive debating team formed and a prisoners' orchestra was developed, which soon began giving regular concerts to the public.

Barnett oversaw a complete overhaul of New Zealand's prison system. These were optimistic, buoyant times, but they did not last. As noted in Chapter 2, from about 1955 crime rates began to rise and with them so did prison numbers. Unable to cope with the pressure, prisons grew overcrowded and this basically stymied further developments. The escape of a dangerous sex killer called 'Slim' Horton from a bowling excursion in 1955, followed by a scandal in 1958 when members of the prison band were found to have been getting out of the prison overnight and committing crimes in Auckland, forced the closure of the Reformative Recreation initiative. A number of other embarrassing escapes and incidents added to Barnett's woes, and he retired a weary and disillusioned man in 1960 (Newbold, 1981, 2007).

The Hanan-Robson Era

The advances of the 1950s were followed by one of the most progressive decades in New Zealand penal history. This period was known as the Hanan-Robson era, referring to the unique relationship that developed between Barnett's replacement as Secretary for Justice, Dr John Robson, and the Minister of Justice, Ralph Hanan. Robson was a career public servant with a PhD in law, while Hanan was a key member of the Second National Government, which defeated Labour in 1960 after just 3 years in office. Both men were passionate reformists. Robson was the ideas man, who mapped out new policy, while Hanan, a person of high integrity who commanded immense respect in Parliament, had the power to convert Robson's suggestions into law.

Once in office Hanan and Robson wasted no time continuing with the reform programme started by National just 11 years earlier. Hanan was an avid opponent of capital punishment and the first thing he did in office was write a new Crimes Act (1961), in which capital punishment for murder was abolished. The following year the non-parole minimum for life, set at 5 years in 1920, was increased to 10. A riot at the Hastings Blossom Festival in September 1960, just before the election, had heightened concern about youth crime and Hanan had promised to address it as one of his election pledges. Accordingly, in 1961 he ordered the opening of a boot-camp-style prison for juvenile males called a detention centre. Aimed primarily at deterrence, detention centres were for teenaged first offenders who were sent to the centres for 3 months of highly structured life, hard work and military-style discipline. In addition, borstal training was reduced to 0–2 years and a new first offenders' borstal was established at Waipiata, Central Otago, in 1961. A community-based sentence called periodic detention, allowing reformable juvenile males to be detained over the weekend instead of being sent to prison, was also created. This was the first community sentence to appear since the commencement of probation in 1886 (Department of Justice, 1971).

Attention was also paid to adults. A first offenders' training programme for reformable adults was established at Wi Tako near Trentham in 1967 (now known as Rimutaka Prison), special remission amounting to one-third of sentence for exemplary conduct commenced in 1964, and a system of home leaves allowing married prisoners to spend weekends at home with their families every 4 months began in 1965. In 1967 parole eligibility was widened to include inmates serving at least 5 years and, in order to increase the chances of an inmate successfully reintegrating to society, in 1961 statutory authority was created for prisoners nearing the end of their sentences to be released during the day to work in the community. In 1963 the first of a series of work parole hostels was established to house parolees on release-to-work schemes.

As had happened in the Barnett era, it was the first half of the decade that was the most productive. In 1965 two crises occurred which turned the Justice Department's head towards security. In January 1965 three dangerous inmates managed to smuggle a sawn-off shotgun into the security division of Mt Eden, where they took an officer hostage and escaped in a prison truck, then barricaded themselves in a nearby house after also capturing the occupants. Although the trio surrendered after a few hours, the security weaknesses of the 80-year-old maximum security prison were underlined. Six months later a worse crisis occurred when two remand prisoners smuggled a .22 calibre pistol into the jail and attempted to escape. When the effort failed they used home-made keys to unlock the rest of the prison and a 3-day riot ensued, during the course of which the entire institution was gutted by fire. Prisoners had to be evacuated to other facilities while a new maximum security facility was built north of Auckland, at Paremoremo. The building of Paremoremo, which when it opened in 1969 was the most sophisticated maximum security institution in the world, dominated the Department's attention for the rest of the decade (Newbold, 1981, 2007).

CORRECTIONS

The 1970s and 1980s

In 1969 Ralph Hanan died suddenly and the next year John Robson retired. By this stage most of the elements of New Zealand's modern correctional system were in place. In 1972 the Third Labour Government was sworn in, and the new Minister of Justice, Dr Martyn Finlay, a progressive humanitarian with a PhD in law, liberalised the country's corrections further. Finlay extended home leaves to become available to minimum security inmates every 2 months, made one-third remission standard for minimum security prisoners, made periodic detention available for women, legislated the abolition of borstal and detention centre training (due to high recidivist rates), increased parole eligibility for prisoners serving finite sentences, reduced the non-parole period for murder from 10 to 7 years, and abolished punishment diets for those in solitary confinement.

Many of Finlay's reforms, however, were unpopular with voters and contributed to Labour's landslide defeat in 1975. From that time forth little was done in prison reform, and in fact in some aspects it began to regress. In 1977 the new government revoked a 1975 law giving prisoners the right to vote, and the new Minister of Justice, David Thomson, removed a liberty that Finlay had given prisoners, which was to write uncensored letters directly to him. Thomson also declared that the new parole law notwithstanding, no lifer would be released in less than 10 years and the minimum for life was statutorily returned to 10 years in 1987. In 1987 parole for finite sentences, which had been extended in 1980 and 1985, was removed entirely for prisoners serving finite sentences for serious violence.

The biggest developments of the 1970s and 1980s had to do with community corrections. Periodic detention, which had been introduced for male juveniles in 1962, was extended to adult males in 1966 and, as noted, to females in 1974. From 1976, however, due to its popularity, residential periodic detention began to decline and was replaced by daytime attendance at periodic detention centres. Until 1980, probation and periodic detention remained the only community sentences available to the courts. But prison populations were increasing rapidly and placing strains on resources. Between 1965 and 1980 musters grew by 69 per cent, to 2800. In order to ease the burden, from 1980 further alternatives to imprisonment were sought. In 1980 a sentence called community service was added, which allowed certain offenders to be ordered to complete up to 200 hours' work within the community. This was followed by a sentence called community care in 1985, allowing courts to sentence low-security offenders to up to 12 months' attendance (up to 6 months

Non-Parole Periods of 25 Years or More

William Bell (20): Life with 30 years in 2002 for beating to death Wayne Johnson, Mary Hobson and Bill Absolum and severely injuring Susan Couch while robbing the Panmure RSA in Auckland.

Graeme Burton (35): Life with 26 years in 2007 for fatally shooting and stabbing mountain biker Karl Kuchenbecker and injuring four others on Wainuiomata Hill, near Wellington. Burton had only recently been paroled for stabbing a man to death in Wellington in 1992.

Bruce Howse (38): Life with 25 years for stabbing his two stepdaughters, Olympia Jetson (11) and Saliel Aplin (12), to death in Masterton, after they had threatened to expose him for sexually abusing them.

Joseph Thompson (37): Preventive detention with 25 years in 1995 for the sexual violation of at least 60 women in South Auckland, over a 12-year period.

---

of which could be residential) at an approved private community centre such as a marae or half-way house. The initiatives had little effect, however, and by 2000 the 1980 prison figure had doubled. In 2002 periodic detention, community service and community care were all collapsed into a single sentence called community work, which is discussed below (Newbold, 1981, 2007).

The final major advent in community corrections was home detention. First introduced experimentally in 1993, home detention was intended to relieve pressure on burgeoning prison populations. In 1999 'home d' was introduced presumptively to replace all sentences of 2 years or less, and also as a release condition for parolees. This changed in 2007, however, with electronic monitoring at a specified residence becoming a community-based sentence in its own right. It is also used as a condition of parole or bail.

The main reason for the massive escalation in prison numbers after 1980 was violent crime, which leapt from 3336 reported offences in 1960 to 22,104 in 1985

– more than a seven-fold increase. The government response was the so-called violent offences legislation, which between 1985 and 1993 expanded preventive detention, mandated imprisonment for violent offences, (temporarily) removed parole eligibility for violent offences, permitted the Secretary for Justice to waive remission for dangerous violent offenders and order that they serve their full terms, increased the maximum penalty for rape from 14 to 20 years, and allowed courts to set non-parole minimums higher than those set at law (Newbold, 2007).

Corrections since 2000

In 2002 some major amendments to parole and sentencing law took place, most of which remain today. The most important changes were that from 2002 all prisoners serving more than 2 years lost remission rights and instead became eligible for parole at one-third of sentence. However, most complete at least two-thirds and recalls for parole violations have become increasingly common. A non-parole minimum of at least 17 years was imposed for murders committed with certain aggravating circumstances, and preventive detention was redefined as a sentence of 5 years to life, available on a first offence for serious violent and sexual offending. In order to reduce sex offender recidivism, in 2004 an amendment to parole law introduced Extended Supervision Orders, allowing the continued supervision of high-risk sex offenders for up to 10 years after completion of sentence (Newbold, 2007). The measures had little impact on offending and between 1985 and 2010 reported violent offences tripled.

In 2010 another major law change was made, with the 'three strikes and you're out' law mentioned in Chapter 2. Briefly, 'three strikes', which refers to a list of 40 specified violent or sexual offences or 'strikes', provides for a normal sentence on a first strike offence, the sentence of the court without parole eligibility on a second strike, and the maximum penalty allowed by law, without parole eligibility, on a third strike. Up to the end of 2016, 1446 offenders had been convicted of first strikes, 171 of second strikes, and one had committed a third strike (Newbold, 2012, 2016; Oleson, 2015).

Since the three strikes law came into effect, reported violent offending has reduced by about 5 per cent. But as discussed in Chapter 2, other forms of offending have receded also and the extent to which the drops in violent crime are attributable to the law as opposed to other factors is unclear. In fact, since reaching a nadir in 2013, reported violence seems to be rising again.

But attempts to control violent offending with tougher sentences have not been without effect. The main impact has been on prison populations. First, of course, longer sentences, combined with deepening parole board conservatism and hair-trigger recalls, has boosted prison numbers, which grew from 5661 in 2000 to over 10,000 at the end of 2016 (up 77 per cent). Second, the ratio of prisoners doing time for violent or sexual offending as their primary offence grew from 20 per cent in 1972 to 63 per cent in 2016. In addition, average sentences have lengthened. In 1972 only 5.2 per cent of inmates were doing sentences of more than 7 years; in 2016 the figure was over 25 per cent. So prisoners today are serving longer terms than before and are more likely to be doing time for violence. Consequently, prisons are more dangerous. All of the thirteen homicides that have taken place in the history of New Zealand corrections have occurred since 1979, with twelve since 1985 (Newbold, 2016).

Along with the changing nature of prisons has been a tightening of security. We have seen that after 1910 there was a gradual de-emphasis of prison security, with a primacy placed on programmes, low-security confinement and productive outside employment. All prisoners were expected to work. The lengthening of prison sentences after 1985 and the more violent composition of the inmate population changed that. First, larger prison numbers made it impossible to find work for all prisoners and unemployment or token employment became a permanent feature of the carceral world from the mid-1980s. Second, the more violent nature of prisons saw a spike in suicides in the 1980s, accompanied by higher numbers of inmates requesting protective segregation. In 1985, only 5 per cent of prisoners were confined in protective custody. Since 2009 the figure has exceeded 25 per cent. The danger that certain inmates present to one another is an added reason why delivering programmes and work has become difficult and why security has tightened. The first big security clamp actually began in the late 1990s when Dr Nick Smith was the National government's Minister of Justice (1997–99). This period saw the commencement of restrictions on visiting, compulsory drug testing, use of drug dogs in prisons and the placement of razor wire and high fences around all facilities. Rations scales were reviewed and reduced. The outcome has been a reduction of visitors, an increase in lockup, a decline in programmes, and an erosion of conditions of confinement. But there has also been a cut in suicides, escapes and positive drug tests (Newbold, 2007).

The Goal of Rehabilitation in Recent Years

Although recent years have focused primarily on higher security and lowering costs, the goal of reform has not been forgotten. Since the late 1980s there has been a number of initiatives in the rehabilitation of prisoners. The first was an experiment that started in 1989 called He Ara Hou (A New Way). He Ara Hou was the brainchild of the then Assistant Secretary (Penal Institutions), Kim Workman. Driven by strong liberal-Christian ideals, Workman's belief was that the custodial nature of prisons cripples their reformative potential. The solution, he felt, was to break down the authoritarian barriers which separate inmates and staff, and place a renewed emphasis on rehabilitation and mutual assistance and cooperation. Staff were discouraged from wearing rank insignia and were urged to develop personal relationships with chosen inmates in order to assist their reform and reintegration. Although bold and imaginative in its intent, in practice He Ara Hou was loosely controlled and it led to a number of embarrassing crises involving staff corruption and malpractice. Thus in 1993 the experiment came to an end. Recidivist rates were unaffected.

The initiative that replaced He Ara Hou was sponsored by Workman's successor, Mark Byers, and was known as Integrated Offender Management (IOM). Byers believed that one failure of He Ara Hou was that it was too idealistic and non-systematic, and instead opted for a scientific approach. He was influenced by his senior advisers, who showed him a raft of international research demonstrating that if the drivers of an individual's offending can be correctly identified and then addressed using scientifically validated and computerised interventions, true reductions in recidivism can be achieved. At the time when IOM became fully operational in 2002, Ministry of Justice figures indicated that 57.7 per cent of all released prisoners would be reconvicted of an offence within 12 months of release, and 85.8 per cent would be reconvicted within 5 years. IOM began in 1996, and Byers and his advisers confidently predicted that if correctly applied, IOM could achieve recidivist rate reductions of at least 30 per cent (Newbold, 2007).

The problem with IOM was its expense. Installing the computerised diagnostic and treatment programme (called IOMs) cost $13.8 million alone and millions more were spent on training and interventions. Even if it had worked properly there is no guarantee that the predicted reductions would have occurred. But in the end the initiative was torpedoed by regular misdiagnosis of offenders' 'criminogenic needs' (CRNs), accompanied by an absence of the programmes necessary for treatment and/or a lack of qualified personnel to deliver them. The Department of Corrections simply could not afford to employ large numbers of fully-trained specialists to apply IOM, nor could it afford to supply the myriad of programmes needed to all of its nineteen institutions. Thus the inmates' CRNs remained largely unaddressed, anticipated outcomes did not occur and recidivist rates remained unchanged. In 2005, IOM effectively came to an end (Newbold, 2007).

The failure of IOM notwithstanding, reform efforts have continued. In 2006 a Labour government strategy called Effective Interventions was announced. Effective Interventions involved an attempt to reduce recidivism by increasing the Department's focus on rehabilitation, the use of restorative justice and an expansion of community sentencing alternatives. In the end, Effective Interventions proved little more than political hype and in the context of rising prison sentences and higher security, nothing significant was achieved. Two years later Labour was replaced by National, which soon announced its own slogan, 'Creating Lasting Change', the focus of which was to be 'working prisons'. The new Minister of Corrections promised that by introducing full employment to prisons she could cut recidivism from the 2011 figure of 57.6 per cent reoffending within 12 months by 25 per cent by June 2017 – that is to a 12-month rate of 43.2 per cent.

The minister set herself an impossible task. First, with prison populations exploding as a result of tough sentencing and parole policies, with 25 per cent of the muster on protective segregation, and with hours of lockup being extended to cut supervision costs, the chances of finding full employment for all sentenced prisoners were virtually nil. Recalling that prior to 1985 there had been full employment in prisons, without any indication of lower recidivist rates than we have now, the prediction was questionable anyhow. By March 2016 the 12-month recidivist rate was only 7.7 per cent lower than the 2011 rate, and that gap was narrowing. In the meantime, between 2011 and March 2016, prison populations expanded by more than 500, or about 7 per cent. In May 2017 the 25 per cent reduction target was abandoned.

New Zealand Corrections Today

Prisons

Today the Department of Corrections has oversight of nineteen penal institutions, including three women's prisons: Auckland Region Women's Corrections Facility (ARWCF), Arohata Prison and Christchurch Women's Prison. Two of the sixteen male facilities are run by the multinational company Serco: Mt Eden Corrections Facility and Auckland South Corrections Facility. Private prisons have been operating in this country since 2000 and while some aspects of contract management have been criticised, the overall results have been positive (Newbold, 2007).

Prisons in New Zealand are relatively small compared with countries like the United States, where facilities frequently exceed 5000 inmates. Nonetheless, in New Zealand prison capacities are growing. Currently there are six prisons in New Zealand with a capacity of about 1000, including the two privately-run institutions. Invercargill is the smallest, with a capacity of 172. The largest female facility is ARWCF, with a capacity of 684. With only about 550 women prisoners in the country, this means that while men's prisons are overcrowded and increasingly moving towards double-celling, women's prisons are currently undersubscribed.

At the end of 2016, as noted, there were over 10,000 men and women in New Zealand prisons – about half of them Māori, who only constitute about 14.6 per cent of the general population. This high percentage is a result of the disproportionate number of Māori involved in crimes of violence. Although ageing considerably, the prison population is still young, with 57 per cent of all inmates aged between 20 and 39. Only a small number are under 20 (4 per cent), reflecting the judiciary's emphasis on keeping youthful offenders out of the formal justice process. As noted, about 63 per cent of prisoners are doing time for a violent or sexual crime as their primary offence. More than two-thirds of all prisoners are serving sentences of over 2 years.

In New Zealand today, prisoners serving 2 years or less are released automatically on remission at half sentence. Those serving finite terms of more than 2 years may be paroled after one-third of sentence, unless a longer non-parole period has been ordered by a court. Where open-ended sentences are concerned, non-parole periods vary. The standard non-parole period for preventive detention is 5 years, and for life imprisonment it is 10 years. Murders committed with certain aggravating circumstances carry a 17-year minimum but as with finite sentences, non-finite penalties may also carry longer minimums imposed by courts. Under the Parole Act 2002, parolees may only be released before their full terms if the parole board believes they no longer present an undue risk to the community. Parolees are released subject to conditions imposed by the parole board up to the expiry of their full sentences and may be recalled at any time for breaching them. Prisoners who serve their full sentences are subject to release conditions for 6 months after their release date.

Conditions in New Zealand prisons vary according to a range of factors, in particular the age of the institution or unit, and the inmate's security ranking and job designation. Four New Zealand prisons – Mt Eden (1882), Invercargill (1911), Waikeria (1911) and Christchurch Men's (1915) – are, or have sections that are, over 100 years old and the capacity for work and programmes in them is low. Here prisoners sit around the wings during hours of unlock with little to do. More modern units built outside the original constructions are sometimes better, although everywhere remand prisoners have almost nothing in the way of recreation or work and spend a great deal of their time locked in their cells or sitting idly about their units. The new prisons built since 2005 – Ngawha (2005), Spring Hill (2007), ARWCF (2006), Milton (2007) and the private prison at Auckland South (Wiri) (2015) – have modern appointments and conditions there are better. The old prison farms at Waikune, Rangipo and Hautu in the central North Island once offered a healthy outdoor environment with 100 per cent employment and plenty of opportunity for sport and recreation, but Waikune closed in 1986 and in 2015 the Minister of Corrections announced that Rangipo was no longer considered 'fit for purpose' and would shut also, while Hautu would be expanded and refurbished.

The toughest prison in the country is Paremoremo, officially known as Auckland Prison (East), which opened in 1969 to replace Mt Eden. Originally a national showpiece of pioneering enlightenment, with five modern workshops, a fully equipped gymnasium and an array of the most organised and diverse recreational programmes ever seen in a New Zealand prison, after 1984 gang influx and several instances of serious violence, including three homicides, caused security to become paramount and programmes to close down. Today the ageing prison, which consists of five cellblocks and a maximum of about 250 prisoners, has only the most basic facilities, no meaningful employment, and 18–22 hours a day of solitary lockup (Newbold, 2016). A new 261-bed maximum security facility is due to open at Paremoremo in mid-2018.

Auckland Prison is the only dedicated maximum security prison in New Zealand. Most institutions cater for a range of security classifications although camps such as Hautu and Rolleston contain only lower-security inmates. Security designations and associated freedoms in New Zealand change frequently but in 2016 there were five security classes based on a computerised score of internal risk (i.e., management compliance) and external risk (i.e., likelihood of escape and danger to the public). The percentages of prisoners in each class are: Maximum (1.2 per cent of prisoners), High (18 per cent), Low-Medium (29 per cent), Low (22.8 per cent) and Minimum (29 per cent).

Management strategy and availability of programmes is largely determined by security levels. For example, maximum security inmates are excluded from most programmes and work. Minimum and low security prisoners may work outside the wire; all higher levels must remain inside. In addition, maximum and high security prisoners must be housed separately from lower security ranks. Since the escape of lifer Phillip Smith from a work release in 2015, all prisoners working outside the wire have had to wear GPS bracelets unless directly supervised. Whereas in the 1970s and 1980s a certain number of prison escapes was seen as somewhat inevitable, today with the emphasis on security, a prison escape is regarded as a serious administrative failing.

Employment and prison programmes are limited by population pressure and inadequate finances, but a number of specialist units exist within the prisons to treat specific types of offender. Perhaps the most famous are the Special Treatment Units (STUs) which have been created to treat sex offenders. The first of these was Kia Marama (Let There be Light), which commenced at Rolleston Prison in 1989 as a 33-week programme for the treatment of child sex offenders. With a 7-year recidivist rate of just 33 per cent, Kia Marama was deemed a great success and was joined by a second sex-offender initiative called Te Piriti (The Bridge) at Auckland Prison in 1994. Inspired by the success of these experiments, in 1998 a Violence Prevention Unit (VPU) was established at Rimutaka. In 2011 VPUs were renamed High-Risk Special Treatment Units (HRSTUs), with a violence programme called Special Treatment Unit Rehabilitation Programme (STURP), which also deals with high-risk repeat rapists using a strategy called the Adult Sex Offender Treatment Programme (ASOTP) (Newbold, 2016).

Other specialist units include Māori Focus Units (MFUs) and Pacific Focus Units (PFUs) which since 1997 have offered cultural immersion for Māori and later Pasifika offenders, and Drug Treatment Units (DTUs) (in operation since 1997) which offer therapy for drug- and alcohol-affected prisoners. Since 1999 there has also been a small number of youth units for prisoners under the age of 20. In 2003 a Faith-Based Unit opened at Rimutaka to offer spiritual guidance programmes for Christian inmates; however, it closed in 2012 due to low responsiveness.

The final type of specialist unit operated by Corrections is the Self-Care Unit (SCU). SCUs commenced in 1998 and consist of groups of self-contained, fully equipped, four-bedroomed flats where trusted prisoners live together, separate from the mainstream but behind a secure wire, in conditions approximating those outside. Prisoners are given a weekly budget which they use to purchase household needs. They do their own cooking, cleaning and laundry and must get themselves to work every day. If deemed suitable, women with children under the age of 2 may have their children living in the units with them. SCUs are particularly useful in preparing trusted prisoners nearing the end of their sentences for life in the free community. Outside of the SCUs, women with infants under 2 can have their children during the day in supervised spaces known as Mothers and Babies Units.

Community Corrections

A cheaper but less punitive alternative to imprisonment is community corrections. Although prisons represent the mainstay of our criminal justice system, community alternatives (sometimes known as intermediate sanctions) are used more often and provide a way of treating minor offenders whose crimes are too serious to be dealt with by fines, or who are unable or unwilling to pay fines. Without community alternatives, the pressure on the prison system would be even higher than it is.

As we have seen, New Zealand has a long history in community corrections, with the First Offenders Probation Act setting up a fledgling probation system in 1886. Probation was renamed supervision in 2002. For many years, probation remained the country's only intermediate sanction, but it was joined in 1962 by periodic detention, by community service in 1980, by community care in 1985 (renamed community programme in 1993) and by home detention in 1995.

Today there are three main types of community sentencing:

1. *Supervision*: Supervision is the second-most common community alternative, serving an average of 7750 clients at any one time and costing $4,486 per person, per year. Supervision is provided by probation officers who perform three main functions: 1) assessment of offenders prior to sentence; 2) monitoring of offenders sentenced to supervision by the courts; and 3) supervision of offenders after release from prison. A variation of supervision is the Extended Supervision Order (ESO), which was created in 2004 for high-risk sex offenders. An ESO allows such a person to be monitored for up to 10 years and can involve highly restrictive conditions. Between 25 and 50 ESOs are issued every year. The ESO was added to in 2007 by a form of

supervision called intensive supervision. Intensive supervision is more rigorous than ordinary supervision and more expensive, costing $6,232 per person, per year. There are about 2380 people on intensive supervision. Another extension of supervision is community detention, which also commenced in 2007. Community detention allows an offender to be placed on curfew with electronic monitoring. It costs about $6,332 per year for each of the 1700 people serving community detention.

2. *Community work*: Community work is easily the most used of all community sentences, catering for about 15,000 offenders at a time. Costing just $2,484 each per year it is also the cheapest. Community work involves offenders working in the community for between 40 and 400 hours, managed by the Community Probation Service which also runs supervision.

3. *Home detention*: As noted, home detention was first trialled in 1993 but was introduced in its current form in 2007. Today home detention is used primarily as a sentence of the court, with electronically-monitored restrictions on movement and a requirement for an offender to live at an approved address. Home detention caters for approximately 1600 offenders on any day and costs about $20,900 per client, per year, to administer. Home detention is also used as a condition of parole or bail.

Community-based sentences cost an average of $8,000 per offender, per year, compared with $91,000 for prison inmates. On any one day, there is an average of about 28,000 offenders serving community-based sentences, compared with over 10,000 prison inmates. So the cost savings of these alternatives to incarceration are considerable. In fact, community sanctions have a number of advantages over imprisonment. The main ones are that:

- They are cheaper to run than prisons
- They give the courts an alternative way of dealing with moderately serious offenders who would otherwise require short prison sentences
- They allow offenders to remain in the community, working, paying taxes and looking after their families
- They avoid some of the deleterious effects that incarceration produces.

But there are also a number of disadvantages. The main ones are that:

- They are less deterrent than prisons
- Victims may be angered when they see offenders on the street who they feel should be locked up
- People on community sentences may continue to offend in some areas such as in fraud or drug dealing
- Some offenders are terrible parents and partners and keeping their families together may not necessarily advantage those families.

Public Protection Orders

The most recent addition to the armoury of criminal sanctions is the Public Protection Order (PPO). PPOs fall between imprisonment and the community sentence in that they are neither. The PPO came about as a result of the particularly brutal murder of a 56-year-old woman called Blessie Gotingco in Auckland in 2014. Gotingco's killer, Tony Douglas Robertson (27), was a high-risk sex offender who had just completed an 8-year prison sentence, was being electronically monitored on release conditions and was about to commence an ESO. In view of the fact that nothing in existing law could have saved Gotingco's life, in 2014 the PPO was created. The PPO allows the High Court to order that offenders subject to ESOs and who are at risk of serious and imminent sexual or violent offending may be detained indefinitely, even though their prison sentences are over. Offenders given PPOs must be kept in units separate from the mainstream, but on Department of Corrections premises, behind a wire. At time of writing in May 2017, the first PPOs had been allocated and units had been prepared at Christchurch Men's Prison for the detention of this new class of client (Newbold, 2016).

Conclusion

This chapter has briefly traversed the history of New Zealand corrections, starting with the disorganisation of the colonial era, the disciplinarianism of Captain Arthur Hume, and the procession of enlightened and optimistic reforms that came after 1910. New Zealand was an early starter in establishing a chain of low-security prison farms, in the abolition of corporal and capital punishment, and in developing effective non-custodial alternatives to prison such as probation and periodic detention. Although attempts to bring about positive changes in offenders continue both inside prisons and within the community, since about 1985 high levels of serious violent offending have caused average sentences to increase and prison populations to rise sharply. The resulting pressure on prisons has necessitated the curtailment of many work and training programmes, while the goal of rehabilitating prisoners has become partially displaced by the cheaper imperative of maintaining order, discipline and security.

REFERENCES

Dallard, B. L. S. 1980. *Fettered Freedom: A Symbiotic Society or Anarchy?* Wellington: Department of Justice.
Department of Justice. 1971. *Waipiata: A Study of Trainees in an Open Borstal*. Wellington: Department of Justice.
Hill, R. S. 1986. *Policing the Colonial Frontier: The Theory and Practice of Coercive Social and Racial Control in New Zealand 1767–1867*. Wellington: Government Printer.
Matthews, C. 1923. *The Evolution of the New Zealand Prison System*. Wellington: Government Printer.
Missen, E. 1971. 'The History of New Zealand Penal Policy', seminar given to the Changes in Attitudes to Punishment Conference, Victoria University of Wellington, 3–4 September.
Newbold, G. 1981. *Punishment and Politics: The Maximum Security Prison in New Zealand*. Auckland: Oxford University Press.
Newbold, G. 2007. *The Problem of Prisons: Corrections Reform in New Zealand since 1980*. Wellington: Dunmore.
Newbold, G. 2012. 'Three Strikes and You're Out in New Zealand', in E. Plywaczewski (Ed.), *Current Problems of the Criminal Law and Criminology/Aktuelle Probleme des Strafrechts und der Kriminologie*. Warsaw: Wolters Kluwer, pp. 487–98.
Newbold, G. 2016. *Crime, Law and Justice in New Zealand*. New York: Routledge.
Oleson, J. 2015. 'Habitual Criminal Legislation in New Zealand: Three Years of Three Strikes', *Australian and New Zealand Journal of Criminology* 48(2): 263–8.
Ringer, J. B. 1991. *An Introduction to New Zealand Government*. Christchurch: Hazard Press.
Spiller, P., Finn, J., and Boast, R. 1995. *A New Zealand Legal History*. Wellington: Brooker's.

Current Practice

This section examines some contemporary aspects of criminal justice in practice. First, Chris Gallavin looks at criminal court procedure and the application of the law of evidence in trials. Jeremy Finn then examines the various criminal courts operating in New Zealand and the functions they perform, and Debra Wilson investigates the rules of sentencing and the types of sentences available to the criminal courts.

6.

Evidence and Human Rights

CHRIS GALLAVIN

Introduction

Dealing with complex cases and the evidence upon which they are based is an everyday reality for law enforcement agencies around New Zealand but also for judges when they make decisions about the use of the evidence gathered and presented at trial. The two areas of law that primarily frame the law of evidence are contained in the provisions of the New Zealand Bill of Rights Act 1990 (NZBORA) and the Evidence Act 2006.

This chapter looks at the framework relating to the law of evidence in New Zealand and specific examples of the application of some of the rights under NZBORA. I will look at real cases in order to illustrate two points: first, that decisions around evidence are not merely concerned with procedural or technical fairness but also have a very real effect upon substantive justice; and second, that the application of criminal justice will often lead investigators, Crown prosecutors and ultimately the courts to consider deep and complex issues of public policy, the correct answers to which are not always straightforward or clear.

The Law of Evidence

The law of evidence regulates the admission or exclusion of evidence in court. It also sets the parameters within which evidence can be used by a judge or adjudicator in reaching conclusions of fact. Complex in its conceptual framework as well as its application, this area of law governs many of the rules under which the common law adversarial system operates. The law of evidence governs both criminal and civil jurisdictions and is therefore not solely focused on the operation of criminal law. The application of the law of evidence is, however, at its most stringent when applied in a criminal trial. Along with the provisions of criminal procedure and a number of common law principles laid down by judges, the law of evidence sets the parameters by which the adversarial system operates.

The Law of Evidence, Reason, and Facts

The law of evidence regulates our legal relationship with evidence or 'facts'. Facts are not law and conversely, the law of evidence is not evidence or facts. Similarly, the law of evidence is not reason and logic; it provides the framework within which reason and logic are to operate. When exploring the relationship between evidence and the law of evidence, Thayer (1898: 263) states that the law of evidence 'does not undertake to regulate the processes of reasoning or argument, except as helping to discriminate and select the material of fact upon which these are to operate; these processes themselves go on, after their own methods, even when all the "evidence" is in, or when there is none and all the facts are admitted'.

In the context of a criminal justice system, evidence can be defined as facts that make matters in issue more or less likely. Examples of such facts include materials found at a crime scene, such as DNA, and murder weapons or tools used to commit a crime. Facts also include oral testimony given by witnesses and expert evidence given by those suitably qualified to assist the court in reaching conclusions on facts that may otherwise not be clear. In order to more lucidly conceptualise the law of evidence, it is helpful to think of the roles of judge and jury. Although only a small minority of criminal cases are dealt with by a judge and jury (as opposed to a judge alone) the analogy remains helpful. Where a case is heard before a judge and a jury it is the role of the judge to determine the law. It is the role of the jury to determine the facts and draw conclusions from those facts. In dealing with the law a judge will make rulings on the admission of evidence and what, if any, limitations are to be placed on the use of that evidence. Therefore, in deciding on whether to allow facts to be put before a jury, a judge will be guided by the law of evidence. A jury is likely never to be aware of the operation of the law of evidence and how that may have informed the thinking of the lawyers or a judge in a case. The jury simply acts upon instructions from, or decisions made by, the judge.

In summary, what facts are put before a jury is decided by a judge – what to do with those facts is the role of a jury. The role of a judge under the law of evidence is therefore often referred to as determining *admissibility* – and whether discrete evidence is to be *admitted* or *excluded*. If evidence is excluded by a judge, a jury will never know of its existence. The relatively hidden nature of the law of evidence belies its fundamental importance to the operation of the adversarial system of criminal justice. Its importance is perhaps best illustrated by the fact that if an appeal is to be lodged it will almost always hinge upon a matter of evidence (e.g., an objection to the admission of particular evidence), or on the judge's direction on the substantive law (the guidance the judge gives the jury on what the law actually requires to be proved).

In establishing the principles by which evidence should be admitted in a case and, if admitted, how it is to be used, the law of evidence is broadly defined as representing two forms of rules or principles. The first of these are those rules relating to epistemic considerations and the second are those relating to non-epistemic considerations. Epistemic considerations are those rules and principles that relate to establishing truth. They include consideration of whether the evidence is *relevant* or *reliable*, whether it has *probative value*, and the *weight* it is to be given. Non-epistemic considerations are those public policy considerations that are not related to fact-finding. They include the principle of *privilege*, where evidence that may otherwise be reliable and probative is nonetheless excluded on the basis that another competing public policy takes precedence. Non-epistemic considerations also relate to matters of *fairness* or *legitimacy*. For example, in the case of privilege there is the principle of protecting confidences between a lawyer and a client (s54, Evidence Act 2006), a doctor and a patient (s59), or on occasion a journalist and an informant (s68). The law of evidence recognises that these principles may at times be more important than the purpose of finding the truth.

There is no definitive list of agreed objectives of the law of evidence, however if there was such a list it might look like this:

- All evidence relevant to a point in issue in a case should be admissible
- All evidence not relevant to a point in issue in a case should be excluded
- Conclusions drawn from facts should be logical and reasonable
- Illogical reasoning is to be avoided.

- Unfairly prejudicial evidence should be treated with caution, if not excluded.

Unfortunately, not all of these principles are made clear under the Evidence Act 2006. Rather, they are gleaned from the myriad of rules under the Act, the legislative framework that preceded the current legislation, and those principles established in case law here in New Zealand together with those from similar common law jurisdictions overseas.

The Evidence Act 2006

Despite the relatively hidden nature of the law of evidence to non-lawyers, the areas it covers contain terms that are likely familiar. Relevance, reliability, probative value, unfair prejudice and terms such as hearsay, privilege, propensity evidence and identification evidence are all evidential concepts that are common within popular culture as well as being important in criminal cases. However, the exclusion of evidence under any of these heads is often referred to in the media as *technical* or just the clever-speak of manipulating lawyers. Far from being mere *technicalities*, however, each of these terms relates to important and justifiable principles that are intended to fulfil the objectives of sound decision making as listed above. That said, many of the principles have, over time, become unwieldy and superfluous. Chief amongst those is the law of hearsay. A hearsay statement is defined as meaning that it:

(a) was made by a person other than a witness; and
(b) is offered in evidence at the proceeding to prove the truth of its contents.
   (s4, Evidence Act 2006)

For many years, evidence caught by the hearsay rule was excluded and therefore not put before a judge or jury. However, there grew a number of exceptions to the hearsay rule. So many exceptions developed that one New Zealand judge stated that the law of hearsay had become so impenetrable that to him it was clear 'the law is an ass' (see Turner J, in *Jorgensen v News Media (Auckland) Limited* [1969] NZLR 961, 990–1 [CA]). The review of the law in the Evidence Act 2006 has been described as 'the most significant overhaul of evidence law in New Zealand's history' (Cull, Fisher and Robertson, 2007: 5). With its enactment the new legislation completed a process of significant simplification. Whilst much work and development are still to occur in our system, the law of evidence is now more transparent and straightforward than it once was.

When discussing the Evidence Act 2006, a convenient starting point is s6, which sets out the purpose of the legislation. The provision states:

> The purpose of this Act is to help secure the just determination of proceedings by—
> (a) providing for facts to be established by the application of logical rules;
> (b) providing rules of evidence that recognise the importance of the rights affirmed by the New Zealand Bill of Rights Act 1990;
> (c) promoting fairness to parties and witnesses;
> (d) protecting rights of confidentiality and other important public interests;
> (e) avoiding unjustifiable expense and delay;
> (f) enhancing access to the law of evidence.

The foundation of all rules of evidence is the principle of relevance. Under the Evidence Act this principle can be found in s7. With limited exceptions, s7 provides that all relevant evidence is admissible. The provision goes on to define relevance as anything that 'has a tendency to prove or disprove anything that is of consequence to the determination of the proceeding' (s7[3]). In positively stating this rule, the provision removes all doubt as to its meaning by stating the opposite: 'Evidence that is not relevant is not admissible in a proceeding' (s7[2]).

The yin to the yang of s7 can be found in s8. Under this section the probative value of evidence is set against any possible illegitimate prejudice. There are two particular aspects to this provision. First, the value of the evidence to the case is to be weighed against the unfair prejudice it may have upon the proceeding. At times this is a difficult test to apply, as one could be mistaken for believing the test does not to compare 'apples with apples', as the saying goes. As outlined above, if evidence is relevant and is of value to an issue in the hearing, it is in the interests of truth that the evidence be admitted. Unfair prejudice on the other hand calls in principles that do not relate to establishing the truth in a particular case. The first part of s8 therefore requires a judge to quantify the value of the evidence to the case and correspond that to the value he or she places on any unfairness in admitting that evidence (if any).

The second element of s8 pits the probative value of particular evidence against the general principle of efficiency in managing the case (s8[1][b]). As with evidence that fails the test of probative value versus unfair prejudice, probative evidence that is so minor that it is not worth the time of admitting it is excluded. This latter part of s8 is important as it establishes a check on s7 – much evidence that might pass the test of basic or mere relevance under s7 may nonetheless be of only marginal value and, if admitted, might unreasonably elongate and complicate a trial.

In navigating one's way around the question of admissibility the first point of call will always be s7. The final point of call will be s8. In between these two polarities lies a myriad of rules and exceptions that may trip evidence in its path to admission. Such areas include hearsay evidence (s18), the rule against the admission of opinion evidence (s23), expert evidence (s25), improperly obtained evidence (s30), veracity and propensity evidence (ss37 and 40), identification evidence (s45) and privilege (ss53–70), including the privilege against self-incrimination and evidence coming from relationships based upon trust and confidence. In this chapter I will discuss only a select group of these. The first aspect I will consider is the base principle of relevance under s7. The second is improperly obtained evidence under s30, and the third and final aspect is propensity evidence under s40. The cases I will use to illustrate the difficulties presented under each heading will be the second (2009) trial of David Bain for the murder of his family, the Urewera 11 case of 2007–12 and the trial of Ewen Macdonald for the murder of Scott Guy in Feilding in July 2010.

The New Zealand Bill of Rights Act 1990

Initially intended to be 'higher' law, NZBORA was ultimately enacted as ordinary legislation (for general discussion see Joseph, 2014). As such it is not higher or supreme law as is the case with the US Bill of Rights under the US Constitution. Under the constitutional structure of the United States, the Bill of Rights can only be amended by a super majority of the Congress and Senate (see Article V). As higher law, the Constitution empowers the US Supreme Court to cast down legislation it believes is inconsistent with the provisions of the Constitution, including those rights under the Bill of Rights. There is no such equivalent under New Zealand law. Although first proposed to be higher or supreme law, such a move proved too radical for New Zealand at the time. In enacting NZBORA as mere ordinary legislation, many commentators declared the Act an effective nullity, predicting that it would be ignored and trampled upon because it lacked the protection of double entrenchment. In reality, the practice has been quite different. Despite sometimes having to apply legislation that is inconsistent with the rights contained under NZBORA, judges have nonetheless given the legislation great weight and do not lightly conclude other legislation to be in conflict with it. What that has meant is that superficially conflicting legislation is likely to be 'read down' (subordinated) so as to avoid conflict with NZBORA (see s6, NZBORA). However, the fact remains that NZBORA, being ordinary legislation, is open to amendment by a simple majority in Parliament. Further, if it is not possible for a court to read down other legislation to ensure consistency with NZBORA, then the other legislation is to stand and NZBORA must give way (see s4, NZBORA; see also *Hansen v R* [2007] NZSC 7; [2007] 3 NZLR 1).

Far from a complete exposé of NZBORA, I will here outline those provisions within it that are most applicable to the criminal justice system. Sections 21–27 of NZBORA fall under the heading 'Search, Arrest and Detention'. Of all the rights within the Act it is this group of seven sections that are the most applied in the context of the criminal justice system. They are not merely relevant to the courts when a case is tried, but provide guidance to the applicable prosecution agency when pursuing an investigation. Errors made at the *investigation* stage, including breach of the rights of an individual, may present significant difficulties at the *prosecution* stage of a case. The seven provisions identified here are: the right to be free from unreasonable search and seizure (s21), the right to liberty (s22), the rights of persons arrested or detained (s23), the rights of a person charged (s24), minimum standards of criminal procedure (s25), the right to be free from the retroactive application of penalties and double jeopardy (s26), and the right to justice (s27). Sections 23–25 contain multiple rights within which one of the most significant is the right to be presumed innocent until proven guilty (s25[c]). This right exists in conjunction with a number of other rights, which include the right to remain silent (s23[4]) and the right not to be compelled to be a witness against oneself or to confess guilt (s25[d]). The presumption of innocence also relates to the privilege against self-incrimination found in the Evidence Act 2006 (s60) (for general criticism of the right to remain silent see Thomas, 1991).

The Burden of Proof

A key component of the presumption of innocence is the burden of proof. Although not a right *per se* and not found either in NZBORA or the Evidence Act, the burden of proof is a vital component of the adversarial system in criminal trials. It is the Crown which bears the burden of proving a case and it is not for a defendant to legally prove their innocence: *Ei incumbit probation qui dicit, non qui negat* ('It is for him who asserts to prove, not him who denies') (see *Woolmington v DPP* [1935] AC 462, [1935] All ER Rep 1 [HL]). Whilst there are exceptions to that rule, the principle is so strong that even when a person charged relies on a defence (e.g., self-defence) it is for the Crown to *disprove* the existence of that defence rather than the defence to legally *prove* the defence (for discussion of the exceptions see Gallavin, 2008: chap. 3). This is why, in a criminal trial, the defence cannot be compelled to call evidence and in a great many cases it may elect not to call any witnesses at all.

This reflects the fact that it is for the Crown to prove its case, and in some situations at the conclusion of the Crown's case the defence may change its mind from a previous intention to call evidence. The submission that would likely follow in such an event is that since the Crown has failed to prove the charge there is no need for the defence to call any evidence. In these cases it can be said that the defence has *put the prosecution to proof*. If a defence team does elect to call evidence it is nonetheless rare for a defendant to give evidence in his/her own defence. The pitfalls of having clients give evidence are too great in most cases to take the risk of them looking bad before a jury. In theory, a trial ought not to be an examination of a defendant's character although character evidence will often be admissible. Even the most unlikeable person has the right to a defence (see s25[e], NZBORA). Likewise, a criminal trial ought not to be about the personality of a victim. Nonetheless, and irrespective of how clear the law may be on this matter, counsel realise that the temptation to draw conclusions as to the likeability of a defendant or a victim may be at times difficult for a jury to avoid.

A further practical danger of having a defendant give evidence is the risk that it will be perceived by a jury as an act in which the defendant takes on the burden of establishing his/her innocence. In law the burden weighs so heavily upon the prosecution that even if no defence witnesses are believed, it does not mean that the prosecution case is proved by default. In reality, however, the jury may not fully appreciate this. This is another reason why calling a defendant to the witness stand is generally avoided.

A notable exception to this rule was Clayton Weatherston, who in the outcome, did himself few favours in giving evidence himself. In his 2009 trial for the murder of his former student and girlfriend Sophie Elliott, Weatherston elected to give evidence in his own defence. Recorded extracts of his evidence in chief and cross-examination were broadcast on television during the trial and are now available on the Internet. They make for uncomfortable watching, as his demeanour is quite frankly repulsive in the context of his acknowledged killing and mutilation of Ms Elliott. However, the defence he relied upon to the charge of murder was provocation, which at the time, if established, would have reduced his culpability from murder to manslaughter (the defence of provocation was removed from the Crimes Act 1961 in 2009). This defence was peculiar in its application to the particular facts of this case in that Weatherston's lawyers argued that the provocation he experienced had an acute effect upon him because he suffered from narcissism. Whilst we do not know the exact reason he elected to give evidence himself, we can speculate that somewhat perversely, it seemed necessary for him to give evidence in order to show the jury that he actually was a narcissist. Indeed, the way he behaved in the dock did lend weight to the narcissist argument.

If this was his motivation for giving evidence the dilemma for the defence was that in establishing himself as a narcissist Weatherston would likely present himself as a thoroughly detestable individual, and thus turn the jury against him. In other words, in presenting the defence of provocation on the basis of his narcissism he could inadvertently ruin any hope of it succeeding in practice. His giving evidence would likely have been a very difficult and hard-thought decision for the defence. Regardless of any submission by defence counsel and reiteration by the judge for the jury to put personal feelings about the defendant aside, it was perhaps of little surprise that Weatherston failed to establish the defence and he was subsequently convicted of murder. Be that as it may, his decision to give evidence was entirely his own choice. Although he probably needed to give evidence in terms of *tactics*, he was not *legally* compelled to do so.

The Standard of Proof

The standard to which the Crown must prove their case presents us with the well-known term *beyond reasonable doubt*. Whilst in the civil jurisdiction the standard of proof is 'on the balance of probabilities', the perhaps more recognisable criminal standard requires proof to a higher degree. The standard does not mean proof beyond *all* doubt. It does not represent absolute certainty. Despite eloquent and at times verbose directions from judges on the meaning of 'beyond reasonable doubt', it is a very simple, common-sense direction that is most often used in law courts today. Of the numerous attempts at a direction, Wigmore (1940, para. 2497) states: 'The attempt to define these qualities of persuasion has great difficulties;

and many useless refinements and wordy quibbles have marked the countless and more or less unsuccessful attempts.' Although lengthy and not mandatory, a useful direction was outlined by the New Zealand Court of Appeal in *R v Wanhalla*. For completeness I replicate it here in full. The direction put the task of the jury in this way (see *R v Wanhalla* [2007] 2 NZLR 573, (2006) 22 CRNZ 843, para. [49]):

> The starting point is the presumption of innocence. You must treat the accused as innocent until the Crown has proved his or her guilt. The presumption of innocence means that the accused does not have to give or call any evidence and does not have to establish his or her innocence.
>
> The Crown must prove that the accused is guilty beyond reasonable doubt. Proof beyond reasonable doubt is a very high standard of proof which the Crown will have met only if, at the end of the case, you are sure that the accused is guilty.
>
> It is not enough for the Crown to persuade you that the accused is probably guilty or even that he or she is very likely guilty. On the other hand, it is virtually impossible to prove anything to an absolute certainty when dealing with the reconstruction of past events and the Crown does not have to do so.
>
> What then is reasonable doubt? A reasonable doubt is an honest and reasonable uncertainty left in your mind about the guilt of the accused after you have given careful and impartial consideration to all of the evidence.
>
> In summary, if, after careful and impartial consideration of the evidence, you are sure that the accused is guilty you must find him or her guilty. On the other hand, if you are not sure that the accused is guilty, you must find him or her not guilty.

The remaining procedural rights that accrue for the benefit of a person detained, arrested or charged are likely familiar to anybody who has watched a crime show on television. The right to consult and instruct a lawyer (s23[1][b] and s24[c]) sits alongside the right to be charged promptly or released (s23[2]), to have adequate time and facilities to prepare a defence (s24[d]), and the right to be treated humanely and with dignity (s23[5]).

The Right to Be Free from Unreasonable Search and Seizure

Turning now from the presumption of innocence and its associated rights and procedures, a further right that has been the focus of much argument in the context of evidence admissibility is s21 under NZBORA. The right to be free from unreasonable search and seizure often frames actions of enforcement agencies, predominantly the police, in a difficult and challenging light. To a great extent our enforcement agencies fight with one hand tied behind their backs, with a citizen's right to be free from unreasonable search and seizure being one example of a significant limitation on investigative agencies. An example of where friction frequently arises in the context of this right is the case of search warrants – or the lack of – in which the property of a suspect is forcibly searched, often resulting in the seizure of items that may later be used in evidence. If such searches are declared unlawful then the admission of the evidence gained from these searches is put in jeopardy. It may be that the evidence seized is unequivocal in its implication of guilt; however, the way it was discovered may result in its exclusion in court, often leaving the Crown with no case. Under this provision much discussion has occurred over where a reasonable expectation of privacy does or does not exist. Furthermore, the discovery of material incidental to the search (e.g., where stolen property is found during a search for drugs) has also posed difficult questions over the lawfulness of some searches and, again, the admissibility of the material in court. In dealing with this provision it is useful to examine its application within the context of a case.

Case Studies

Having given a brief overview of the law of evidence and a selection of important rights under NZBORA, I will now discuss the application of the provisions of both NZBORA and the Evidence Act in relation to three high-profile cases.

The David Bain Emergency 111 Call

In May 1995 David Bain was convicted and sentenced to life imprisonment for the murder of five members of his family in June 1994 – his father Robin, his mother Margaret, sisters Arawa and Laniet and his brother Stephen. He claimed he was innocent and that he found all five dead upon returning home from his early morning paper round. The defence proceeded on the basis that the deaths were the result of a murder-suicide by Robin Bain – a third-party intruder theory appears never to have been pursued, likely due to a lack of supporting evidence. With the success of the Crown case in 1995 David was convicted of all five murders and sentenced to life in prison. He served approximately 13 years before his conviction was quashed by the Privy Council and a new trial was ordered (see *Bain v R* (New Zealand) [2007] UKPC 33). At his second trial, Bain was acquitted, meaning he walked from the courthouse a free man.

Part of the evidence called by the Crown at both trials was the recorded 111 telephone call of David Bain ringing for the assistance of emergency services. The recording makes for difficult listening. He sounds distraught. He breathes heavily throughout the call. The operator is calm and measured and steps him through the questions he needs answered in order to deal with the emergency at hand. There are pauses. There are questions that seem basic if not irrelevant – Bain seems remote and detached; he clearly wants help and fast. The transcript of the call reads as follows:

AO [Ambulance Officer]   Ambulance, can I help you?
C [Caller]   Help.
AO   Yeah.
C   They're all dead.
AO   What's the matter?
C   They're all dead. I came home and they're all dead.
AO   Whereabouts are you?
C   Erm– erm Every Street.
AO   W-w– Every Street?
C   Sixty-five Every Street. They're all dead.
AO   Who's all dead?
C   My f– my family. They're all dead. Hurry up.
AO   It's okay. Every Street and it runs off s– off Summerville Street?
C   (Yeah.) Yes.
>>> [POSITION OF QUESTIONED UTTERANCE]
AO   And what phone number you're calling from?
C   Four-four five four.
AO   Mm-hm.
C   Two five two seven. [Whispered on out-breath]
AO   Four five four?
C   Two five two seven.
AO   Two five two seven. And your last name?
C   (Ig-er) Bain.
AO   Bain. Okay. We're on our way. Okay Mister Bain.

C   Please hurry up.

AO Yeah, we'll be there very shortly. (*Bain v R* [2009] NZSC 16 at [10])

At the first trial the transcript of the call raised no particular alarm, save for its harrowing nature and the eeriness that inevitably accompanies such an extreme real-world event. However, in preparation for the second trial the Crown made a discovery within the recording that if true would have been a powerful element in their case. In slowing down the recording the Crown alleged that at one point the words 'I shot the prick' or 'I shot that prick' could be made out. If correct, then this was a confession to one of the killings for which Bain was charged. The Crown moved to adduce the evidence but it was challenged by the defence. The question of whether this evidence was admissible proceeded through the Courts and ultimately came before the Supreme Court for consideration in March 2009 (see *Bain v R* [2009] NZSC 16).

At that hearing, argument was heard from both sides on whether the evidence ought to be admitted. The defence challenged admissibility on two main grounds. The first was that the confession to one murder did not accord with the Crown theory that David had killed all five members of his family. This was clearly a difficult argument to run. It was not likely to result in exclusion merely because the confession did not suggest guilt for the killing of all five. What it did do was highlight the important part played by a Crown theory in a case. As stated above, investigations are voyages of discovery that hopefully lead to the correct identification of a suspect. A trial is not. The presentation of the Crown case at trial is far from a voyage of discovery; it is the result of detailed work in which lawyers for the Crown piece together the evidence gathered into a narrative that links the evidence and explains what happened before, during and after the event in question. In some cases the Crown theory might change from one trial to the next (see, e.g., the trials of Mark Lundy for the murder of his wife and daughter in which the Crown theory changed significantly between the first and second trials). In the Bain case, the Crown theory was that David Bain had killed all five of his family. Therefore, the defence argued that the confession evidence was not relevant as it did not match the theory advanced by the Crown. Unfortunately for the defence, an admission of killing one person did not exclude the possibility of David killing all five, so the admission evidence was accepted as relevant on this point.

However, the defence's second argument was more compelling. The recording had been forensically analysed by linguistic experts for both the Crown and the defence. Their conclusions were remarkably similar. Chief Justice Elias and Blanchard J summarised the opinion of the experts in this way:

> None of the experts is able to say that the sounds relied upon in the recording are words, rather than meaningless exhalation of breath. If they are words, none of the experts is able to say that they amount to the words the Crown wishes to rely upon as evidence. Some consider such words can be heard in the recording, with effort. But all experts caution as to the dangers of hearing something that may not in fact be there, because of accident in arrangements of sounds. The principal Crown expert uses the analogy of an image glimpsed in a cloud formation to illustrate the dangers. (*Bain v R* [2009] NZSC 16 at [5])

Importantly, the Supreme Court noted the view of the experts that 'it is not possible for experts or lay people to resolve the question whether the sounds are speech by listening to the recording'. This conclusion was vital to the court's decision that the recording was not admissible. Only with the aid of being primed was it likely that a jury would hear the sounds alleged and then, with no rational basis upon which to conclude whether the sounds were even speech, the jury would be left with guessing whether they were in fact the words alleged. With no rational basis for a jury to conclude this point, the Supreme Court ruled the evidence inadmissible due to irrelevancy since it did not meet the basic minimum threshold of reliability needed to satisfy the test of relevance under s7 of the Evidence Act 2006. The reasoning was that if it was not speech then it was not relevant, and there was no rational basis for the jury to decide whether it was speech or not.

But the issue is not clear-cut. If, for example, of all the experts consulted there had been just one who concluded that the sounds were words, and that the words were those alleged, the decision may well have been different. This is because the existence of at least one dissenting expert, if believed by the jury, would have provided the rational basis otherwise lacking. But even without such an expert, the decision was contentious. Prior to the Supreme Court ruling, both the High Court and the Court of Appeal had ruled that the evidence *was* admissible, saying that the jury should hear the evidence un-primed and make their own mind up as to what words, if any, were heard. However, given that deciding whether the sounds amounted to words would certainly have been guesswork on the part of the jury, in my view it was right for the Supreme Court to exclude the evidence either under s7 (relevance) or s8 (unfair prejudice). This case clearly illustrates that first, decisions are not always universal, particularly when dealing with powerful evidence, and second, that although it may seem a mere technicality, the reasoning of the Court was rational, clear and robust, and anything but a technicality.

The Urewera 11 that Became the Urewera 4

From the time that it broke in 2007, the Urewera case received significant media attention as one in which domestic terrorism had been thwarted by the strident intervention of the police. The raids resulted from evidence gathered by the police suggesting that paramilitary training camps had been operating between 2006 and 2007 in the bush on Tuhoe-owned land in the Urewera Ranges. Initially involving eleven defendants, the case became known as the Urewera 4 after the Supreme Court excluded evidence against seven of them on the basis that the evidence had been gathered in breach of the right to be free from unreasonable search and seizure (s21, NZBORA). All of the initial eleven defendants had been charged with offences under the Arms Act 1983, and some with participating in an organised criminal group under s98A of the Crimes Act 1961.

As part of a series of search warrants authorising them to enter Tuhoe land, police had sought to install motion-activated cameras in areas where their intelligence suggested further camps were to be established. Roadside cameras were also stationed to capture evidence of traffic movements to and from the areas. Unfortunately, the warrants obtained by the police did not specifically authorise the installing of motion-activated cameras, even though the applications for those warrants appeared to refer to them. These were the warrants that the police used to enter the land and position the cameras and later to retrieve them.

The warrants were applied for pursuant to s198 of the Summary Proceedings Act 1957 (SPA). The first question for the Supreme Court was whether the warrants authorised the use of motion-activated cameras to capture evidence that at the time did not exist. In other words, the question was whether the police had authority to act in *anticipation* of evidence coming into existence rather than authority to enter private land and uplift evidence *already* in existence (see Gallavin and Wall, 2012). On this question the Supreme Court concluded that there existed no authority under New Zealand law for the granting of anticipatory warrants, since s198 did not allow for such action. As a consequence, the court concluded that the activity of the police was not lawful. Although the police actions may have been necessary and justified, the fact remained that no authority for anticipatory warrants existed at the time the warrants were granted (see *Hamed & Ors v R* [2011] NZSC 101).

The defence challenge to the admission of the evidence was based upon s30 of the Evidence Act 2006. The marginal note to s30 reads 'Improperly obtained evidence' and guides a judge through the process of first, determining whether evidence has, in fact, been improperly obtained, and second, whether exclusion of that evidence is the correct and proportional response to the impropriety (these two limbs of the section are outlined at s30[2][a] and [b]) (see Gallavin and Wall, 2012).

Improperly obtained evidence is defined under s30(5) of the Act. It provides that impropriety may arise under three circumstances. The first relates to any breach of NZBORA (s30[5][a]). The second relates to evidence obtained as a result of a statement made by a defendant that would be inadmissible if offered in evidence by the prosecution (s30[5][b]). The third relates to evidence obtained unfairly (s30[5][c]). If impropriety is established by a judge then he or she must decide whether exclusion of the evidence is a proportional response. Here weight must be given to the breach or unfairness but with a view to the importance of maintaining an 'effective and credible system of justice' (s30[2][b]). In considering this balance the Evidence Act gives guidance as to what a judge *may* have regard to, including:

(a) the importance of any right breached by the impropriety and the seriousness of the intrusion on it;
(b) the nature of the impropriety, in particular, whether it was deliberate, reckless, or done in bad faith;
(c) the nature and quality of the improperly obtained evidence;
(d) the seriousness of the offence with which the defendant is charged;
(e) whether there were any other investigatory techniques not involving any breach of the rights that were known to be available but were not used;
(f) whether there are alternative remedies to exclusion of the evidence that can adequately provide redress to the defendant;
(g) whether the impropriety was necessary to avoid apprehended physical danger to the Police or others; and
(h) whether there was any urgency in obtaining the improperly obtained evidence. (s30[3])

In the Urewera case the Supreme Court determined that impropriety had occurred. This was not simply because anticipation warrants were not authorised under s198 of SPA but because of a corresponding breach of the right to privacy under s21. How the court reached this conclusion is muddled between the judges' different lines of reasoning. Although brief, s21 of NZBORA is powerful in its influence. The section protects a fundamental right enjoyed by peoples of free countries and is not interfered with lightly by Parliament, nor easily sidestepped by the courts. The right provides that

> Everyone has the right to be secure against unreasonable search or seizure, whether of the person, property, or correspondence or otherwise.

The court in this case agreed that the test of what was unreasonable under s21 involved three aspects. The first centred upon the nature of the place being searched, the second involved the level of intrusiveness into the privacy of the persons being searched, and third the purpose of the search itself.

The primary judgment of the court was delivered by Justice Blanchard. He opined that s21 required the asking of two questions: first, whether a search had in fact occurred, and second, whether that search was reasonable. For him, whether a reasonable expectation of privacy existed was an issue that was relevant to both questions (see para. 167). Therefore whether covert filming was a 'search' depended on where that filming had occurred. If it occurred on private land it would be a search but if it took place in a public place then it would likely not be a search for the purposes of s21. Thus, the judge concluded that the covert filming on Tuhoe land was a search but the filming of the public access road into the land was not (see para. 171). Justice Tipping, on the other hand, applied different reasoning. For him the issue of whether there existed a reasonable expectation of privacy was not relevant to the question of whether there was a search for the purposes of s21. But he did think the existence of an expectation of privacy was relevant to the second question – whether the search was reasonable. On the question of whether there was a search Justice Tipping preferred to apply a plain interpretation of the word 'search' (see paras 221 and 222). Applying this, he concluded that there was a search for the purposes of s21. He then concluded that the filming of the camps was unreasonable given the expectation of privacy. The filming of the road on the other hand was not, given its public nature. Importantly, just because the search had no legislative authority and was unlawful this did not mean that it was automatically 'unreasonable' (see 226).

Having clumsily established that there was impropriety, the court moved to the second limb of the test under s30 – the balancing test (see Gallavin and Wall, 2012). I will not here go through each judgment outlining their approach to s30(3); suffice to say that they were equally if not more clumsy than the disparate approaches to the first limb of the test. In short, the balancing test is one that weighs the importance of justice being done against the need to maintain integrity of the system. If impropriety in the obtaining of evidence were allowed to become commonplace then the central elements of the system would be undermined. For example, permitting breaches of rights by prosecution agencies would allow police to use any means necessary to get evidence against people they thought were guilty. This may seem fair enough if the assumption of guilt is correct but the police are not always right, and evidence obtained following a faulty assumption could destroy an innocent life. We have seen clear examples in the wrongful convictions of Arthur Allan Thomas for double murder in 1971 and of Teina Pora for rape and murder in 1994. The rules governing the admissibility of evidence are there to minimise the occurrence of judicial miscarriages of this type.

The Murder of Scott Guy

Scott Guy was murdered at the end of his rural driveway in the Manawatu in July 2010. He was shot in the throat and face with a shotgun. False leads sent police around the country looking for possible witnesses. None were found. Scott Guy's past and his associates were investigated and every part of his life unpacked in order to find anyone who might have had a grudge against him. The investigation soon focused on his brother-in-law, Ewen Macdonald. Other offending by Macdonald suggested an orchestrated plan to scare Guy and his wife Kylie away from the farm, so that Macdonald could manage it and take over. This offending suggested that Macdonald was a man of particular callousness. It was discovered that he had killed nineteen calves owned by a neighbour following a dispute. He had killed these calves with a ball-peen hammer by inflicting a blow to the head of each calf. This evidence was not put before the jury although the reason is unclear since the trial transcript is not on public record. I use this as an example of what the prosecution may have wanted to call in evidence but would likely have been ruled inadmissible by the court due to questions over its 'propensity' relevance.

Under the Evidence Act 2006 there are circumstances in which the past conduct of an accused can be called in evidence by the prosecution to support the existence of a particular trait or disposition. This can result in previous convictions or even acquittals being adduced in support of those traits. This form of evidence is called propensity evidence and is dealt with under s40 of the Act. Section 40 provides a definition of propensity as meaning:

> ... evidence that tends to show a person's propensity to act in a particular way or to have a particular state of mind, being evidence of acts, omissions, events, or circumstances with which a person is alleged to have been involved;

Significant restrictions exist on the ability of the prosecution in a criminal case to positively advance evidence of bad character in the case of a defendant (see ss41 and 43).

Focusing on s43 in particular, the law allows for admission of such evidence against a defendant only where the probative value outweighs the illegitimate prejudice (s43[1]); in this respect it is similar in practice to s8 discussed above. Guidance is given to a judge in the application of this test under s43(3) and (4). These provisions provide:

(3) When assessing the probative value of propensity evidence, the Judge may consider, among other matters, the following:
(a) the frequency with which the acts, omissions, events, or circumstances that are the subject of the evidence have occurred;
(b) the connection in time between the acts, omissions, events, or circumstances that are the subject of the evidence and the acts, omissions, events, or circumstances which constitute the offence for which the defendant is being tried;
(c) the extent of the similarity between the acts, omissions, events, or circumstances that are the subject of the evidence and the acts, omissions, events, or circumstances which constitute the offence for which the defendant is being tried;
(d) the number of persons making allegations against the defendant that are the same as, or are similar to, the subject of the offence for which the defendant is being tried;
(e) whether the allegations described in paragraph (d) may be the result of collusion or suggestibility;

(f) the extent to which the acts, omissions, events, or circumstances that are the subject of the evidence and the acts, omissions, events, or circumstances which constitute the offence for which the defendant is being tried are unusual.

(4) When assessing the prejudicial effect of evidence on the defendant, the Judge must consider, among any other matters:
(a) whether the evidence is likely to unfairly predispose the fact-finder against the defendant; and
(b) whether the fact-finder will tend to give disproportionate weight in reaching a verdict to evidence of other acts or omissions.

Applying these provisions to the evidence of the killing of the nineteen calves, the reasoning of the judge, if argued in the case of Macdonald, may have developed along the following path: remember that the judge first needs to determine that the evidence is relevant and then that it has probative value (i.e., they need to quantify the value of the evidence to the case). The prosecution may have contended that the evidence was relevant because it supported Macdonald as having some or all of the following character traits:

- Capable of committing crime
- A very nasty piece of work
- Can bludgeon animals and can therefore kill a human
- Cross him and he will go to extraordinary lengths to exact revenge
- A good hunter (see Gallavin and Arnold, 2014).

The prosecution would have needed to be clear, as once they had established relevance the precise reason for admitting the evidence would have become important to the question of its probative value. For any of the above propositions the value of the evidence will be different. The higher the value the more chance it will be admitted. Next the judge would have had to quantify the illegitimate or unfair prejudice that may accrue. It is best to illustrate this by way of example.

Let us choose one from the list above – that the evidence was relevant because it showed Macdonald to be vindictive and callous. The killing of the calves supported this because he killed the calves for no good reason and merely out of spite after a dispute with his neighbour. It is relevant to a point in issue in the case because shooting one's brother-in-law at point blank range with a shotgun over a dispute regarding farm succession illustrates a particular level of callousness. Succession planning disputes occur all the time in New Zealand without resulting in the shooting of a family member, so without character evidence shedding light on what type of man Macdonald was a jury may be less inclined to believe the Crown case. In light of this the calf episode would have been of some probative value. However, it would come with considerable collateral damage (unfair prejudice). The value of the evidence of killing the calves, and the way in which that occurred, would have likely brought disgust in the eyes of the jury and led it to give that evidence too much weight – beyond its true probative value if looked at dispassionately. Thus giving the evidence more weight than it was worth is an example of unfair prejudice. This would have then been weighed against its probative value. In conclusion, if considered by the judge in this way and, on applying s43, a ruling of inadmissability may have been a fair decision.

Likely because of this, the evidence of calf-killing and other deviant activities that Macdonald had engaged in, which could have strengthened the Crown case, was not presented to the jury. Had the jury heard the calf-killing evidence it may well have returned a different verdict. However the principles of fairness and reasonableness applied in this instance as much as they do in any other, and thus on the evidence presented to it the jury concluded that the Crown had not proven its case beyond a reasonable doubt.

Conclusion

In this chapter I have looked at the interplay between the law of evidence and human rights. I have distinguished the law of evidence from evidence itself and emphasised the role of logic and reason in the question of admission of evidence. The exclusion of evidence, although often not accepted by the public and often referred to as a technicality by the media, is far from technical. Although much work in the development of the rules of evidence is still to be done, the rules cannot be criticised for lack of foundation in logic or reason. They have developed over centuries and represent a fine and difficult balance between considerations of truth and resolution of individual cases, and the maintenance of the integrity of our system of justice. Criticism, whilst easy to make, must therefore engage with the foundation of the rules and recognise the fact that no human system is fool-proof.

REFERENCES

Arnold, T., and Gallavin, C. 2014. 'Evidence Act Update', *Criminal Law Symposium* [Wellington] (November): 1–32.
Cull, H., Fisher, R., and Robertson, S. 2007. 'Overview', in W. Young and J. Chambers JJ (Eds), *Evidence Act 2006*. Wellington: New Zealand Law Society, pp. 3–16.
Gallavin, C. 2008. *Evidence*. Wellington: LexisNexis.
Gallavin, C., and Wall, J. 2012. 'Hamed: Anticipatory Warrants'. *New Zealand Law Journal* (March): 40–41.
Gallavin, C., and Wall, J. 2012. 'Hamed: s21 BORA'. *New Zealand Law Journal* (April): 85–86.
Gallavin, C., and Wall, J. 2012. 'Hamed: Section 30'. *New Zealand Law Journal* (May): 116–17.
Hunter, K. 2007. *Trial by Trickery*. Auckland: Keith Hunter Productions.
Joseph, P. 2014. *Constitutional and Administrative Law in New Zealand* (4th ed.). Wellington: Thompson Reuters.
New Zealand Law Commission. 2016. *Understanding Family Violence: Reforming the Criminal Law Relating to Homicide*, Report 139, 12 May. Wellington: New Zealand Law Commission.
Thayer, J. 1898. *A Preliminary Treatise on Evidence at the Common Law*. Boston: Little, Brown.
Thomas, E. 1991. 'The So-Called Right to Silence', *New Zealand Universities Law Review* 14: 299–322.

7.

Where Cases Are Tried, and How

JEREMY FINN

Introduction

New Zealand law has created a very large number of criminal offences, scattered across hundreds of statutes and statutory regulations. Determining which court will deal with any particular offence requires a systematic application of a number of rules which appear in the Criminal Procedure Act 2011 (CPA) and in other statutes. Fortunately the process is in most cases relatively straightforward, provided all the rules are considered. Occasionally matters are more complex because, as will be discussed later in the chapter, in some areas the courts have been given discretion to send cases down a particular pathway, or not to do so, on the basis of the particular factual and legal issues involved. Even so it is possible to chart the different pathways available and mark off the decision points and processes.

Deciding which court will hear a case will usually also settle the mode of trial. In New Zealand we have two modes of trial. One is judge-alone trial, where the case is heard by a judge who decides all issues of both fact and law. The other is jury trial where a judge decides all legal issues and a jury decides on the facts. As we will see, for a significant number of offences, including many very serious offences, the choice of the mode of trial is made by the defendant, rather than by a judge or court official.

An Overview of the Process and the Rules to Be Applied

The process of setting cases down for trial is described here in broad terms, with a more detailed discussion and analysis of the various points given later. The key points are that deciding where a case will be tried, and by whom, involves first looking at the nature of the offence, the alleged role of the defendant in the offending and the maximum possible punishment provided for it by statute, then that statutory description and penalty must be matched with one of the four categories of offences described in s6 CPA. Under ss71–74 CPA the selection of the appropriate category will, for three of the four categories, provide a working assumption both as to where the case will be tried and the means of trial, as later sections of the CPA match modes of trial to the various categories. The odd one out here is category 3, as with these offences further processes are needed to determine both the court of trial and the method of trial.

The working assumption provided by selecting the appropriate category of offence must then be checked against several rules of general application which may affect or override the usual rules in some particular cases. These will be referred to as 'potentially overriding rules'. The most significant of these are the rules affecting defendants who are facing a range of charges spread across different categories and the rules where several persons are charged with involvement in a particular episode of offending (discussed below). It is also essential to consider the age of the particular defendant, because the rules affecting persons aged 17 or over at the time of trial are generally different from those affecting persons under 17. Once again, more care is needed where a young defendant (under 17) is facing a range of charges and/or is alleged to have been acting with others who are older. The rules relating to trials of young defendants are also discussed below.

Finally, it is necessary to consider the possible options for the prosecution or the defence if they want to have any decisions about the place and mode of trial reconsidered. These include possible changes to the place of trial. Lastly, but only relevant in the cases where the normal rules would mean there will be a jury trial, it is necessary to consider the possibility that a defendant who wishes to have a jury trial may be deprived of it through the application of special statutory provisions in ss102 and 103 CPA.

Section 6 of the Criminal Procedure Act 2011

The four categories of offences are set out in s6(1) CPA. The detailed definitions are set out and discussed more fully below. A rather over-simplified overview is that:

- Category 1 offences are punishable by a fine or other penalties but not by a community-based sentence or a term of imprisonment.
- Category 2 offences are those where the maximum penalty is a community-based sentence or a term of imprisonment of less than 2 years.
- Category 3 offences are punishable by 2 years' or more imprisonment but the category does not include the offences listed in Schedule 1 to the CPA.
- Category 4 offences are those listed in Schedule 1. All of them are punishable by substantial terms of imprisonment.

Conspiracies, Attempts, and Parties to Offences

The division of offences into the four above categories in s6(1) CPA must be read in conjunction with the further provisions of subsections (2) and (3) which state:

> (2) If an offence is in a given category, then the following is also an offence in that category:
> (a) conspiring to commit that offence;
> (b) attempting to commit that offence, or inciting or procuring or attempting to procure any person to commit an offence of that kind that is not committed;
> (c) being an accessory after the fact to that offence.

To understand s6(2) we must briefly look at some basic rules about criminal liability for involvement in an offence. Under s66(1) of the Crimes Act 1961, an offence is committed by any person who actually commits the offence – the principal offender – and by any person who aids, abets, incites, counsels or procures the offending (often called 'secondary parties' or just 'parties' to the offence). Once it has been decided what category the offence in question belongs to, it is follows that any person who is charged with being a party to the offence will be treated in the same way as the principal offender. However, s66 of the Act does not cover cases where the full offence had not been completed or the defendant was charged as an accessory after the fact. Under s72 of the Act, trying unsuccessfully to bring about an offence is still an offence. Conspiring to commit an offence (s310) requires no more than an agreement between two or more persons to bring about the offence. Section 311 of the Act creates liability for inciting or procuring or attempting to procure persons to commit an offence even when no offence is actually committed. In all these cases the attempt, procurement or incitement is an offence in itself. The same is true where a defendant is charged with being an accessory after the fact to an offence; that is, where person X knows that person Y has been involved in a crime and then helps to cover up the offending or avoid detection.

Section 6(3) and Increased Penalties for Repeat Offenders

Sometimes s6(3) CPA will be important. It provides:

> (3) If an offence is punishable by a greater penalty where the defendant has previously been convicted of that offence or of some other offence, the offence is an offence in the category that applies to offences punishable by that greater penalty only if the charge alleges that the defendant has such a previous conviction.

This subsection deals with a fairly small group of offences where the maximum penalty increases when the defendant has been previously convicted of the same offence. An example is s32(1) of the Land Transport Act 1998, relating to drink-driving. This section provides a maximum penalty for a first or second conviction of not more than 3 months in prison or a fine up to $4,500, as well as a driving disqualification of 6 months or more. However the section provides a much more severe maximum penalty for a third or subsequent offence, with a maximum penalty of up to 2 years' imprisonment or a fine of up to $6,000, as well as disqualification for a year or more. Thus, where a defendant is facing a first or second conviction the offence is category 2 but for subsequent possible convictions it becomes a category 3 offence.

Where a defendant could face a greater penalty because of two prior convictions, s22(3) CPA allows the prosecution to specify this in the charging document but does not make it compulsory. If the prosecution does state the prior conviction(s) in the charging document, the higher penalty applies; however, if the charging document does not state the prior conviction, the lower penalty applies.

Categories of Offending

As noted above, under the CPA there are four categories of offending, distinguished by the possible penalties and/or by their listing in Schedule 1 to the Act. These categories are discussed below.

Category 1 Offences

Section 6(1) CPA defines category 1 offences thus:

> Category 1 offence means—
> (a) an offence that is not punishable by a term of imprisonment, other than—
>   (i) an infringement offence; or
>   (ii) an offence described in paragraph (b) or (c) of the definition of a category 2 offence; or
>   (iii) an offence described in paragraph (b) of the definition of a category 3 offence; or
> (b) an infringement offence, if proceedings in relation to that offence are commenced by filing a charging document under s14, not by the issuing of an infringement notice.

This statutory definition of category 1 offences, read together with the references to other categories, means that the starting point – involving all offences not punishable by imprisonment – is significantly modified. First, the combination of paragraphs (a) and (b) means that most infringement offences are excluded, but some remain within category 1. Second, the definition excludes offences which provide for a maximum penalty of a community-based sentence. As discussed in Chapter 5, those sentences include community work, supervision, intensive supervision or community detention. This leaves only those punishable solely by imposition of a fine. There are not many such offences, but the graffiti- or tagging-related offences in ss11A and 11B of the Summary Offences Act 1981 are examples.

The definition also avoids problems where the alleged offender is a body corporate (i.e. an artificial legal person such as a company, a Māori incorporation, a trade union or a charitable trust). The principles under which bodies corporate can be held criminally liable for offences are set out in Simester and Brookbanks

(2012: chap. 7) and France (2017: para. CA2.27). The definition of category 1 offences makes it clear that offences which may be punished by imprisonment fall outside category 1 even where the defendant is a body corporate and even though a body corporate cannot be imprisoned if it is convicted. In such cases the body corporate is punished by a fine.

Infringement Offences Initiated by a Charging Document under s14 CPA

The term infringement offences covers a wide range of minor offending which is generally dealt with outside the court system through infringement notices (such as illegal parking or exceeding the speed limit). These give the offender an option to pay an infringement fee without going to court. However, the offender may go to court if he/she wishes to challenge the charge. Payment of the infringement fee ends the matter without a conviction being imposed. Infringement offences are therefore treated under the CPA as falling outside the normal categories of offending.

However, some statutes provide the enforcement agency with a choice of immediately bringing a prosecution under s14 CPA, or of issuing an infringement notice and then bringing a prosecution. There is an informative discussion of infringement offences of this kind in the Supreme Court decision *Down v R* [2012] NZSC 21; [2012] 2 NZLR 585. The most important of the statutes containing this mechanism is the Resource Management Act 1991. This kind of infringement offence is included within the s6 CPA categories and, because the relevant offences can be punished only by imposing a fine, they fall into category 1.

Category 2 Offences

Section 6(1) CPA defines category 2 offences thus:

> Category 2 offence means—
> (a) an offence punishable by a term of imprisonment of less than 2 years; or
> (b) an offence that, if committed by a body corporate, is punishable by only a fine, but that would be punishable by a term of imprisonment of less than 2 years if committed by an individual; or

(c) an offence punishable by a community-based sentence and not punishable by a term of imprisonment.

The scope of category 2 is rather more easily explained than that of category 1. Category 2 covers offences which have a maximum penalty of a community-based sentence or imprisonment for a term of less than 2 years. The category also encompasses cases where a body corporate can only be fined although a human defendant could be sentenced to a term of less than 2 years' imprisonment. The 'less than 2 years' phrasing is important. If the maximum penalty is 2 years exactly, the offence falls into category 3. The sentence limit parallels that for the right to elect jury trial under s50 CPA. As a result, jury trial is never available for category 2 offences. In practice, the 2-year limitation may require care by prosecutors in framing changes involving some forms of dishonesty offending where the maximum penalty is related to the value of the property involved. Thus, for theft under s219 of the Crimes Act 1961 or obtaining by deception under s240 of the same Act, the maximum penalty where the property is worth less than $1,000 is 1 year's imprisonment, but for property valued at $1,000 or more it is 7 years. The specification of a value of $1,000 or over therefore means that the offence is category 3; failure to specify the value or specifying a sum below $1,000 will leave the offence in category 2.

Category 3 Offences

Section 6(1) CPA defines category 3 offences thus:

Category 3 offence means an offence, other than an offence listed in Schedule 1—
(a) that is punishable by imprisonment for life or by imprisonment for 2 years or more; or
(b) that, if committed by a body corporate, is punishable by only a fine, but that would be punishable by imprisonment for life or by imprisonment for 2 years or more if committed by an individual.

This definition is a little more complex than it first appears. The first point is that the category is very large, covering as it does almost all offences punishable by a maximum sentence of 2 years' imprisonment or more, although the number is limited somewhat by the exclusion of the offences listed in Schedule 1 CPA, which come within category 4. The definition includes, in line with the earlier provisions, paragraph (b) in relation to offending by a body corporate. Curiously, some of the most serious offences are included in category 3. In particular, offences under s6 of the Misuse of Drugs Act 1975 of importing, manufacturing and selling class A drugs, all punishable by life imprisonment, are within category 3 and will be tried by a judge alone in the District Court if the defendant does not elect a jury trial.

Category 4 Offences

Section 6(1) CPA defines category 4 offences thus:

> Category 4 offence means an offence listed in Schedule 1.

Schedule 1 is the first schedule to the CPA and is in two parts. The first lists a number of Crimes Act 1961 offences, while the second lists various offences from a range of other statutes. The Crimes Act offences included in the first part of Schedule 1 are very varied, but fall into four broad groups. First, there are several sections which criminalise activity in ways which might or might not be covered by s6(2) CPA, for example s69(2) of the Crimes Act, which makes it an offence to incite someone else to commit a murder outside New Zealand, whether or not the person actually commits the murder, and s74(3) of the same Act, which creates a specific offence of being a party to treason. These appear to have been included in Schedule 1 as a precaution and to avoid any doubts that might arise.

Second, there are several sections which create offences with an international aspect, criminalising conduct which is recognised by international law as being serious offending against the world community. Examples include slave dealing under s98 of the Crimes Act and piracy under s92 of the same Act. There is a clear parallel with the offences included in part 2 of Schedule 1, as discussed below.

Third, there is a group of sections related to homicide in its different forms of murder, manslaughter and infanticide. As this group includes some offences of party liability and conspiracy there is some overlap with the first group identified earlier. Last, there are several sections dealing with peace, order and good government of New Zealand, including such drastic crimes as treason and more prosaically a range of offences involving judicial or political corruption. These offences may be assumed to have been included in the schedule because of their extreme public importance. Requiring that such offences be tried in the High Court and by jury recognises that public-impact element.

The second part of Schedule 2 lists an eclectic range of offences from twelve different statutes, all of which contain provisions required to be part of New Zealand law by international treaties or conventions New Zealand has signed. For example, the Mercenary Activities (Prohibition) Act 2004, one of the listed twelve statutes, ensures New Zealand will comply with the International Convention against the Recruitment, Use, Financing and Training of Mercenaries 1989, to which New Zealand became a party in September 2004. Placing these offences in category 4 reflects the fact that such conventions require signatory countries to ensure the offences and their penalties reflect the grave harm the offences may produce. Ensuring any trial will take place in the High Court signifies New Zealand's commitment to its treaty obligations.

Modes of Trial

The various categories of offending are each assigned specific modes of trial by ss71–74 CPA. As we will see, these assigned modes of trial may be displaced in some cases by other, overriding, rules. In three of the categories, trial requirements are initially straightforward because there is no provision for choice.

Category 1 offences must be tried in the District Court. There is no right to jury trial and issues of fact and law are decided by the presiding judge or other judicial officers. In many cases the judicial officer will be a District Court Judge, but offences within the category may also be tried by one or more Community Magistrates or one or more Justices of the Peace. Category 2 offences are also tried only in the District Court, but they must be dealt with only by a judge of that court. There is no right to jury trial so the judge decides both fact and law. By contrast, category 4 offences must be heard in the High Court before a judge and jury (unless, as we shall see, the option of jury trial is removed on the grounds in ss102 and 103 CPA).

This leaves the much more complex provisions of s73 CPA which govern how category 3 offences are to be tried. The default position is that the trial will be in the District Court by judge alone. That default may be varied in two ways. The High Court is given jurisdiction to try category 3 offences and a High Court Judge may under s68 or s70 CPA order a case be transferred from the District Court to the High Court. This may be for convenience and better use of resources or, more commonly, because it will allow a defendant charged only with category 3 offences to be tried jointly with a person charged with a category 4 offence – who must therefore be tried in the High Court. The question of trying co-offenders is discussed below. When this is done the trial will be by judge and jury in the High Court, unless an overriding rule, as discussed below, applies to remove the right to jury trial. The CPA authorises the Chief High Court Judge and the Chief District Court Judge to enter into a protocol for the treatment of such offences so as to enable the smooth transfer of cases. The most recent iteration of that protocol came into force in May 2017.

If the case remains in the District Court, as the large majority of category 3 cases do, it is tried by a District Court Judge sitting without a jury unless the defendant chooses to elect jury trial under s50 CPA. That option applies for all offences carrying maximum sentences of 2 years or more. A defendant who has elected jury trial may retract that election later under s53 CPA, but only with the leave of the court. The case then goes back to the judge-alone track.

Potentially Overriding Rules

So far this discussion has largely proceeded, as do s6 and ss71–74 CPA, on the artificial basis that criminal proceedings normally involve a single defendant and a single offence, or at least offences within a single category. Reality is, of course, very different. When the position is more complex we need to take into account some potentially overriding rules which may change the way some cases are tried.

When One Defendant Faces Multiple Charges

In many cases a defendant will be facing a number of criminal charges in a single proceeding. The prosecution has a choice under s138 CPA to bring multiple charges against a single defendant in one set of charging documents. If the prosecutor does so, all the charges against the defendant will be dealt with in a single trial, unless the defendant successfully seeks an order under s138(4) for one or more of the offences to be tried separately. In any case, when a defendant faces multiple charges, there is an obvious question as to where the trial should take place and in what fashion. The starting point is clear. Under s139(1) CPA if one charge is to be tried by jury, all the other charges in those proceedings must also be tried by jury. This will be so even if some or all of the other charges are category 1 or category 2 offences which would otherwise be tried by a judge alone. The rule prevents an unnecessary multiplication of trials, with attendant stresses on witnesses and additional costs. It also prevents attempts by a defendant to game the system by opting for jury trial for only some of the offences and not for others.

Section 139(1) also provides that if any one of the offences is to be tried in the High Court (either as a category 4 offence or as a category 3 offence transferred to the High Court), all the other offences must also be tried in the High Court. Again this avoids multiplication of proceedings and attempts to manipulate the system, but again it means that offences which would normally not go to the High Court may sometimes now arrive there. Since s139(1) in effect trumps the normal rules, what happens if the most serious charges, which trigger a trial in the High Court or give a right of jury trial, are dropped or otherwise terminated before trial? The answer is that if all offences carrying 2 years' imprisonment or more are dropped or terminated prior to trial, the defendant loses the right to elect jury trial, and the case reverts back to trial by judge alone. Similarly, if all charges which were required to be in the High Court are dropped or terminated, the case goes back to the District Court.

Multiple Defendants Facing the Same Charges

In the case of multiple defendants, there is little difficulty where all are facing the same category 1 or category 2 charges. The cases must all be heard in the District Court and there is no possibility of a jury trial. Nor is there a difficulty with category 4 cases because it is mandated that these be in the High Court with a jury.

However, there is an obvious problem with category 3 offences where it is desirable to try the defendants together but the defendants are not agreed on the mode of trial. Once again, Parliament has provided a solution which can override the normal process under ss6 and 73 CPA. Under s139(2) CPA, where two or more defendants are to be tried together and one is to be tried by jury, then all must be tried by jury. In effect, any decisions by defendants not to elect a jury trial will be overridden if any one of them exercises the option of jury trial. Section 139(2) also contains a provision that where one or more co-defendants are to be tried in the High Court, all defendants must be tried in the High Court. Although there is, as yet, no decided case on point, it seems logical that if some co-defendants are ordered to stand trial separately, or have the charges against them resolved or terminated prior to trial, the other co-defendants will be able to make fresh choices.

Multiple Defendants Facing a Range of Charges

It is common for the prosecution to bring a range of charges against multiple defendants even if this means they do not all face the same charges. For example, if methamphetamine has been manufactured and sold, it is highly likely that the police will charge some defendants with manufacturing, some with selling, and some with both, as well as other charges such as procuring chemicals, allowing premises to be used for selling/manufacture, and various other party offences. Under s138 CPA it is highly likely that the courts would refuse to separate the trials of the various defendants, even if the charges were different and even if some of the defendants were only peripherally involved – for example by unlawfully possessing firearms in order to protect the drug-sellers. In such a case s139 CPA will again apply: if any one of the co-defendants elects jury trial, all will be tried by jury; if some are to be tried in the High Court, all will be tried in the High Court.

Changing the Place of Trial

The statutory starting point in change of trial venue cases is that a criminal trial should be held in the court nearest to where the offending took place. This recognises the desirability of justice being done, and being seen to be done, in the community which was most affected by the offending.

This is reflected in the requirement that a charging document be filed in the closest District Court to where the alleged offence took place. The same principle underlies s5(5) of the Juries Act 1981, which states that so far as practicable, a jury should be drawn from the community in which the alleged offence occurred. Because not all District Courts are physically able to hold jury trials, cases which may require a jury trial in the District Court are automatically shifted to the nearest District Court where a jury trial is possible. All High Court venues can hear jury trials so there is no similar problem for category 4 offences which have been sent to the High Court for trial.

However, Parliament recognises that sometimes the closest-court principle can cause inconvenience or can risk creating an unfair trial, so the principle cannot always apply. Under s157 CPA the Court can order that proceedings be transferred to the same court at a different place. All further stages of the case up to and including trial will then occur at the new venue.

An application to change the venue can be made by either prosecution or defence. A judge may also initiate a change of venue but this is rare. Normally the decision is made by a District Court Judge or a High Court Judge but in the case of category 1 or 2 offences the parties may agree that any issue of transfer be decided by a Justice of the Peace, a Community Magistrate or the Registrar of the District Court.

A change of venue may be ordered on either of two broad grounds. Firstly, a case may be transferred if there is a real risk that a fair trial will not be possible at the original venue. Courts have been reluctant to make such orders where a trial will be by judge alone, because judges are considered to be immune to community pressure. Transfer is sometimes ordered when a trial will be by jury. This may be because there has been such strong local feeling in the community that it will be very difficult to assemble a panel of jurors who are not affected by that community sentiment – either towards the defendant or the reverse. A good example is provided by *R v Te Kahu* [2006] 1 NZLR 459; (2005) 22 CRNZ 133, where there was a risk that jurors would have connections to, or hostility towards, one or the other of two rival gangs involved in significant violent offending in an area with a limited jury pool.

A change of venue may also be ordered where a defendant is being retried after a successful appeal against conviction, if there is a concern that members of the community – who are likely to be on the jury – will have their judgements affected by memory of the earlier trial. This is not usually seen as a problem in a large city where a jury will be drawn from a larger pool, but can be a problem in provincial centres.

The other basis for changing the place of trial is administrative convenience. Sometimes it may happen that, although the offence took place in one particular region, the parties to it and the witnesses are largely from another region and it is simply more convenient to move proceedings to the location of the people involved. Imagine, for example, two groups of holidaymakers from Christchurch who become involved in a brawl in Nelson during the summer holiday period. If most of the parties and witnesses to the alleged offending all live in or near Christchurch, it is easier to try the case in Christchurch.

Overriding the Defendant's Right to Jury Trial

While generally a defendant facing charges carrying a sentence of 2 or more years' imprisonment has a right to jury trial, that right is not absolute. Parliament recognises that sometimes circumstances may render a jury trial impractical or unfair, and has provided in ss102 and 103 CPA two grounds on which a judge may decide that the defendant's right to a jury trial is to be overridden. Both are closely modelled on English statutory provisions.

Section 102, which has been used on a number of occasions, allows for judge-alone trial, even where the defendant wants a jury trial, where:

(a) the offence charged carries a maximum penalty of less than 14 years' imprisonment; and
(b) the trial is likely to take more than 20 sitting days; and
(c) the normal right to jury trial is outweighed by the likelihood that a jury could not perform its functions properly.

The power to rely on judge-only trials in long-running cases was created in response to two often-encountered problems. First, some long trials have had to be abandoned because too many jurors have become ill or otherwise unable to serve, reducing the jury to one below the minimum allowable size. In New Zealand, under s22(1A) of the Juries Act 1981 a jury trial may only continue with fewer than ten of the original twelve jurors if all parties agree and the judge considers it is in the interests of justice to continue. (Once the numbers fall below ten, the verdict must be unanimous, but where there are ten, eleven or twelve jurors s29C of the Act allows a verdict to be returned even though one juror dissents.) Some overseas jurisdictions deal with the problem by empanelling reserve jurors who attend the trial and can be called into the jury if needed, but New Zealand does not do so.

More seriously, there has been concern that when trials are very long, particularly if they involve complex issues and large volumes of information, jurors find it hard to retain the material, with the result they either fail to reach a verdict or reach one which did not reflect the evidence. These problems have been particularly acute in cases of large-scale fraud. This was noted by the courts in a leading decision on s102 CPA, the case of *R v Wenzel* [2009] 3 NZLR 47; [2009] NZCA 130, where Wenzel and a co-defendant had been charged with a large-scale fraud. There were 20 charges against Wenzel alone, and a further 16 charges jointly against Wenzel and the co-defendant, all of which related to a complex series of transactions involving 18 properties. The prosecution intended to call 41 witnesses, several of whom were expected to take several days each to give their evidence, and estimated the trial would take 10 weeks. The Court of Appeal at para. [54] described the case as having 'all the hallmarks identified by Parliament as being sufficient to outweigh the advantages which are otherwise obtained by trial by jury' and confirmed the order for judge-alone trial. While the greatest use of s102 has definitely been in fraud cases, orders under the section have been made in other circumstances such as serious domestic violence or firearms offences, and participation in an organised criminal group with an alleged political agenda.

Estimates of the length of a trial must take into account the number of witnesses and the likely time that will be taken in hearing their evidence, particularly if there may be any legal challenges, as well as the other elements of the trial including jury selection before evidence is heard, the judge's summing up at the end of the evidence and an appropriate period for jury deliberations. The estimated length of the trial is best seen as a pre-condition for the use of the s102 power, with the primary issue for the court being whether the usual right to a jury trial is outweighed by the risk the jury may not be able to perform its duties effectively and thereby risk a trial which is procedurally defective and thus unfair. Section 102 can, on this basis, be seen as a clear and justified limitation on the right to jury trial otherwise conferred by the general law and recognised by s24(e) of the New Zealand Bill of Rights Act 1990. The Supreme Court noted in *Porter v R* [2009] NZSC 107, at para. [6], that the New Zealand Bill of Rights Act 1990 provision should be given priority if the issue was 'finely balanced'.

Juror Intimidation or Interference

A judge may make an order under s103 CPA, before or during the trial, that the case be heard by judge alone instead of by a jury if there is a real risk that jurors will be intimidated or otherwise interfered with. The section covers attempts by any person or group to affect the verdict, whether or not they are parties to the case. An order under the section has not yet been made in New Zealand, but in the one case where an order was unsuccessfully sought (*R v Pritchard*, 23/2/09, Dobson J, HC Napier CRI 2008-020-002387) it was said that the importance of the right to jury trial meant that an order should only be made where there was no other procedural option which would be likely to be effective to prevent the interference. Thus, a step such as changing the venue to avoid intimidation will normally be favoured over ordering a judge-alone trial. Either prosecution or defence may appeal against an order made under either of ss102 or 103, or a decision not to make an order under the section.

Youth Justice: Overriding Rules When Trying Young Defendants

The Children, Young Persons and Their Families Act 1989 (CYPTFA) is the most important New Zealand statute dealing with state interaction with children (persons aged up to and including 13) and young persons (those aged 14, 15 or 16) and with the families of such alleged offenders. The procedure for trying young offenders is decided by their age at the time of the offence, not the age when the matter comes to court. The Act contains a number of sections which are of great importance when dealing with offending by children and young persons. CYPTFA has the overarching aim of achieving the outcomes that are best for the child or young person and it treats children charged with offences in a very different way from the way it treats young persons. That difference has major consequences in terms of where, and by what process, criminal proceedings occur. Cleland and Quince (2014) provide an excellent introduction to youth justice in this country in *Youth Justice in Aotearoa New Zealand: Theory, Practice, Critique*.

As discussed below, most criminal proceedings against children or young persons occur in the Youth Court, which is a division of the District Court. The Youth Court is designed to be less formal in its procedures than the other branches of the District Court, so as to allow greater participation by and on behalf of the defendant. Youth Court Judges are District Court Judges with a warrant to hear Youth Court cases, and adopt generally a more activist role in shaping the course of proceedings, particularly in making sure issues around the child or young person's physical or mental health are ventilated.

Since 2008, a growing number of Youth Courts have conducted some of their proceedings as Te Kooti Rangatahi, hearing cases at marae with modified procedures which draw on and emphasise Māori cultural practices and customs. There are also two Youth Courts which operate Pasifika Courts, with procedures drawing on Pasifika culture.

Standard District Court procedures are heavily modified in Youth Court criminal cases by CYPTFA. In particular those modifications have very significant implications for defendants outside the normal scope of the Act but who are charged as co-defendants with a child or a young person, or jointly with both a child and a young person. These possibilities are discussed below.

Children (Persons Aged 10–14)

Persons aged 10–14, referred to as children for the purposes of the criminal law, rarely come before the courts as criminal defendants because the vast majority of their offending is dealt with by police Youth Aid or by state care and protection proceedings, with the courts having no jurisdiction to try child offenders. However s272 CYPTFA provides three exceptions where children may face prosecution and specifies the court of trial. The three exceptions are:

(a) a child aged 10–13 who is charged with murder or manslaughter. The child will tried in the High Court by judge and jury, although all pre-trial matters are dealt with in the Youth Court. The court and mode of trial are not affected by the presence or absence of co-offenders as any co-defendant will also be tried in the High Court;

(b) a child aged 12 or 13 charged with an offence (other than murder or manslaughter) for which the maximum penalty available is imprisonment for life or for at least 14 years. Any such offence will be in category 3 or category 4. Here all proceedings will be in the Youth Court, therefore involving trial by judge alone, unless the child elects jury trial under s50 CPA or the Youth Court Judge makes an order the child be tried together with one or more co-defendants in the regular District Court or in the High Court;

(c) a child who is 12 or 13 years of age and is a previous offender charged with an offence (other than murder or manslaughter) for which the maximum penalty is between ten and 14 years. The term previous offender is given an extended definition in s272(1A) and (1B) CYPTFA. The child will be tried in the Youth Court unless the child elects jury trial.

Young Persons (Defendants Aged 14, 15 or 16)

Young persons are all persons aged 14, 15 or 16 other than those who are or have been married or are in a civil union. The latter are treated as adults. Young persons have none of the age-related immunities from prosecution enjoyed by children.

Almost all criminal proceedings against young persons are held in the Youth Court, with trial being by a Youth Court Judge with no jury. A small number of exceptions are provided for in s272(3) CYPTFA. The position can be summed up thus:

(a) A young person charged with murder or manslaughter will be tried in the High Court by judge and jury (although, as with children accused of homicide, preliminary matters will be dealt with in the Youth Court);
(b) a young person can elect jury trial in relation to any category 3 or 4 offence under s274 CYPTFA, in which case the jury trial will be in the District Court or High Court as appropriate. Many defendants will forgo the election because they may be exposed to more serious penalties if tried by jury. A defendant may withdraw an election of jury trial (s276 CYPTFA);
(c) traffic offences not punishable by imprisonment (category 1 offences) will be heard in the District Court;
(d) infringement offences against the Psychoactive Substances Act 2013, the Sale and Supply of Alcohol Act 2012, the Summary Offences Act 1981 or s239A of the Local Government Act 2002 will be heard in the District Court unless a Youth Court Judge orders under s272(5) CYPTFA that the infringement offences be joined with other charges to be heard in the Youth Court;
(e) the charge or charges against the young person are ordered under s277 CYPTFA to be transferred from the Youth Court to the High Court or the District Court jury jurisdiction, in order to resolve difficulties in cases involving co-defendants.

Children and/or Young Persons Charged Jointly with Others

There are complex provisions in s277 CYPTFA to govern the common position where a child or a young person is charged jointly with one or more people from other age groups. The complexity is partly a function of the three different regimes for children, young persons and older offenders and partly of the ability of offenders facing category 3 charges to elect jury trial. The procedural rules are summarised below.

Children
A child who is jointly charged with any other person, of whatever age, and is to be tried by a judge and jury must be tried in the same court as any co-defendant

who is also to be tried by jury. In such cases the child will be part of a joint trial by jury, in the High Court or in the District Court. Under s277(3) CYPTFA a child who has not been charged with murder or manslaughter, has not elected jury trial in the case of any other offence and who is jointly charged with any other person, of whatever age, must be tried in the Youth Court together with any co-defendants who are not being tried by jury. This means that an adult defendant who has not elected jury trial, but could have done so, will be tried in the Youth Court.

Young Persons
A young person who is jointly charged with co-defendants, of any age, who have elected jury trial must be tried in the same court as those co-defendants unless the Youth Court orders that the trials be separated and the young person be tried by judge alone in the Youth Court (see s277[5] CYPFTA). Recent Youth Court decisions have given great weight to the presumption in favour of joint jury trial and held that young persons should be tried by jury with their alleged co-offenders. The judges have therefore not severed the trials as the section empowers them to do. While a wide range of factors must be taken into account, the stress on witnesses and complainants of having to give evidence at multiple trials has perhaps been the single most important factor. A less than obvious consequence of this rule is that where a young person is charged together with another young person, the trials will be held separately in the Youth Court.

Adults
An adult who has been charged jointly with a child or young person will be tried by jury in the same court as that child or young person if the child is to be tried by jury. However, under s277(6) CYPTFA if the child or young person co-defendant is not to be tried by jury but in the Youth Court, the adult will also be tried in the Youth Court if he/she either did not have a right of jury trial or has chosen not to elect jury trial. In effect, if the child co-defendant is to be tried by jury an adult will be required to face trial by jury for category 3 offences, irrespective of his/her wishes. However, if the child or young person co-defendant is not be tried by jury and the adult has a right to elect jury trial, the adult can do so and will then be tried separately in a jury trial court. Otherwise all parties will be tried in the Youth Court. In any case not covered by the points raised above, the defendant will be tried in the Youth Court by a Youth Court Judge.

If an adult defendant is tried in the Youth Court, any conviction will be deemed to have been a conviction in the District Court and the judge can impose any sentence or make any order which could have been made in that court (see CYPTFA s277[9]). Pre-trial processes as regards the adult defendant will largely be the same as for the District or High Court (see s277[1] and [11]).

Conclusion

Getting cases to the right court is an essential part of making the justice system work. In criminal cases the process is complicated by the range of different offences and by the need to allow for both jury trial and trial by judge alone, as well as the fact that both the District Court and the High Court try criminal cases. The CPA contains a number of provisions which collectively provide a pathway for each case. Finding that pathway is a matter of carefully and systematically going through the different matters described above. It is essential to check at each point where the pathway divides whether one party or the other has a right to determine which part of the path is to be followed, and then to cross-check whether there are any overriding factors (such as one of the offenders being a child or young person) which will change the outcome of applying the usual factors.

REFERENCES

Cleland, A., and Quince, K. 2014. *Youth Justice in Aotearoa New Zealand: Theory, Practice, Critique.* Wellington: LexisNexis.
Finn, J., and Mathias, D. 2015. *Criminal Procedure in New Zealand* (2nd ed.). Wellington: Thomson Reuters.
France, S. B. (Ed.). 2017. *Adams on Criminal Law* [Online]. Wellington: Thomson Reuters. Accessed 21 May 2017. http://www.thomsonreuters.co.nz/proview
Simester, A., and Brookbanks, W. 2012. *Principles of Criminal Law* (3rd ed.). Wellington: Thomson Reuters.

8.

Sentencing

DEBRA WILSON

Introduction

When a person is found to have committed an offence – the legal term for what we commonly refer to as a crime – following a trial by either a judge or a jury, the person is said to have been convicted of that offence. The next step in the criminal justice process is for a judge to determine the appropriate punishment, known as a sentence, for this offender. Sentencing can be a complicated process, and can be considered as more of an art than a science. The sentencing judge must consider numerous factors before deciding on an appropriate sentence. These factors might include the circumstances of the offending, the impact of the offending both on the victim and on wider society, and the personal circumstances of the offender. The judge must also consider what he or she is trying to achieve by punishing the offender, and the consequences of such punishment. When all of the relevant information is considered, a decision can be made as to which of a number of potential sentences is the most appropriate.

This chapter will begin by considering the reasons why society punishes offenders and the aims of sentencing. It will then consider the various types of sentences available in New Zealand. Finally, it will consider how these sentencing options have been applied in New Zealand in recent years, and whether there are any identifiable trends developing.

Why Do We Punish People?

Imagine a simple scenario:

> One evening a husband and wife are eating dinner. The wife serves the husband a bowl of soup. While preparing the soup, she had crushed several tablets into powder and had carefully stirred these into her husband's serving. Not long after he finishes eating, he passes out. He does not regain consciousness, and dies later that night. She later admits her actions to the doctors and to the police.

Has the wife done something for which she should be punished? Your immediate thought on reading this might have been that it was a clear case of murder (defined as the intentional killing of one person by another). If so, you might also have thought that she is deserving of punishment, and that this is a case that requires a high level of punishment. But what if you only know some of the story? Read the following additional alternative scenarios and consider whether your opinion about the need for, or the amount of, punishment, changes:

> *Scenario (a):* Doctors provide evidence that the husband was suffering from a medical condition, and that the pills were prescribed treatment for that condition. As the husband did not like the taste of the pills, his wife often crushed them into powder and stirred them into his food. She gave him the correct dosage on the evening in question.

> *Scenario (b):* Most of the facts in (a) apply, with the one difference being that the wife gave him more than the prescribed dosage (three pills instead of two). Her husband had been complaining of pain earlier that day, and she thought that increasing the dosage would help him.

> *Scenario (c):* The husband was physically abusive towards his wife. This abuse usually occurred at night following a few beers after dinner. After many years of abuse his wife knows the signs of impending trouble well. When he came in from work that night and she saw those signs, she decided to feed him some sleeping pills, so she would be safe that evening.

> *Scenario (d):* Most of the facts in (c) apply, with the one difference being that when the wife saw the warning signs, something inside her snapped. She realised that

nothing was ever going to change, and believed that if she didn't kill him, he would kill her.

Scenario (e): There are hints that the wife may suffer from an undiagnosed mental condition. She often hears a voice inside her head, whom she calls 'Tom', who tells her to do things. In the week prior to the night in question, 'Tom' had repeatedly told her that her husband was possessed by the devil but that he could be saved if she gave him these pills. She gave her husband the pills thinking it would save him from the devil.

In some of these alternative scenarios the additional information might change whether we think the wife is deserving of punishment, or might lead us to re-evaluate the level or amount of punishment that we think is appropriate. In scenario (a), she appears to have done nothing wrong. She is unlikely to be found guilty, and will probably not even be charged. In scenario (e), she may be found not guilty due to a defence of insanity. In the other scenarios, she could well be found guilty of murder or manslaughter under their legal definitions. The additional information will likely be considered as relevant, however, in determining the appropriate sentence. The idea of sentencing being an art and not a science might now begin to make a little more sense. There are multiple reasons which might have led to the wife acting in the way that she did, and our system of justice requires that these be taken into account.

Theories of Punishment

The starting point in understanding sentencing is to accept two statements as being true:

1. The effect of sentencing is to punish someone.
2. Punishing someone is an inherently wrongful act, whether this punishment is carried out by individuals or by the state.

It is worth considering the second point in more detail. Bentham ([1789] 1907: chap. XIII.2) comments that 'all punishment in itself is evil . . . if it ought at all to be admitted, it ought only to be admitted in as far as it promises to exclude some greater evil'. A person who is punished through the imposition of a criminal sentence will have his or her human rights and freedoms interfered with for the duration of that sentence (e.g., under a sentence of imprisonment, freedom of movement and freedom to make one's own decisions are severely limited). Alternatively, the person may have some other burden imposed on him for a period of time (e.g., a fine imposes a financial burden, and a sentence of community work requires a person to work without financial compensation).

Any restriction of rights or imposition of burdens should be considered unacceptable, unless there is a sufficient justification for doing so. If I was to lock someone in a small room for a couple of years because they stole something from me, society would not consider that acceptable and I would likely be imprisoned for it. What, then, permits society (through the courts) to respond to my actions by effectively doing the same thing to me as I did to the thief, through a sentence of imprisonment? The only way that society's response can be considered acceptable is if its punishment is justified in a way that my punishment of the other person was not. Rawls (1955: 13) writes, for example, that 'it is morally fitting that a person who does wrong should suffer in proportion to his wrongdoing'. To put it another way, the state must have the moral authority to punish me in order for its actions to be justified. This moral authority is lost if society punishes me in a manner that is unreasonable or disproportionate to my actions.

There are four generally accepted theories for why punishment can be considered justified. The first three theories can be described as consequentialist theories. This means that they are focused on the future consequences of the punishment: they view the purpose of punishment for the current offence as an attempt to influence future events and to prevent future offending. I now deal with each of the above four theories in sequence.

1. *Deterrence theory*. According to Bentham ([1789] 1907), deterrence is based on the assumption that people are rational actors who weigh up the positive and negative consequences of an act before deciding to carry it out. An appropriately severe sentence will therefore operate as a sufficient disincentive to commit crime. Posner (1992: 223–8) agrees, explaining further that people will commit crime if the expected net benefit of committing that crime exceeds the expected net benefit of behaving lawfully. Therefore, if the expected punishment is greater than the expected benefit gained from the criminal activity, the person will logically decide that it is not worthwhile committing the crime. There are two forms of deterrence: specific deterrence, which aims to deter the

offender personally from reoffending; and general deterrence, which aims to deter other people from committing crimes through making an example of offenders.

2. *Incapacitation theory.* American Judge Hugo Black (*Powell v. Texas* 392 US 514, 539 [1968]) described the second theory, incapacitation, by commenting that 'isolation of the dangerous has always been considered an important function of the criminal law'. Under this theory, if a person proves himself (or herself) sufficiently likely to reoffend in the future, society may be justified in protecting itself by incapacitating that person through imprisonment. While the person is in jail, his/her chance of reoffending against the free community is minimal.

3. *Rehabilitation theory.* Rehabilitation starts from the presumption that criminal offending is not an inherent characteristic of a person, but is a consequence or result of certain previous (known as antecedent) causes. If these causes can be addressed and remedied, the person will be less likely to commit crime in the future. This theory is therefore based on the idea that people can learn from their mistakes and change, given the right opportunities. It is particularly useful where one of the identifiable causes of the offending is drug or alcohol dependency, anger management issues, or undiagnosed or untreated mental health issues.

4. *Retributionist theory.* The final theory is a retributionist theory (also known as 'just deserts', *jus talionis*, or 'an eye for an eye'). Its focus is on the past and its purpose is to punish in retribution for the conduct of the offender and the harm this conduct has caused. Whether or not this punishment will deter future conduct is irrelevant. Kant ([1785] 2011) states that in determining whether a conduct is moral or not, we must disregard all of its consequences. In Kant's opinion, therefore, an action is morally right or wrong because of the nature of the act, not of the consequences. It is important to understand that in Kant's formulation, retribution is not the same as vengeance. Vengeance, which can be understood as retaliation against the offender (you hurt me, so I should be able to hurt you in return), is not morally permissible. Retribution is instead about communicating to the offender that what they did was unacceptable. Society's moral authority to punish through retribution only exists if the punishment is proportionate to the offending, and is imposed on a rationally-acting person (see Kant [1790] 2014: 199). Punishment should be 'pronounced over all criminals in proportion to their internal wickedness'.

Consequences of Punishment

There are two consequences to being convicted of an offence. First, a conviction means that the offender will have a criminal record, upon which this conviction is entered. This criminal record will normally remain in place for the rest of the offender's life. The one exception to this is if the Criminal Records (Clean Slate) Act 2004 applies. Under this Act, a person who meets certain specific criteria may have their criminal record wiped clean after 7 years. The existence of a criminal record can have severe implications for an individual. Prospective (and even current) employers can require the disclosure of this information. There are certain occupations in New Zealand that cannot be undertaken by people with criminal convictions. In other occupations, a conviction may create hurdles to gaining employment, while not necessarily preventing it. Travel overseas will become more difficult, as many countries refuse visitor visas to people with convictions for certain offences. Second, an additional punishment (known as a sentence) will also be imposed in the majority of cases. These potential sentences are discussed below.

The Sentencing Act 2002

In New Zealand, the Sentencing Act 2002 is a judge's guidebook to sentencing. It explains the purposes of sentencing, the factors to take into account when determining the level of sentencing, and the different types of sentence available.

Purposes of Sentencing

Section 7 of the Sentencing Act describes the purposes of sentencing. It reads:

1. The purposes for which a court may sentence or otherwise deal with an offender are—
    (a) To hold the offender accountable for harm done to the victim and the community by the offending; or
    (b) To promote in the offender a sense of responsibility for, and an acknowledgement of, that harm; or
    (c) To provide for the interests of the victim of the offence; or
    (d) To provide reparation for harm done by the offending; or

(e) To denounce the conduct in which the offender was involved; or
(f) To deter the offender or other persons from committing the same or a similar offence; or
(g) To protect the community from the offender; or
(h) To assist in the offender's rehabilitation and reintegration; or
(i) A combination of 2 or more of the purposes in paragraphs (a) to (h).
2. To avoid doubt, nothing about the order in which the purposes appear in this section implies that any purpose referred to must be given greater weight than any other purpose referred to.

Some of these purposes clearly fit within one of the four theories described above. Deterrence, for example, can be seen in purpose (f), incapacitation in (g), rehabilitation in (h), and retribution in (a) and (d). Other purposes, however, seem to be fulfilling a different goal. Purposes (b), (c) and (d) seem more focused on the victim than the offender. It is thought that these three factors represent the emerging theory of restorative justice, a process which focuses on the idea that the victim and also perhaps the offender have needs that are not met under the traditional criminal justice system. It focuses on addressing the harm caused to the victim and on allowing the offender to make amends.

It is clear that in some cases the application of these theories can provide us with conflicting answers as to whether punishment is justified. Take scenario (d) above, for example. In relation to deterrence theory, punishing the wife would send an important message to society (general deterrence) that we do not resolve situations like this through 'self-help' type remedies, but that we seek help from the police. On the other hand, punishment is unlikely to be necessary in order to deter her from acting in the same way in the future (specific deterrence). Unless she remarries into another abusive relationship, she is unlikely to continue to be a threat to society.

Under incapacitation theory, it is unlikely that society needs protecting from this woman, assuming we believe that her actions were a specific reaction to long-term abuse. Rehabilitation theory, meanwhile, would suggest that she is a victim of domestic violence, and in fact needs assistance in relation to this. Low level Intimate Partner Violence is beginning to be recognised as a condition that should result in treatment through counselling rather than punishment.

With regard to retribution theory, think of the husband's family. There may be no proof that there was violence in the relationship (indeed, hidden domestic abuse is an unanswerable claim, since the accused abuser is dead and cannot defend him/herself). In this case, the wife has deliberately taken the life of another person, and retribution requires punishment for this.

Finally, restorative justice might suggest that it is more important to address the underlying needs of the victim's family (in circumstances where an individual has died as a result of the offending, the victim's family are also considered to be victims) and the needs of the offender, particularly in this case since the victim and the offender were part of the same family. It will often be considered important to the family in this situation to understand why these events occurred.

This brief analysis demonstrates that these theories can give us conflicting views on whether the state should punish, and if so, the type and level of punishment which is desirable. Other arguments can also be identified. Sentencing can therefore be a complicated issue. The sentencing judge must weigh up all of the implications of applying each of these theories. As s7(2) of the Sentencing Act states, no purpose 'must be given greater weight than any other purpose referred to'. One theory is not more important than the others.

Principles of Sentencing

Once a judge has considered the purposes of sentencing according to law, the next step is to consider which sentencing option is the most appropriate. Again, the Sentencing Act provides guidance. Section 8 contains a series of principles of sentencing that are to be taken into account:

> In sentencing or otherwise dealing with an offender the court—
> (a) must take into account the gravity of the offending in the particular case, including the degree of culpability of the offender; and
> (b) must take into account the seriousness of the type of offence in comparison with other types of offences, as indicated by the maximum penalties prescribed for the offences; and
> (c) must impose the maximum penalty prescribed for the offence if the offending is within the most serious of cases for which that penalty is prescribed, unless circumstances relating to the offender make that inappropriate; and
> (d) must impose a penalty near to the maximum prescribed for the offence if the offending is near to the most serious of cases for which that penalty is prescribed, unless circumstances relating to the offender make that inappropriate; and

(e) must take into account the general desirability of consistency with appropriate sentencing levels and other means of dealing with offenders in respect of similar offenders committing similar offences in similar circumstances; and

(f) must take into account any information provided to the court concerning the effect of the offending on the victim; and

(g) must impose the least restrictive outcome that is appropriate in the circumstances, in accordance with the hierarchy of sentences and orders set out in section 10A; and

(h) must take into account any particular circumstances of the offender that mean that a sentence or other means of dealing with the offender that would otherwise be appropriate would, in the particular instance, be disproportionately severe; and

(i) must take into account the offender's personal, family, whanau, community, and cultural background in imposing a sentence or other means of dealing with the offender with a partly or wholly rehabilitative purpose; and

(j) must take into account any outcomes of restorative justice processes that have occurred, or that the court is satisfied are likely to occur, in relation to the particular case (including, without limitation, anything referred to in section 10).

There are two overall themes in these principles. The first is found in principles (a) to (e), and appears to focus on the severity of the offending in question (reflecting the appropriate level of moral responsibility) and the importance of sentencing in a manner consistent with other similar offences. If the wife in our example is convicted of murder, the penalty imposed should be consistent with the penalty given to others also convicted of murder in similar circumstances, but it must be proportionate to the seriousness of her particular offending. In simple terms, the sentencing judge must decide whether the wife's actions were equivalent to the most serious examples of murder in our society, the least serious examples, or an identifiable place somewhere in the middle. The appropriate sentence for her ought therefore to be similar to other murders of similar seriousness. The second theme, reflected in principles (g), (h) and (i), focuses on the individual. This ensures that the offender is considered as a unique individual, and not merely as part of a mathematical equation which results in a number representing a prison term.

Aggravating and Mitigating Factors

Section 9 of the Sentencing Act provides further guidance for this second theme. It lists aggravating and mitigating factors in offending. Aggravating factors (those that make the offending more serious) include:

- The actual or threatened use of violence or of a weapon
- Unlawful entry into a dwelling house
- That the offender was on bail at the time of offending
- Particular cruelty in the way the offence was carried out
- The fact that the offender was in a position of trust in relation to the victim
- The fact that the victim was particularly vulnerable due to age or health
- The fact that the offending was motivated by hatred towards a group of people who share a common characteristic (race, colour, nationality, gender identity, sexual orientation, etc)
- Whether the offending occurred as part of organised crime
- Whether the offender had planned the offending (premeditation)
- Previous convictions of the offender.

Mitigating factors (those that make the offending less serious) include:

- Age of the offender
- Whether and when the offender pled guilty
- If several people committed the offence, how large a part was played by the offender
- Whether the offender showed remorse
- Previous good character of the offender.

Types of Sentence Available

The Sentencing Act provides for a number of potential sentences which can be imposed following conviction. These are (in order from least serious to most serious):

- Discharge without conviction
- Conviction and discharge
- Conviction and order to come up for sentence if required

- Fine
- Reparation
- Community work
- Supervision
- Intensive supervision
- Community detention
- Home detention
- Imprisonment.

Generally, as has been suggested above, provided that the judge takes into account the purposes and principles of sentencing, the appropriate sentence is a matter for the judge to determine at his or her discretion. This general statement is, however, subject to three points. First, the legislation which creates the offence might require a particular sentence to be imposed following conviction. In this case, the judge must comply with this. Second, a judge may decide that justice is best served by imposing more than one type of sentence on an offender. As an example of this, the most appropriate sentence for someone who causes damage to a public playground might be a combination of reparation (to fix the damage) and community work (cleaning up the playground on weekends might make the impact of the offending clear to the person). Logically, some combinations of sentences are not possible. Section 19 of the Sentencing Act discusses permitted (and therefore not-permitted) combinations of sentencing. As an example, a person sentenced to imprisonment or home detention cannot also carry out community work, as they are not permitted to leave the prison or place of home detention. Alternatively, it would be unfair for a person sentenced to imprisonment (thereby losing their income) to also pay a fine in most cases.

Third, the Act provides additional guidance on how to approach the selection of a sentence. As we have seen in s8 above, principle (g) states that a sentencing judge must impose the least restrictive sentence possible. Imprisonment is therefore a last resort. Section 11 clarifies that a sentencing judge must first consider discharge without conviction, then conviction and discharge, then conviction and order to come up for sentencing. Section 13 then states that if the offence committed is sufficiently serious that one of the sentences mentioned in s11 are not considered appropriate, a fine should be presumed to be the appropriate penalty (unless imprisonment is required by the definition of the offence). The various types of sentence are discussed below in the same order that the sentencing judge is required to consider them.

Discharge without Conviction

This is seen as a 'last chance' for offenders. We have seen above that one consequence of being found guilty is normally a conviction. As the name of this sentence suggests, however, a conviction may not be considered necessary in a particular case. Instead, a sentencing judge will simply discharge the offender, meaning the offender is free to leave court without a conviction being imposed. If the offender has caused damage to any property, such a sentence may be conditional on the offender compensating the property owner for this damage.

This sentence is often granted when the gravity (or seriousness) of the offending is low and the consequences of the conviction are high, resulting in the punishment being out of proportion to the seriousness of the offending. A common example of this is where a teenager is arrested for minor offending (e.g., minor property damage or disturbing the peace). A conviction in this case might hinder or prevent the teenager from gaining employment in their preferred field (e.g., the Army, or teaching). While a conviction might be appropriate in many cases, for minor offending a conviction can result in far more serious consequences than the offending merits. The teenager's fear that his or her future could be so severely affected by one poor decision often serves as a wake-up call and can be sufficient in itself to deter any future wrongdoing.

Conviction and Discharge

In this case, the offender is given a conviction, but it is considered that the conviction is itself a sufficient punishment, and that no additional punishment is either reasonable or required. This sentence is often an option where an offender is charged with multiple offences in relation to one action. As an example of this, imagine the case of a driver pulled over for speeding who is subsequently found to have excess breath alcohol and to be driving while disqualified. These are three different offences. The judge might feel that all three warrant conviction, but that it would not be reasonable or proportionate to also impose three separate fines. The driver might be convicted and fined for the most serious offence, and then convicted and discharged for the other two.

Conviction and Order to Come Up for Sentence If Required

Under this type of sentence the offender is convicted, but any further punishment is placed on hold. The offender is told that if they learn from this experience and commit no further offences within a specified period (usually in the 6–9 months following the sentencing), the conviction will be the only penalty imposed. If, however, the offender does not learn and is found guilty of a further offence committed during this period, they will be penalised for both the first offending and also the second offending. The sentencing judge for the second offending can impose two separate sentences (one for the first offending and one for the second) but more commonly will increase the sentence for the second offending and comment that this is because of the order to come up for sentencing from the first offending.

Fine

A fine is a financial penalty, with the money being paid to the government. As stated above, under s13 of the Sentencing Act a fine is presumed to be the normal mode of punishment. The amount of the fine might be indicated by the specific offence. If the relevant legislation states a maximum or minimum fine, the sentencing judge must comply with this. Otherwise, the judge has discretion as to the amount ordered. The judge also has discretion as to how the fine is to be paid (whether by a one-off payment or by instalments). The financial circumstances of the offender are a relevant and important consideration.

If the offender has limited means, then imposing a substantial fine will be seen as unjust, and potentially disproportionate, and the amount should therefore be reduced. While this might initially seem unfair, reducing the amount of the fine in these circumstances does have a logical justification. If the amount of the fine is far beyond the offender's disposable income (money left after essentials are paid), this puts the offender in a difficult position. How do they find the money? The offender may choose not to pay for essentials like food or power, which might put their family's health at risk, or they might commit further crime in order to pay, or they may simply not pay the fine, which might lead to a more serious sentence like imprisonment. It is more appropriate to impose a fine that the offender can pay without imposing an undue burden.

If the offender has substantial means, then the amount of the fine can be increased. Again, there is a logical justification for this. In order to achieve a deterrent effect, the amount of the fine must be high enough to disincentivise future offending. If the offender has a high income, the amount needed to effectively act as a deterrent must logically be higher than the amount imposed on someone with a lower income.

Reparation

Reparation involves the payment of money to the victim to compensate for loss or damage to property or for emotional harm. Physical harm to a person cannot be the subject of reparation, although amounts consequential to physical harm (e.g., hospital bills) can be. Under s12 of the Sentencing Act, if a court is permitted to impose reparation to compensate for loss, damage or harm, it must do so unless the financial circumstances of the offender would result in undue hardship. Again, the limited financial means of the offender is relevant, and payments can be made by instalment.

Community-based Sentences

The next four sentences are designed for more serious offending. They are called community-based sentences because the offender remains part of the community during the sentence (as opposed to being isolated from it as is the case with a prison sentence). These sentences aim to achieve a balance between three objectives: enabling the offender to build or maintain working and personal relationships in the community; holding the offender to account; and the safety of the community. The specific nature of each sentence is discussed below.

Supervision
A sentence of supervision targets low-level offending. It is suitable where the offending has an identifiable underlying cause which can be addressed through straightforward rehabilitation. This sentence primarily requires attendance at specific rehabilitation programmes (e.g., drug or alcohol treatment). The offender will be assigned a probation officer, to whom they must report regularly. The offender must also comply with any conditions imposed by the probation officer in addition to attending any rehabilitation programme. Supervision can last from 6 to 12 months.

Intensive Supervision
Intensive supervision targets medium- to high-level offending where the offender has more complex rehabilitation needs. As with supervision, a probation officer is assigned and special conditions can be imposed. Intensive supervision can last for a minimum of 6 months, but can extend beyond the 12-month maximum for supervision.

Community Work
Community work involves the offender carrying out unpaid work in the community as a form of reparation for harm done to that community. It involves anywhere between 40 and 400 hours, which must be completed within 2 years (12 months for any period less than 200 hours). Often these hours are completed in 9-hour shifts on Saturdays to avoid clashes with work, education or religious commitments. Relevant work is assigned, and often occurs on government or local authority land (e.g., cleaning community parks or removing graffiti) or with charitable, religious, educational or health organisations.

Community Detention
Community detention involves the imposition of a curfew which is often enforced through the use of electronic monitoring. An offender will be required to remain at a specified residence during specified curfew periods. A curfew period must be of at least 2 hours' duration, and while numerous curfew periods can be specified, the total time cannot exceed 84 hours per week. The offender may leave the residence outside of these curfew periods, allowing for work or education to continue.

Home Detention

Home detention is the next most serious sentence. While it can be considered rehabilitative (as the offender remains in the community), it is also a punitive sentence (as the offender cannot leave the house without permission). The Court of Appeal (*R v D* [2008] NZCA 254, [65]) has referred to this as a 'hybrid sentence, regarded as neither custodial nor community based'. Offenders on home detention are required to remain at a specified residence at all times unless leave is approved by their probation officer. They may be permitted to leave the property to attend work, education or rehabilitation programmes, but they will be monitored both electronically and otherwise (through phone calls verifying their location). Home detention can be ordered for a period between 14 days and 12 months. It can be the primary sentence imposed, or it can be made available once an offender has served most of a long sentence in jail as a way of beginning reintegration into the community. Because of the potential impact on other people, all adults living in the property must agree to the offender being granted home detention.

Imprisonment

This is the most serious sentence that can be imposed in New Zealand. The only sentence that is more severe, the death penalty, was abolished in New Zealand by the Crimes Act 1961 for all offences except treason. In 1989 the Abolition of the Death Penalty Act removed death as a sentencing option for treason.

If a court is thinking of imposing a sentence of imprisonment, it will usually begin by obtaining further evidence. The first piece of evidence is a Pre-Sentence Report. This will be prepared by a probation officer, and will include information about the offender's personal background, any obvious reasons for the offending, the need for any rehabilitation, the likelihood of reoffending, and a recommendation as to the appropriate sentence. The second piece of evidence is a Victim Impact Statement. This allows victims (which includes family members if the victim was killed) to address the court in writing and explain how they have been affected by the offending.

When determining the appropriate length of the prison sentence, the sentencing judge must first identify a 'starting point'. The wording of the relevant legislation might indicate this. Additionally, the judge will hear arguments from both the prosecution and defence. Finally, the judge will look at the particular offence and see if there are any relevant Sentencing Guidelines issued by the Court of Appeal (which will, from time to time, review the sentences imposed for a particular offence in recent years.) As the sentencing judge will be conscious of the need for consistency in sentencing with other similar offences, the chosen starting point should be similar to those in the Sentencing Guidelines. Once a starting point has been identified, this will be adjusted up or down, depending on the aggravating and mitigating factors of the case, the Pre-Sentence Report and the Victim Impact Statement.

In the majority of cases, the judge will impose a determinate sentence. This is a sentence with a fixed end date (e.g., 9 years, or 1 year and 3 months). If a determinate sentence is for 2 years or less, the offender must be released from prison after serving half of the sentence. They will, however, be required to comply with conditions for the remainder of the sentence term. In such cases the offender is said to be on probation, rather than on parole. If the sentence is for longer than 2 years, then the judge must state a minimum term of imprisonment before the offender is eligible for parole. This term, known as a non-parole period, must not be longer than two-thirds of the total sentence, or 10 years (whichever is lesser). For example, a judge might sentence an offender to a sentence of 10 years imprisonment, with a non-parole period of 6 years. The offender must serve 6 years in prison, but will then be eligible for parole.

There is one situation in which the judge loses the discretion to decide on the appropriate determinate sentence. This is commonly known as the 'three strikes and the maximum' rule, which was introduced in the Sentencing and Parole Reform Act 2010. Section 86A of the Sentencing Act lists 40 'qualifying' (serious violent or sexual) offences to which 'three strikes' applies. The first time an offender commits one of these offences, he is sentenced following the process described previously, and is additionally given a 'first-strike' warning. If the offender subsequently commits another of these qualifying offences, he will not be eligible for parole and must therefore serve the entirety of the sentence imposed. A 'second-strike' warning will also be issued. If the offender then commits a third qualifying offence, the judge must sentence the offender to the maximum sentence permissible for that particular offence.

While a determinate sentence is normally appropriate, in some cases a judge might impose an indeterminate sentence. This is a sentence without a specific end date. Under such a sentence, the offender may be eligible for parole at some stage and therefore be released. Alternatively, she may never be eligible for parole (or may never be granted parole) and will remain in prison for the rest of her life. There are two main examples of indeterminate sentences, which are discussed below.

Life Imprisonment
This is the presumptive sentence for murder. 'Presumptive' in this case means that it is presumed that someone convicted of murder will be sentenced to life. In addition, manslaughter and class A drug dealing also carry discretionary life sentences, which a judge may impose if he or she feels the case warrants it. As the name suggests, life imprisonment means that the offender may remain in prison for the rest of his life and if released will remain on life parole. The sentencing

judge can impose a determinate sentence for murder only if it is felt that life imprisonment would be manifestly unjust in the circumstances, and clear reasons must be given. In some cases, the sentencing judge may decide that the offender can be eligible for parole, and state a minimum non-parole period (which must be at least 10 years). Although theoretically a judge might decide that the offender may never be paroled, this has never happened. The longest non-parole period ever given in this country is 30 years, given to William Bell for killing three people at the Panmure RSA in 2001.

Preventive Detention

This is a sentence available for offenders who, since the age of 17, have committed one or more of a list of specified sexual or violent offences, and who appear likely to commit further offences in the future. For the protection of the community, the offender is given an indeterminate sentence, with a non-parole period of at least 5 years. If the offender is ever released back into the community, they will be managed by the Department of Corrections for the rest of their life (in other words, they will effectively be on parole for the rest of their life). They can be recalled to prison at any time.

Sentencing in Practice

Every year the Department of Corrections and the Ministry of Justice publish relevant statistics on offending and sentencing. On occasion, they also publish detailed studies of particular types of sentencing. The most recent published statistics range from 2014 to 2016, and they provide an interesting look at how sentencing occurs in practice.

General Statistics on Convictions

In the years 1991–2016, between 63,699 and 99,723 people were convicted of offences each year. The highest number of convictions occurred in 2009 and the lowest in 2015 (Ministry of Justice, 2016). The year 2015 also saw the lowest number of adults (76,582) charged with offences (and therefore appearing in court). With just over 77,500 people charged in 2016, this represents a 83 per cent conviction rate. Such a high conviction rate suggests that the police are careful to charge people only once a reasonable amount of evidence has been obtained. The number of people being charged in 2016 reflects a 27 per cent decrease from 2011. (Ministry of Justice, 2016).

Gender and Ethnicity

In 2016, 78 per cent of those convicted of an offence were male. Of all convicted persons, 41 per cent identified as Māori, 37 per cent as European and 9 per cent as Pasifika. These proportions appear to have been reasonably consistent since 1985 (Ministry of Justice, 2016).

Cost of Sentencing

It is interesting to note the cost to the community of each sentence. In 2011, these were estimated to be as follows (rounded to the nearest dollar) (Ministry of Justice, 2011):

- Community work: $7 per day ($2,484 per year)
- Supervision: $12 per day ($4,484 per year)
- Community detention: $17 per day ($6,092 per year)
- Intensive supervision: $17 per day ($6,232 per year)
- Home detention: $58 per day ($20,972 per year)
- Imprisonment: $249 per day ($91,000 per year)

Types of Sentence Imposed

Of the 64,625 offenders convicted in 2016, the most common sentences imposed were (Ministry of Justice, 2016):

- Fine   21,497
- Community work   15,198
- Imprisonment   8238
- Community detention   4162
- Conviction and discharge   3560
- Reparation   3724

- Home detention   2874
- Supervision   3501
- Intensive supervision   1887

Women and offenders under the age of 20 are the most likely to serve a community-based sentence (Department of Corrections, 2015).

Specific Statistics on Sentence Type

The following section considers some specific trends and statistics noted in 2014 in three types of sentence: a community-based sentence (community work), the hybrid home detention sentence, and imprisonment.

Community Work

A total of 17,732 offenders were sentenced to community work in 2014 (Ministry of Justice, 2014a). Of these:

- Approximately 80 per cent were male
- Approximately 43 per cent were Māori, 33 per cent were European and 10 per cent were Pasifika
- Over 40 per cent were aged between 20–29 years of age, with the youngest being in the 15–19 year range (approximately 6 per cent) and the oldest being in the 80–84 year range
- The most common offences attracting this type of sentence were traffic offences (25.6 per cent), violent offences (23.3 per cent) and dishonesty offences (22.2 per cent).

Home Detention

Since its introduction in 2007, the number of sentences of home detention per year has increased from 1822 to 3142 (Department of Corrections, 2015). Of those beginning a sentence in 2014:

- 22 per cent were women (a consistent proportion since 2007)
- 46 per cent were Māori and approximately 40 per cent were European
- The average age of an offender beginning home detention was 34 years, however, the highest proportion (39 per cent) were aged between

20–29 years (the average age of 34 is explained by the fact that the number of over-50s being sentenced to home detention has also increased each year)
- The most common offences attracting home detention are traffic offences, followed closely by violent offences.

Imprisonment
The total prison population at the end of 2014 was 8641. Of these:

- 93.5 per cent were male (8080), 6.5 per cent female (561) and 0.1 per cent other (Ministry of Justice, 2014a)
- Approximately 50 per cent of offenders were under the age of 35, with only 4 per cent under the age of 19 years (Department of Corrections, 2014)
- Approximately 51 per cent were Māori, 33 per cent were European and 11 per cent were Pasifika (Department of Corrections, 2014)
- Over one-third of all offenders claimed gang affiliation, with 71 per cent of gang members being Black Power (Department of Corrections, 2015)
- The most common offences resulting in imprisonment were violent offences (37.9 per cent) followed by sexual offences (25.6 per cent).

It is interesting to note that the number of convictions for violent offences in 2014 was the lowest since 2002.

In 2014, 7114 offenders were sentenced to imprisonment (Department of Corrections, 2015). Of these:

- The average age of a person beginning a sentence was 32 years
- The average length of finite sentence was 18 months
- Approximately 19 per cent of offenders were sentenced to a short-term sentence (less than 2 years)
- Over two-thirds of those sentenced to imprisonment had previously been incarcerated.

It is interesting to note that there has been a general decrease since 2006–7 in offenders being sentenced to imprisonment (Department of Corrections, 2015). Despite this, the number of prison sentences started by women (despite being only 6.5 per cent of the prison population at the end of 2014) has almost doubled every year since 1984–5 and has increased by 55 per cent since 2003 (Department of Corrections, 2015). Also of interest is the fact that by December 2016 the total prison population had risen from the 8641 recorded at the end of 2014 to over 9900 (Department of Corrections, 2016). The reasons for the jump include fewer remand accused being granted bail, longer proportions of sentences being served and increasing numbers of parole recalls.

Indeterminate sentences (life imprisonment and preventive detention) are imposed on between 40–50 offenders each year. While this only amounts to approximately 0.4 per cent of sentences imposed, these offenders now comprise 12 per cent of the total sentenced prison population. There have been 1299 indeterminate sentences since records began in 1945 until 2014 (Department of Corrections 2014a), although note that the Department warns that records from 1945 to 1980 may be incomplete). Of these offenders:

- 45 per cent had been released into the community
- 28 per cent of those released had been recalled
- 43 per cent were European, 42 per cent were Māori and 10 per cent Pasifika
- 12 per cent claim gang affiliation.

It was noted in 2014 that 772 offenders remained in prison, 99 had died, 28 had been deported and 265 were on release into the community (Department of Corrections, 2014a). In relation to age at the start of the sentence, there is a notable distinction between the two forms of indeterminate sentence. Those serving life imprisonment are on average younger than those receiving preventive detention, with the average ages being 27 years and 38 years respectively.

Conclusion

The aim of this chapter has been to provide a brief introduction to the complex nature of sentencing following conviction for an offence. It began by commenting that sentencing is more of an art than a science or mathematical equation. It showed that sentencing judges are required to consider theories of punishment, the Sentencing Act principles and purposes of sentencing in general, as well as the specific aggravating and mitigating circumstances of the offences and the offender. The chapter then discussed the various types of sentence available to be imposed on an offender, and when each sentence (or a combination of sentences) might be appropriate. It concluded by reference to some recent statistics relating to convictions and types of sentencing as a way of demonstrating the use of available sentences and also to provide demographic material on offenders in New Zealand.

REFERENCES

Bentham, J. [1789] 1907. *An Introduction to the Principles of Morals and Legislation*. Oxford: Clarendon Press.
Department of Corrections. 2014a. *Offenders on Indeterminate Sentences*. Wellington: Department of Corrections.
Department of Corrections. 2014b. *Prison Facts and Statistics*. Wellington: Department of Corrections.
Department of Corrections. 2015. *Trends in the Offender Population 2014–2015*. Wellington: Department of Corrections.
Department of Corrections. 2016. *Prison Facts and Statistics*. Wellington: Department of Corrections.
Kant, I. [1785] 2011. *Groundwork for the Metaphysic of Morals*. Oxford: Oxford University Press.
Kant, I. [1790]. 2014. *Science of Right*. Charleston, SC: CreateSpace.
Ministry of Justice. 2011. *Home Detention: A Review of the Sentence of Home Detention (2007–2011)*. Wellington: Ministry of Justice.
Ministry of Justice. 2014a. *Conviction by Sentence Type*. Wellington: Ministry of Justice.
Ministry of Justice. 2014b. *Trends in Conviction and Sentencing*. Wellington: Ministry of Justice.
Ministry of Justice. 2016. *Conviction by Sentence Type*. Wellington: Ministry of Justice.
Posner, R. 1992. *Economic Analysis of the Law*. Boston: Little, Brown.
Rawls, J. 1955. 'Two Concepts of Rules', *Philosophical Review* 64: 3–32.

Key Issues

This final section of the book consists of six chapters dealing with key issues in criminal justice. Randolph C. Grace, Anthony McClean and Sarah Beggs Christofferson begin by surveying psychological treatment models and the principles that lie behind them. Sacha McMeeking then describes the disproportionately high rates of recorded Māori offending before interrogating the factors behind them. Andrew Becroft and Sacha Norrie explore youth crime, the youth justice system and some of the responses available to the courts, before Jarrod Gilbert enters the thorny field of judicial miscarriage and some of the factors that lead to false convictions. In the penultimate chapter, Tara Ross and David Fisher examine how news agencies work, who decides what gets published, how this influences crime reporting and how crime reporting in turn affects public opinion. Finally, Jarrod Gilbert describes the laws of the criminal underworld and how this world operates below and beyond the reach of official law enforcement agencies.

9.

Psychology and Criminal Justice

RANDOLPH C. GRACE, ANTHONY McLEAN AND SARAH BEGGS CHRISTOFFERSON

Introduction

Can crime be cured? Whether or not it can is moot, but once a person commits a crime there is often much that can be done to decrease his or her likelihood of future offending. Ever since the publication of a famous early study of delinquency in American youth by Sheldon and Eleanor Glueck (Glueck and Glueck, 1950), it has been known that delinquent and non-delinquent youth differ in many psychologically important ways. For example, relative to non-delinquents, delinquent youth in the Gluecks' sample held more antisocial attitudes such as defiance, ambivalence to authority and hostility. There were also temperamental differences such as restlessness, inattentiveness, lower conscientiousness and poorer self-control. These differences were found even though the groups of participating youth were of similar age, racial composition, socioeconomic status and intelligence. Furthermore, much of what the Gluecks reported makes good sense in light of psychological theory, and has been replicated in subsequent research. Overall, there is strong evidence that at least some of crime's contributing factors lie among the psychological differences identified in these studies between those who commit crime and those who do not. If such factors are amenable to psychological treatment, then it would seem to follow that future crime could be reduced or avoided.

This chapter will review the basic principles which inform psychological treatment and risk assessment of offenders. These principles are evidence-based because they have been developed from empirical research, and we give examples of their application in New Zealand. The chapter concludes with a discussion of treatment programmes for offenders provided by the New Zealand Department of Corrections.

The Risk-Needs-Responsivity Model

The development of psychological treatment programmes for criminal offenders in New Zealand and overseas owes much to a straightforward framework promoted by Canadian psychologists Donald Andrews and James Bonta and their colleagues since the early 1990s (Andrews and Bonta, 2010; Andrews, Bonta and Hoge, 1990; Andrews et al., 1990). This framework is known as the risk-needs-responsivity model and in its simplest form consists of three elements that need to be considered in developing psychological treatment programmes that aim to reduce reoffending. The first concerns the level of risk the individual presents with regard to future offending, and what this says about case management for the individual. The second concerns the specific factors that interventions should aim to change, termed 'needs' or 'treatment targets'. The third acknowledges that human learning proceeds more easily when the manner in which the treatment is delivered, including how it is 'pitched', is suited to the learning styles, world view, and the general day-to-day concerns of the offender. Thus, treatment delivery needs to take account of responsivity factors to maximise the uptake of treatment content. Let's consider each of these in more detail.

Risk

According to Andrews and Bonta (2010), intensive psychological treatment should be reserved for high-risk cases; in other words, those who are assessed as bearing a higher likelihood of reoffending than other offenders. Stated more generally, the intensity of intervention should be matched to the offender's level of risk: it should be low in the case of low-risk offenders and high in the case of high-risk offenders. Mismatching intensity and risk level might produce a treatment programme for the offender that is counterproductive and could actually increase their risk of reoffending (Andrews and Dowden, 2006).

What is meant by the intensity of treatment? The frequency or duration of treatment sessions (i.e., dosage), the level of professional training of therapists, and the degree to which assessment and treatment 'intrude' into core features of the individual's thinking and feelings are all matters that might vary across intervention programmes, and contribute to their overall intensity. For an example of how risk might inform intervention planning, with a low-risk youth offender who does not yet have established patterns of delinquency, it might be sufficient and appropriate to pair them with a responsible, prosocial and caring adult, who arranges productive leisure activities and accompanies the youth, offering advice and encouragement. However, if the same youth was instead mislabelled 'seriously delinquent' or 'high-risk' and recommended for professionally run intensive group treatment for antisocial behaviour, he or she would inevitably spend time and develop friendships with other youth who are more antisocial. These friendships may persist after the programme is completed, and increase the likelihood of further trouble. However, for cases in which risk is high, more intensive (and more psychologically intrusive) treatment is more appropriate, and likely necessary. Thus, the importance of understanding an individual's level of risk of reoffending when planning interventions is clear. The next section provides an introduction to the ways in which risk is typically assessed in the criminal justice system.

Static Risk Factors: Computer Models to Predict Risk
Research in New Zealand has pioneered the use of risk scales that can be automatically scored using information in computer databases. In 1999 Department of Corrections psychologists Leon Bakker and David Riley, in collaboration with statistician James O'Malley, developed a method of measuring risk level on the basis of criminal offence history called Risk of Conviction, Risk of Imprisonment (RoC*RoI; Bakker, Riley and O'Malley, 1999). The Department of Corrections routinely uses the RoC*RoI with all offenders who receive custodial or community-based sentences. The RoC*RoI is based on criminal history variables already coded into a nationwide conviction database (e.g., number of convictions, age at first conviction, frequency and seriousness of convictions, and total time spent in prison), and provides a single score ranging from 0 to 1 which can be interpreted as the probability that the individual will be imprisoned for a further offence within 5 years. According to interpretive guidelines, a RoC*RoI score of 0.7 or

higher reflects a 'high' level of risk (>70 per cent chance of reimprisonment), scores between 0.3 and 0.69 are in the 'moderate' range, and those who score less than 0.3 are 'low' risk (<30 per cent chance of reimprisonment). The RoC*RoI score is calculated by a computer program, making it a highly efficient screening tool, and is one of the inputs to a wide range of decisions made in the course of sentence management. However, it is important to note that RoC*RoI scores are not valid for certain offender populations, such as youth, and are also not predictive of the risk of specific kinds of reoffending, such as sexual reoffending.

The RoC*RoI is a 'one size fits all' measure for predicting general recidivism among broad categories of offenders. Instruments can also be developed for predicting recidivism with specific offender subtypes. For example, Skelton et al. (2006) developed a scale for predicting risk of sexual recidivism for sex offenders in New Zealand that could also be scored automatically from criminal conviction records. The starting point for their work was a Canadian scale known as the Static-99 (Hanson and Thornton, 2000). The Static-99 is the most widely used and best-validated instrument for predicting recidivism for sexual offenders. Skelton et al. identified seven items from the Static-99 that could be coded from offence history information in the Courts Management System database: Number of Prior Sexual Offences (scored from 0–3), Number of Unique Prior Sentencing Dates (0–1), Convictions for Non-contact Sexual Offence (0–1), Current Sentence Non-sexual Violence (0–1), Prior Sentence Non-sexual Violence (0–1), Sexual Offence Convictions with a Male Victim (0–1), and <25 Years Old at Release (0–1). The item scores are summed to yield a total that ranges from 0 to 9 points and is typically scored in terms of four risk categories: Low (0), Medium-Low (1–2), Medium-High (3–4) and High (5+). These items formed the new computer-scored New Zealand scale, which the researchers called the Automated Sexual Recidivism Scale (ASRS).

Skelton et al. (2006) assessed the predictive validity of the ASRS in three cohorts of offenders who were released from New Zealand prisons in 1998, 1992 and 1987, respectively. Results showed that 10-year recidivism rates were 4 per cent for offenders whose risk was scored as Low, 17 per cent for Medium-Low, 30 per cent for Medium-High, and 50 per cent for High. Because the recidivism rates increased systematically across risk categories, Skelton et al. concluded that the ASRS provided an efficient and successful method for making initial risk screenings for sexual offenders. Subsequently, the ASRS has been implemented within the Corrections Analysis and Reporting System database used by the Department of Corrections to provide actuarial risk information for all sexual offenders in New Zealand to staff responsible for their case management.

For example, ASRS assessments are used to help determine whether an application for an extended supervision order is made under the Parole Act 2002.

An important goal for risk assessment is to be able to identify young persons in the system who are likely to continue to offend as adults, so that appropriate interventions can be provided. However, unlike adult offenders, many youth may have no prior criminal records so risk scales cannot be based on offence history. For this reason, a number of risk measures such as the Youth Level of Service – Case Management Inventory (YLS/CMI; Hoge, Andrews and Lescheid, 2002) and the North Carolina Assessment of Juvenile Risk (NCAR; Schwalbe et al., 2005) have been developed. These are typically scored on the basis of a semi-structured interview which covers topics such as offending behaviour, substance abuse, family issues, and antisocial peers. Using a statistical review method called meta-analysis, Schwalbe (2007) showed that these scales had moderately good predictive accuracy for future offending.

Because of the time required for their assessment (e.g., the semi-structured interview for the YLS-CMI requires on average 30–40 minutes), it would be helpful to have an automatically scored risk measure that could serve as an initial screen for high-risk youth. McKinlay, James and Grace (2015) investigated whether such a measure could be developed for New Zealand using information obtained from the Department of Child, Youth and Family (CYF) and the police. They identified a nationally representative sample of 936 young persons aged 13–17 years who received a youth justice sentence in 2002, and obtained records of their prior contact with CYF and the police. Reoffending was defined as having been subject to a further criminal charge or to an additional youth justice sentence. During a 1-year follow-up, 57.9 per cent of the sample reoffended. McKinlay et al. then devised a predictive model which showed that young persons who were male, younger at the time of their first CYF contact, had more prior court dates and had greater frequency of contact with police were more likely to reoffend. Results showed that the model had good predictive validity. Figure 9.1 shows the survival curves (i.e., proportion of cases that had not reoffended by follow-up time) for four groups of cases defined by their risk scores (Low, Low-Medium, Medium-High and High). McKinlay et al.'s results show that an automatically scored model for predicting high-risk youth is a realistic and practical goal.

The bulk of the information used in the risk assessments described above is 'fixed', and nothing can be done to change it (e.g., a first conviction at a young age indicates a poor prognosis and cannot be changed). Such factors are called static risk factors. Other risk-related variables such as thinking styles, attitudes

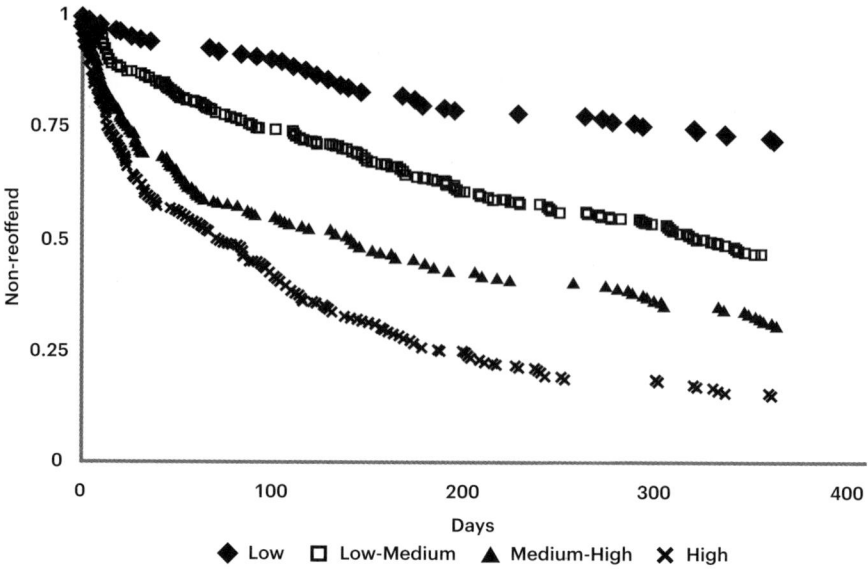

FIGURE 9.1 Survival curves for the four groups (Low, Low-Medium, Medium-High and High) of young offenders in New Zealand based on risk score

Source: McKinlay, James and Grace (2015); used with permission.

and substance use can in theory be changed (although sometimes only with difficulty). These are called dynamic risk factors and are discussed next.

Dynamic Risk Factors

Dynamic risk factors contribute to risk assessment in the same way as static risk factors do, but are also informative in the selection of treatment targets. Risk assessments incorporating dynamic factors are also able to take into account changes made by the offender through participating in treatment and/or with the passage of time, making them potentially more accurate than static-only tools following treatment (Olver and Wong, 2011). For these reasons, it is important to consider both static and dynamic factors in an offender risk assessment.

Several dynamic risk assessment instruments are used in conjunction with static tools by psychologists, probation officers and others working with offenders in New Zealand in order to obtain a more complete picture of their risk level and their treatment needs. These include the Dynamic Risk Assessment for Offender Re-entry (DRAOR; Serin, 2007), the Violence Risk Scale (VRS; Wong and Gordon,

2006) and, for sexual offenders, the Violence Risk Scale: Sexual Offender version (VRS:SO; Olver et al., 2007) and the STABLE 2007 and ACUTE 2007 (Hanson et al., 2007). Research, including from New Zealand, has shown that dynamic factors can improve the accuracy of risk assessments (e.g., Allan, et al., 2007; McGrath and Thompson, 2012; Olver et al., 2007).

Allan et al. (2007) studied a sample of sexual offenders ($N = 495$) from the Kia Marama Special Treatment Unit near Christchurch. Upon entry to the programme, offenders completed 21 self-report assessment tests to measure psychological variables that might be related to sexual offending. The 21 scales covered several broad domains, including sexual attitudes and beliefs (e.g., the Rape Myth Acceptance Scale [Burt, 1980] and the Sex Fantasy Questionnaire [Wilson, 1978]), emotional functioning (e.g., the State-Trait Anger Expression Inventory [Spielberger, 1988]) and interpersonal competency (e.g., the Social Self-Esteem Inventory [Lawson, Marshall and McGrath, 1979]). Allan et al. used factor analysis to identify four broad dynamic factors across the tests, which together accounted for 61.7 per cent of the variance in the data: Social Inadequacy, Sexual Interests, Anger/Hostility and Pro-Offending Attitudes. They showed that higher scores on these dynamic risk factors were correlated with recidivism, and that the dynamic risk factors increased the accuracy of risk prediction beyond the level that could be achieved by static risk factors alone.

Allan et al.'s (2007) results show that offenders' self-reports can provide valid information about risk. Beggs and Grace (2011) tested whether self-reports could also provide a valid measure of treatment change by comparing responses to the psychometric tests both before and after treatment. Although in terms of raw change scores offenders reported considerable gains across treatment, correlations between change and recidivism were variable, and were often opposite to expectation – that is, for some scales greater apparent pro-social change was associated with an increased chance of reoffending. Beggs and Grace suggested that this occurred because offenders with higher scores at pre-treatment (i.e., greater risk) had more opportunity to show improvement. Once this effect was taken into account by controlling for pre-treatment scores (via partial correlations), the change scores were significantly predictive of recidivism in the expected direction, therefore showing that greater pro-social change was associated with a reduced risk of reoffending. Importantly, they also found that treatment change measured by the self-report tests was correlated with change using measures designed to be rated by therapists, such as the VRS:SO (Olver et al., 2007). Beggs and Grace's results therefore show that valid measures of treatment effectiveness can be obtained from offender self-reports. The validity of VRS:SO-assessed dynamic change was also supported by Beggs and Grace, in line with the previous findings of Olver et al. (2007).

Needs or Treatment Targets

Once an individual's risk level in terms of future offending is established, how should this be addressed through treatment? As noted, it is impossible to modify an offender's static risk factors, but the dynamic ones are potential treatment targets. Andrews and Bonta (2010) state that among the many treatment targets a psychologist might work on to promote change, only some are likely to have an appreciable effect on future offending. These targets are termed 'criminogenic needs' because their presence in an individual's life generally increases their risk of criminal offending. Knowledge of criminogenic needs has been further refined by results of studies where needs have been addressed and have impacted on future offending. Such studies (including Glueck and Glueck, 1950) have identified a rich array of factors that, if successfully addressed in treatment, appear likely to produce reductions in offending, including drug and alcohol abuse/dependence, delinquent thinking styles and antisocial values. These criminogenic factors do not reflect criminal behaviour *per se*, but they can be associated with likelihood of offending. For example, an important criminogenic need noted by Andrews and Bonta (2010) is poor achievement in employment or educational contexts, which is of course not a crime. But people with poor work records and low educational attainment often become involved in crime. For this reason, criminogenic needs are sometimes called 'intermediate treatment targets'. The logic is that changing these factors will, in turn, reduce criminal activity. Research has also identified a number of factors that, although intuitively appealing, do *not* seem very promising at all as treatment targets. These factors can therefore be considered to be non-criminogenic (e.g., low self-esteem, depression, anxiety). Targeting them will not necessarily reduce reoffending. As Andrews and Bonta (2010: 261) put it: 'We may help an offender feel better, which is important and valued, but this may not necessarily reduce recidivism.'

Assessing offenders on the full range of criminogenic needs as described above is one of two main approaches used in New Zealand to identify appropriate treatment targets. The other approach is much more focused on the idiosyncratic patterns of behaviour displayed in an offender's criminal history. This is called the 'offence process approach'. Here, the factors requiring treatment are identified from a detailed reconstruction of past offences, and the cognitive and behavioural patterns that are apparent in these. For example, an offender may have completed a previous sentence with the intention to avoid further offending, but later on a series of bad decisions made in the heat of a moment led to another crime. Interestingly, these decisions sometimes indicate to a therapist that the real problem may be, for example, low self-esteem or anxiety. If so, he or she may decide to treat these symptoms rather than the classic criminogenic needs. Similarly, while it might be found that the offender sometimes uses alcohol or illicit drugs, if this has never been a contributing factor in their offending, it would not be a critical treatment target.

Once an offender's criminogenic needs are identified, treatment normally involves strategies to reduce the number or intensity of such factors in the individual's life. Of course, there are often additional steps needed. The offender may not initially see, for example, that something they habitually do is leading them to reoffend. They may therefore need to be assisted to explore this for themselves and develop motivation to make changes. Thus, there is sometimes a good deal of work needed in addressing such 'responsivity barriers', either alongside treatment or, in some cases, before an offender actively engages in treatment.

Responsivity

Responsivity has received less attention from researchers than the other principles in Andrews and Bonta's (2010) framework, perhaps because it is the most complex. Responsivity concerns the offender's ability to respond to a programme and make the desired changes. A mismatch between the offender's learning style, world view, personal and culture-dictated concerns on the one hand, and the therapy context and delivery style on the other, may prevent a positive response and may even lead to outright resistance. Inevitably, this would undermine treatment effectiveness. Some of the results from the Gluecks' 1950 study provide guidance here. They found the young offenders they studied to be normally concrete (rather than abstract or symbolic) thinkers. For this reason, programmes should normally make use of specific, everyday-life examples when analysing problematic situations. Theory, particularly social learning theory, provides more guidance about how effective therapists should behave in treatment settings. Considerable research has shown that highly structured programmes are better suited to the typical offender's learning style, and that programme content should be presented more than once, using several different modalities (e.g., psycho-education, reading material, practice in role-plays; see Gendreau, Little and Goggin, 1996, for review).

A particularly interesting responsivity issue is raised by the offenders' cultural heritage. Consider a substance-abuse treatment programme that is pitched to offenders in a way that emphasises the benefits *to them* of breaking substance use habits. With some offenders, this is all well and good. But what about people whose culture emphasises the importance of responsibility to the extended family – particularly in the context of individual self-improvement? A programme that emphasises personal benefits may seem odd to someone whose primary commitment is to their extended family. Indeed, several programmes in New Zealand have responded to this problem by presenting treatment programmes in ways that are informed by an understanding of indigenous culture. Results suggest that this strategy has benefited reoffending rates (Nathan, Wilson and Hill, 2007).

An Alternative: The Good Lives Model

While Andrews and Bonta's risk-needs-responsivity model has been highly influential for a number of decades, a more recent development is the so-called 'strengths-based' approach to offender treatment, such as the 'Good Lives Model' developed by Tony Ward and colleagues (Ward and Stewart, 2003). Some in the field, such as Ward and Stewart, object to the stance that offenders behave as they do because of 'deficits' in their personal functioning, or that focusing treatment around such deficits will be effective in changing behaviour. Instead, they argue, treatment focusing on their personal strengths and goals will be more effective in motivating change, partly because of the more positive tone that such an approach lends to the treatment process. Rather than targeting a person's deficits, however, the Good Lives Model concentrates on the goals and 'primary human goods' that are highly valued by the individual offender. Good Lives Model proponents argue that in their approach, criminogenic needs will still be addressed, albeit incidentally, and that focusing on positive values will prove more effective in communicating with offenders (Ward and Gannon, 2006).

Given the relative novelty of this model, research has not yet ascertained whether it is in fact more effective than the traditional Andrews and Bonta approach. Nevertheless, a focus on personal strengths, and the adoption of the offender's own personal life goals (instead of avoiding reconviction *per se*) as ultimate treatment goals, might indeed be a valuable way of addressing responsivity barriers. For persistent offenders, criminogenic deficits in individuals do seem undeniable however, and it may take some creativity to mobilise offenders to pursue personal goals in order to remedy deficits that are not immediately relevant.

To conclude, Andrews and Bonta's model has been influential because it offers guidance in answering, in an evidence-based way, three important questions: who gets treatment (it depends on risk level), what should the treatment aim to achieve (it should address criminogenic factors), and how is it best delivered (in accordance with recognised responsivity factors). In each case, the answers initially seem rather vague, because we need much more specific information about risk, criminogenic factors and responsivity factors. Some detail is provided by general research data on offenders, offering a way ahead that will suit many cases. More detailed and individual-focused specification of risk, criminogenic factors and responsivity factors is offered by the offence process approach, which is used with more serious cases in keeping with both the risk principle and the high costs associated with it. If a better alternative is forthcoming in the future, it seems likely that it will contribute new information that still fits within the three-element framework proposed by Andrews and Bonta.

Treatment Programmes for New Zealand Offenders

The New Zealand Department of Corrections is responsible for managing the sentences of individuals convicted of criminal offences, both custodial and community-based. Governed by the Corrections Act 2004, the Department has an important role in contributing to the rehabilitation of the offenders in its care, for the purpose of enhancing public safety. The Department operates a suite of rehabilitative programmes itself and contracts others to supplement this process. In accordance with the Andrews and Bonta framework, these programmes encompass a range of intensity levels, treatment targets and delivery methods. This section provides an overview of the main rehabilitative interventions currently in operation.

The Moderate-intensity Programmes

In New Zealand, participation in programmes begins with assessment. For offenders at the moderate risk level for general and/or violent offending (e.g., based on their RoC*RoI score), this typically includes an assessment of each person and their patterns of offending against a list of known general dynamic risk factors, in order to identify those of most concern for the particular individual. While this allows a degree of individualised treatment planning, the moderate-intensity programmes are run throughout the country (within resource constraints) in group format, precisely because they address a range of criminogenic risk factors known to be common among New Zealand offenders. The programmes are run by trained facilitators who administer a standardised treatment manual under the supervision of professional psychologists as well as cultural advisors. The group treatment modality has clear advantages in terms of efficient service provision. However, there are additional benefits, including the ability for group members to vicariously profit from each other's therapeutic interactions, and receive valuable peer input (Ware, Mann and Wakeling, 2009).

Male offenders at the moderate risk level (excluding sex offenders) are typically eligible for a programme called the Medium Intensity Rehabilitation Programme (MIRP). The MIRP is offered both in prisons and to offenders on community-based sentences or who have been paroled from prison. MIRP participation typically involves attending four 2.5-hour sessions per week for a 3-month period. Targets are modularised, and include offence-supportive attitudes, managing emotions, substance abuse, criminal associates, self-control skills and relationship skills. Participants are guided to explore the various factors that led to their offending in the past, and develop plans for living an offence-free life in the future. For offenders who would be suitable for the MIRP but who are only doing short sentences, there is the Short Rehabilitation Programme (SRP), run on an as-needed basis in smaller groups over a shorter period.

A number of authors (e.g., King, 2011) have argued that while standard rehabilitation models are applicable to females in a general sense (despite being based predominantly on male research samples), specialised 'gender-informed' interventions are needed to take into account a number of gender-specific features of female offenders. For these reasons, the Department of Corrections has developed a specialised programme for females called Kowhiritanga. Also delivered in group format both in prisons and in the community, Kowhiritanga is co-facilitated by a psychologist and trained facilitator. While this programme has many similarities to the MIRP, differences include Kowhiritanga placing more emphasis on relational aspects in group processes, and taking into account common aspects of the New Zealand female offender profile, including the greater likelihood of multiple offence-related, cultural and psychological needs being present, and a higher prevalence of a trauma/abuse history. The SRP has also been adapted for females with short sentences or who are living in areas where Kowhiritanga is not available.

Offenders are provided with programmes on a volunteer basis, although participation is often a requirement for parole. For offenders who are not motivated to attend a treatment programme, the Short Motivational Programme (SMP) has been developed. This consists of five sessions, and can be delivered on an individual or group basis depending on demand. The goal of the SMP is simply to enhance offenders' motivation to participate in rehabilitation by applying the principles of motivational interviewing (for a description of motivational interviewing, see Miller and Rollnick, 2012).

Psychological Services and Special Treatment Units

Of course, the individualised offence process approach described above is more arduous and time-consuming than a standardised criminogenic needs assessment approach. It also requires the involvement of more specialised staff because standardised approaches are less generally applicable and treatment must be tailored more closely to the individual's particular patterns of behaviour. For this reason, individualised responses are normally reserved for offenders who are at particularly high risk of reoffending, or who are likely to commit particularly serious offences.

For many years, individualised treatment was more or less the exclusive domain of professional psychologists working within the Psychological Services division of New Zealand Department of Corrections. Since the late 1980s, however, a number of Special Treatment Units (STUs) have been developed where psychologists (and others) have the opportunity to specialise in particular areas of criminal behaviour (e.g., sexual offending, violent offending or drug-related offending), enabling them to keep up to date with best practice in treatment and with the burgeoning research on the characteristics of different types of offenders. These psychologists not only assess offenders and administer high-intensity programmes, they are also enabled to conduct research projects that may inform future initiatives. In this way, the role of psychologists within the New Zealand Department of Corrections is a clear example of the 'scientist-practitioner' model in action (Waikaremoana et al., 2016).

Currently there are six STUs operating in New Zealand, as well as a number of specialist Drug Treatment Units. Two of the STUs, Te Piriti in Auckland and Kia Marama in Christchurch, exclusively treat men imprisoned for sexual offences against children as stand-alone therapeutic communities. Therapy within these programmes is of high intensity, involving three 2.5 hour sessions per week across a 9-month period, with the remainder of inmates' time spent in therapeutic community activities such as prison employment, community meetings and selected adjunct groups. Treatment follows an extensive individual psychological assessment including an offence process approach, general clinical screening and risk assessment. The treatment is cognitive-behavioural with relapse prevention underpinnings, and targets include offence-related insight, cognitive distortions, deviant sexual interest, emotional regulation and self-regulation skills, intimacy skills and victim empathy. Evaluation research has found these programmes to be effective at significantly reducing the rate of reoffending among those who complete the programme (Moore, 2012; Nathan et al., 2003).

In order to adhere to Andrews and Bonta's (2010) risk principle, a lower-intensity programme for child sexual offenders has recently been developed, and those assessed as being of a low risk level can now be diverted to a 12-week prison-based Short Intervention Programme instead. Moderate-risk offenders on community sentences or released on parole can complete a community-based child sex offender treatment programme as part of their sentence requirements.

The other STUs, which operate in prisons near Christchurch, Wellington, Hamilton and Waikato, target high-risk individuals with serious violent and/or general offending patterns. These programmes are of a similarly high intensity, operate as stand-alone therapeutic communities, and are facilitated by psychologists and trained facilitators. Treatment targets include increasing insight into the cognitive-behavioural patterns underlying their offending, distress tolerance and emotional management skills, offence-related attitudes and beliefs, relationship skills, and the link between substances and offending. Three of these STUs also operate a high-intensity programme for men who have committed sexual offences against adults.

Psychologists employed by the Department of Corrections also engage in treatment with offenders on an individual basis, if one of the group treatment programmes is not available to them. This could be due to, for example, barriers related to low cognitive functioning, behavioural volatility, or other factors making them unsuitable for groups. Psychologists also work with those on community sentences who are assessed as high risk and therefore require a more intensive intervention than the MIRP or Kowhiritanga.

Conclusion

The above programmes do not represent an exhaustive list of offerings run by the Department of Corrections, and offenders are also often provided with programmes run by external agencies on departmental contracts. What is apparent, however, is that the New Zealand criminal justice system prioritises rehabilitation following the risk-needs-responsivity framework developed by Andrews and Bonta (2010). The Andrews and Bonta approach is internationally regarded and carries a high volume of empirical support in terms of effectiveness in reducing recidivism. It seems, therefore, that New Zealand will continue to pursue this method in the hope of achieving significant results in terms of reduced reoffending and the control of crime.

REFERENCES

Allan, M., Grace, R. C., Rutherford, B., and Hudson, S. M. 2007. 'Psychometric Assessment of Dynamic Risk Factors for Child Molesters', *Sexual Abuse: A Journal of Research and Treatment* 19: 347–67.

Andrews, D. A., and Bonta, J. 2010. *The Psychology of Criminal Conduct* (5th ed.). New Providence, NJ: LexisNexis.

Andrews, D. A., Bonta, J., and Hoge, R. D. 1990. 'Classification for Effective Rehabilitation: Rediscovering Psychology', *Criminal Justice and Behavior* 17: 19–52.

Andrews, D. A., and Dowden, C. 2006. 'Risk Principle of Case Classification in Correctional Treatment: A Meta-analytic Investigation', *International Journal of Offender Therapy and Comparative Criminology* 50(1): 88–100.

Andrews, D. A., Zinger, I., Hoge, R. D., Bonta, J., Gendreau, P., and Cullen, F. T. 1990. 'Does Correctional Treatment Work? A Clinically Relevant and Psychologically Informed Meta-analysis', *Criminology* 28: 369–404.

Bakker, L. W., Riley, D., and O'Malley, J. 1999. *ROC, Risk of Reconviction: Statistical Models Predicting Four Types of Re-offending*. Wellington: Department of Corrections.

Beggs, S. M., and Grace, R. C. 2011. 'Treatment Gain for Sexual Offenders against Children Predicts Reduced Recidivism: A Comparative Validity Study', *Journal of Consulting and Clinical Psychology* 79: 182–92.

Burt, M. R. 1980. 'Cultural Myths and Supports for Rape', *Journal of Personality and Social Psychology* 38: 217–30.

Gendreau, P., Little, T., and Goggin, C. 1996. 'A Meta-analysis of the Predictors of Adult Offender Recidivism: What Works!', *Criminology* 34(4): 575–608.

Glueck, S., and Glueck, E. 1950. *Unraveling Juvenile Delinquency*. New York: Commonwealth Fund.

Hanson, R. K., Harris, A. J. R., Scott, T. L., and Helmus, L. 2007. *Assessing the Risk of Sexual Offenders on Community Supervision: The Dynamic Supervision Project*. Corrections Research User Report No. 2007-05. Ottawa: Public Safety Canada.

Hanson, R. K., and Thornton, D. 2000. 'Improving Risk Assessments for Sex Offenders: A Comparison of Three Actuarial Scales', *Law and Human Behavior* 24(1): 119–36.

Hoge, R. D., Andrews, D. A., and Leschied, A. 2002. *Youth Level of Service/Case Management Inventory: YLS/CMI Manual*. Toronto: Multi-Health Systems.

King, L. 2011. 'Interventions for Women Offenders', in K. McMaster and D. Riley (Eds), *Effective Interventions with Offenders: Lessons Learned*. Christchurch: HMA, pp. 207–27.

Lawson, J. S., Marshall, W. L., and McGrath, P. 1979. 'The Social Self-esteem Inventory', *Educational and Psychological Measurement* 39: 803–11.

McGrath, A., and Thompson, A. P. 2012. 'The Relative Predictive Validity of the Static and Dynamic Domain Scores in Risk-need Assessment of Juvenile Offenders', *Criminal Justice and Behavior* 39: 250–63.

McKinlay, A., James, V. L., and Grace, R. C. 2015. 'Development of an Actuarial Static Risk Model Suitable for Automatic Scoring for Predicting Juvenile Recidivism', *Legal and Criminological Psychology* 20: 288–305.

Miller, W. R., and Rollnick, S. 2012. *Motivational Interviewing: Helping People Change*. New York: Guildford Press.

Moore, L. 2012. 'A Comparison of Offence History and Post-release Outcomes for Sexual Offenders against Children in New Zealand Who Attended or Did Not Attend the Kia Marama Special Treatment Unit', MA thesis, University of Canterbury, Christchurch. Accessed 21 May 2017. http://ir.canterbury.ac.nz/handle/10092/7105

Nathan, L., Wilson, N., and Hill, D. 2003. *Te Whakakotahitanga: An Evaluation of the Te Piriti Special Treatment Programme for Child Sex Offenders in New Zealand*. Wellington: Department of Corrections.

Olver, M. E., and Wong, S. C. P. 2011. 'A Comparison of Static and Dynamic Assessment of Sexual Offender Risk and Need in a Treatment Context', *Criminal Justice and Behavior* 38: 113–26.

Olver, M. E., Wong, S. C. P., Nicholaichuk, T., and Gordon, A. E. 2007. 'The Validity and Reliability of the Violence Risk Scale-Sexual Offender Version: Assessing Sex Offender Risk and Evaluating Therapeutic Change', *Psychological Assessment* 19: 318–29.

Rice, M. E., and Harris, G. T. 1995. 'Violent Recidivism: Assessing Predictive Validity', *Journal of Consulting and Clinical Psychology* 63: 737–48.

Schwalbe, C. S. 2007. 'Risk Assessment for Juvenile Justice: A Meta-analysis', *Law and Human Behavior* 31: 449–62.

Schwalbe, C. S., Fraser, M. W., Day, S. H., and Arnold, E. M. 2005. 'North Carolina Assessment of Risk (NCAR): Reliability and Predictive Validity with Juvenile Offenders', *Journal of Offender Rehabilitation* 40: 1–22.

Serin, R. C. 2007. *The Dynamic Risk Assessment of Offender Re-entry (DRAOR)*. Unpublished user manual.

Skelton, A., Riley, D., Wales, D., and Vess, J. 2006. 'Assessment Risk for Sexual Offenders in New Zealand: Development and Validation of a Computer-Scored Risk Measure', *Journal of Sexual Aggression* 12: 277–86.

Spielberger, C. D. 1988. *State-Trait Anger Expression Inventory (STAXI) Professional Manual*. Odessa, FL: Psychological Assessment Resources.

Waikaremoana, W. W., Feather, J. S., Robertson, N. R., and Rucklidge, J. J. (Eds). 2016. *Professional Practice of Psychology in Aotearoa New Zealand* (3rd ed.). Wellington: New Zealand Psychological Society.

Ward, T., and Gannon, T. A. 2006. 'Rehabilitation, Etiology, and Self-regulation: The Comprehensive Good Lives Model of Treatment for Sexual Offenders', *Aggression and Violent Behavior* 11: 77–94.

Ward, T., and Stewart, C. A. 2003. 'The Treatment of Sex Offenders: Risk Management and Good Lives', *Professional Psychology: Research and Practice* 34: 353–60.

Ware, J., Mann, R. E., and Wakeling, H. C. 2009. 'Group versus Individual Treatment: What Is the Best Modality for Treating Sexual Offenders?', *Sexual Abuse in Australia and New Zealand* 2: 2–13.

Wilson, G. 1978. *The Secrets of Sexual Fantasy*. London: Dent.

Wong, S. C. P., and Gordon, A. E. 2006. 'The Validity and Reliability of the Violence Risk Scale: A Treatment-Friendly Violence Risk Assessment Tool', *Psychology, Public Policy, and Law* 12: 279–309.

10.

Māori and Justice

SACHA McMEEKING

Either you defend the status quo, or you invent the future.
—Seth Godin

Introduction

Māori over-representation in criminal justice has been a national problem for 80 years. That means for four generations New Zealand has become accustomed to Māori being more likely than non-Māori to be arrested, convicted and imprisoned. Each generation has witnessed the patterns of over-representation become progressively more pronounced, embedded and ever more complex to both understand and solve. How did New Zealand become a nation that is internationally criticised for the experience of Māori within our criminal justice system? How, as a society, did we seem to reach an unstated acceptance of these realities as normal? How is it that we not have solved these issues when we have had 80 years to do so?

This chapter starts with a statistical portrait of the experience of Māori within the criminal justice system, followed by an exploration of factors contributing to the significant over-representation of Māori. Tracing causation is complex and contested because there is no singular reason for the situation we have inherited and created as a nation: there are multiple, interdependent and poorly evidenced contributors, creating a Gordian knot within a vicious cycle. As a corollary, responses and potential solution-building for Māori over-representation in criminal justice have been many, varied and have seldom produced convincing evidence of positive impact. After reviewing some prominent responses, the chapter invites readers to reimagine the principles, processes and outcomes of New Zealand's criminal justice system by looking at tikanga Māori (Māori customary law). The chapter concludes with a provocation to the new generation of people who will work within the criminal justice sector to be bold in creating meaningful and enduring transformation. As a nation, we cannot wait another 80 years for solutions to manifest.

The 'Problem': Embedded Over-representation

At every stage in the criminal justice system – apprehension, arrest, prosecution, conviction and custodial sentencing – Māori are over-represented. With Māori only comprising 15.6 per cent of New Zealand's population, this means that the number of Māori appearing in the criminal justice statistics is higher than the proportion of Māori in the population as a whole (Statistics New Zealand, 2015b). At each stage of the criminal justice system, Māori experience a much higher likelihood of a negative outcome:

- Apprehension: Māori are 3.3 times more likely than non-Māori to be apprehended for a criminal offence than non-Māori (Doone, 2000).
- Prosecution: Māori are 3.8 times more likely than non-Māori to be prosecuted (Ministry of Women's Affairs, 2001).
- Conviction: Māori are 3.9 times more likely than non-Māori to be convicted (Burton, 2006).
- Custodial sentences: Māori men are seven times more likely to be given a custodial sentence than non-Māori (Burton, 2006), and Māori women are nine times more likely to be imprisoned than non-Māori women (Te Puni Kōkiri, 2011).

The result is that 51 per cent of the male prison population is Māori and 58 per cent of the female prison population is Māori (Statistics New Zealand, 2012). Within the Māori community, 30 per cent of all Māori males between the ages of 20 and 29 have been imprisoned at some time, which contrasts with 10 per cent of the non-Māori population (Department of Corrections, 2007). This pattern of disproportionately making up the prison population has been progressively worsening since the 1930s: in 1936, Māori were approximately 5.7 per cent of the national population (Pool and Kukutai, 2011; 'Total Population', 1966) and 11 per cent of the prison population (Workman, 2016). Over the next decade, that percentage more than doubled to 26.4 per cent, and in the two following decades, from 1950 to 1970, it doubled again (Workman, 2016).

From the 1950s, there has been a series of government-initiated inquiries and reports that sought to understand the worsening and progressively more visible patterns of Māori over-representation across the criminal justice system (Hunn, 1961; O'Malley, 1973; Workman, 2016). These reports comprehensively catalogued consistent trends: Māori are more likely to be prosecuted and imprisoned than non-Māori and, as a corollary, are less likely to have cases dismissed than non-Māori (Workman, 2016). The extent of the problem has therefore been well known and well described for over 60 years.

The future trajectory for Māori over-representation, without transformative change, is that these patterns will endure and amplify. Māori are a young and rapidly growing segment of the population: by 2038 the Māori population is forecast to account for up to 20 per cent of the total national population and of that population half will be under 28 years old (Statistics New Zealand, 2015a). It is also expected that nearly a third of New Zealand's children by 2038 will identify as Māori (Statistics New Zealand, 2015a). If the current pattern of 6 per cent of the Māori population being imprisoned or sentenced to community work at any one time (Te Puni Kōkiri, 2011) remains, we can expect approximately 50,000 Māori to be imprisoned or on a community sentence in 2038. This is likely to disproportionately impact on young Māori, who currently make up 54 per cent of the youth prosecutions.

The consequences of disproportionate Māori representation within the criminal justice system, now and in the future, are profound for families and for our nation as a whole. For families, imprisonment means lower household income, less support for children and more stress and disruption, with a ricochet impact on health and wellbeing outcomes for the family as a whole. Māori recidivism rates are also disproportionately high, meaning that for many families this experience is repeated with cumulative impacts on the family and ever lessening potential for the person who carries convictions to gain secure employment in the future. The human reality of these statistics is that security of income, housing and access to services are all compromised, with a further impact on the level of hope, aspiration and achievement within the home, a phenomenon which Sir Mason Durie (2003) has described as 'trapped lifestyles'.

As a nation, the over-representation of Māori has direct and indirect costs. The criminal justice system is expensive: the annual cost in 2016 per inmate in prison was around $100,000. Any growth in prison population, number of prosecutions and number of associated police and correction staff has a direct impact on New Zealand's ability to afford the educational, health and retirement costs of the nation. Indirectly, people trapped within the criminal justice system have limited opportunities to contribute the national interest, as tax payers or in other ways unlocking their talents to make positive contributions to the community. Ultimately, the over-representation of Māori in the criminal justice system is not a 'Māori problem', it is a New Zealand problem that impacts on our social cohesiveness as a nation, the financial prosperity and choice available to future governments, and the integrity of our national belief in justice and equality.

The First Layer of the Onion: Drivers and Bias

Knowing the extent of Māori over-representation in the criminal justice system and being attuned to the cumulative impacts on communities and our nation does not, however, explain the causes or provide direction for potential solutions. The media have tended to portray causation in one of two simplistic terms: 'Māori are mad, bad and sad' and possess heightened criminal tendencies; or the system is racist, resulting in over-criminalisation of Māori. The answer, however, is not so simple. There is a complex interplay between the drivers of criminal offending (the factors shown to trigger criminal activity) and systemic bias within the criminal justice system, both of which have a deeper causal relationship with the process and consequences of colonisation.

Drivers of Criminal Behaviour

Experiencing socio-economic disadvantage is well recognised as contributing to criminal behaviour. Poverty, low educational achievement and long periods of unemployment have been strongly evidenced as having a causal correlation with criminal activities (Doone, 2000; Tauri and Webb, 2012). There are also lifestyle risk factors that are known to contribute to offending, including alcohol addiction, drug use, gambling, experiences of abuse and domestic violence (Durie,

2005). Specifically in relation to Māori, drivers of criminal offending have been identified as including:

- Having few social ties or antisocial peers
- Family breakdown
- Poor self-management, aggressiveness, poor school attendance and performance
- Unemployment or low-skilled and low-income jobs
- Demonstrating anti-social and violent attitudes
- Living in overcrowded housing, and/or in transient, poor neighbourhoods
- Disconnection from cultural institutions such as whānau, hapū and iwi. (Quince, 2007, citing a report from former Police Commissioner Peter Doone)

This list should in no way be seen as exhaustive and is arguably a partial manifestation of socio-economic disadvantage.

Māori disproportionately experience socio-economic disadvantage with a cumulative, and in some circumstances intergenerational, interplay of factors: lower levels of income, employment security, education, health and housing, contributing to the presence of various lifestyle risk factors. This has led to many commentators arguing that Māori over-representation in the criminal justice system is not a result of Māori identity, rather it is a product of deprivation, poverty and socio-economic disadvantage (Quince, 2007). The argument is that Māori are more likely to engage in criminal behaviour because they are poor, not because they are Māori.

A critical criminology encourages a deeper interrogation of whether socio-economic disadvantage, and the accompanying lived realities of people experiencing disadvantage, is the singular or paramount cause of criminal behaviour. These theorists argue that there is a complex interaction between a number of social processes which create, perpetuate, amplify and overlay the impacts of social disadvantage. For example, the politics of law-making and law enforcement can further marginalise and disenfranchise disadvantaged communities, as well as contributing to systemic bias, such as over-surveillance of these communities (Quince, 2007). Equally, critical theories question the cause of socio-economic disadvantage, particularly considering whether enduring experiences of disadvantage reflect structural inequalities within society and the institutions of our nation that perpetuate disadvantage within particular communities. In a New Zealand context, any structural causes of ongoing Māori socio-economic disadvantage are intimately connected to the ongoing process and consequences of colonisation.

Systemic Bias

Systemic bias is embedded discrimination against a particular segment of the community. It typically manifests as any discretion being used against the community concerned. In the criminal justice system there are multiple points of discretion: whether or not to stop a person who may potentially be engaged in criminal behaviour, whether to prosecute or discharge someone who has been arrested, whether to imprison or release on a community sentence, and so on. In New Zealand, there is ongoing debate about whether Māori experience systemic bias in the criminal justice system. One argument is that the disparity which Māori experience reflects the nature of the offending and that any discretion used against Māori is as a result of factors of socio-economic disadvantage, rather than Māori identity *per se*. The contrary argument is that there is direct and indirect discrimination against Māori in both the criminal justice system and our society more broadly (Ministry of Justice, 2009). These arguments have circulated for over 30 years without resolution, due in part to strong perceptions of bias but limited substantiated evidence of bias (Fergusson, Horwood and Swain-Campbell, 2003).

Perceptions of systemic bias have been extensively recorded in a range of qualitative studies. One of the earliest and most comprehensive reports that engaged with issues of systemic bias was *He Whaipānga Hou*, which drew on three years of research and interviews with the Māori community, police, correctional officers, inmates, community workers and academics (Jackson, 1988). The report concluded that there was marked institutional bias throughout the criminal justice system, particularly in policing and sentencing trends, which materially increased the likelihood of Māori becoming trapped within the system (Jackson, 1988). This report was followed by thirteen other reports between 1998 and 2009, all of which concluded that there was clear systemic bias against Māori (Workman, 2016).

Specific research on bias within the practice of policing has collated numerous examples from both the police and Māori of tangible expressions of bias. Police officers have identified their own bias, with some officers reporting that they are more likely to suspect Māori of an offence than a non-Māori (Maxwell and Smith, 1998). In the same study, 25 per cent of police reported having negative attitudes about Māori and two-thirds of police reported hearing colleagues use racist language against Māori (Maxwell and Smith, 1998). These patterns are repeated in Māori community perceptions of police practice, which include examples of Māori being arbitrarily stopped on the pretext of offending; abuse, both verbal and physical, by police officers; and being provoked by police officers to justify arrests (Te Whaiti and Roguski, 1998).

The potential presence of bias within the police is significant because police officers possess discretion over whether to arrest and charge a person with an offence (Department of Corrections, 2007). Studies have indicated that ethnicity does influence police-officer decisions to stop and question potential offenders (Quinton, Bland and Miller, 2000), which has led to perceptions of police over-surveillance of Māori communities, resulting in disproportionate apprehension of Māori (Quince, 2007). Subsequent discretion points include whether to charge and the seriousness of the offence the offender is to be charged with: the perception is that Māori are less likely to benefit from being warned and not charged, and more likely to be charged with a more serious offence. The Independent Police Conduct Authority (IPCA, 2016) reviewed the use of pre-charge warnings, which are a police discretion to not prosecute an offender despite there being enough evidence to do so. The IPCA identified in that review that Māori were significantly less likely to receive a pre-charge warning than non-Māori, but the Authority was reluctant to attribute this to ethnic bias within the police, noting that additional factors such as severity of the offence, offending history and other factors could have been the material determinants. This position reflects an enduring contestation and reticence about whether perceptions of bias are real, or whether the perceptions are spurious, with the real issues being socio-economic disadvantage which can result in less bargaining power or legal advice, or whether the disparity merely reflects real differences in the rates and type of offending between Māori and non-Māori (Fergusson, Horwood and Swain-Campbell, 2003).

One of the few robust empirical studies that engaged with these three possible causes of disparate conviction rates for Māori concluded that there is statistical evidence for all three causes, including bias (Fergusson, Horwood and Swain-Campbell, 2003). The inquiry used a comparison of self-reported criminal activity against criminal activity that led to prosecution. Statistical controls for individual characteristics included gender, socio-economic status and educational qualifications. The report concluded that Māori patterns of offending, socio-economic disadvantage and systemic bias independently and cumulatively placed Māori at a higher risk of conviction for criminal offending because:

- Irrespective of social background, Māori were at higher risk of offending.
- Young people from low socio-economic backgrounds had a greater risk of conviction than people from advantaged backgrounds, which disproportionately impacts on Māori.
- Independent of self-reported criminal activity and social background, Māori had increased risks of conviction which reflected systemic bias in the criminal justice system. (Adapted from Fergusson, Horwood and Swain-Campbell, 2003: 363–5)

The presence of multiple causes of Māori experiences of the criminal justice system should not surprise: like any complex contemporary phenomenon, there is a web of interdependent, mutually reinforcing and amplifying factors, all of which are products of history and context.

The Second Layer of the Onion: Colonisation as Causation

Māori experiences of structural disadvantage and systemic bias have long roots in New Zealand's colonial past. Colonisation is a multi-dimensional process of taking over a country that involves importing new cultural values, acquiring land and creating new systems of power and law-making which, typically, advantage the coloniser. The consequence of colonisation on indigenous peoples generally is forced impoverishment resulting from the taking of lands and other economic resources, with land loss also resulting in communities breaking apart as families migrate away from traditional homelands to find economic opportunities. Wider cultural disenfranchisement results from laws and policies which criminalise and dissuade the retention of language and cultural practices. Impoverishment, community breakdown, the loss of cultural identity and the wider colonial agenda have directly shaped contemporary Māori experiences of socio-economic disadvantage, the various lifestyle risk factors linked to criminal offending, and bias in the criminal justice system. The criminal justice system has also been used at times as an intentional instrument of the colonial agenda, creating a legacy of tensions between Māori and the criminal justice system.

The taking of Māori land in Aotearoa New Zealand had a swift start and a pernicious tail that lasted until the 1990s. The bulk of Māori land was taken between the late 1840s and the early 1890s, through three main mechanisms: confiscation by the Crown, sale by contract following which the Crown did not honour its obligations under the contract (such as the reservation of particular lands or Crown supply of contracted goods, commonly including provision of hospitals and schools), and the operation of the Native Land Court, which turned collectively held land interests into individualised ownership, facilitating future sales that may or may not have abided collective expectations. Māori resistance to Crown and settler encroachment onto land created the first significant tensions with the criminal justice system. Early Māori offending often involved tribes seeking to protect their land interests, with the Crown using the law to criminalise resistance (Bull, 2004). For example, the Suppression of Rebellion Act 1863 made it an offence for any person to fight in defence of their lands, which was directly targeted at Māori. In addition to creating a new criminal offence, the Act suspended the right to fair trial before imprisonment. In a similar vein, the Māori Prisoners Act 1880 was used in that year against the peaceful movement at Parihaka. The movement occurred between the years 1879 and 1882 and involved passive resistance in the form of the Māori ploughmen of Parihaka ploughing through government survey lines. The ploughmen were arrested, held without trial and imprisoned in the South Island, many hundreds of kilometres from Parihaka. The Māori Prisoners Act was retrospectively used to legitimate and legalise the indefinite postponement of the imprisoned ploughmen's right to a fair trial (Bull, 2004). The movement at Parihaka is recognised as being one of the earliest examples of a non-violent resistance movement, a precursor to and perhaps even an inspiration for well-known passive resistance advocates such as Martin Luther King and Mahatma Gandhi (Buchanan, 2011; England and Torrance, 1991; Page and Sonnenburg, 2003; Scott, 1975). By the turn of the twentieth century, approximately 4.9 million acres of Māori land had been taken in the North Island, while 99 per cent of the South Island had been lost to the Crown and the New Zealand Company, amounting to around 35 per cent of land still in Māori possession (Ministry for Culture and Heritage, 2017; Orange, 2004).

During the twentieth century, the taking of Māori land progressed steadily and became more subtle in its means. Māori land which has been continually held by Māori since prior to colonisation is owned under a separate legal tenure system which recognises the collective ownership of the land and creates a separate administrative system under the Māori Land Court (formerly Native Land Court). Once the various colonial processes of land-taking had been completed, Māori land tended to be concentrated in less productive and remote blocks, which limited the ability of Māori to develop the land for economic gain, a problem which was further exacerbated by legal and practical barriers to raising finance (Boast, 2004). From the 1930s, Māori land became increasingly exposed to forfeiture by local government when rates could not be paid due the land being locked into a state of economic underdevelopment. In this way, over several decades the slow but steady taking of Māori land continued. By the 1950s approximately 26.9 million acres of Māori land had been taken in the North Island, amounting to 96 per cent of Māori land, resulting in 4 per cent of land remaining in Māori ownership. In the South Island only around 1 per cent remained in Māori possession (Ministry for Culture and Heritage, 2017; Orange, 2004).

The taking of land caused multiple dimensions of devastation within indigenous communities. The most practical dimension was that the tools of economic independence were forcibly removed: Māori went from living in prosperous, financially secure communities to having limited to no means of wealth generation and independence within traditional hapū and iwi territories. Over time, land loss triggered an urban migration of Māori from traditional territories with strong community cohesion to city centres. Here migrants were settled under the 'pepperpotting' policy, designed to prevent the formation of 'Māori ghettos', by interspersing Māori families into non-Māori neighbourhoods, resulting in low community cohesion and high isolation (Kingi, 2005; Walker, 1990). The acceleration of urban migration in the 1940s correlated with the debt burdening of Māori land through rates is also aligned with the rapid growth in Māori criminal offending rates from the 1940s (see above).

The colonial agenda was also driven by a belief that Māori and the fledgling state were both best served by breaking down Māori cultural identity to facilitate assimilation into the Western cultural 'ideal'. Māori language, cultural practices and spirituality were intentionally eroded through a range of policies, such as the Native Schooling System, within which Māori were beaten for speaking te reo Māori, and the enactment of the Tohunga Suppression Act 1908 which criminalised the practices and status of tohunga. These policies compounded the impact of physical dislocation from kin-based communities and access to traditional sites associated with cultural practices. It is important to state the obvious: that culture is experienced and perpetuated only within communities of people who share history, language, memories and trust. As Māori communities broke apart due to landlessness and the pull of urban economic opportunities, however notional, it became practically more difficult to maintain language and culture, compounded by a national disregard and denigration of cultural validity and value.

The pernicious consequence of colonisation is that despite it being an historical phenomenon, its legacy has a long-lasting hangover that still manifests today. The current under-representation of Māori as police officers, policy-makers engaged with the criminal justice system, lawyers and judges did not arise overnight; it is a product of successive generations of Māori being expected to fill and be educated for low-skilled career pathways (Quince, 2007). Equally, the tensions and distrustful perceptions between Māori and the criminal justice system can be connected to various periods of criminalisation of Māori, often as a result of an excessive police response to Māori protests against land loss running right through to the late twentieth century (Quince, 2007). More contentiously, the outlook of colonisation, which positions indigenous peoples as inferior, arguably pervades some of the contemporary stereotypes which essentialise Māori as 'mad, bad and sad' (Quince, 2007).

In composite, colonisation is seen to have resulted in social disintegration, stemming from the breakdown of Māori communities and social norms, and the blocking of cultural transmission of language and ideologies (Quince, 2007). Leading Māori academics have described colonisation as an 'attack on the Māori soul' that leads to Māori experiencing in the contemporary era 'trapped lifestyles' (Durie, 2003). Multiple generations of Māori have now lived with the legacy of colonisation, which some commentators assert has resulted in spiritual and psychological damage to Māori through the compounding impact of loss of land, the trauma of surviving violent experiences, and the loss of language and cultural identity (Durie, 2003; Jackson, 1988; Quince, 2007). This argument conflicts with the meritocratic ideal New Zealand upholds: that we all have equal opportunities to achieve success in life, because it fundamentally challenges the assumption that there is an equal playing field to begin with. Consequently, some politicians, the media and many members of the community are uncomfortable drawing a correlation between contemporary Māori experiences and the colonial legacy, dismissing the relationship as too old and too tenuous to be germane to current-day realities. Furthermore, there are also a number of decolonial theorists who argue that the colonial ethic is perpetuated through the contemporary status quo and is not merely an historical artefact (Maldonado-Torres, 2004; Mignolo, 2000).

The causal relationship between Māori offending, socio-economic disadvantage, systemic bias and the intergenerational impacts of colonisation is likely to remain contested and infused with ideological elements. What cannot be contested is that Māori experiences with the criminal justice system are problematic and a product of multiple interacting factors. The United Nations has repeatedly expressed concern about the extent of Māori offending and imprisonment and recommended that the government urgently address institutional and societal determinants contributing to Māori experiences with the criminal justice system (Human Rights Committee, 2016; Working Group on Arbitrary Detention, 2015; Working Group on the Universal Periodic Review, 2014).

Responses: Stepping Stones to Solutions

Over the last 30 years, New Zealand has explored a range of responses to the experiences of Māori within the criminal justice system, many of which have merit. But as the statistics attest, these have not proven to materially abate the enduring patterns of Māori offending and imprisonment. The responses have tended to focus on one of three areas: the people working within the criminal justice system, processes used within the criminal justice system, or programmes which aim to work with people engaged in criminal activity.

People

People-related strategies to address deleterious Māori experiences in the criminal justice system have tended to focus on one of two approaches: increasing the recruitment of Māori staff, and creating culture change within organisations in order to address issues of systemic bias.

Recruitment of Māori staff has been a particular priority for the New Zealand Police and is substantiated by international literature which argues that recruiting people from minority communities is effective in building trust and challenging elements of police culture which may perpetuate bias (Ministry of Justice, 2009). The New Zealand Police have expressed commitment to having a representative workforce, which they consider to be an important contributor to public perceptions of police legitimacy and the trust and confidence placed in the police (O'Reilly, 2014). As of 2014, Māori were under-represented in the police as a whole and particularly in leadership positions: 10 per cent of the total police force were of Māori descent and there were only a handful of Māori in District-, Area- or Executive-level leadership positions (O'Reilly, 2014). The New Zealand Police have instigated a number of strategies to increase recruitment of Māori into the organisation, to facilitate more Māori progressing to leadership roles and to restructure roles with specific responsibilities for Māori responsiveness (O'Reilly, 2014).

In parallel, the police have also instigated a number of strategic interventions aimed at improving organisational culture within the force. Common approaches used internationally in circumstances of bias are the development of responsiveness strategies, cultural awareness training, changing reward structures within the organisation to incentivise greater responsiveness to the community affected by bias, reducing individual discretion through more directive policies or monitoring procedures, and greater public accountability for performance relating to the affected community (Ministry of Justice, 2009). The New Zealand Police are implementing a suite of such programmes, including partnering with iwi and Māori within regions to increase collaborative preventive and responsive work programmes (O'Reilly, 2014). The Turning of the Tide Strategy, developed in 2012 by the Police Commissioner's Māori Focus Forum (a high-level Māori advisory board) is one such strategy, which enables iwi and urban Māori organisations to lead the development of crime prevention plans within their area, bringing in all organisations and community leaders who have the potential to contribute to crime reduction (New Zealand Police, n.d.).

The efficacy of these approaches is difficult to gauge due to organisational culture and bias being difficult to objectively assess, and the multiple causality of Māori offending and imprisonment. Some commentators also question whether these types of strategies are capable of effecting substantial change. In their view, populating institutions with Māori and creating more amenable culture change does not engage with the fundamental causation of Māori experiences with the criminal justice system and is little more than a tokenistic response (Tauri, Walters and Bradley, 2005).

Processes

Over the last 40 years there have also been procedural changes within the criminal justice system which have sought to integrate tikanga Māori elements as a means of ameliorating some of the disproportionate conviction and imprisonment outcomes Māori experience. The first processes emerged in the 1970s, with urban marae managing an alternative to court processes for less serious offences (Quince, 2007). The model is held on marae and uses a community panel to facilitate a restorative justice process that agrees to a plan of action which can result in the offender being discharged without conviction and no further criminal action being pursued (Quince, 2007). Since that time, marae-based processes have grown, particularly in the area of youth justice.

Rangatahi Courts for youthful offenders were first established in 2008. Rangatahi Courts sit on marae with a presiding judge who applies standard law but incorporate elements of tikanga Māori and te reo Māori into court processes and outcomes (Taumaunu, 2014). The Rangatahi Court commences with a pōwhiri, followed by a mihimihi from all of the participants in order to cement relationships between all parties (Taumaunu, 2014). Kaumātua and kuia from the marae commence the proceedings through a mihi, and remain in attendance for the proceedings, often providing life advice as appropriate. The young person is required to learn in advance and deliver their pepeha at the start of the proceedings, which is one way of rebuilding cultural identity and connectivity. The outcomes of Rangatahi Court processes can also include tikanga Māori-based programmes which further build upon a positive cultural identity. A Ministry of Justice-commissioned evaluation of the Rangatahi Courts in 2012 found that they were not seen as an easy option and were contributing multiple positive outcomes, both to offenders and communities. Notable outcomes included offenders being more likely to perceive the process as legitimate and an increased likelihood of reduced future offending (Davies, Whaanga and Kaipuke Consultants, 2012).

These processes exist within a broader programme of adopting restorative processes, many of which arguably draw upon principles of tikanga Māori and are being applied across the criminal justice system as a whole (Quince, 2007). Other examples include the Family Group Conference, which was an early approach to youth offending that brings together victim, offender and whānau to discuss the offending and impacts, and to produce an action plan; and the more recent Victims of Offences Act 2002, which encourages face-to-face engagement between the offender and the victim (Quince, 2007). These processes, while designed for all participants in the criminal justice system, have particular resonance for Māori. From 2002 there has also been the ability for offenders at the time of sentencing to call a witness to present on their behalf regarding any elements of their cultural background that may have impacted on their offending (Quince, 2007).

Notwithstanding their apparent utility, the efficacy and desirability of these process changes within the criminal justice system have also been contested. Advocates cite examples of personal transformation occurring as a result of marae-based processes and argue for their merit as an effective intervention in the perpetuation of Māori disadvantage within the system. Critics, however, argue that marae processes amount to cultural co-option that grafts cultural elements in a piecemeal way without addressing the underlying structural and institutional contributors to Māori disadvantage (Jackson, 1995; Tauri, Walters and Bradley, 2005). These commentators encourage a more fundamental reconsideration of the place of marae and communities within a criminal justice system (Quince, 2007).

Programmes

Since the early 1980s there have a number of programmes developed from both inside and outside the criminal justice system which draw upon tikanga Māori, Māori identity, and community development to address causes of offending.

Māori Focus Units inside prisons are among the most well-known examples of these programmes. The first Māori Focus Unit was established in 1997 at Hawke's Bay Prison, a significant milestone given that until the early 1990s it was prohibited to speak or write in te reo Māori inside prisons (Workman, 2016). Māori Focus Units are residential units that use intensive te reo and tikanga Māori elements in their programmes to build cultural connectivity and culturally sourced resilience in the hope of reducing future offending (Quince, 2007). There are also programmes available to inmates not housed in Māori Focus Units that integrate tikanga Māori into various therapeutic programmes in order to reduce the causes of recidivism (Quince, 2007). These programmes operate within a Framework for the Reduction of Māori Offending (FReMO), which is a globally pioneering approach to integrate tikanga Māori with Western science to assess future risks of recidivism and recommend targeted interventions. For example, FReMO assesses whether Māori inmates have issues with their Māori identity or whānau cohesion and recommends programmes accordingly (Quince, 2007). Many commentators commend these programmes as a constructive response to reduce recidivism, complemented by supporting programmes within the Department of Corrections to build relationships between inmates and their whānau, with kaumātua and kuia being available to inmates, and cultural awareness training for staff (Quince, 2007). However, other commentators express caution about the value of programmes which focus on individuals rather than the whānau as a whole, and about the integrity of how tikanga is integrated into both assessments and programmes (Mihaere, 2015).

More broadly, Te Puni Kōkiri (2011) has questioned the efficacy of programmes for Māori that are not designed and led by Māori. Existing government and non-Māori programmes are considered to have low probability of success for the following reasons:

- Interventions tend to be based on risk factors and individual treatment, which are inconsistent with the need for integrated solutions that work with whānau and the offender.
- The complex and dynamic nature of offending as a social problem means that a linear relationship between evidence and outcomes is unlikely to apply.
- There is a failure to address broader social, economic and intergenerational issues for whānau and Māori communities that drive offending.
- There is limited engagement of 'at risk', hard-to-reach whānau and communities in the programmes. (Adapted from Te Puni Kōkiri, 2011)

There are also a wide range of programmes driven by Māori organisations that use Māori methods to reduce offending and reoffending. These programmes often incorporate elements of tikanga Māori, building cultural identity, and working with the whānau as a whole, rather than solely with the offender (Te Puni Kōkiri, 2010). The presence and diversity of Māori programmes can be expected to grow significantly with the maturation of Whānau Ora. Whānau Ora is a culturally embedded concept of 'family wellbeing' that is now the rubric for a compendium of nationwide initiatives including public policy reforms, the redesign of social service delivery and new opportunities for 'bottom-up' transformation. The premise and architecture of Whānau Ora is arguably grounded in the academic work of Sir Mason Durie. His body of work, stretching over decades, has propounded a key thesis that Māori transformation must be led by Māori, premised in Māori knowledge and infused with belief in the capability of Māori to develop sustainable change on their own terms. This thesis reflects an inherent and critical value being placed on self-determined approaches that are founded in Māori values, knowledge and philosophies (Durie, 2003, 2011). Equally, his work elegantly reframes the popular positioning of Māori as a 'problem people' to people who experience challenges, many of which have a chain of causation rooted in colonisation, and who have the requisite resources and capabilities to forge solutions. The corollary of Durie's work is that government-led solutions are confined to limited efficacy unless and until they are reconceptualised from within Māori cultural knowledge and involve significant Māori leadership in their design and delivery.

Whānau Ora makes two significant departures from the dominant government-led approach to addressing social disadvantage. Firstly, Whānau Ora is premised on a whānau-centred approach to achieving social gains: the focus should be on working with the collective holistically rather than solely with an individual. Secondly, Whānau Ora resolutely advances a 'strengths-based' approach to working with whānau: recognising and building on the existing capabilities and aspirations within whānau to generate their own solutions and pathways. These two critical elements of Whānau Ora stand in marked contrast to the positivist, expert-led interventionist approach of mainstream approaches to social needs. The New Zealand government has recognised the dissonance between existing government-led services and Whānau Ora and, importantly, that the existing approach is not achieving social gains for Māori:

> Government health and social services for Māori have not typically been designed to take a whānau-centred approach, focusing instead on individuals and single-issue problems. As a result, delivery of services to whānau has often been fragmented, lacking integration and coordination across agencies and social service providers, and unable to address complexities where several problems coexist. (Te Puni Kōkiri, 2015: 9)

Consistent with this philosophy, government has devolved responsibility for funding programmes that address Māori experiences of disadvantage to three Commissioning Agencies that are led by the local community. The Whānau Ora Commissioning Agencies established in 2014 are independent of government and have a reasonable degree of latitude in their model of commissioning and prioritising for investment. These characteristics enable a localised, responsive approach to whānau-centred, strengths-based initiatives that generate social, cultural and economic gains by and for Māori communities. The Whānau Ora Commissioning Agencies are now collectively responsible for approximately

$30 million per annum, comprised of a quantum of ongoing Whānau Ora-tagged commissioning funds and *ad hoc* amounts of additional government funds transferred for specified areas of social gain. The scale and relative autonomy in commissioning has enabled significant advances in whānau-led transformation initiatives and novel service models, producing a body of social value creation and social change within Māori communities that is both critical to address known disparities and inspiring in its courage, diversity and impact. The devolution model itself is arguably one of, if not the, most significant transfers of responsibility from the government to Māori in New Zealand's history as it allows Māori to lead their own transformation journeys, premised on cultural knowledge and holistic concepts of wellbeing.

From publicly available information, it is difficult to assess how much commissioning money has been invested in programmes which aim to reduce Māori offending, criminalisation and imprisonment. However, it is clear that addressing the determinants and experiences of social disadvantage is a shared priority for all three Commissioning Agencies. There is cause for optimism that Whānau Ora investment opportunities will catalyse and support innovative programmes which are capable of generating transformational change for and with Māori.

Ultimately, solving the national problem of Māori over-representation across the criminal justice system is likely to require a collage of solutions that collectively address the multiple elements of causation, which will require contributions from government, Māori and other organisations connected to the criminal justice system. However, if we are to engage with the critical commentary, more may also be needed. To create enduring change to a complex, embedded problem we may need to explore more fundamental change to the principles of our criminal justice system and the causes of structural inequality and disadvantage.

Reimagining the Criminal Justice System: What Could Be?

The criminal justice system that we have inherited is premised on a suite of principles that are rarely questioned, and operates within a wider societal construct that is equally rarely addressed as part of the solution to problems with the criminal justice system.

Principles

New Zealand's criminal justice system is premised on individual responsibility and is designed to achieve deterrence and retribution for offending (Tauri, Walters and Bradley, 2005). Traditional tikanga Māori, in contrast, supported a pre-contact criminal justice system which was premised on collective accountability and designed to achieve restoration of mana and social bonds (Tauri, Walters and Bradley, 2005). These principles have the potential to infuse a contemporary New Zealand criminal justice system if the architects and practitioners within it are willing to explore bolder solutions than we have done to date.

Criminal justice within traditional tikanga Māori was framed by the principles of whanaungatanga, tauutuutu, tapu, noa, mana and muru. Whanaungatanga is the principle of relationship-building and maintenance, which is paramount within tikanga Māori because of the genealogical relationships between people, whānau, hapū, iwi and the natural environment. There is a fundamental driver to maintain equilibrium and reciprocity in relationships, which is achieved through the principle of tauutuutu (Quince, 2007). In pre-European times, the processes of social control sought to maintain equilibrium through the balancing principles of tapu and noa, which in a legal context designate what is lawful behaviour and what is not (Quince, 2007). Within tikanga, serious offences were considered to injure personal tapu and the mana of an individual or collective. Historical accounts include a number of hara (akin to the notion of an offence), such as murder, suicide, infanticide, rape, incest, adultery, domestic violence and theft (Joseph, 1999). Injury to tapu and mana called for restoration through the process of tauutuutu, which aimed to effect recompense to restore mana and repair relationships damaged by the offending (Quince, 2007).

One of the key institutions through which recompense and restoration occurred is muru. Muru involves the taking of personal property as compensation, and the nature of muru, whether peaceful or violent, was determined by a range of factors that included the mana of the victim and the offender and the seriousness of the offence (Ministry for Culture and Heritage, 2012). In what has been described as the greatest muru on record, in August of 1872 an Opunake Chief Te Kahui Te Kararehe, who lived with his wife at the settlement of Te Namu, eloped with Lydia, the wife of chief Aperama of Parihaka (Taranaki Veteran, 1919). Kahui had been forbidden to marry Lydia due to his and Aperama's high rank and arranged marriages, so Kahui and Lydia's elopement was the cause for muru, and the villagers of Te Kahui Te Kararere became liable for plunder (Taranaki

Veteran, 1919). Some valuable items such as guns and food were hidden in the local sawmill, but the bulk of the villagers' precious possessions were placed in bundles at the front of the marae, ready for the taking. The first taua muru (raiding party) from Matakaha, the closest village, took 'old clothes, blankets, boxes, kits, eel-baskets, cooking utensils and anything moveable that they could carry away'. Taua muru from Umuroa, Nuku-Te-Apiapi and Waitaha arrived the following day, taking 'fowl, duck, goose, turkey and pig in the vicinity of or on the lands belonging to the village' (Taranaki Veteran, 1919: 99). Kahui's people began to look 'exceedingly gloomy'. The next day, a taua muru from Taungatara, Punehu and Ouri confiscated 'every horse, bullock, cow and calf they could find' (Taranaki Veteran, 1919). When the taua muru of Parihaka, the main aggrieved party arrived, there was little remaining of any possessions. Two 'old naked women' from Parihaka cut themselves while setting the village alight. The Te Namu people sat and allowed this happen. Of note is that when a local woman falsely claimed there was a sick person in one of the whare, the muru was immediately suspended and everyone, including the taua muru, worked to rescue the person from the house. Once it had been established that the house was empty, the muru proceeded (Taranaki Veteran, 1919: 100). After all had burnt, the taua muru was fed by the Te Namu people, who themselves ate nothing. Once the meal had been consumed, the Parihaka taua muru rose and left. 'Everything had been done in perfect order, and in accordance with the best of their old traditions', and 'the muru had dissolved the marriages of Kahui and Betty, of Aperama and Lydia, and had solemnized the marriage of Kahui and Lydia; she became his legal wife according to Maori custom, and she remained his wife so long as he lived' (Taranaki Veteran, 1919: 102).

The elements of muru and tauutuutu that contrast with our contemporary expectations of criminal justice are that the community as a whole was accountable for and provided recompense for the hara, and that at the conclusion of the muru, relationships were restored in an enduring way. It is interesting to contemplate how these principles could meaningfully frame a contemporary criminal justice system. One of the key elements of imprisonment that has been criticised is removing the inmate from their whānau, which is considered to perpetuate a cycle of offending by isolating the offender and preventing solutions being formed which engage with contextual factors that trigger offending (McIntosh and Radojkovic, 2012). What if offenders were not removed from their environments? What if whānau as a whole bore some level of responsibility for a family member's offending? What if the offender's wider community had a role in enforcing accountability? What if the treatment of an offender directly responded to the victim's needs? Would these principles change the nature, extent and type of Māori offending and could they provide some level of enduring transformation to the national problem of Māori disproportionate disadvantage in the criminal justice system? There are no knowable answers to these questions because there has been no appetite to revisit the fundamental principles of our criminal justice system. However, there have been repeated calls from Māori and critical commentators for mechanisms that would allow tikanga Māori to be reinvigorated as a system of law that applies in our criminal justice system with greater autonomy for Māori-framed solutions (Jackson, 1988; Tauri and Webb, 2012; Workman, 2016). Given the scale and consequence of the Māori over-representation in criminal justice which shows no sign of relenting, it is perhaps contingent on the next generation of participants in the criminal justice system to explore bolder, systemic change to the principles under which we operate.

Causation

The structural causation of embedded socio-economic disadvantage is well recognised as contributing to Māori experiences of the criminal justice system, as a trigger for offending and as a contributor to disproportionately heavy treatment and outcomes in the criminal justice system and the formation of intergenerational cycles. However, responses to Māori disadvantage have concentrated on direct interventions which address discrete, individualised experiences, such as therapeutic engagement or increased recruitment of Māori police officers. These solutions, while having merit, do not engage with the causes of structural inequality and disadvantage, with their roots in colonisation and an insidiously broad contemporary impact across all measures of health and wellbeing. If we are serious as a nation that we want to curb, and over time solve, Māori over-representation in our criminal justice system, we will need to invest in solving structural disadvantage and recognise that intergenerational cycles of disadvantage will not be cured within a political cycle or with solutions known to the status quo of today.

Conclusion

Māori over-representation in the criminal justice system is a significant contemporary issue with profound impacts for individuals, families, communities and our nation as a whole. It is caused by a complex interplay of factors which are politically and ideologically contested by all sides. The extent to which Māori over-representation is attributed to higher Māori offending, socio-economic disadvantage, systemic bias or the legacy of colonisation will depend in part on the persuasion of rhetoric and commentary. Owing to the lack of robust evidence and the complexity of assigning attribution for any complex contemporary issue, there is a high chance that the status quo will continue when it comes to the theorised causation of Māori offending. Equally, the solutions for this very problem are contested and seemingly incomplete in isolation. Perhaps the only certainty is that this reality should not be allowed to continue, and that on existing patterns it will not only continue but will exacerbate over time. The status quo perpetuates the status quo, which is a disservice to us all. Perhaps it is time for bold and transformative approaches to a problem that has haunted us for over 80 years.

Glossary of Māori Terms

Aotearoa	New Zealand
hapū	sub-tribe
hara	offence or crime
iwi	tribe
kaumātua	elder, often a person of status within whānau/families
kuia	elderly woman, grandmother
mana	influence, prestige, reputation
mihi	to greet, pay tribute, acknowledge or thank
mihimihi	speech of greeting, introductory speeches at the beginning of a gathering
muru	ritualistic redistribution of property, compensation through confiscation, a form of restorative justice
noa	unrestricted, safe, profane
pepeha	the saying or recitance of one's whakapapa or tribal history
pōwhiri	welcome ceremony at marae

rangitahi	younger generation, youth
take	claim or right
tapu	restricted, set aside, dedicated for a purpose
taua	war party, group
taua muru	raiding party
tauutuutu	concept of reciprocity, payment or recompense
te reo/te reo Māori	the language/Māori language
tikanga	law, correct and proper practices, customary law/lore
whānau	extended family
whare	house
whanaungatanga	familial obligations, kinship

REFERENCES

Boast, R., Erueti, A., McPhail, D., and Smith, N. F. 2004. *Māori Land Law* (2nd ed.). Wellington, NZ: LexisNexis.

Buchanan, R. 2011. 'Why Gandhi Doesn't Belong at Wellington Railway Station', *Journal of Social History* 44(4), 1077–93.

Bull, S. 2004. 'The Land of Murder, Cannibalism, and All Kinds of Atrocious Crimes? Maori and Crime in New Zealand, 1853–1919', *British Journal of Criminology* 44(4): 496–519.

Burton, M. 2006. 'The Effective Interventions Initiatives and the High Number of Maori in the Criminal Justice System', *Beehive.govt.nz*. Accessed 21 May 2017. https://www.beehive.govt.nz/speech/effective-interventions-initiatives-and-high-number-maori-criminal-justice-system

Davies, L., Whaanga, J., and Kaipuke Consultants. 2012. *Evaluation of the Early Outcomes of Ngā Kooti Rangatahi*. Wellington: Ministry of Justice.

Department of Corrections. 2007. *Over-representation of Māori in the Criminal Justice System: An Exploratory Report*. Wellington: Department of Corrections.

Doone, P. 2000. *Report on Combating and Preventing Māori Crime: Hei Whakarurutanga Mō Te Ao*. Wellington, NZ: Crime Prevention Unit.

Durie, M. 2003. 'Imprisonment, Trapped Lifestyles, and Strategies for Freedom', in *Ngā Kāhui Pou: Launching Maori Futures*. Wellington: Huia, pp. 59–73.

Durie, M. 2005. *Ngā Tai Matatū: Tides of Māori Endurance*. Melbourne: Oxford University Press.

Durie, M. 2011. *Ngā Tini Whetū: Navigating Māori Futures*. Auckland: Huia.

England, J. C., and Torrance, A. J. 1991. *Doing Theology with the Spirit's Movement in Asia*. Singapore: Association for Theological Education in South East Asia.

Fergusson, D. M., Horwood, L. J., and Swain-Campbell, N. 2003. 'Ethnicity and Criminal Convictions: Results of a 21-year Longitudinal Study', *Australian and New Zealand Journal of Criminology* 36(3): 354–67.

Human Rights Committee. 2016. 'Human Rights Committee Considers the Report of New Zealand'. Accessed 17 May 2017. http://www.ohchr.org/EN/NewsEvents/Pages/DisplayNews.aspx?NewsID=17228&LangID=E

Hunn, J. K. 1961. *Report on Department of Maori Affairs with Statistical Supplement*. Wellington: Government Printer.

Independent Police Conduct Authority. 2016. *Review of Pre-charge Warnings*. Accessed 21 May 2017. http://www.ipca.govt.nz/Site/publications/Reports-on-investigations/Reports-2016/2016SEP14-Pre-Charge-Warnings.aspx

Jackson, M. 1988. *Māori and the Criminal Justice System: He Whaipaanga Hou: A New Perspective*. Wellington: Department of Justice

Jackson, M. 1995. 'Justice and Political Power: Re-asserting Māori Legal Processes', in K. Hazlehurst (Ed.), *Legal Pluralism and the Colonial Legacy*. Aldershot, UK: Avebury, pp. 243–65.

Joseph, R. 1999. *Māori Customary Laws and Institutions: Crimes against the Person, Marriage, Interment, Theft*. Hamilton: Te Matahauraki Research Institute, University of Waikato.

Kingi, T. K. 2005. 'Indigeneity and Māori Mental Health', paper presented at the International Symposium on Indigenous Inspiration in Health, 25 November, Waitangi.

Maldonado-Torres, N. 2004. 'The Topology of Being and the Geopolitics of Knowledge: Modernity, Empire, Coloniality', *City* 8(1): 29–56.

Maxwell, G., and Smith, C. 1998. *Police Perceptions of Maori*. Wellington: Institute of Criminology, Victoria University of Wellington.

McIntosh, T., and Radojkovic, L. 2012. 'Exploring the Nature of the Intergenerational Transfer of Inequalities Experienced by Young Māori People in the Criminal Justice System', in D. Brown (Ed.), *Indigenising Knowledge for Current and Future Generations: Symposium Proceedings*. Auckland: Ngā Pae o te Māramatanga, New Zealand's Indigenous Centre of Research Excellence, University of Auckland, pp. 38–48.

Mignolo, W. 2000. *Local Histories/Global Designs: Coloniality, Subaltern Knowledges, and Border Thinking*. Princeton, NJ: Princeton University Press.

Mihaere, R. 2015. 'A Kaupapa Māori Analysis of the Use of Māori Cultural Identity in the Prison System', PhD thesis, Victoria University of Wellington.

Ministry for Culture and Heritage. 2012. 'Māori Values and Practices'. *NZ History*. Accessed 21 May 2017. https://nzhistory.govt.nz/culture/frontier-of-chaos/maori-values

Ministry for Culture and Heritage. 2017. 'Maori Land Loss, 1860–2000.' *NZ History*. Accessed 21 May 2017. https://nzhistory.govt.nz/media/interactive/maori-land-1860-2000

Ministry of Justice. 2009. *Identifying and Responding to Bias in the Criminal Justice System: A Review of International and New Zealand Research*. Wellington: Ministry of Justice.

Ministry of Women's Affairs. 2001. *Maori Women: Mapping Inequalities and Pointing Ways Forward*. Wellington: Ministry of Women's Affairs.

New Zealand Police. n.d. 'The Turning of the Tide: A Whānau Ora Crime and Crash Prevention Strategy 2012/13–2017/18'. Accessed 21 May 2017. http://www.police.govt.nz/about-us/maori-police/turning-tide

O'Malley, P. 1973. 'The Amplification of Maori Crime: Cultural and Economic Barriers to Equal Justice in New Zealand', *Race* 15(1): 47–57.

Orange, C. 2004. *An Illustrated History of the Treaty of Waitangi*. Wellington: Bridget Williams Books.

O'Reilly, J. 2014. *A Review of Police and Iwi/Maori Relationships: Working Together to Reduce Offending and Victimisation among Maori*. Wellington: New Zealand Police.

Page, M. E., and Sonnenburg, P. M. 2003. *Colonialism: An International, Social, Cultural, and Political Encyclopedia*. Santa Barbara, CA: ABC-CLIO.

Pool, I., and Kukutai, T. 2011. 'Taupori Māori – Māori Population Change', *Te Ara – Encyclopedia of New Zealand*. Accessed 21 May 2017. http://www.TeAra.govt.nz/en/interactive/31311/maori-population-1841-2006

Quince, K. 2007. 'Māori and the Criminal Justice System in New Zealand', in J. Tolmie and W. Brookbanks (Eds), *The New Zealand Criminal Justice System*. Auckland: LexisNexis, pp. 333–58.

Quinton, P., Bland, N., and Miller, J. 2000. *Police Stops, Decision-making and Practice*. London: Home Office.

Scott, D. 1975. *Ask That Mountain: The Story of Parihaka*. Auckland: Heinemann/Southern Cross.

Statistics New Zealand. 2012. 'New Zealand's Prison Population', *StatsNZ*. Accessed 21 May 2017. http://www.stats.govt.nz/browse_for_stats/snapshots-of-nz/yearbook/society/crime/corrections.aspx

Statistics New Zealand. 2015a. 'How Is Our Māori Population Changing?', *StatsNZ*. Accessed 21 May 2017. http://www.stats.govt.nz/browse_for_stats/people_and_communities/maori/maori-population-article-2015.aspx

Statistics New Zealand. 2015b. 'National Ethnic Population Projections: 2013(Base)–2038', *StatsNZ*. Accessed 21 May 2017. http://www.stats.govt.nz/browse_for_stats/population/estimates_and_projections/NationalEthnicPopulationProjections_HOTP2013-38.aspx

Taranaki Veteran. 1919. 'The Great *Muru*', *Journal of the Polynesian Society* 28(110): 97–102.

Taumaunu, H. 2014. 'Rangatahi Courts of Aotearoa New Zealand – an Update'. *Māori Law Review*. Accessed 21 May 2017. http://maorilawreview.co.nz/2014/11/rangatahi-courts-of-aotearoa-new-zealand-an-update/

Tauri, J., Walters, R., and Bradley, T. 2005. 'Indigenous Perspectives and Experiences: Maori and the Criminal Justice System', in R. Walters and T. Bradley (Eds), *Introduction to Criminological Thought*. Auckland. Pearson Education, pp. 129–45.

Tauri, J., & Webb, R. 2012. 'A Critical Appraisal of Responses to Maori Offending', *International Indigenous Policy Journal* 3(4): 1–16.

'Total Population'. 1966. [From A. H McLintock (Ed.), *An Encyclopaedia of New Zealand*. Wellington: Government Printer] *Te Ara – Encyclopedia of New Zealand*. Accessed 21 May 2017. http://www.TeAra.govt.nz/en/1966/population/page-4

Te Puni Kōkiri. 2010. *Nā Ngāi Māori te Rongoā i Tipu, Hei Whakakore i te Mahi Tūkino: Māori Designed, Developed and Delivered Initiatives to Reduce Māori Offending and Re-offending*. Wellington: Te Puni Kōkiri.

Te Puni Kōkiri. 2011. *Ko te Aro ki ngā Pūtake Hara mō Ngāi Māori: Addressing the Drivers of Crime for Māori*. Wellington: Te Puni Kōkiri.

Te Puni Kōkiri. 2015. *Understanding Whānau-centred Approaches: Analysis of Phase One Whānau Ora Research and Monitoring Results*. Wellington: Te Puni Kōkiri.

Te Whaiti, P., and Roguski, M. 1998. *Māori Perceptions of the Police*. Accessed 21 May 2017. http://www.police.govt.nz/sites/default/files/publications/maori-perceptions-of-police.pdf

Walker, R. 1990. *Ka Whawhai Tonu Matou – Struggle without End*. Auckland: Penguin.

Working Group on Arbitrary Detention. 2015. *Report of the Working Group on Arbitrary Detention: Addendum 2: Mission to New Zealand*. Geneva: Office of the United Nations High Commissioner for Human Rights

Working Group on the Universal Periodic Review. 2014. *Report of the Working Group on the Universal Periodic Review: New Zealand*. Geneva: United Nations Human Rights Council.

Workman, K. 2016. 'From a Search for Rangatiratanga to a Struggle for Survival: Criminal Justice, the State and Maori, 1985 to 2015', *Journal of New Zealand Studies* (22): 89–104.

11.

Youth Justice

ANDREW BECROFT AND SACHA NORRIE

Introduction

The youth justice system in Aotearoa New Zealand has been described as 'revolutionary' and 'an international trendsetter' (Wundersitz, 2000: 110). In an attempt to understand why, this chapter will pose and answer a number of questions about the youth justice system in Aotearoa. First, the chapter will discuss why we treat youth offenders differently to adult offenders and who our young offenders are. Second, the chapter will outline how the youth justice system in Aotearoa treats young offenders differently, principally through the twin pillars of diversion and Family Group Conferences. Finally, some of the strengths of the Youth Court will be outlined, as well as some of the challenges that face our top-end youth offenders.

Who Are Our Youth Offenders and Why Do We Treat Them Differently?

Science and the Developing Teenage Brain

Although it seems common sense that most teenagers 'act up' to some degree before maturing into adulthood, neurological science about the developing teenage brain explains why this is the case. The science also forms the principled basis for why it is so important to treat young offenders differently.

The development of the teenage brain is vastly different to that of an adult. The prefrontal cortex, responsible for executive function (including coordination of thoughts and behaviour, response inhibition, the ability to foresee consequences of one's actions and impulse control), is still developing during adolescence and does not mature until well into a person's twenties. During puberty the brain's social and incentive processing develops at a faster rate. This means that adolescents are drawn to sensation-seeking and risky behaviour without the necessary self-control or maturity to ensure their behaviour is not harmful (Lambie, Ione and Best, 2014). Unsurprisingly, adolescents are often characterised as impulsive, temperamental, immature and unable to consider the feelings of others or the consequences of their actions. In fact, often they are neurologically much less capable of doing so than adults.

Peer influence also has a significant effect on the adolescent brain. Unlike adults, peer influence leads to activation of areas of the teenage brain associated with reward-processing, increasing both the sensitivity to potential immediate rewards of risky choices and the likelihood of engaging in risky behaviour. As is now well recognised in the criminal justice system, the likelihood of adolescents engaging in risky behaviour actually *increases* when they think that the result of that behaviour will be harmful (*Churchwood v R* [2011] NZCA 531).

This critical phase of adolescent development is described as the 'white water rafting years' – a time when young people face a number of risks and challenges that require careful navigation to escape without harm or injury. For 'adolescent-limited offenders' some common factors that heighten the risk of offending include mixing with antisocial peers, substance abuse, family problems such as poor parental monitoring and negative parent–child relationships, poor performance and attendance at school, and negative feelings about school (Cleland and Quince, 2014).

Not All Youth Offenders Are the Same

Desisters
In Aotearoa, the law treats young offenders differently to those in the adult criminal justice system. And for good reason. Around 75 per cent of young people in Aotearoa will never commit a crime. Of the 25 per cent that do, the vast majority (roughly 80 per cent) will offend only once or twice and this offending behaviour generally peaks at the age of 17 (Ministry of Youth Justice, 2000). These youth

offenders are referred to as 'adolescent limited offenders' or 'desisters', meaning the offending is limited to the adolescent stage of life and stops before adulthood. Desisters usually start offending after 13 years of age and tend to stop or 'age out' of offending by age 24 to 28 (Moffit, 1993).

Given that most desisters will grow out of their offending and go on to be engaged members of society, it is of critical importance that the justice system responds to them appropriately. Labelling theory suggests that the stigmatising label of introducing a young person to criminal proceedings during this key developmental stage can foster further criminal behaviour (Cleland and Quince, 2014). Labelling theory is based on the idea that the way that young people are labelled by the community creates a self-fulfilling prophecy. Because young people are less experienced and more impressionable than older people, they are more likely to respond to a given label (White and Haines, 2004). Inevitably, the response of the justice system and its officials towards a young person will affect that young person's perceptions of, and willingness to engage in, criminal behaviour. Counterproductively, labelling a young person an 'offender' may actually increase their engagement with the criminal justice system.

The vast majority of the literature suggests that the less contact young people have with the formal justice system during their teenage years, the better the likelihood of a successful outcome. Furthermore, those young people who are dealt with less severely after having come into contact with the justice system are less likely to reoffend (Ministry of Social Development, 2004). If we accept that contact with the criminal justice system can propel a young person along the trajectory towards becoming a 'career criminal', it follows that effective and prompt diversion away from the formal system can minimise that risk and help ensure that the young person ages out of their offending.

Persisters
The second group of youth offenders are 'persisters', also known as 'early onset' or 'life course' offenders. This small, hard-core group may make up only roughly 5–15 per cent of young offenders but account for more than half of all youth offending. Unlike desisters, who will grow out of offending behaviours, persisters will start exhibiting antisocial behaviours from a young age, will usually start offending around 10 years of age and will continue to offend into adulthood.

Statistics provided by the New Zealand Ministry of Justice and the New Zealand Police, and presented in Becroft (2015: 2), suggest that there are a number of characteristics commonly associated with persisters:

- 81 per cent are male. However, the number of young women who offend, especially violently, is increasing.
- Many, estimated up to 70–80 per cent, have a drug and/or alcohol problem.
- Most, estimated up to 70 per cent, are not engaged with school or even enrolled at a secondary school. Non-enrolment, rather than truancy, is the problem.
- Most experience family dysfunction and disadvantage, and lack positive male role models.
- Many, up to 76 per cent, have some history of abuse and neglect, and previous involvement with Child, Youth and Family.
- Many have some form of psychological disorder, especially conduct disorder, and display little remorse, let alone any victim empathy.
- Many will also have a neurodevelopmental disorder such as prior traumatic brain injury, foetal alcohol spectrum disorder, autism, attention deficit disorder, speech and communication disorders, a specific learning disability (e.g., dyslexia), or a combination of these. This will impact their ability to engage in any justice process.
- Māori are disproportionately represented at every stage of the youth justice process:
    - 24 per cent of the 10–16-year-old population is Māori.
    - Māori make up 58 per cent of apprehensions of 14–16 year olds and 64 per cent of Youth Court appearances.
    - Māori made up 100 per cent of all appearances in four small Youth Courts in 2014. In a further 20 Youth Courts, young Māori constituted over 70 per cent of all appearances.
    - Māori are given 65 per cent of supervision with residence orders (youth prison), which is the highest custodial Youth Court order before conviction and transfer to the District Court.
    - The disproportion of Māori representation in the Youth Court is getting *worse* not better (an increase from 44 per cent in 2005 to 61 per cent in 2014).

For this group of offenders, Aotearoa's specialist youth justice system offers a small window of opportunity to effectively engage with some of our most complex and challenging young people. Often it is the 'last best shot' to steer these youth offenders away from a future of escalating violence, crime and imprisonment.

How Does the Youth Justice System Treat Young Offenders?

The youth justice system in Aotearoa is unique. It has been described as world-leading (Wundersitz, 2000). At its inception in 1989, the statutory framework underpinning the system, the Children, Young Persons and Their Families Act 1989 (CYPTFA), was hailed as 'a new paradigm' for going beyond traditional philosophies of youth justice and offering a completely new conceptual approach (Morris and Maxwell, 1993: 1).

There are two foundational pillars of CYPTFA. First, there is an emphasis on not charging young offenders and, if at all possible, using police-led and community-based alternative responses. Second, where police diversion is not possible, the Family Group Conference acts both as a diversionary mechanism to avoid charging and as the prime decision-making mechanism in every case that comes before the Youth Court that is either admitted or proved after a trial.

Jurisdiction in the New Zealand youth justice system depends, almost exclusively, on age. Offenders aged 10–13 years are called 'child offenders'. Child offenders are generally dealt with in the Family Court on the basis that their offending is caused by lack of parental care and protection. Some 12- and 13-year-old child offenders may also be dealt with in the Youth Court if they are charged with very serious offending or have persisted to offend at a high level. Offenders aged 14–16 years are called 'youth offenders'. They are dealt with by the youth justice system, which can include being charged in the Youth Court. Curiously, non-imprisonable traffic offences are usually not within the youth justice system and must be dealt with in the adult court. Both child and youth offenders can be charged with murder or manslaughter and, if so, their cases are dealt with in the adult jurisdiction in the High Court.

Diversion

Diversion is the first, and arguably most fundamental, statutory goal of Aotearoa's youth justice system. The principle of diversion in our local context can be summarised as the avoidance of formal youth justice interventions (such as appearing in court) and, if such formal interventions cannot be avoided, the minimisation of any harmful impact (Doolan, 1993). This approach is based on the idea discussed above that it is better to keep a young person away from the formal justice system.

The first of nine youth justice principles in CYPTFA is that, unless the public interest requires otherwise, criminal proceedings should not be instituted against a child or young person if there is an alternative means of dealing with the matter (s208d). There is a statutory requirement that a young person who commits an offence should be kept in the community so far as it is practicable and consistent with the need to ensure public safety (s208d). Any sanctions imposed on the child or young person who commits an offence should also take the form most likely to maintain and promote the development of the child or young person within his or her family group, and take the least restrictive form that is appropriate in the circumstances (s208f).

The meaning of the term 'diversion' has evolved and is often misunderstood in the modern context (Morris and Giller, 1987). Historically, diversion often meant that a young offender avoided formal interventions (like arrest or court appearances) and was diverted away from the criminal justice system completely. By contrast, the modern approach is to divert a young offender *towards* a particular process or programme. As Geraldine Van Bueren (1998: 174) notes, 'the term diversion is misleading as children are not diverted away from a legal system itself but merely from its more formal aspects'. In the formal Youth Court context, diversionary principles and processes are also engaged in order to avoid convictions, court orders and custodial sanctions in favour of community-based alternatives.

The emphasis on diversion in CYPTFA has significantly reduced reliance on charging young people after apprehension by police. A specialist youth-focused police division ensures that approximately 80 per cent of all youth offending is dealt with through prompt, community-based alternative intervention. This means that the young person never has to go to court. This process is often called 'alternative action', deriving from the wording of the statutory provision (s208a).

Family Group Conferences (FGCs)

If the police wish to charge a young person who has not been (or cannot be) arrested, an FGC must be convened to consider whether a charge should be laid in the Youth Court. This type of FGC is known as the 'intention to charge' FGC. If the young person admits the alleged offending at the intention to charge FGC, a voluntary 'alternative action' plan for the young person to undertake can be recommended. If the plan is satisfactorily completed, this will usually end the matter. If the alternative action plan is not successfully completed, or the offending is very serious, then a charge may be laid in the Youth Court.

Every young person who is charged and comes before the Youth Court is referred to a FGC. This mandatory FGC allows for less reliance on judicial decision making and instead places families, victims and the community at the heart of the decision-making process. A consensus-based plan is created to hold young people accountable for their behaviour while addressing the underlying causes of offending. Rehabilitative, wraparound, community-based sentences are a priority and detainment in secure custody is an absolute last resort.

If arrested and charged in the Youth Court, the young person must have an FGC either if the charge is admitted or if the charge is proved after a trial (ss246 and 281, CYPTFA). It is worth noting that if the offending is particularly serious or if the FGC plan is not followed, the young person will usually receive a formal Youth Court order (which is conceptually similar to the sentence in the adult courts but modified for Youth Court purposes). Therefore, the FGC is a fundamental part of the process for deciding whether police should charge the young person in the first instance, as well as being the primary decision-making forum when a charge is formally laid in the Youth Court. This accounts for roughly 25 per cent of all youth justice cases.

The FGC is the hub of the Youth Court process – it is not peripheral to the court procedure (Cleland and Quince, 2014). FGCs are the primary and mandatory decision-making forum for all types of serious offending before the Youth Court (except for charges of murder and manslaughter, and most non-imprisonable traffic offences) (CYPTFA, s273). Despite subsequent adaptation and replication of the conferencing system in many jurisdictions around the world, Aotearoa remains unique in that the FGC is the primary and mandatory decision-making process in the Youth Court.

Most cases in the Youth Court are resolved through an FGC plan without the need for a formal court order. For example, in 2013 only 26 per cent of Youth Court appearances resulted in a formal order. However, some FGC plans will recommend a formal order. The Youth Court has a residual power to make certain formal orders when the offending is so serious that a formal order is deemed appropriate, or where the FGC plan has either not been fulfilled or has been only partly fulfilled, or when no agreement has been reached at the FGC. Many of the Youth Court orders are comparable to sentences available in the adult court, but there are some unique aspects. Youth Court orders include, but are not limited to:

- Absolute discharge
- A discharge that is noted on the young person's record
- An order to come up for sentence if called upon within one year
- Disqualification from driving
- Reparation
- Community work
- Supervision
- Directed activities in the community followed by supervision
- Youth justice residence (youth prison) followed by supervision
- Conviction and transfer to the District Court for sentencing.

What Are the Strengths of the Youth Justice System?

The 'Bad Old Days'

When CYPTFA came into force in 1989, the landscape of youth justice changed dramatically. In the 'bad old days', the youth justice system in Aotearoa was the subject of growing public dissatisfaction and criticism. In direct contrast to what we now know about the benefits of diversion and the need for a multidisciplinary response, in the decades preceding CYPTFA there was a heavy emphasis on police charging young people for all levels of offending. There was also a disproportionately high reliance on the institutionalisation of young offenders due to the fact that, generally, more consideration was given to the welfare concerns of the young person rather than the offence that they committed. For example, at its worst, the system saw young people caught shoplifting a chocolate bar locked up in custody for months because they came from unsafe home environments and had nowhere else to go. Families and communities felt frustrated and disempowered by the formalised and official decision-making processes from which they were alienated.

In particular, Māori were marginalised and disadvantaged by the system's monocultural processes. State systems and processes failed to take account of Māori values and cultural practices (Cleland and Quince, 2014). The decision-making mechanisms used by the Department of Social Welfare and other government agencies when making decisions about children, particularly Māori children, were seen as culturally inappropriate and possibly racist. Describing the concerns at this time, Mike Doolan (1993: 18), the first Chief Social Worker for Child and Youth Services, commented:

In New Zealand, Māori and Pacific Island youth are more fundamentally at risk of the coercive, intrusive welfare dispositions, under the guise of treatment and in pursuit of rehabilitation, than are their Caucasian counterparts. The fact that most professional decision-makers in the youth justice system are from the dominant white culture and are rarely identified as working class, contributes directly to this state of affairs.

These concerns were captured in the *Pūao-Te-Ata-Tū (Day Break)* report released in 1987 (Māori Perspective Advisory Committee, 1986). This report exposed many deficiencies in the youth justice system in relation to its treatment and dealings with Māori, and found evidence of institutional racism within the Department of Social Welfare. Emerging from this report, and subsequent consultation with Māori groups, was the strong message that whānau, hapū and iwi must be at the centre of decision-making processes for children (Cleland and Quince, 2014). The recommendations from *Pūao-Te-Ata-Tū* became the backbone underpinning the period of then radical legislative reform and, arguably, much of the spirit of the report has been embodied in CYPTFA.

Enacted amid such a turbulent political and social background, the new youth justice system, as expressed in CYPTFA, had much to live up to. First, it had to achieve a balance between the polarised goals of child welfare (which sees youth offending entirely as a symptom of family dysfunction) and criminal justice models (which views young offenders as independent and autonomous decision-makers who should be held accountable). The new system also had to realise the objectives of effective diversionary strategies by steering young people away from becoming potential career criminals; empower whānau and families by providing processes allowing for mediation between victims, offenders and their families; and offer appropriate rehabilitative services that are culturally sensitive. Some of the ways in which the modern youth justice system attempts to achieve these objectives are set out below.

Cross-over and Flexibility of Response

The youth justice system avoids an unhelpful, artificial, rigorous split between the youth justice (criminal) and care and protection (welfare) systems by acknowledging their mutual causal relationship and that much of the offending by young people will be connected with their home environment and is a product of abuse and neglect. It achieves this by allowing cross-over between the two courts that deal with these issues: the Youth Court and the Family Court. Flexibility between the two systems allows youth offenders with care and protection issues (typically familial abuse and neglect) to be dealt with appropriately. There is also the ability for the Youth Court to decide whether an incidence of offending is really driven by care and protection and should be dealt with by the Family Court. For example, a young person might be caught breaking into a number of houses in order to steal food from the fridge because there is none at home. This enables the justice system to concentrate on justice issues and avoid getting involved in care and protection work.

Recently, a Cross-over List, pioneered by Judge Tony Fitzgerald, has evolved for children and young persons who are appearing in the Youth Court and have been identified as having 'care and protection' status. On a Cross-over List day, a judge with both a Family Court and Youth Court warrant will manage a young person's case by addressing both youth justice and care and protection issues at the same hearing. The Cross-over List streamlines proceedings, reduces court appearances and minimises the chances of either court unintentionally subverting actions taken in the other. It also gives reality to the highly desirable principle of 'one family; one judge; one Court appearance' (Pierse O'Byrne, 2014).

Reduced Institutionalisation

There are currently four youth justice residences (youth prisons) and four care and protection residences (secure facilities for children or young people with acute care and protection needs) in Aotearoa. There is also a secure residential facility for young sexual offenders.

Immediately preceding CYPTFA in 1988, 2000 children in New Zealand were in state-run institutions. By late 1996 the figure was under 100. Research had firmly established that putting young offenders into state institutions was more likely to reinforce their criminal identities and restrict their opportunity to choose a non-criminal lifestyle through normal integration into the community. It became apparent that the warehousing of mostly violent yet vulnerable young men in concrete cells was not conducive to enduring rehabilitation. As a result of the new approach, many boys' homes and residences closed down.

Significantly Reduced Rates of Imprisonment

CYPTFA requires its agents to consider alternatives to court proceedings, to impose the least restrictive sentence, and to keep young offenders in the community whenever public safety allows. Consequently, the use of imprisonment and corrective training (a 3-month disciplinary sentence in secure custody for 16–19 year olds, which was abolished in 1996) has fallen dramatically. This trend has continued almost unabated since 1990 due to the reduced reliance on incarceration and the increased use of community-based sentences. In 2013, less than 0.5 per cent of young people appearing in the Youth Court received a sentence for detainment in secure custody (Ministry of Justice, 2013).

Specialist Youth Court Judges

One of the greatest strengths of the Youth Court is the highly experienced and specialised bench of Youth Court Judges. All judges with a Youth Court warrant are also full time District Court Judges, bringing with them a wealth of knowledge and experience from the criminal, or Family Court, jurisdictions. Youth Court Judges receive specialist training on their role, covering the philosophy and principles underpinning the system, the legal and technical aspects of the Youth Court and tools to more effectively engage with young people and their families. Most Youth Court judgments are delivered orally and, almost invariably, written judgments are recorded as if the judge is speaking directly to the young person. This helps ensure that the young person understands exactly what is going to happen and the reasons for this.

Diversion and Specialist Youth Police

As previously discussed, a diversionary approach is a key focus of the youth justice system and one of its biggest successes. The decision to divert or charge in the Youth Court is made by one of the approximately 250 specialist Youth Aid police officers to whom all young offenders are referred after apprehension or arrest. The officers are sworn constables, are given additional training to deal with young people and receive higher salaries than other constables of a similar rank.

FGCs

As discussed above, it is through the mandatory use of FGCs for all those who come before the Youth Court that control over, and responsibility for, youth offending is partially transferred and given back to the community and families. There are six types of FGC. The most common are those ordered by the court when the young person does not deny the charge.

Youth Advocates

Another reason for the success of Aotearoa's youth justice system is that Youth Advocates (lawyers for the youth offender) are universally appointed by the Youth Court and are paid for by the government, irrespective of the financial means of the young person's family. Youth Advocates are specifically trained in the youth justice system. When appointing lawyers to the Youth Advocates Panel, the court takes into account a range of matters including knowledge of the objects and principles of CYPTFA; knowledge of the roles and practice of various professionals within the youth justice system; and ability to relate to young people and their families. This makes them better lawyers because they are able to take complex legal information and processes and explain them in a way that the young person understands.

Rangatahi Courts

Rangatahi Courts are sittings of the Youth Court that are judicially directed to be held on the marae. Rangatahi Courts operate within the jurisdiction of the Youth Court and are not a separate system of youth justice. After a young person has first appeared in the Youth Court and a FGC plan has been subsequently formulated and approved by the court, the young person may have their FGC plan monitored by the Rangatahi Court.

The Rangatahi Court initiative was first pioneered by Judge Heemi Taumaunu in 2008 as a response to the disproportionate rates of young Māori in the Youth Court. The aim of the Rangatahi Courts is to provide a more culturally appropriate process and the best possible rehabilitative response, encouraging strong cultural links by involving local Māori communities in the youth justice process.

Each Rangatahi Court sitting is held on a marae and the court process incorporates the use of te reo Māori (the Māori language), tikanga and kawa (rituals and protocols). Kuia and kaumātua (respected elders) sit alongside the judge and provide valuable insights and advice to the young person and his or her whānau.

Those responsible for the establishment of Rangatahi Courts consider that offending by many Māori youth is related, in part, to a lack of self-esteem, a confused sense of self-identity and a strong sense of resentment and cultural dislocation (Taumaunu, 2014). As part of the Rangatahi Court process, the young person is encouraged to learn and deliver a pepeha (an expression of tribal identity), which requires them to explore three central pillars of self-identity:

1. Ko wai koe? (Who are you?)
2. Nō whea koe? (Where are you from?)
3. Nā te aha koe? (What is your purpose?)

The final element that completes the Rangatahi Court model is the provision of tikanga wānanga (cultural programmes) which provide specialist kaupapa Māori (informed by Māori worldviews) interventions and opportunities for Māori young offenders. These include te reo Māori, tikanga, kapa haka, waka ama, taiaha wānanga, noho marae and other wānanga. Given that the underlying causes of offending are rarely confined to the young person individually, programme providers work with the young person's whānau and community as well as working with the young person individually.

There are currently fourteen Rangatahi Courts (and two Pasifika Courts) around the country, with an additional number of hapū and iwi Māori asserting strong support for the establishment of a Rangatahi Court in their region.

Lay Advocates

Lay advocates were 'created' with the CYPTFA in 1989 and have no known counterpart in any other legislation anywhere in the world. The role of the lay advocate includes two principal functions:

- To ensure that the court is made aware of all cultural matters that are relevant to the proceedings.

- To represent the interests of the child's or young person's whānau, hapū, and iwi (or their equivalents [if any] in the culture of the child or young person) to the extent that those interests are not otherwise represented in the proceedings.

Lay advocates represent a visionary new role for the Youth Court and, like Youth Advocates, are funded by the state, irrespective of the financial means of the young person's family. In spite of this, lay advocates were simply not used in the youth justice process in any meaningful way until 2008 and the launch of the first Rangatahi Court:

> It is clear that the ... Act envisaged a person of mana (status/reputation) who could support the person's whānau, hapū and iwi and advise the court of any whānau context of which it would not be aware, which would be relevant to any decision-making about the young person. (Cleland and Quince, 2014: 121)

Lay advocates demonstrated such value in the Rangatahi Courts, and the youth justice process generally, that they quickly became mainstreamed into many Youth Courts. Lay advocates are now an established and growing part of the Youth Court process and are adding real value to it. Reports provided by lay advocates often uncover family issues and dynamics that government social workers cannot penetrate, especially when families take a closed-rank position to government agencies. Families are given a voice by lay advocates, relieving youth advocates of the dual, and often conflicting, tasks of presenting the views of young offenders and their families. Lay advocates ensure that insightful advice as to cultural factors involved in the offending, or which are necessary as part of any subsequent intervention package, is being provided (Becroft, 2014: 6).

This gives the court a deeper pool of information that it can use to craft appropriate responses to the young person and his or her family. It also helps the judge and kaumātua in the Rangatahi Courts to draw connections to the young person's family. Often, elders can inform a young person, using the lay advocate's information, of ancestors who have played an important role in the local community.

Corey's Story

Corey, aged 15, faces a charge in the Youth Court of aggravated robbery. At about 2:00 a.m. on a Friday night, Corey and two other male co-offenders assaulted a French tourist who was sleeping in his van in the car park at Maraetai Beach in Auckland. After smashing open the passenger window of the van and dragging out the occupant, one of the co-offenders held the victim down while Corey and the other co-offender kicked the victim a number of times to the head and body. A short time into the attack, Corey smashed an almost empty bottle of Jim Beam over the victim's head, causing him to lose consciousness. The three offenders then took the victim's van, which contained all the victim's belongings including his wallet and passport. The victim suffered a traumatic brain injury caused by a number of blunt force traumas to the head, one of which fractured his skull. He may never remember short-term events or be able to drive again. He also suffered a broken jaw and cheekbone, three broken ribs and significant internal damage to his kidneys and liver caused by multiple kicks to the abdomen.

At the time of the offending, Corey was high on synthetic cannabis and had shared two boxes of Cody's, a premixed bourbon drink, with his two co-offenders. Corey's dad gave him his first joint at age 6 and he has been drinking regularly since age 7. At age 15, Corey is addicted to both alcohol and synthetic cannabis. He is able to steal these from his mum and her mates, who come around most days to drink. When he is not able to do so, Corey shoplifts and sells the goods to make enough money to buy drugs.

Corey has been in and out of state care since he was 3 years old. Corey's dad is connected to the Mongrel Mob and has been in and out of prison since before Corey was born. Corey's mum is an alcoholic and struggles with methamphetamine addiction. Her current partner is also gang-affiliated. Corey witnesses him beat his mum regularly. Corey and his four siblings also receive regular beatings. On account of the abuse and neglect Corey faced growing up he was placed in a number of foster care arrangements and state homes. He always ran away back to his mum.

Corey hasn't been in school since he was 12. After being excluded from three mainstream schools for behavioural issues, he was put into an Alternative Education programme, but failed to engage. The genesis of Corey's bad behaviour is partly attributable to a number of neurodevelopmental issues. Corey has a strand of foetal alcohol spectrum disorder caused by his mother drinking heavily, and smoking methamphetamine, while pregnant. This has never been diagnosed. At age 7, Corey also developed glue ear from living in damp, cold and overcrowded state housing. This too was never diagnosed. To disguise the fact that he could not hear the teacher in class, or understand the lessons, Corey began to act up.

Corey is Māori, although he does not know which iwi or hapū he is connected to. He has some relatives up North and went to a tangi on a marae once, but doesn't know which one. He grew up in Mangere and the only times he has lived outside of South Auckland are the periods he has spent detained in a Child, Youth and Family residence, or when Child, Youth and Family placed him with an aunty in Kaikohe. A week after being placed in Kaikohe, Corey stole a car and drove back to Mangere to be there when his dad got out of prison. Corey's dad is one of the co-offenders in the aggravated robbery.

Corey's story is one that those working in the Youth Court encounter almost daily. It is also somewhat paradoxical. On one hand, it represents a number of the challenges faced by the youth justice system (and wider community generally) in Aotearoa. On the other hand, however, it also highlights some of the entry points into a young offender's life and opportunities for our system to more effectively respond to our young offenders.

Youth Court as a Therapeutic Model

Therapeutic jurisprudence is a philosophy that examines the role of the law as a therapeutic agent in relation to legal rules, legal processes and the role of the legal profession. In relation to the court process, therapeutic jurisprudence focuses on the role of the court and court processes in improving the wellbeing of parties to its processes (Wexler, 2016).

One of the basic premises of the therapeutic movement has been to move away from a focus on the outcome of the court process to a focus on the court process itself. The court is directed to respond to offending in a way that identifies the underlying causes of offending and takes a problem-solving and solutions-focused approach to criminal offending. Toki (2005: 173) cites His Honour Judge Thorburn:

> Therapeutic jurisprudence proposes a broadening of the role of the Judge, which has traditionally been limited to fact-finding and law-applying. Therapeutic jurisprudence asks why the judicial role should not extend to the search for solutions to an individual's cycle of offending.

In the context of youth justice, the main therapeutic premise is that effectively reducing offending requires the underlying causes of offending to be addressed via a holistic approach taking into account family context, social background, mental health, drug and alcohol issues and other environmental factors (Evans, 2012).

The principles of CYPTFA allow scope for a therapeutic response by providing that any measures for dealing with a child or young person's offending should, as far as practicable, address the underlying causes of offending (s208f). Perhaps more than any other court in New Zealand, the Youth Court and its founding legislation are best suited and placed to utilise a therapeutic jurisprudence approach. There are also clear efforts to incorporate therapeutic principles in the operation of the Youth Court, such as:

- Regular monitoring of a young person's FGC plan in court (usually every 2 weeks)
- Having the same judge monitor the young person's case (where possible) throughout the proceedings
- Having a coordinated, multidisciplinary team approach with access to the necessary wraparound social services

- Direct engagement and dialogue between the judge and the young person
- Routine forensic and education screening.

Therapeutic principles and approaches have also been the impetus for the development of a number of specialised Youth Courts including the Youth Drug Court, Cross-over List, Intensive Monitoring Group and Rangatahi Courts.

What Challenges Does Our System Face?

Education

There is a clear link between a lack of engagement in education and youth offending. While there are no completely accurate figures, anecdotally it is thought that up to 65–70 per cent of offenders in the Youth Court are not formally engaged with the education system. 'Not formally engaged' includes those who are not truants, because they are not meaningfully enrolled at any secondary school to be truant from. They are simply not registered in the formal education system.

Any effective and meaningful youth justice response *must* include education. All those involved in the youth justice community accept that educational involvement is one of the most significant protective factors in a young person's life. Re-engagement in education is probably the most effective response that the youth justice system can make to repetitive youth offending. The statutory mandate contained in CYPTFA to address the causes underlying a child or young person's offending is one way that the youth justice system can mobilise comprehensive and effective educational intervention. While there is no magic bullet to reduce youth offending, if there was, it would be to keep every young person meaningfully involved in education, preferably mainstream education, for as long as possible.

The increased provision of education officers in Youth Courts around the country has proven invaluable. There are now nine Youth Courts and four Rangatahi Courts that are serviced by specialist employees of the Ministry of Education, with a further seven courts that are able to access written education reports, with plans to expand to a further eleven courts. The education officer's role is to:

- Provide timely, useful and accurate information about a young person's education status for the Youth Court

- Help address a young person's education needs
- Assist the FGC Coordinator to determine whether a more detailed education assessment is required
- Assist the young person to re-engage in education or vocational training (if suitable).

The Education Officer will draw on information such as:

- Enrolment status and schooling history
- History of any suspensions or exclusions
- Specialist education services received
- Achievement data
- Relevant education information (e.g., attendance, attitude, strengths etc.).

Encouragingly, there is a growing and shared recognition of the importance of education for young offenders, and the commitment to prevention, early intervention and effective transitioning of young offenders back into education. Over the years, there have been significant changes in the attitudes of New Zealand secondary schools to retaining their most difficult young people. Increasingly, it seems to be accepted that excluding or expelling a problem student does not solve the problem for the community, it only relocates it. There really has been a sea change in the attitude of most schools and the benefits are being seen in youth justice. Youth Court numbers have halved in the last five years. The rates of appearances in court have reduced dramatically. While it is difficult to isolate a single factor, the view of most is that the increased commitment by the Ministry of Education and schools around Aotearoa to retaining students within the school community has been a significant contributing factor.

Perhaps the greatest challenge for this area of youth justice in the future will be for schools. Schools are the community's ultimate, and certainly its frontline, 'crime fighters'. Schools that engage and involve as many young people as possible, and for whom exclusions/expulsions are a rarity, provide an enormous service for the justice system and their country. Their efforts bring down the crime rate. Schools are not usually cast in this role. The language of crime fighting is seldom attributed to the educational community. But it should be. Simply put, young people who are at school, or who are able to access some form of meaningful educational or vocational training, are unlikely to become adult criminals.

Neurodisability

> The cognitively challenged are before our Courts in unknown numbers. We prosecute them again, and again, and again. We sentence them again, and again, and again. We imprison them again, and again, and again. They commit crimes again, and again, and again. We wonder why they do not change. The wonder of it all is that we do not change our expectations rather than trying to change them.
> (*R v Harris* [2002] BCPC 0033, at para. 167)

Youth justice has entered the 'era of the teenage brain'. The connection has now been made between neurodevelopmental disorders and youth offending. A recent study by the Children's Commissioner for England (2012) found a staggering prevalence of neurodisability in the youth offending population. While no similar comprehensive research has taken place in Aotearoa, there is every reason to suggest that similar prevalence rates exist.

Research demonstrates that many young offenders will have some form of neurodisability such as traumatic brain injury (TBI), foetal alcohol spectrum disorder (FASD), autistic spectrum disorder (ASD), attention deficit hyperactivity disorder (ADHD), epilepsy, speech and communication disorders, a specific learning disability (e.g., dyslexia), or often a combination of these. Some will also have a neuropsychological disorder, particularly conduct disorder.

Judge Catherine Crawford of the Western Australia Children's Court has conducted studies which show that children adversely affected by neurodisability resulting from alcohol exposure during pregnancy are at an increased risk of committing crime or being a victim of crime. Such outcomes are 'doomed to be repeated when there is systematic failure to identify and appropriately accommodate their disability into adulthood' ('Fetal Alcohol Spectrum Disorder Kids', 2015).

Some specific neurodisabilities are particularly challenging to current practice. For example, current research shows a high prevalence (up to 60 per cent) for oral language and communication (OLC) difficulties in young people within the youth justice system (Hennessey and Snow, 2013). The Youth Court, and especially FGC processes, rely heavily on the oral language abilities (everyday talking and listening skills) of the young offender, who needs to listen to complex and emotionally charged accounts of a victim's perspective and formulate his or her own ideas into a coherent narrative. This narrative is then judged by the parties affected by the wrongdoing as either adequate or not, and has a strong effect on the outcome of the FGC. A language or speech difficulty will significantly impact upon a young person's ability to understand and positively engage with youth justice processes.

Our challenge is to better recognise and support young people with OLC disabilities, and to take into account that some appearing in the Youth Court may only have the level of comprehension of a 7 or 8 year old, meaning they might struggle to participate in the FGC and court process. This will influence the appropriate support provided and strategies for breaking down information regarding what the FGC plan means he or she has to do. Such strategies might include presenting information visually, checking understanding and comprehension, and teaching important vocabulary (e.g., what 'breaching bail' means). A young person may also need additional support to interpret the language and emotions expressed at the FGC and, in turn, may need help to express themselves in a way that can effectively communicate remorse or empathy.

Helpfully, every Youth Court in New Zealand is now equipped with youth forensic services. The mandate of the youth forensic services includes, but is not limited to, screening and assessment of young offenders, court liaison services, delivery of specific mental health and drug and alcohol assessments and suggested treatment, clinical care for young people in youth justice residences, and specialist consultation for health and justice personnel (Coleman, 2011).

As the twenty-first century advances, the challenge will be for the youth justice system to provide a comprehensive health response to neurodevelopmental issues, with an emphasis on early identification and early intervention. At the same time, the Youth Court must continue to be supported by appropriate experts and community groups who can identify these issues amongst young offenders and ensure that the response by the youth justice system is appropriate in all the circumstances.

Female Offenders

In 2014, only 20 per cent of Youth Court charges were female, making up a relatively small minority of youth offending (Ministry of Justice, 2014a). However, proportionately, there are more female youth offenders in the youth justice system now than 25 years ago. While youth offending generally is decreasing, female offending, and particularly violent offending, is decreasing at a much lower rate than male offending, meaning there are proportionately more young female offenders in the system. Between 2006 and 2012, the rate of apprehensions for males decreased by 21 per cent, but only by 14 per cent for females.

Violent offending by young female offenders has also been a particular concern. Between 2010 and 2014, the proportion of young females charged with violent offending increased from 29 per cent to 37 per cent (Ministry of Justice, 2014a).

There is an almost complete lack of comprehensive research on the particular situation of girls in the youth justice system in Aotearoa (Lynch, 2008). It has been suggested that young female offenders have unique concerns that the system needs to be wary of and careful to address. These include family dysfunction, childhood and adolescent maltreatment, mental health disorders, substance abuse and gang involvement (Lambie, Ione and Best, 2014). Sexual abuse is particularly prominent among young women who offend. Donna Swift (2011: 99), who carried out research through interviews of 1704 girls and 1720 boys in Nelson, notes that:

> It is well documented in New Zealand that 1 in 4 females have been victims of sexual violation and both international and national research acknowledges that many females who end up in the justice system have also been survivors of sexual violation. During their interviews, many girls spoke about their unwanted sexual experiences. The girls' quotes scattered throughout this report provide the evidence. A girl's reputation for violence almost always paralleled her experience of sexual abuse.

The government's *Youth Offending Strategy 2002* noted a scarcity of programmes targeting young female offenders in New Zealand (Ministry of Justice and the Ministry of Social Development, 2002). This continues today. Swift (2011: 103) advocates for the development of female-specific programmes in her research, stating that her findings 'highlight the need for New Zealand to follow international prevention and intervention strategies. These use a gender-specific, gender-responsive and trauma-informed approach to address girls' use of violence and antisocial behaviour. This means programmes must be designed specifically for our girls and young women.'

In order to do better for our young female offenders, the youth justice system needs to be fully equipped with a suite of female-specific intervention programmes that are based on current evidence as to what rehabilitation programmes and approaches work for young female offenders. These programmes should be accessible to all stages of the youth justice process, from community-based intervention, intention to charge FGC referrals, through to formal court intervention and custodial orders.

Māori Disproportionality

The disproportionate overrepresentation of young Māori in our youth justice system is long-standing and worsening. Despite apprehension rates decreasing for both Māori and non-Māori young offenders, the rates are decreasing much faster for non-Māori than Māori. Consequently, the disproportionality of Māori young offenders within the system is getting worse, not better.

In Aotearoa, 23 per cent of the youth population are Māori. Of this group of young Māori, only a small portion (approximately 5 per cent) appear in the Youth Court. However, despite occupying a very small proportion of the youth population, 52 per cent of all young people who are apprehended are Māori, and 64 per cent of all young people who appear in the Youth Court are Māori. Māori youth offenders receive 66 per cent of all custodial orders (youth prison) (Ministry of Justice, 2014b). In some Youth Courts, the ratio of Māori young offenders appearing is over 90 per cent of the total number of appearances. These figures show us that at every stage of the youth justice process in which a discretionary decision is made, Māori are increasingly likely to receive an unfavourable outcome. It is therefore possible to infer that some degree of institutional bias operates within our justice system to the disadvantage of Māori.

This disproportionality is highly problematic. Attempts to tackle the issue of Māori overrepresentation in the youth justice system must necessarily consider the wider historical and modern context of Māori social, economic, political and cultural marginalisation. Issues of poverty, intergenerational incarceration and the enduring effects of colonisation cannot be ignored. Any meaningful solution requires our system to be critically self-reflective, to identify the root causes of the issues, and respond in a principled and innovative way. Indeed, when reflecting on Māori overrepresentation in the criminal justice system, Justice Joe Williams (2013, at para. 29) has noted that 'the statistics suggest trying to do something different on a wider scale cannot possibly do any harm'.

The Rangatahi Court, through the involvement of local marae communities and incorporation of tikanga-based programmes, is working towards a more culturally responsive Youth Court process. The early evaluations of this approach are very positive and the model will continue to evolve and grow over time. In this respect, the Rangatahi Court provides an example of a step in the right direction with respect to re-visioning how our youth justice system can do better for young Māori. It also gives effect to the long overlooked statutory enjoinders to involve whānau, hapū and iwi in all decision making and in the implementation of all measures for dealing with youth offending (see ss5a and 208c, CYPTFA).

Our Tough Kids Come from Tough Backgrounds

As evident with the case of Corey above, serious youth offending often presents a tricky paradox. On one hand, the offending committed by the young person is high-end, often violent and causes long-lasting harm to the victim and the community. For example, in 2011 a 16-year-old-boy broke into an elderly woman's home in the early hours of the morning and repeatedly raped her at knife point (*Police v J O* [2011] CRI-2011-263-00072). It is important to remember that when we talk about 'serious crime' in the Youth Court, we do mean 'serious'.

However, on the other hand, we must acknowledge that our toughest kids come from our most fractured and disadvantaged family backgrounds and will invariably have been the victims themselves of horrific abuse and neglect. Henwood and Stratford (2014: 56) cite Youth Justice Coordinator Paul Hāpeta:

> Most young people I work with live in a violent world. Their home is violent. Maybe the mother's not violent, but the mother's successive partners have been violent towards them, kicked them, beaten them up, whacked them with baseball bats, dog chains and all the sort of stuff, you know. Not all of them, but a significant amount of them have been horrendously abused, sexually abused. They've had more whippings than you can even think about.

Many families of young offenders do not subscribe to normative values regarding offending behaviours. The causes for this are complex and far-reaching. Many of these families have themselves been marginalised by state institutions, education and social welfare systems, and have been incarcerated at disproportionate rates. Many are unable to provide, or model, caring and supportive family structures. For example, many young males who offend do not have an older male who can be a role model and show by example how to live a better life. If the father is in prison or has left the family, the mother might have subsequent partners with little interest in someone else's children. Indeed, they may be actively hostile to the children. There are also longitudinal issues as well, where antisocial attitudes and behaviours are passed on from generation to generation within a family. Henwood and Stratford (2014: 153) cite former prisons boss Kim Workman:

> We may be dealing with third generation stuff here, very high-risk families where kids have been brought up by violent parents who've been brought up by violent mothers, so this whole culture of violence is in there and very difficult to change.

Part of that violence is an absolute abhorrence of authority, and reluctance and resistance to engaging with the police or authorities of any kind – or even service providers of any kind. These totally marginalised families are hostile towards most authorities, schools, health services and all the rest of it. There is no quick fix for that.

As Justice Joe Williams has reflected, the youth justice system is expecting changes from young people in their behaviour when their environment – their household and the values that are around them at home – remains exactly the same (cited in Henwood and Stratford, 2014: 153). The major difference in the degree of positive outcomes for young people who come into contact with the youth justice system is the degree of family involvement in both the justice and therapeutic processes. Research indicates quite strongly that some form of multisystemic family intervention is a particularly productive approach to reducing recidivism in young offenders (Ministry of Youth Justice, 2000). Indeed, a recurrent catchcry amongst youth justice practitioners in Aotearoa is 'if you don't fix the family, you can't fix the child' (Henwood and Stratford, 2014: 153).

However, it is an undeniably big task for a legal process to strengthen an offender's family. CYPTFA asks the state, in the context of a criminal justice response, to reach out to and affect positive change in the lives of our most challenged young people and our most challenging families. The key statutory mechanism to do this is the FGC. Much is expected from the FGC process and its agents, including identifying, bringing together and strengthening a young person's immediate and/or extended family, which will each have its own unique and complex needs. Practitioners reflect that, a lot of the time, if the family issues are not dealt with, there is unlikely to be lasting change for the young person. However, strengthening a young offender's family must be a broader interdisciplinary long-term goal. That goal needs to go hand in hand with real social and economic reform to change the conditions in which offending behaviours are fostered (Cleland and Quince, 2014).

Conclusion

Ko te pae tawhiti whāia kia tata
Ko te pae tata whakamaua kia tīna

As for the distant horizon, pursue it and make it close
As for the close horizon that has been reached, hold fast and secure it

This whakataukī (proverb) echoes the successes of and opportunities for Aotearoa's youth justice system. It reminds us that first we must strengthen and nurture what has already been achieved. Our youth justice system is unique. It understands that young people's brains work differently and that most will make risky decisions during the 'white water rafting years' of adolescence. Most desisters will grow out of their offending behaviour, and for this group any contact with a formal justice system will actually increase their chances of reoffending. The New Zealand Police has a specialist youth-focused division to ensure that approximately 80 per cent of all youth offending is dealt with by prompt, community-based and highly successful alternative interventions.

For the small group of persisters who are charged and come to the Youth Court, the mandatory FGC places families, victims and the community at the heart of the decision-making process. A consensus-based plan is created to hold the young person accountable for their behaviour while addressing the underlying causes of offending. Rehabilitative, wraparound, community-based sentences are a priority and custody is an absolute last resort.

The whakataukī also encourages us to have vision and to continue to do better for our young people. Our most serious offenders come from our most marginalised, damaged and damaging families. We cannot ignore the influences of socio-economic disadvantage, cultural marginalisation, mental health and neurodevelopmental issues, intergenerational violence and abuse, colonisation and drug and alcohol dependency. Effectively, the youth justice system is being asked to fix a social problem, or at least provide the infrastructure to do so. In this respect, the Youth Court is the ultimate ambulance at the bottom of the cliff and early identification and intervention must be the solution. This is an undeniably enormous task that must go hand in hand with real social, economic and political evolution.

Nevertheless, the Youth Court continues to face these challenges head on. We know that meaningful engagement in education is the single most protective factor for young offenders. Specialist education officers work with schools and the Youth Court to help address a young person's education needs and assist with re-engagement. The Youth Court is also becoming increasingly aware and equipped to identify and respond to those young offenders who have underlying neurodevelopmental disorders, with forensic screening now routine in every Youth Court.

The youth justice system also has a principled and pragmatic duty to do better for our young Māori. On this score, to walk into the future, our gaze must also be fixed on the past – the overrepresentation of Māori in the youth justice system is just one strand of a much broader story of modern and historical social, economic and political marginalisation. Both CYPTFA and *Pūao-Te-Ata-Tū*, its founding document, recognise the potential for whānau, hapū and iwi to have a greater role in responding to their rangatahi. In this respect, the Rangatahi Court is a step towards realising these aspirations.

While reflecting on Aotearoa's youth justice system at the launch of the Rangatahi Court in Christchurch, the Right Honourable Chief Justice Dame Sian Elias (2014) eloquently summarised her thoughts:

> Young people get into trouble and that has always been so. But now more than ever, we know about the connections between offending and neuro-disability, alienation from whānau, school and community, substance abuse, and young people who have been victims themselves of abuse and neglect. This knowledge must be seized upon.
>
> Most young people grow out of their offending behaviour – they are at a transitional phase in their development. However, some young people are irreparably damaged by their circumstances and also by the system. In this respect, it is vital that we in the youth justice system 'get it right' when we respond to these young people.
>
> It is through socialisation, inclusion and connection, not punishment, that young people learn to obtain respect for others by respecting themselves. As a community, we are all invested in growing healthy, respectful and supported young people.
>
> The Rangatahi Courts acknowledge a certain kind of alienation for young Māori – alienation caused by inter-generational processes of urbanisation, the loss of tribal connections and the loss of te reo Māori. In this respect, the Rangatahi Court is about fostering a sense of belonging and an attempt to bring rangatahi 'home'.

REFERENCES

Becroft, A. J. 2014. *Lay Advocates Handbook*. Wellington: Ministry of Justice.
Becroft, A. J. 2015. *Child and Youth Offending Introductory Notes*. Office of the Principal Youth Court Judge, Wellington.
Children's Commissioner for England. 2012. *Nobody Made the Connection: The Prevalence of Neurodisability in Young People Who Offend*. Birmingham: Children's Commissioner for England.
Coleman, J. 2011. 'New Youth Forensic Mental Health Services Announced', *Beehive.govt.nz*, 17 November. Accessed 21 May 2017. https://www.beehive.govt.nz/release/new-youth-forensic-mental-health-services-announced
Cleland, A., and Quince, K. 2014. *Youth Justice in Aotearoa New Zealand: Law, Policy and Critique*. Auckland: LexisNexis.
Doolan, M. 1993. 'Youth Justice – Legislation and Practice', in B. J. Brown and F. W. M. McElrea (Eds), *The Youth Court in New Zealand: A New Model of Justice*. Auckland: Legal Research Foundation.
Elias, T. 2014. Speech delivered at the launch of the Christchurch Rangatahi Court at Ngā Hau e Whā Marae, Christchurch.
Evans, K. 2012. 'The Intensive Monitoring Group and Youth Justice', MA thesis, Auckland University of Technology.
'Fetal Alcohol Spectrum Disorder Kids 19 Times More Likely to Cause Trouble'. 2015. *New Zealand Herald*, 26 May. Accessed 1 August 2016. http://www.nzherald.co.nz/nz/news/article.cfm?c_id=1&objectid=11454886
Hennessey, H., and Snow, P. 2013. 'Oral Language Competence and Restorative Justice Processes: Refining Preparation and the Measurement of Conference Outcomes', *Trends and Issues in Crime and Criminal Justice: Australian Institute of Criminology* 463: 1–6.
Henwood, C., and Stratford, S. 2014. *New Zealand's Gift to the World*. Wellington: Henwood Trust.
Lambie, I., Ione, J., and Best, C. 2014. '17 Years Old and Youth Justice', *New Zealand Law Journal* 8: 316–17.
Lynch, N. 2008. 'Youth Justice in New Zealand: A Children's Rights Perspective', *Youth Justice* 8(3): 215–228.
Māori Perspective Advisory Committee. 1986. *Pūao-Te-Ata-Tū (Day Break): Report of the Ministerial Advisory Committee on a Māori Perspective for the Department of Social Welfare*. Wellington: Department of Social Welfare.
Ministry of Justice. 2013. *Youth Court Quarterly Report*. Wellington: Ministry of Justice.
Ministry of Justice 2014a. *Trends in Child and Youth Prosecutions*. Wellington: Ministry of Justice.
Ministry of Justice. 2014b. *Youth Court Quarterly Report*. Wellington: Ministry of Justice.
Ministry of Justice and the Ministry of Social Development. 2002. *Youth Offending Strategy*. Accessed 21 May 2017. https://www.msd.govt.nz/documents/about-msd-and-our-work/publications-resources/archive/2002-youth-strategy.pdf
Ministry of Social Development. 2004. *Achieving Effective Outcomes in Youth Justice*. Wellington: Ministry of Social Development.
Ministry of Youth Justice. 2000. *Tough Is Not Enough – Getting Smart about Youth Crime*. Wellington: Ministry of Youth Justice.
Moffit, T. 1993. 'Adolescence-Limited and Life-Course Persistent Antisocial Behavior: A Developmental Taxonomy', *Psychological Review* 100(4): 674–701.
Morris, A., and Giller, H. 1987. *Understanding Juvenile Justice*. London: Croom Helm.
Morris, A., and Maxwell, G. 1993. 'Juvenile Justice in New Zealand: A New Paradigm', *Australian and New Zealand Journal of Criminology* 26(1): 72–90.
Pierse O'Byrne, K. 2014. 'Identifying and Responding to Neurodisability in Young Offenders: Why, and How This Needs to Be Achieved in the Youth Justice Sector', LLB (Hons) dissertation, University of Auckland.
Swift, D. 2011. *The Girls' Project. Girl Fighting: An Investigation of Young Women's Violent and Antisocial Behaviour*. Nelson: Stopping Violence Services Nelson.
Taumaunu, H. 2014. Rangatahi Courts of Aotearoa New Zealand – an Update. *Māori Law Review*. Accessed 21 May 2017. http://maorilawreview.co.nz/2014/11/rangatahi-courts-of-aotearoa-new-zealand-an-update/
Toki, V. 2005. 'Will Therapeutic Jurisprudence Provide a Path Forward for Māori?', *Waikato Law Review* 13: 169–89.
Van Bueren, G. 1998. *The International Law on the Rights of the Child*. The Hague: Nijhoff.

White, R., and Haines, F. 2004. *Crime and Criminology*. Melbourne: Oxford University Press.
Wexler, D. 2016. 'Therapeutic Jurisprudence: An Overview', *International Network on Therapeutic Jurisprudence. Law.arizona.edu*. http://www.law.arizona.edu/depts/upr-intj/
Williams, J. 2013. 'Lex Aotearoa: An Heroic Attempt to Map the Māori Dimension in Modern NZ Law', *Waikato Law Review* 21: 1–34.
Wundersitz, J. 2000. 'Juvenile Justice in Australia: Towards the New Millennium', in D. Chappell and J. Wilson (Eds), *Crime and the Criminal Justice System in Australia: 2000 and Beyond*. Sydney: Butterworths.

12.

Justice and Injustice

JARROD GILBERT

> *Injustice anywhere is a threat to justice everywhere.*
> —Martin Luther King Jr.

Introduction

Injustice can take many forms but an area of great interest and concern is injustice rising from wrongful convictions. This chapter will examine the causes of miscarriages of justice as well as their remedies, and outline a number of high-profile cases that have occurred in New Zealand. It will also review the ways in which unsafe convictions are challenged here and internationally.

Background

An important principle of justice in Western democracies is that the state carries the burden of proof. In other words, the prosecution must prove the case for guilt – and to a very high standard – and defendants are considered to be innocent until proven guilty. The importance of ensuring innocent people are not punished has a long history and was famously encapsulated by English jurist Sir William Blackstone in the 1760s. Blackstone's (1765: 352) formulation (sometimes called the Blackstone ratio) states: 'It is better that ten guilty persons escape than that one innocent suffer.'

Although the criminal justice system is ostensibly set up to protect innocent people, sometimes processes are corrupted, either by accident or on purpose, leading to wrongful convictions. There are no data on how often wrongful convictions happen in New Zealand, but international examples provide a reasonable indication. In the United States, for example, there have been at least 1900 convicts exonerated since 1989, with those people on average spending 8.8 years behind bars (National Registry of Exonerations, 2016), and 4.1 per cent of defendants sentenced to death have later been shown to be innocent (Gross et al., 2014). That means that one in every 25 people sentenced to death was not guilty of the crime. While many are absolved before execution, another study found that 2.3 per cent of those judicially executed in the United States were wrongfully convicted (Gross and O'Brien, 2008). But those extreme cases are only the tip of the iceberg, and it can be difficult to determine how many wrongful convictions actually occur. Because it can be extremely expensive and time-consuming to investigate and overturn a wrongful conviction, often only the most serious cases are uncovered.

While the percentages are small, the large number of cases that go through the courts means that miscarriages of justice are actually rather common. Michael Naughton, a leading UK advocate for the wrongly convicted, offered a sobering perspective to the *Telegraph*: 'People think that miscarriages of justice are rare and exceptional, but every single day, people are overturning convictions for criminal offences. Miscarriages of justice are routine, even mundane features of the criminal justice system. They are systematic' (quoted in Goldhill, 2014).

Although the breadth of the issue is not widely known, high profile cases have sparked the public imagination – and often outrage. Many cases have become famous due to news media and popular culture. In America, professional boxer Rubin 'Hurricane' Carter became an unfortunate *cause célèbre* after his 1967 triple homicide conviction. In 1975 Bob Dylan wrote the song 'Hurricane' to publicise the injustice of his conviction, but he wasn't freed from prison until 1985. The notoriety of the case peaked with the 1999 film *The Hurricane* starring Denzel Washington. In the United Kingdom, the case of the Guildford Four captured the public imagination, and directly led to the establishment of a Criminal Cases Review Commission, which will be discussed later. The case involved the convictions of four people for an IRA bombing of a pub in Surrey, England, in 1974. Their convictions were overturned in 1989, after they had served 15 years in prison, and became the subject of major film starring Daniel Day-Lewis called *In the Name of the Father* (1993).

The Crewe Murders

The spectre of unsafe convictions in New Zealand came to national prominence after the grisly – and baffling – murder of a husband and wife in the small Waikato community of Pukekawa in 1970. The 'Crewe murders' and the name Arthur Allan Thomas became seared into the consciousness of the country at that time.

Jeanette and Harvey Crewe came to a violent end when they were shot at their farm house and their bodies bound and submerged in the Waikato River in June 1970. It is one of New Zealand's most controversial criminal cases and it remains unsolved. The crime scene was reported to police some five days after the couple were believed to have died. Adding a layer of intrigue, the couple's 18-month-old baby Rochelle had been tended to during that period (Yallop, 1978). Initial suspicions centred around Jeanette's father, Len Demler, with whom the couple had been in a dispute about land. He was viewed by many as having acted strangely on the discovery of the crime scene and in the subsequent search for his daughter and brother-in-law.

Police attention soon turned, however, to a local famer named Arthur Allan Thomas. Initially, the case against Thomas was not strong, the motive was weak, and the only physical evidence linking him to the crime was an axle that had weighted down Harvey Crewe's body, which was believed to have come from Thomas's property. Despite this, police were convinced they had their man, even if they didn't have enough to prove the case in court. On 27 October 1970, police searched the Crewe property for a third time and produced a .22 calibre cartridge case found in a garden – despite that area having previously been meticulously grid-searched. The markings on the shell casing were consistent with having been fired by Thomas's gun. Thomas was arrested and in 1971 he was found guilty of the murders following a 12-day trial. After a successful appeal, a new trial was ordered. In 1973, Thomas was found guilty again.

While the court was satisfied with his guilt, sections of the public were unconvinced. For the first time, the integrity of the police became widely questioned. A campaign challenging the safety of Thomas's conviction was driven in large part by the *Auckland Star* newspaper and reporter Pat Booth. Campaigners believed that police had planted the shell casing. Forensic analysis showed that the casing's condition was too good to have been in the garden for as long as police claimed it had been, and that both of the bullets in the bodies had been manufactured at a different time to the shell casing. Thus, they could not have come from that shell casing at all. Following a recommendation from the Prime Minister in 1979, the Governor-General pardoned Thomas. Headed by a retired Australian judge, the Honourable Robert Taylor, a Royal Commission of Inquiry released its report in November 1980. It found that the police had planted the cartridge case and that the arrest and prosecution of Thomas was unjustified (Royal Commission, 1980).

Despite the Commission concluding that Detective Inspector Bruce Hutton and Detective Sergeant Len Johnston's actions in planting the casing were an 'unspeakable outrage' (Royal Commission, 1980: 116), no officers were charged in relation to the investigation or prosecution of the case. Thomas spent 9 years in prison, during which time his wife left him. He eventually received a judicial pardon and $950,000 in compensation.

Common Factors That Lead to Miscarriages of Justice

There are a number of reasons why miscarriages of justice occur, and while one element may be sufficient, often a number of factors, the most significant of which are outlined below, work in concert to create an injustice.

False or Incorrect Testimony

Misidentification of offenders by eyewitnesses is one of the leading causes of wrongful convictions (Huff, 2003). While memory is often treated as being reasonably objective and certain, it is subject to influence and degradation over time (Knoops, 2006: 59). Witnesses and victims may mistakenly identify bystanders as offenders, and can be unintentionally influenced by investigators. Studies have found that people can be encouraged to recall events that did not happen (Chrobak and Zaragoza, 2008; Loftus and Pickrell, 1995), and that a person's prejudices or beliefs about events may lead to them recalling events incorrectly (Lenton, Blair and Hastie, 2001). Where witnesses may be initially unsure about their memories of events, positive feedback can cause them to become more confident over time, regardless of how accurate their recollection is (Bradfield, Wells and Olson, 2002).

Witnesses may perjure themselves – give false testimony – in order to avoid incriminating themselves or others, or to deliberately incriminate another person. In some cases a witness may exaggerate their testimony because they believe, or have been led to believe, that an accused person is guilty and may go free without it (Huff, 2003: 17).

Witnesses may also give false evidence in order to claim a reward or they might be incentivised by police. Incentivised witnesses – often called 'snitches' or 'narks' – may be rewarded to give evidence, and often they have a clear incentive to fabricate or alter their stories in order to avoid prosecution for their own crimes, or to be released from prison early (Bloom, 2003: 20). 'Jailhouse snitches' – informants who claim that an accused confessed details about a crime to them while they were sharing a prison cell – are a common cause of wrongful convictions (Huff, 2003: 18) because their testimony is often compelling but extremely difficult to prove or disprove.

False Confession

Although it seems acutely counterintuitive, miscarriages of justice cases often involve innocent people making false self-incriminating statements or wrongfully confessing to a crime (Knoops, 2006: 41). One study has found that in the United States false confessions or self-incriminating testimony were involved in 29 per cent of cases where erroneous convictions were later overturned by DNA evidence (Innocence Project, 2016). In other words, nearly one in three of those wrongful convictions was caused or exacerbated by a false confession or similar.

There are a number of reasons why this can happen. Often suspects are led to believe (either by accident or deliberately) that there is evidence that puts them at the crime scene or that a confession is in their best interests. Many such confessions are recanted soon after the end of an interrogation, but may still be used as evidence. These issues are substantially more likely in cases where a suspect has diminished mental capacity, was intoxicated at the time, or has a poor understanding of the law.

Plea Bargaining

Plea bargaining is when an accused person is offered a lesser punishment in exchange for pleading guilty (Huff, 2003: 17). This has the advantage of avoiding the need for a trial, which can be expensive and time-consuming for both the state and the accused.

Accepting a plea bargain may be sensible in many instances, but in some cases the prosecution offers a deal because it has poor evidence and wants to avoid the uncertainty of a trial. If the accused is innocent, he/she may feel pressured to accept a deal if led to believe that the case is strong. In some cases a lawyer may incorrectly advise making a guilty plea or accepting a plea bargain when it is against a client's interests. Once given, a guilty plea can make it more difficult to secure a retrial (Elks, 2008: 326). This is sometimes known as 'the innocent prisoner's dilemma', and can also be an issue if an innocent prisoner is required to accept guilt in order to be eligible for parole.

Contaminated Evidence and Expert Testimony

Because forensic science is often assumed to be unbiased and largely infallible, it can be a powerful contributor to proving guilt or innocence. Unfortunately, this reputation for clarity and infallibility is something of a misconception and issues of contamination, faulty testing and poor expert testimony can lead to forensic science contributing to wrongful convictions.

Items from the scene of a crime may be contaminated accidentally, causing forensic testing to produce incorrect results. Furthermore, forensic science, as with any other scientific method, does not always generate clear answers on its own. Experts are often required to analyse and disentangle the scientific findings, and even then their conclusions can vary significantly. Even when they generate an apparently clear result, forensic tests such as fingerprint and DNA analyses must be interpreted in regard to other evidence in order to build a theory of how a crime was committed, and there are many ways that DNA can be present at the scene of a crime without it necessarily arriving there during the crime itself.

Investigators, emergency services, passers-by and those involved in an event can easily contaminate a crime scene by inadvertently or deliberately leaving damaging evidence such as fingerprints or altering the position of items, and by dispersing smaller evidence such as hair and skin cells (Walker and Stockdale, 1999: 127). Crime scene sample contamination can lead to forensic scientific evidence that a guilty person was involved in a crime, prevent the conviction of a guilty party, or invalidate evidence that might have exonerated an accused.

Withheld, Destroyed or Falsified Evidence

In some cases, material evidence may be illegally falsified or altered by investigators in order to secure a conviction when other evidence is poor. Similarly, if investigators discover evidence that may be used against them to prevent a conviction, they may illicitly withhold or destroy that evidence so that it cannot be used in the trial. In the case of wrongful convictions, this might happen because bias has led investigators to strongly suspect the wrong person, or because of institutional corruption.

Investigator Bias

Investigators, as with all people, may be unconsciously biased against certain suspects, and therefore be more likely to pursue them. They may be biased for reasons such as race or class, or may be influenced by a suspect's conduct (e.g., if they are belligerent when questioned) or through previous dealings that they have had with police. The police are careful to control for these biases, but often they are difficult to avoid: a gang member with previous convictions, for example, is naturally more likely to be the subject of suspicion than a company director with a clean record, but that suspicion may not necessarily be valid. This may lead to a guilty but less obvious person being ignored.

Additionally, confirmation bias may lead investigators to pursue false hypotheses even after conflicting information has arisen. Confirmation bias is the tendency to select evidence that supports an existing hypothesis or belief, and to minimise evidence that disagrees with it. This can lead to a condition known as 'tunnel vision', which is common in many areas of human behaviour (Snyder and Swann, 1978). It can cause people to maintain polarised political opinions, to uphold discredited beliefs, or to hold on to conspiracy theories that have little basis (Leman and Cinnirella, 2007). In the context of a criminal investigation, confirmation bias can mean that once investigators begin to suspect somebody of a crime, that suspicion may lead them to ignore contradictory evidence or fail to pursue other possible lines of inquiry (Ask and Granhag, 2007; Ask, Rebelius and Granhag, 2008). In extreme cases, this can lead to police using coercive interrogation tactics to secure an expected confession (perhaps leading to a false confession), or withholding or falsifying evidence in order to convict someone that they strongly believe is guilty.

Indeed, one key element is police interviewing procedures and one method that has been put under the spotlight is the Reid Technique, which originated from the United States. Reid is a nine-stage interview method that is highly effective at gaining confessions. At face value this is a good thing – after all, you want guilty people to confess. But numerous cases and scientific experiments have shown the Reid Technique to be coercive and far too likely to produce false confessions, especially among youth. Step 6, for example, ends with 'if the suspect cries at this point, infer guilt', which seemingly ignores the idea that being accused of committing a horrific crime may conceivably produce tears in some people.

In 2012 a Canadian judge concluded that the 'Reid Technique is a guilt-presumptive, confrontational, psychologically manipulative procedure' (*Montreal Gazette*, 9 November 2012). Suspect interrogation using the Reid Technique is less about truth and more about confession at all costs, and Reid has been banned for use on youth suspects in several European jurisdictions. In recent years the New Zealand Police have adopted a British interrogation method called PEACE, which stands for Planning and Preparation, Engage and Explain, Account, Closure and Evaluation, and which is far less coercive.

Poor Legal Representation

Many of the issues described above relate to the organisation and use of evidence in court, and can be unravelled or counteracted by a clever and dedicated defence lawyer. In the case of many miscarriages of justice, however, the legal representation provided to a defendant is insufficient. An overworked, inexperienced or uninterested lawyer may fail to carry out sufficient investigation, fail to call important witnesses, or provide poor advice around plea deals.

Poor resources are a common cause of this problem: accused people may be unable to hire their own lawyer (or change lawyers if they prove to be ineffective) or unable to afford to undertake necessary investigations or hire forensic experts (Joy and McMunigal, 2003). On the other hand, prosecutors, as employees of the state, have access to much greater investigatory and forensic resources. If we now turn to three high-profile New Zealand cases, we can easily identify many of these factors at play.

David Dougherty and DNA

In October 1992 an 11-year-old girl was abducted from her home and raped. The victim told police that her attacker said he was 'David from next door', at which point the child's neighbour David Dougherty became the prime suspect. Dougherty denied any involvement but despite his pleas of innocence he was convicted of abduction and rape in June 1993 and sentenced to 7 years and 9 months of imprisonment.

Few crimes are as repugnant as that of child rape. To be falsely accused and convicted of it must be an unimaginable nightmare and one that David Dougherty said he was experiencing. In October 1994, an appeal bid was thrown out. The case was kept alive, however, in large part due to a campaign undertaken by journalist Donna Chisholm. Alarmed by weaknesses in the scientific evidence, Chisholm told Dougherty in prison: 'I'm going to write a story about you every week until you're out' (*Sunday Star-Times*, 7 March 2009). As was the case with Arthur Allan Thomas, the media played a key role in searching for justice. As Chisholm (2016, pers. comm.) said:

> I'd always understood the power of the media in injustice cases after working with Pat Booth of Arthur Allan Thomas fame at the *Auckland Star* in the '70s, so I knew the value of perseverance even when the campaigns aren't popular. The Dougherty case didn't sell papers, but thank God, like Booth, this didn't deter the then-*Sunday Star-Times* editor Michael Forbes, who kept putting the stories on the front page.

The case hinged on a key piece of evidence: the semen left in the victim's underwear. DNA testing used at the original trial was said to be inconclusive, and the Department of Scientific and Industrial Research scientist called by the Crown said Dougherty could not be excluded. The defence lawyers sourced other scientists and their testing was definitively at odds with the Crown case. In 1996, Dougherty was granted leave for another appeal and in that same year the Court of Appeal quashed his convictions. Science had eventually rescued an innocent man.

When he was released from Mt Eden Prison, a large media contingent was there to meet him. As Chisholm (2016, pers. comm.) explained:

> There was a media scrum – the thought crossed my mind that this was the first time any of the others had been interested in him. I think I was more excited than he was – he was a broken man and remained so for many years until I ultimately lost touch with him.

Dougherty was awarded $868,728 in compensation, and in 2000 new testing established the DNA profile of the true offender. In 2003 Nicholas Reekie was found guilty of the crime. He was sentenced to preventive detention with a 20-year minimum for this and two other rapes.

Teina Pora's False Confession

In recent times the most significant case to gain headlines is that of Teina Pora, who was convicted of raping and murdering Susan Burdett in 1994. A retrial in 2000 also found Pora guilty. At face value, the result was unsurprising: the then 17 year old had told police he was at the scene, and had implicated some Mongrel Mob associates in the crime.

For nearly everybody, that was that. It was not until Tim McKinnel, a private investigator and former police officer, began to make some independent inquiries about the case that things began to change. Pora claimed that he had said he was at the scene of the crime in an attempt to claim the $20,000 reward on offer by the police. An examination of the police interview tapes – interviews that spanned days and often lasted for hours – showed that he had no knowledge of the scene or the circumstances of the crime. When police took him to the street he failed to identify Burdett's house. Suffering from foetal alcohol spectrum disorder (FASD), Pora had been seeking the reward with seemingly no idea that his false statement would lead him to prison.

The work of McKinnel, counsels Jonathan Krebs and Ingrid Squire and others was crucial in getting the case reheard, but Pora's argument was significantly aided by the media, notably Phil Taylor at the *New Zealand Herald*, and Paula

Penfold and Eugene Bingham from the TV3 current affairs show *3rd Degree*. Even the New Zealand Police Association voiced doubts about the case, a significant move from a union that rarely deviates from a conservative line.

The DNA evidence at the crime scene had been identified as belonging to Malcolm Rewa, a serial rapist who had stalked South Auckland for years before his eventual capture. He was convicted of raping Burdett in 1999, but not of her killing. Notably, Rewa had always operated alone and, more than that, Pora had associations with the Mongrel Mob while Rewa was a senior member of Highway 61, two gangs that were sworn enemies at the time Burdett was killed. It was highly unlikely, therefore, that the two would have collaborated.

In 2014, the Privy Council heard Pora's appeal and in 2015 found that 'the combination of [Pora's] frequently contradictory and often implausible confessions with the diagnosis of [FASD] leads to the conclusion that reliance on his confessions gives rise to a risk of a miscarriage of justice' (Privy Council, 2015: 21). The Council therefore ordered that the conviction be quashed. Pora was set free and the Crown decided not to retry him. In 2016 the government announced that Pora was to be awarded $2.5 million in compensation after a review by Justice Hansen found that 'on the balance of probabilities' (the threshold for compensation) Pora was innocent. However, Hansen (2016: 100) went further, saying: 'Indeed, the state of the evidence is such that, in my view, he could have proved his innocence to an even higher standard.' While Teina Pora was set free, Tim McKinnel (2016, pers. comm.) now bristles at any suggestion that this shows that the system of appeals works to free innocent people: 'Teina spent 22 years in prison as an innocent man. That is not an example of the system working.'

One interesting component of the Pora case was the extremely broad degree of public support he enjoyed, which reminds us of another controversial case where compensation was sought. Former Otago University music student David Bain had been found guilty of killing five members of his family in 1995 and had served 13 years in prison before being acquitted in a retrial. The public remained deeply divided over Bain's guilt or innocence, and in 2016 he was denied compensation for the time he had spent in prison. He was, however, given nearly $1 million because the reviews assessing his case had been poorly handled. He was, in effect, paid to stop pursuing compensation claims. While many consider David Bain to be very lucky to be out of prison, let alone to gain a settlement, another equally contentious case has yet to reach a definitive conclusion: the satanic child-abuse case of Peter Ellis.

Peter Ellis and False Testimony at the Christchurch Civic Crèche

This case originates in 1991 when a child at the Christchurch Civic Child Care Centre told his mother: 'I don't like Peter's black penis' (cited in Hood, 2001: 226). This led to sexual abuse claims being made against Peter Ellis, an unabashedly gay man with an over-the-top personality whose style at the crèche was described as 'unconventional . . . sometimes to the point of being risqué and outrageous' (*R v Ellis* [2000] 1 NZLR 513). As news of the first allegation spread, other children began making more allegations, many of which were utterly remarkable. They included claims that:

- Crèche workers had stood in a circle watching children dance naked
- Children had been placed in ovens and others suspended in a cage
- One boy had been forced to kill another boy in a ritual
- One child had been turned into a frog and a cat
- Children had been killed with axes
- Children had been buried alive in coffins.

By the time the 10-month police investigation was over, investigators believed there were up to 80 child victims and up to ten crèche staff involved (McLoughlin, 1996). Ellis was arrested and joined later by four female crèche workers. The charges against the women were subsequently dropped but Ellis was brought to trial facing 28 charges involving 13 children. At trial the most outlandish claims were not heard by the court – these having been excluded by the trial judge as irrelevant to the case in hand. But much of the testimony the jury did hear was highly questionable, having been elicited through the use of extremely poor interviewing and now discredited techniques. It was on this contaminated evidence that the jury found Ellis guilty on 16 charges and he was sentenced to 10 years in prison. The ramifications of the case were wide and fundamentally changed how many men interacted with children, fearful that similar accusations would be made against them. This was particularly true in the education sector.

Ellis was given leave to appeal, and in 1994 the Court of Appeal quashed three of the convictions but upheld his sentence, and the same court was unmoved by a further appeal in 1999. In February 2000, Ellis was released on statutory remission after serving two-thirds of his sentence. Prior to that he had refused to appear before the Parole Board, knowing that he would not get parole without an admission of guilt.

A month after his release, it was announced that a ministerial inquiry was to be undertaken by Chief Justice Sir Thomas Eichelbaum. Eichelbaum found no fault with the verdicts, and on the back of that the Justice Minister, Phil Goff, recommended to the Governor-General that a pardon be denied. That decision has not satisfied many, however, given the investigative work done by journalists and others, most notably Lynley Hood (2001), who wrote an award-winning book about the case. Concerns around the safety of the convictions are many and complex but they include: concerns around the interviewing techniques used to gain evidence from the children; a wave of moral panic around satanic abuse at the time; and problems with the investigation; for example, one of the lead police investigators in the case had sexual relationships with the mothers of two of the complainants. For many people, the Peter Ellis case remains a dark stain on justice in New Zealand.

Addressing Miscarriages of Justice

One person who took interest in the Civic Crèche case was former High Court Judge Sir Thomas Thorp. It had been an investigation by him that had sparked the Eichelbaum inquiry. Unlike Eichelbaum, however, Thorp had the gravest of misgivings about the case. In fact, he was convinced of Peter Ellis's innocence. His concerns led him to investigate miscarriages of justice generally, publishing a report on the matter in 2005. Basing his estimate on UK data, Thorp (2005) concluded there could be as many as 20 people in New Zealand's prisons who had been wrongly convicted (Taylor, 2006), with a wrongful conviction rate of around 1 per cent. Thorp (2015, pers. comm.) told me that his estimate may even have been too low. In the United States the wrongful conviction rate has been estimated as high as 3.3 per cent to 5 per cent (Risinger, 2007). Whatever the situation, it was nevertheless enough for the retired judge to call for the establishment of a Criminal Cases Review Commission (CCRC) in New Zealand. He maintains that position to this day.

In the United Kingdom the idea of a CCRC came about after a number of high-profile cases heightened public concern around false confessions and police misconduct, notably that of the Guildford Four mentioned earlier. CCRCs are government-funded but independent of the judicial system, and they have the power to refer cases for retrial if they believe that a conviction may be unsafe or sentences excessive. A single CCRC handles all cases in England, Wales and Northern Ireland, while Scotland, which has a separate legal system, has its own commission, known as the Scottish Criminal Cases Review Commission. These commissions began work in 1997 and 1999 respectively, and may also take cases where guilt has been established but the sentence given was unfair.

The CCRCs undertake an extensive review process before accepting a case, requiring that there be a 'real possibility' of a positive outcome before referring cases for retrial. Although the English, Welsh and Northern Irish CCRC receives over 1500 applications each year, only around 3.4 per cent of cases are taken up, indicating that in the vast majority of cases there is insufficient evidence to justify attempting a retrial. Cases must involve new or untested evidence, or a legal principle or argument that was not used originally. Because of the high costs of investigation, testing evidence, and finally challenging a conviction in court, only the most compelling cases can be accepted.

As well as being government-funded, the CCRCs have special powers to request information from public bodies, and can request court orders to gain information from private organisations, significantly enhancing their ability to investigate and gather evidence. To date, calls for a CCRC in New Zealand have fallen on deaf ears, and while Opposition parties now support one, the current National government has been unmoved, seeing the current system of appeals as adequate (Matthews, 2015).

Once the appeals processes have been exhausted the final step is an application for a Royal prerogative of mercy. The Royal prerogative of mercy exists as a final safeguard against miscarriages of justice. It is exercised by the Governor-General as the Queen's representative on advice from the Minister of Justice. The Royal prerogative of mercy has the power to give a pardon, reduce a sentence or insist that the case be reheard by the courts. As noted above, this was the remedy that was applied to Arthur Allan Thomas.

I have noted that Teina Pora had his concerns heard by the Privy Council. The Privy Council is based in the United Kingdom and was New Zealand's highest court until it was replaced with our own Supreme Court in 2004. Notwithstanding that, cases that occurred before the establishment of the Supreme Court, such as Pora's, can still be heard by the Privy Council. So while there are perhaps a handful of cases that might still go to the Privy Council, its days as a last resort in New Zealand are numbered.

Internationally, there are non-governmental organisations (NGOs) that have stepped up to assist in the process of correcting miscarriages of justice. The most significant of these is the Innocence Project, which was founded at the Cardozo School of Law at Yeshiva University in New York in 1992. The Innocence Project was established in response to accumulating evidence that relatively simple causes such as eyewitness misidentification were responsible for many wrongful convictions. The Project uses DNA testing to establish guilt or innocence, and primarily takes cases where evidence exists that can be tested or retested for DNA. Although still centred in the United States, local variations of the project, connected through the Innocence Network, have started in many countries around the world.

All of the Innocence Project organisations are non-profit NGOs that have no special powers, unlike the CCRCs. As such, they survive through donations and volunteer contributions. Despite this, between 1992 and September 2016 in the United States the Innocence Project worked to exonerate 343 wrongfully convicted people, all on the basis of DNA evidence. Among these were people who were serving extremely long prison sentences, including 20 who were on death row, and its DNA testing has identified the real perpetrators in 147 cases (Innocence Project, 2016).

In New Zealand an Innocence Project was established at Victoria University of Wellington in 2007 but it fell into recess and was moved to Otago University where it is currently dormant. The New Zealand Public Interest Project (NZPIP) was established in 2015, and is based at the University of Canterbury. It looks at criminal and civil matters perceived to be in the public good, which includes miscarriages of justice. Within 12 months the NZPIP had received 89 requests for help. The trustees have stated that they would happily have the organisation made redundant by the establishment of a CCRC which is properly funded and given adequate power and authority.

Conclusion

There are a number of important elements that contribute to miscarriages of justice, but rarely is only one factor at play. Often these factors work in combination to create terrible consequences for individuals and undermine the justice system.

While miscarriages of justice on their own are not evidence of a broken system, they are proof of its fallibility. Acknowledging the risk of such imperfections should encourage us to be mindful of the dangers of shifting the burden of proof, and of the need for continual checking of investigative and judicial systems. Nonetheless, it is unrealistic to expect errors never to be made. Given that reality, an important measure of the quality of a judicial system must be how it deals with potential miscarriages when they are discovered. In this area New Zealand rates poorly. While a number of high-profile cases have shown, usually with the help of campaigners and the media, that injustices can be corrected, they often take a very long time. Furthermore, it is unclear how many cases are not brought to public attention because the victims are incapable of pursuing cases by themselves.

REFERENCES

Ask, K., and Granhag, P. A. (2007). 'Hot Cognition in Investigative Judgments: The Differential Influence of Anger and Sadness', *Law and Human Behavior* 31: 537–51.
Ask, K., Rebelius, A., and Granhag, P. A. (2008). 'The Elasticity of Criminal Evidence: A Moderator of Investigator Bias', *Applied Cognitive Psychology* 22: 1245–59.
Blackstone, W. 1765. *Commentaries on the Laws of England*. Oxford: Clarendon Press.
Bloom, R. M. 2003. 'Jailhouse Informants', *Criminal Justice* 18(1): 20–27.
Bradfield, A. L., Wells, G. L., and Olson, E. A. 2002. 'The Damaging Effect of Confirming Feedback on the Relation between Eyewitness Certainty and Identification Accuracy', *Journal of Applied Psychology* 87: 112–20.
Chrobak, Q., and Zaragoza, M. S. 2008. 'Inventing Stories: Forcing Witnesses to Fabricate Entire Fictitious Events Leads to Freely Reported False Memories', *Psychonomic Bulletin and Review* 15(6): 1190–95.
Elks, L. 2008. *Righting Miscarriages of Justice? Ten Years of the Criminal Cases Review Commission*. London: Justice.
Goldhill, O. 2014. 'When Innocent Men Go to Jail: Miscarriages of Justice in Britain', *Telegraph*, 4 September.
Gross, S. R., and O'Brien, B. 2008. 'Frequency and Predictors of False Conviction: Why We Know So Little, and New Data on Capital Cases.' *Journal of Empirical Legal Studies* 5: 927–962.
Gross, S. R., O'Brien, B., Hu, C., and Kennedy, E. H. 2014. 'Rate of False Conviction of Criminal Defendants Who Are Sentenced to Death', *Proceedings of the National Academy of Sciences of the United States of America* 111(20): 7230–35.
Hansen, R. 2016. Report for the Minister of Justice on Compensation Claim by Teina Anthony Pora. Accessed 21 May 2017. https://www.justice.govt.nz/assets/Documents/Publications/pora-teina-compensation-claim-innocence-report.pdf
Hood, L. 2001. *A City Possessed: The Christchurch Civic Crèche Case*. Dunedin: Longacre.
Huff, R. C. 2003. 'Wrongful Conviction: Causes and Public Policy Issues', *Criminal Justice* 18(1): 15–19.
Innocence Project. 2016. *DNA Exonerations in the United States*. Accessed 2 November 2016. http://www.innocenceproject.org/dna-exonerations-in-the-united-states/
Joy, P. A., and McMunigal, K. C. 2003. 'Inadequate Representation and Wrongful Conviction Ethics', *Criminal Justice* 18(1): 57–59.
Knoops, G. A. 2006. *Redressing Miscarriages of Justice: Practice and Procedure in National and International Criminal Law Cases*. Ardsley, NY: Transnational.
Leman, P. J., and Cinnirella, M. 2007. 'A Major Event Has a Major Cause: Evidence for the Role of Heuristics in Reasoning about Conspiracy Theories', *Social Psychological Review* 9: 18–28.
Lenton, A. P., Blair, I. V., and Hastie, R. 2001. 'Illusions of Gender: Stereotypes Evoke False Memories', *Journal of Experimental Social Psychology* 37: 3–14.

Loftus, E. F., and Pickrell, J. E. 1995. 'The Formation of False Memories', *Psychiatric Annals* 25: 720–25.

Matthews, P. 2015. 'Miscarriages of Justice Targeted by NZ Academics, Lawyers', *Stuff*, 23 May. Accessed 21 May 2017. http://www.stuff.co.nz/national/crime/68745556/miscarriages-of-justice-targeted-by-nz-academics-lawyers

McLoughlin, D. 1996. 'Second Thoughts on the Christchurch Civic Creche Case: Has Justice Failed Peter Ellis?', *North and South*, August.

National Registry of Exonerations. 2016. *National Registry of Exonerations*. Accessed 2 November 2016. https://www.law.umich.edu/special/exoneration/Pages/about.aspx

Privy Council. 2015. *Pora (Appellant) v The Queen (Respondent) (New Zealand)*. Privy Council Appeal No 0081 of 2013.

Risinger, D. M. 2007. 'Innocents Convicted: An Empirically Justified Factual Wrongful Conviction Rate', *Journal of Criminal Law and Criminology* 97(3): 761–806.

Royal Commission. 1980. *Report of the Royal Commission to Inquire into the Circumstances of the Convictions of Arthur Allan Thomas for the Murders of David Harvey Crewe and Jeanette Lenore Crewe*. Wellington: Government Printer.

Snyder, M., and Swann, W. B. 1978. 'Hypothesis-testing Processes in Social Interaction', *Journal of Personality and Social Psychology* 36: 1202–12.

Taylor, P. 2006. 'Up to 20 Wrongly in Jail Says Judge', *New Zealand Herald*, 21 January.

Thorp, T. 2005. *Miscarriages of Justice*. Auckland: Legal Research Foundation.

Walker, C., and Stockdale, R. 1999. 'Forensic Evidence', in C. Walker and K. Starmer (Eds), *Miscarriages of Justice: A Review of Justice in Error*. London: Blackstone, pp. 119–50.

Yallop, D. 1978. *Beyond Reasonable Doubt*. Auckland: Hodder and Stoughton.

13.

Crime and News Media

TARA ROSS AND DAVID FISHER

Introduction

The coverage of crime in the news media has a long history dating back to the earliest European newspapers' reports on sixteenth-century witchcraft trials and US colonial newspapers' reports on crimes like counterfeiting, robbery and piracy (Zelizer and Allan, 2010: 26). Though crime reporting has differed in style and focus across time and across different media, it has become a significant part of the contemporary news diet. A 2014 study of online news in New Zealand, for instance, found that stories about crime, courts, police and justice made up a fifth of all stories and were the most common news lead (Burgess, 2014).

    For those with an interest in criminal justice, understanding how crime is reported is important as most people have little firsthand experience of crime, and the news media are, by default, a crucial source of information about crime, justice and social order. This chapter looks at how crime is reported in the media and the issues and constraints that journalists face. It discusses how newsrooms work and how journalists source and produce different types of crime story; how various factors, including legal, institutional and newsroom influences, can shape their stories; what crimes get covered (not all do); why they tend to be reported in ways that distort our understanding of crime; and what that might mean for audiences and the wider public.

How Newsrooms Work

To understand crime news, it helps first to understand newsrooms – how they operate and how they decide what is news. Typically, newsrooms are hierarchical, with an editor at the top who serves a range of roles: he or she will assign stories, decide on story ranking and treatment, and set the overall tone of coverage. Editors must also make tough calls, under the pressure of frenzied deadlines, about how far to push their reporters' stories. If stories are too aggressive and beyond people's comfort boundaries they risk alienating the audience, but if they are too passive they can fail to engage or deliver what the community requires. As well as being concerned with news content, editors must worry about its cost, and they must balance coverage within tight financial and resource constraints. Again, balancing risk is key. Which legal boundaries – be they defamation, suppression or a host of other issues – can be pushed and which must be observed strictly can sometimes come down to the size of the potential legal bill.

Typically, newsrooms are divided into content creators (reporters, photographers, videographers, camera operators) and production journalists (producers, sub-editors, video editors) who check and polish reporters' copy and package the final news product. Specialist editors, such as news editors, sports editors and lifestyle editors typically straddle creation and distribution and supervise the production team as well as the chief reporters, who manage the minutiae of a reporting team's focus and workflow. They assign stories, help with edits and ensure a flow of content to meet the continuous deadlines of their newsroom's website, newspaper and television and/or radio bulletins. Their reporting team will typically include generalists, who cover an eclectic range of news events, and specialists who work 'rounds' or 'beats' such as business, court, environment, local government, police and politics. There tends to be a mix of experience among reporting teams, with a heavy majority usually having less experience than the few who have been a decade or more in media. A 2007 survey of New Zealand reporters found half had less than 5 years' reporting experience, and only a quarter had 15 years' experience or more (Hollings et al., 2007: 181).

Newsrooms typically cover crime stories by assigning reporters to rounds such as police and courts or to the breaking news desk, which deals with unfolding 'this just happened' news that is often crime-related. Larger organisations may also assign senior reporters to investigative roles to cover bigger, more difficult stories (such as Phil Kitchin's years-long investigation into a rape culture within the New Zealand Police), but these roles are increasingly under threat from the commercial pressures of falling circulation and ratings and intensifying competition for audiences. In recent years, most New Zealand media organisations have restructured their newsrooms and cut back on the staff and resourcing needed to sustain large investigations (Myllylahti, 2015).

As a result, most crime news is produced by police and court rounds reporters. The police round can be a difficult one to navigate. As well as having to master the many skills now expected of journalists – cultivate sources, analyse information quickly, write compelling stories, take great photos and video, edit your own work and promote it on social media – police reporters, say Samson and Hollings (2008), must be on top of the laws of trespass, privacy, *sub judice* and defamation; deal with the emotion and stress of talking to relatives of crime victims or witnessing violence themselves (such as happened with the 1990 killings at Aramoana); and forge relationships with police without being too friendly or swayed by political agendas. And they must do all this within an environment that is increasingly controlled by media minders.

Court reporters tend to report mainly on court proceedings. As news media, they have a right to be present in court and can widely report what happens as long as their stories are fair, accurate and balanced (which is not easy to get right when reporters might be parachuted into court for only a day or two of what might be months-long proceedings). Court reporters must understand the complexities of the justice system – its legal terminology, bureaucracy and structure (District and High Courts, the Court of Appeal and Supreme Court, as well as the Environment Court, Youth Court, Family Court, Coroner's Court, Māori Land Court, and a variety of tribunals and hearings). They must also abide by the strict rules of the courtroom, which restrict photography and recording in court, interviews with jurors and, often, the publication of names. There are generally more reporting restrictions in the criminal courts, mainly to shield defendants from publicity that might jeopardise their right to a fair trial (though critics say such restrictions can allow the wealthy and powerful to escape public scrutiny and name suppression is often fought by newsrooms on that basis).

What Gets Covered, and Why Crime?

Is it new? Is it interesting? Is it about – or does it affect – people? News doesn't have to be all of these things but it is usually at least one of them. Decisions about each are highly subjective and to a large degree those decisions are moderated by chief reporters who budget staff and time according to their assessment of their audience's actual need for certain information and the media outlet's need to supply content that resonates. For instance, an audience needs to know who won a national election, what rates will be, or if there has been a chemical spill in a local river. They probably do not *need* to know about the actions and behaviour of well-known celebrities, but many people will often *want* to know and it might be on that basis that stories are assigned to reporting staff.

The decision making behind selection is akin to feeding from a dinner buffet scaled from salad at one end to fast food at the other. Too much from one end or the other is likely to have an effect on diners: constant salad will have people looking to eat elsewhere, while a total fast-food diet of news is likely to have its own impact on an audience. The sayings 'if it bleeds, it leads' and 'bad news sells' have long been wry references to editors' arguably cynical story-selection policies, particularly around crime which can often produce the McDonald's of news. Like McDonald's, there is a healthy option on offer but it's often a lot easier to serve burgers.

Done well though, crime reporting can provide communities with critical information that helps them understand where and how they live. It can also provide information that allows people to gauge the cohesiveness of their community and to identify – maybe even solve – its problems. It allows the community to be informed about how society deals with crime and punishment, and ask important questions about crime trends or court judgments. But it can also be subject to hyperbole, provoke unrealistic fear and concern about security, and engage with a public appetite for morbid, horrific and macabre stories (and, for some, titillation) about the darker sides of our nature. Lawyer and lecturer Judy McGregor noted that coverage of Raymond Ratima's 1992 killing of seven members of his family, including his three young sons, lifted newspaper sales, which she attributed to the public's need to be reassured of their essential 'goodness' in opposition to the 'badness' symbolised by Ratima (Walrond, 2012).

There is a strong public service ethic underpinning newsrooms' crime reporting. The routine reporting of court proceedings, for instance, is a function of the notion that justice must not only be done but also be *seen* to be done and journalists have privileged access to our courts for this reason. Court coverage can also expose unfairness in the system (to both victims and defendants) and help prevent injustices by putting the justice system itself (judges, lawyers and justice officials) under the spotlight. This Fourth Estate role as a defender of public interests and a watchdog on social and political institutions also underpins the media's focus on holding institutions like the police and prisons to account. High-profile examples of this sort of coverage include an investigation by the UK *Guardian* ('The Counted', 2015–16), which revealed the true number of people killed by law enforcement in the United States, and 'An Unbelievable Story of Rape', the Pulitzer Prize-winning investigation by non-profit news organisations ProPublica and the Marshall Project into the story of a young woman who was punished by police for reporting a rape they did not believe happened but which was eventually proven true when the serial rapist was caught (Christian Miller and Armstrong, 2015). New Zealand journalists have led similarly high-profile media campaigns to highlight the cases of innocent people jailed for crimes they did not commit, such as Arthur Allan Thomas, David Dougherty and Teina Pora.

What Is Crime News?

Crime news can take various forms, and the following examples are but a small sample:

1. *Breaking:* This is when news breaks around an unfolding event such as an armed robbery, the discovery of a body or a riot. Sources typically include police and eyewitnesses. This type of crime news is fast-moving, and reportage, particularly in the online media environment, is measured in seconds and minutes. Reporters are expected to file reports within minutes of an event breaking and continue to file frequent updates through the day. The demand for up-to-the-minute news on 24/7 mobile and online news platforms has created extra challenges for reporters who must update stories quickly when events are running fast and it is difficult to digest and verify information (Craig, 2011). In the chaotic aftermath of the 2013 Boston Marathon bombing, for instance, several media outlets mistakenly reported that Boston police had made an arrest and within hours had to retract their reporting.
- *Developing:* This is when the breathless first few hours of a breaking news story change gear and allow a more measured assessment of the information. These stories give an opportunity to incorporate context and to flesh out leads that might have emerged during the breaking news phase. Sources are usually expanded to include those involved in the breaking news event – perhaps victims and those with personal connections to

Snapshot of a Crime Story: The Case of Tony Robertson
DAVID FISHER

The killer of Blessie Gotingco dumped her body about 20 metres away from my grandparents' grave. It was a detail which tugged at my mind when the news broke that she had been found and when Tony Robertson was arrested.

It was 2014 and once arrested and charged, journalists knew almost immediately the man accused of killing Mrs Gotingco had a history of sexual offending. Robertson, who was named on court charge sheets when he was arrested, had only just received parole. One of the *New Zealand Herald*'s journalists had written a story from the parole decision, which stated he was at a high risk of reoffending on release.

Then there was more coverage when the Department of Corrections applied to the court to have Robertson subject to electronic monitoring for the next decade. At that stage, we were bound from reporting the back story. Court rules prevented us from detailing Robertson's abduction and indecent assault against a 5 year old in Tauranga in 2005. But there was no doubt that Robertson's release had put an angry, dangerous man into a community which would likely suffer as a result.

Robertson was barely out for 6 months when he killed Mrs Gotingco. He ran her down with his car, took her back to his home and raped her before stabbing her to death. He then wrapped her body in a sheet and dumped it in long grass and bush neighbouring the Birkdale Cemetery in Auckland.

The case was a slam-dunk. It was possible to track Robertson by his electronic GPS bracelet from the moment Mrs Gotingco went missing, back to his house and then to the place her body was found. He left DNA evidence on Mrs Gotingco and the knife in his house had her blood on it – as did his car and his garage. The items she had been carrying he dumped under bushes in his front yard.

For all that, he pleaded not guilty then fired his lawyers before presenting an outlandish conspiracy theory to the jury.

While the justice system worked, I dug into Robertson's back story. When such awful things happen, there is a community desire to ask if it could have been prevented. I won access to court files from the 2005 attack, was able to access the evidence presented (cast-iron and yet he still pleaded not guilty) and see the judge's reason for not imposing preventive detention at the time.

I studied parole reports and court records presented for the eventual GPS monitoring order made 8 years later and found Robertson had served his entire sentence. There was no way to keep him inside longer. He had denied, consistently, that he was guilty and refused all forms of treatment. He wasn't a sex offender, he said.

The story which the *Herald* eventually ran explained that everyone involved did everything they could to keep the public safe. He was eventually released when it would have been unlawful to keep him locked up.

It didn't stop others pursuing that line. A former advocate with the Sensible Sentencing Trust – a 'lock 'em up' lobby group – had formed a relationship with the Gotingco family and a number of stories followed in which there were calls for accountability. An inquiry found no one was to blame, backing up the *Herald* reporting, but it was labelled a whitewash by the Gotingco family. In the wake of the conviction, the family was planning civil action against the Department of Corrections.

I've often wondered why Robertson denies in the face of extraordinary evidence. In the 2005 case, he was found alone in his car with the 5-year-old girl on a deserted country road. Her first words to her rescuer were: 'The man hurt my heart.' Her underwear was found in the back of his car.

His mother, whom I interviewed, told me she tried to take her life after police told her he had been arrested over the incident. She was unsuccessful. A short while later, she visited Robertson in prison where he awaited trial and he assured her he was innocent. In all those years, and after all that evidence, she still believed him. When he ran down Mrs Gotingco, he told his mum it was an accident.

It was almost as if the two gave each other purpose. As long as Robertson was innocent, his mum was free of whatever motivations drove her to seek an end to her life. For Robertson, perhaps he felt he needed to deny, deny, deny, to free his mum of those motivations.

Whatever reason, he was released. At the time he was convicted, there were 46 other child sex offenders released with GPS. More than half had breached their release conditions.

---

them – as well as those with experience or expertise in the type of event or related issues.
- *Concluding:* Crime stories often have a life cycle, with the court system bookending many events. The structure of the justice system means a hearing, trial and outcome provide set pieces for reporters. The conclusion of a trial usually frees reporters from the restraint of *sub judice*, which bars news media from reporting matters that could unduly influence the course of justice, and it is common for reporters to make public at this point the material they have gathered since the original incident (such as someone's history, previous offences, insights into their character and so on). Aside from coverage of the testimony and discussion within the court, there is no predictable sourcing in these stories.
- *Investigative:* Any crime – solved or otherwise – will have unanswered questions, and reporters will work to answer those questions before and after the court process. Stories might focus on the entire incident – for example, the Ben Hope and Olivia Smart murders – or specific aspects of the crime (e.g., Was there a mystery ketch?). Again, sourcing in these stories is diverse. Other investigative stories might dig into crime trends and statistics, as did the *Guardian* for its 'The Counted' exposé discussed above; wrongdoing among police, corrections and/or justice officials; or policy issues, as did Amy Maas (2014) in her Canon Media Award-winning investigation into the rise of American-style plea bargains,

which save the taxpayer the cost of lengthy trials but arguably hide the true face of crime.

As most people have little first-hand experience of crime news, the news media are, for many, their only source of information about crime, justice and social order. Yet what we see in the news is a highly selective and distorted account of reality (Greer, 2010: 201; Wykes, 2001). Crime news differs from the 'reality' of criminal offending and its representation in official crime statistics (Jewkes, 2011: 41) by focusing on some, and not all crime, and certain types of crime. That's partly because news is shaped by the complex production processes of news organisations. Time pressures, cost, publication space and the need for visuals all play a role in determining what is reported and what is left out. A story that takes more time and money to cover or that is too big for the available news slot, for instance, is less likely to make the news (Abel, 2004).

Crime news is also shaped by journalists' news values, a subjective set of criteria that journalists learn through a process of informal socialisation (reading newspapers, talking to more experienced colleagues, and observing the selection decisions of editors) and use to assess the newsworthiness of events or topics, such as the public appeal of a story and whether it is in the public interest (Chibnall, 1975, 1977; Jewkes, 2011). Jewkes (2011) identifies twelve key news values that determine the structure and content of crime stories. To be newsworthy, she says, events must meet a certain level of perceived importance or drama (*threshold*), which rules out reporting on most common and minor crimes. Stories are more likely to be newsworthy if they are current, unusual or dramatic, which means that the past, the normal and the mundane are typically neglected by news media (Chibnall, 1975: 58). For example, if your home was broken into 6 months ago, that is not news. If your home and those of all your neighbours were broken into at the weekend, that might be news for your local community newspaper. If the burglars set out breakfast for each household before they left with their stolen goods, that's unusual enough to be reported on even more widely.

Conversely, a story that is *predictable* is also more likely to be reported on because it guarantees usable news, as did the 8-week Chris Cairns perjury trial in late 2015, and enables journalists to plan their coverage in advance – the big feature that wraps up the trial or the footage for daily television bulletins. Crimes that have *graphic imagery* are also more likely to be reported as television and newspaper front pages needs strong visuals. In fact, the availability of an image can not only determine whether or not a story is run, but also help elevate a

Snapshot of a Crime Story: The Fall of Mark Lyon
DAVID FISHER

I had a 14-year relationship with Mark Lyon before he went to jail for a long time. We didn't meet, or at least not in any meaningful way, but I knew him well enough to know his methamphetamine addiction had taken him down some twisted roads.

Enemies, friends and those who passed through his crazy lifestyle combined with court records to provide access to the life of a man who was one of Auckland's wealthy masters of the universe.

Lyon was a property dealer, a smart investor and one of those who helped shape parts of modern Auckland with boldness and vision. He is now serving a 15-year sentence, which includes convictions for sex offences against a number of victims including a 14-year-old girl.

I first encountered Lyon, or his life anyway, in 2002 amid the burned-out ruins of the mansion he owned on the slopes of Auckland's Mt Eden, neighbouring Government House. He had been hosting a constant party – working girls and gang members were a regular feature, with members of the Head Hunters taking up residence in some of the bedrooms.

The house was a shell and Lyon had disappeared but some of those hangers-on were around – enough people to tell me what happened. The signs were pretty obvious. His bedroom was filled with empty bottles of spirits, meth pipes and carefully cut-out pornography arrayed in a vast mural above his bed.

My pursuit of Lyon took me to a few places he lived. One of those was a bunker, levels below an underground car park he owned. The entrance appeared to be booby-trapped – no idea who by – with a large sheet of metal precariously balanced across the entrance. Opening the door brought it swinging down like a guillotine.

Then he was in an apartment – another collage of pornography – and then a disused apartment above a central city pub which had the same wallpaper. Every few months someone from the scene would call and pass on the latest. If that didn't happen, Lyon would pass through court on some technicality and his slow, constant slide to rock bottom would pass another descent marker.

Lyon became a familiar inner-city Auckland sight. For a while, he adopted a black dreadlocked wig. He wore singlets and jeans which seemed to have never been washed. His teeth seemed to have disappeared inside his mouth. The talk was they had been eaten away by meth abuse.

Lyon flirted with disaster. He had his head smashed in outside a brothel one night and it seemed unlikely he would pull through. It wasn't an unusual place to find Lyon. He was known to go looking for prostitutes when he was on a bender. His meth addiction compelled him to seek out sex and also brought anger when he was unable to get from it all he wanted.

Lyon survived and went on to target young women and girls lost in life. He would find them in the inner city – runaways, drifters, party girls and gang hangers-on. He had all the drugs anyone might want, and sexual demands driven to a frenzy by his abuse of meth. In a building he owned – having retained his wealth through all this – was an area he called his 'dungeon'.

Victims would be taken there and what was not surrendered willingly would be forced. One victim told of what was effectively a torture device – she was shackled by the neck and bound and forced into an uncomfortable, hunched position. Lyon forced oral sex on her until she begged to be raped, she later said in court, in the hope her ordeal would be over.

It took two and a half years for that case to go through the courts. For detectives who laid the charges, it was a long time to keep witnesses on track. Lyon spent his time on bail and drugs. Young women and his frustrated sexual demands were a constant until his conviction and imprisonment in 2014, at age 59.

crime victim or offender to iconic status (Greer, 2010: 227). The picture of 3-year-old Madeleine McCann, who disappeared in 2007 from her bed in a holiday apartment in Portugal, became instantly recognisable to a generation of news audiences. *Violent* crimes, crimes of a *sexual* nature and crimes involving *children* are all more likely to be reported, as are mundane crimes if they involve a *high-status* or *celebrity* figure, such as Star Trek actor Chris Pine, whose 2014 appearance in the Ashburton District Court on drink driving charges garnered widespread media attention.

There are no hard-and-fast rules to reporting the news, however. Jewkes's list helps us to identify typicalities, but there are clearly differences in the way crime is reported within and between different news media, which reflects the inherent differences of different media markets and target audiences. In the United Kingdom, for instance, Schlesinger, Tumber and Murdock (1991) found that national television tended to focus on public order offences while tabloid newspapers tended to focus more on sexual and violent crime and rely more on the views of criminals, victims of crime and their relatives (compared with the quality press which relied more on experts, elites and pressure groups). It's important, then, not to over-generalise the construction and content of crime news, especially given today's media are highly diversified and the ways in which they source, select, produce and disseminate news are changing rapidly (Greer, 2010: 262). Nonetheless, research on crime reporting has revealed some key patterns.

Understanding Crime News

Many scholars agree that crime is over-represented in the media and bears little relation to actual crime statistics (see, e.g., Boda and Szabo, 2011; Chadee and Ditton, 2005; Greer, 2007; Jewkes, 2011). In the United Kingdom, Ayres and Jewkes's (2012) study of media coverage of crystal meth found that coverage was not only overblown but also unfounded. The news media reported 'ice' as 'Britain's deadliest drug problem', despite the fact that indicators measuring *actual* drug use suggested its use was almost non-existent and crystal meth had not been identified as a problem by any scientific, policy or crime-measuring organisation.

As well as over-reporting certain crimes, the news media also treat different crimes, offenders and victims unequally. Studies suggest that the news media place disproportionate emphasis on violent crime and give sparse attention to the property offences that make up the majority of recorded crime (Greer, 2007). Aside from driving offences, the majority of offences reported to police in New Zealand are property crimes such as theft and burglary, yet the media under-report these and disproportionately focus on the minority of crime that is violent (Walrond, 2012), particularly the small percentage of crimes that are murders. The media focus on violent crime is also highly selective. Stranger crime is emphasised more than domestic or family violence, as are particularly high-profile or serious crimes that resonate with wider society (Greer, 2007). The 1993 murder of UK toddler James Bulger by two 10-year-old boys, for instance, generated fierce public debate at the time – and intense coverage and vilification of the offenders by the popular media for decades afterwards (Jewkes, 2011).

Generally, crime news has to be simplified to fit tight space (and keep the limited attention of audiences), and it is often personalised to give stories 'human interest' appeal and narrative impact. As a result, crime stories tend to focus on individual motivations rather than broader social, political and economic issues. They can also tend to stigmatise criminals as monsters or absolute 'others'; that is, completely unlike 'us', the general public (Jewkes, 2011). Think of how convicted rapist Stewart Murray Wilson was dubbed the 'Beast of Blenheim', or how Robert Thompson and Jon Venables, who were 10 when they killed James Bulger, were variously labelled in the British newspapers as 'evil', 'beasts' and 'bastards'.

On the other hand, the news media tend to sentimentalise some victims of crime, especially elderly women and young children who are perceived as vulnerable, innocent and worthy of sympathy. Young men, the homeless, and those with drug problems or otherwise on the margins of society receive little, if any, media attention by comparison (Greer, 2007: 24). But, again, there are no hard-and-fast rules to such coverage. The popular and award-winning investigative podcast *Serial*, produced by US radio show *This American Life*, was criticised for the absence of murder victim Hae Min Lee in its coverage of her killer's case, while the *New York Magazine* was applauded for bringing each of the 35 accusers in Bill Cosby's sexual assault allegations dramatically to the fore by putting each of them on the cover of its magazine.

Research has long identified racist trends in crime reporting (Dixon and Linz, 2000; Entman and Rojecki, 2001; McCreanor et al., 2014; Nairn et al., 2006), though recent studies have noted some changes. Dixon's (2015) analysis of US news broadcasts between 2008 and 2012 revealed Hispanic and African American depictions had greatly improved, with African Americans accurately portrayed across all roles of offender, victim and police officer, though Whites were more likely to be portrayed as police and homicide victims than was the case in reality. Another study of US national news broadcasts (Dixon and Williams, 2015) found that African Americans were *under*-represented as perpetrators (and victims) of crime, but new troubling dynamics were emerging for Latinos and Muslims.

In many ways, these trends reflect wider social attitudes – journalists are diarists of the culture of the period in which they live (Wykes, 2001: 26). For example, media reports today are shared, discussed and amplified across media networks in ways that reveal the same biases among the wider public. Lampolsthammer et al. (2014) examined all geo-referenced crime tweets posted in the United Kingdom in 2012, along with all worldwide tweets related to crime news. They found that if the victim of a crime was a woman or the crime type was theft/burglary, there was less chance the crime incident would be posted on Twitter than if the victim was a man or the type of the crime incident was violent, which mirrored the media's biases towards violent crime and against sexual violence.

Researchers have also found evidence that crime news can tend to reflect the agenda and interests of those in power. Factors such as time, cost and ease of access mean reporters tend to over-rely on official and elite sources in all their reporting. Lugo-Ocando and Brandão (2016) argue that the faster pace of news has created a sort of 'mimicry' in the news media where press releases and crime data are reported almost unchanged in some cases, making coverage less an exercise of accountability of public policy and more a repetitive ritualistic performance. Allen and Savigny's (2012) analysis of newspaper coverage of price-fixing prosecutions after its criminalisation in the United Kingdom found the voice of business elites (and not marginalised consumers) dominated coverage and, as a result, news reports tended to 'decriminalise' the activity. Because of its reliance on official and elite sources such as the police, Jewkes (2011: 62) says crime news is also more likely to have an essentially conservative agenda that emphasises deterrence and repression. Indeed, by highlighting behaviours or issues that have not always been crimes, such as boy racing, teenage binge drinking or party pills, crime reporting tends to amplify what news media perceive to be community concerns (Walrond, 2012). Intense, media-fuelled bursts of collective concern, known as 'moral panics' (Cohen, 2011), are seen by some to increase the public's fear of crime and predispose people to more punitive law and order policies and national security measures (Greer, 2010: 379).

When following crime stories, it pays to ask how they have been put together. What information has been included and what has been left out? Does it answer

Snapshot of a Crime Story: The Benefit Fraudster
DAVID FISHER

Information has ways of finding journalists. In 2006 I had a tip from someone on the inside of a police investigation about a large amount of cash and gold found in a house in Massey. The tip came by way of a staff member at the *New Zealand Herald*, who knew someone who was working on the case. When stories are extraordinary, there are no secrets kept.

I reached out to contacts I knew who might have a connection to criminals, wealth and 'weird' – there's nothing normal about a large amount of gold. One of those I contacted was able to give me an address and the outline of the remarkable story of Wayne Thomas Patterson.

Eventually convicted on a string of fraud charges, Patterson had manufactured about 120 false identities to steal more than $3 million. Each false identity was for someone over the age of 65 – 18 years older than Patterson was when convicted. Using a range of disguises and the false identities, he applied for and received $54,000 a fortnight.

The details unfolded over a few short days – the number of identities, the amount of money and the involvement of a specialist police team brought in for the search of Patterson's home.

By the time I turned up at Patterson's home – a modest $230-a-week terraced rental in Massey, Auckland – he had already been charged and was in prison on remand awaiting trial. His neighbours knew him as Geoffrey Patterson, one of a multitude of identities he had to keep straight. They all had stories to tell – about how he was a gold trader and loved exotic plants, and about the 'eureka' moment when police found $750,000 buried in the garden.

The police had finished and the landlord let me inside Patterson's home. From there, with help from a contact in the know, Patterson's life of crime was able to be reconstructed. His home office was kitted out for his full-time job of defrauding the taxpayer.

The cash, gold and silver was hidden throughout the home – small cubby holes, nooks and crannies. Patterson showered under nearly $800,000 in gold.

The landlord was sorry to lose his tenant – no surprise given the amount of money Patterson had lavished on the flat. He spent $50,000 alone on the garden, which was little more than 10 metres wide and 15 metres deep. It was packed with expensive, exotic plants and – as much as possible in the small space – landscaped.

When it came to publishing, the degree of public interest and length of time until Patterson's trial were considered enough to trump *sub judice* rules. Every detail that was learned was printed – including Patterson's conviction for a strikingly similar welfare fraud in Australia 20 years earlier.

By the time the story came to court, it seemed most of it had already been told. But there was more – Patterson had successfully invested his stolen money, making about $3 million. His lawyer argued in court that he had earned the money so should be allowed to keep it.

Patterson, also, found new ways to break the law. When he appeared for parole, he provided letters from referees who, it turned out, did not exist or who had never written to support the conman.

all your questions? Why these sources and not those? Why now? How do we know what's true? Understanding crime reporting starts with knowing how to evaluate, analyse and fact-check the trustworthiness of crime news. The following strategies can be used as a guide:

- *Sources:* Is the evidence direct or indirect (e.g., is information truly a 'fact' or something that is said by someone quoted in the story)? What sources or perspectives are present? What sources or perspectives are missing? Whose voices aren't being heard? Who should have been interviewed to give a more well-rounded story?
- *Language:* What language is used to describe the action or story subject? Are there any loaded words that unfairly describe or characterise a person or event?
- *Structure:* How is the story organised? What is considered the most important information? What choices have gone into selecting the lead paragraph?
- *Context:* Does the story place the news into a broader context? What limitations of the 24-hour/breaking news cycle are evident?
- *Framing:* What values inform the writing of the story? Is the story treated with respect and neutrality? Is the story fair?
- *Visual:* Consider the photographs, captions, infographics and headlines that accompany a story. How do they grab attention and appeal to emotion? What extra information do they convey?

Debates over Media Effects

One of the key criticisms of crime stories is that by focusing on the worst crimes they produce a highly skewed picture that leads many to mistakenly believe violent crime is increasing or that they are at risk. Indeed, concerns about the impact of media on society has spawned a vast literature on media effects. However, much of the research on behavioural effects, which asserts a direct causal connection between exposure to media violence and subsequent violent behaviour, has been widely criticised (see Gauntlett, 2001), largely for the suggestion that audiences are passive recipients of media messages and its failure to account for the wider structural and cultural factors behind violent behaviour (Greer, 2010: 401).

In fact, it is very difficult to study media effects. We are so saturated with mass media that it is nearly impossible to find people who do not consume media of some kind and studies typically lack a control group. A review of research on media and fear of crime (Ditton et al., 2004, cited in Greer, 2010) concluded that media effects research is at best scattered and vague. Heath and Gilbert (1996: 380), meanwhile, have suggested that causal direction may not start with the media, but go from fear to media viewing. In other words, people who are apprehensive about crime may seek out crime representations as some sort of coping, calming or information mechanism. Indeed, the relationship between media consumption and fear of crime is complex. Factors such as the audience's credulity and prior apprehension about crime, the randomness of the crime, the proportion of the newspaper devoted to crime (as opposed to the raw number of articles about crime), location of the crime, and the type of programming (drama versus news) all affect the relationship with fear of crime (Heath and Gilbert, 1996: 384).

Other researchers have attempted to look more at what audiences *do* with media – how they access, consume and interpret it in their everyday lives – to get a more nuanced understanding of media 'influence' (Greer, 2010: 442–3). Particularly in today's multi-mediated world, where media content is constantly being shared and recycled and patterns of influence are less predictable (Greer, 2010: 483), we need to think differently about news media and their relationship to crime.

Particularly, as news is increasingly filtered through social media, platform companies and apps (e.g., Facebook, Twitter, Snapchat, Google, Apple, Amazon, WhatsApp) and it gets harder to determine what is news and what is an advertisement or propaganda piece, it becomes even more important that news consumers and citizens learn how to evaluate the credibility of the news and information they consume. By understanding the elements that shape how crime is reported and thinking critically about what you read, hear and see in the media, you will be better able to distinguish good crime reporting, which presents information fairly, accurately and contextually, from opinion and misinformation.

REFERENCES

Abel, S. 2004. 'All the News You Need to Know?', in L. Goode and N. Zuberi (Eds), *Media Studies in Aotearoa/New Zealand*. Auckland: Pearson Longman, pp. 183–91.

Allen, H., and Savigny, H. 2012. 'Selling Scandal or Ideology? The Politics of Business Crime Coverage', *European Journal of Communication* 27(3): 278–90.

Boda, Z., and Szabo, G. 2011. 'The Media and Attitudes towards Crime and the Justice System: A Qualitative Approach', *European Journal of Criminology* 8(4): 329–42.

Burgess, J. 2014. 'What Makes News Online: A New Zealand Perspective', MA thesis, Massey University, Palmerston North.

Chadee, D., and Ditton, J. 2005. 'Fear of Crime and the Media: Assessing the Lack of Relationship', *Crime, Media, Culture* 1(3): 322–32.

Chibnall, S. 1975. 'The Crime Reporter: A Study in the Production of Commercial Knowledge', *Sociology* 9: 49–66.

Chibnall, S. 1977. *Law and Order News: An Analysis of Crime Reporting in the British Press*. London: Tavistock.

Christian Miller, T., and Armstrong, K. 2015. 'An Unbelievable Story of Rape', *ProPublica and the Marshall Project*, 16 December. Accessed 21 May 2017. https://www.propublica.org/article/false-rape-accusations-an-unbelievable-story

Cohen, S. 2011. *Folk Devils and Moral Panics* (3rd ed). London: Routledge.

Craig, D. 2011. *Excellence in Online Journalism: Exploring Current Practices in an Evolving Environment*. Thousand Oaks, CA: Sage.

Dixon, T. 2015. 'Good Guys Are Still Always in White? Positive Change and Continued Misrepresentation of Race and Crime on Local Television News', *Communication Research* 27(5): 547–73.

Dixon, T., and Linz, D. 2000. 'Overrepresentation and Underrepresentation of African Americans and Latinos as Lawbreakers on Television News', *Journal of Communication* 50(2): 131–54.

Dixon, T., and Williams, C. 2015. 'The Changing Misrepresentation of Race and Crime on Network and Cable News', *Journal of Communication* 65(1): 24–39.

Entman, R., and Rojecki, A. 2001. *The Black Image in the White Mind: Media and Race in America*. Chicago: University of Chicago Press.

Gauntlett, D. 2001. 'The Worrying Influence of "Media Effects" Studies', in M. Barker and J. Petley (Eds), *Ill Effects: The Media/Violence Debate* (2nd ed.). Abingdon, UK: Routledge, pp. 47–62.

Greer, C. 2007. 'News Media, Victims and Crime', in P. Davies, P. Francis and C. Greer (Eds), *Victims, Crime and Society*. London: Sage, pp. 22–45.

Greer, C. 2010. *Crime and Media: A Reader*. London: Routledge.

Heath, L., and Gilbert, K. 1996. 'Mass Media and Fear of Crime', *American Behavioral Scientist* 39(4): 379–86.

Hollings, J., Lealand, G., Samson, A., and Tilley, E. 2007. 'The Big NZ Journalism Survey: Underpaid, Under-trained, Under-resourced, Unsure about the Future – but Still Idealistic', *Pacific Journalism Review* 13(2): 175–97.

Jewkes, Y. 2011. *Media and Crime* (2nd ed.). London: Sage.

Lampoltshammer, T. J., Kounadi, O., Sitko, I., and Hawelka, B. 2014. 'Sensing the Public's Reaction to Crime News Using the "Links Correspondence Method"', *Applied Geography* 52: 57–66.

Lugo-Ocando, J., and Brandão, R. 2016. 'Stabbing News', *Journalism Practice* 10(6): 715–29.

Maas, A. 2014. 'The Real Cost of Cut-Price Justice', *New Zealand Herald*, 14 May. Accessed 21 May 2017. http://www.nzherald.co.nz/nz/news/article.cfm?c_id=1&objectid=11256874

Machado, H., and Santos, F. 2009. 'The Disappearance of Madeleine McCann: Public Drama and Trial by Media in the Portuguese Press', *Crime, Media, Culture* 5(2): 146–67.

McCreanor, T., Rankine, J., Barnes, A., Borell, B., Nairn, R., and McManus, A. 2014. 'The Association of Crime Stories and Māori in Aotearoa New Zealand Print Media', *Sites* 11(1): 121–44.

Myllylahti, M. 2015. *JMAD New Zealand Media Ownership Report 2015*. Accessed 26 January 2016. http://www.aut.ac.nz/__data/assets/pdf_file/0011/608366/JMAD-2015-Report.pdf

Nairn, R., Pega, F., McCreanor, T., Rankine, J., and Barnes, A. 2006. 'Media, Racism and Public Health Psychology', *Journal of Health Psychology* 11(2): 183–96.

New Zealand Police. 2015. *New Zealand Crime Statistics 2014*. Accessed 26 January 2016. http://www.police.govt.nz/sites/default/files/publications/crime-stats-national-20141231.pdf

Samson, A., and Hollings, J. 2008. 'The Police Round: Crime, Emergencies and Disasters', in J. Tully (Ed.), *Intro: A Beginner's Guide to Professional News Journalism*. Wellington: New Zealand Journalists Training Organisation, pp. 175–200.

Schlesinger, P., Tumber, H., and Murdock, G. 1991. 'The Media Politics of Crime and Criminal Justice', *British Journal of Sociology* 42(3): 397–420.

'The Counted'. 2015–16. *Guardian*. Accessed 21 May 2017. https://www.theguardian.com/us-news/series/counted-us-police-killings

Walrond, C. 2012. 'Crime and the Media: Crime News', *Te Ara – The Encyclopedia of New Zealand*. Accessed 26 January 2016. http://www.teara.govt.nz/en/crime-and-the-media/page-1

Wykes, M. 2001. *News, Crime and Culture*. London: Pluto Press.

Zelizer, B., and Allan, S. 2010. *Keywords in News and Journalism Studies*. Maidenhead, UK: Open University Press.

14.

Gangs and Underworld Justice

JARROD GILBERT

Introduction

Patched gangs, both outlaw motorcycle clubs and street gangs, formed in New Zealand in the 1960s and 1970s (Gilbert, 2013) but it was not until the 1990s that their dominance within many parts of the underworld became apparent. At this time, gang strength had grown to the point that gangs could define and enforce their own justice system of what we might term 'street rules'. Following this, it was during the 1990s that the related term 'taxing' entered the country's lexicon. Taxing is essentially a form of extortion, whereby people are stood-over for payments regarding real or perceived debts owed to the gang. Often little more than crude robberies, acts of taxing exemplify the unique culture and rules that govern criminal life. Also related to street rules, but perhaps more concerning, have been gang efforts to escape prosecution. The most significant of these involved the murder of state witness Christopher Crean in 1996. This case, discussed in more detail below, highlights the extreme lengths that some gang members will go to when their interests are threatened. This chapter will look at taxing and at measures gangs may take to escape justice, and highlight what happens when the criminal justice system is forgone and is replaced by the rules of the street. It also discusses recent steps taken by the state to neutralise gang power when street rules threaten the legitimacy of the judicial process.

The Rules of the Street

Within criminal fraternities, redress of disputes is not ordinarily available via the process of law. Either due to an allegiance to criminal codes of behaviour (see Newbold, 1989) that forbids them from complaining to police, or through fear that a complaint to police will draw attention to one's own criminal undertakings, criminals are unlikely to seek the traditional law and order remedies that are available to most members of society. Therefore, those involved in criminal activity exist in a world where the strong can govern the weak. In communities where a gang has dominant strength, the gang will often regulate or exploit crime undertaken through taking the earnings of local criminals or claiming a percentage of their earnings.

Within the criminal world the gangs have seized *de facto* authority by using their strength to create and enforce their own rules. Within communities where gang influence is strong, criminals – primarily drug dealers – often have to negotiate with this authority in order to trade, in a way not entirely dissimilar to the way legitimate businesses need to deal with regulatory hurdles of city councils or government agencies. Without gang approval, and most often paying a fee to undertake certain activities, criminals open themselves up to be taxed. Because such activities are, by their very nature, secretive, most forms of taxing occur with little public knowledge and therefore most often only come to light when the police become involved.

Indeed, the act of taxing largely dissolves once the authorities do become involved. Although no specific research has been done in this area, it is widely acknowledged within the criminal fraternity that the New Zealand Police are incorruptible. There are claims that they will break the law in order to secure a conviction, but they are very unlikely to break the law to the benefit of criminals. Support for this view is reflected in Transparency International's (2016) Corruption Perceptions Index, which consistently rates New Zealand as one of the least corrupt countries in the world. The lack of corruption in the police is a key element in ensuring that taxing is generally confined to the criminal underworld that is resistant to police intervention. Those who are able and likely to seek protection from the law – that is the vast majority of the general population – will not be targeted as the significant risk of prosecution outweighs the potential benefits of the 'earn'.

The Rise of Taxing

During the early 1990s, the Nomads were one of the first gangs to gain a reputation for taxing, particularly in the town of Foxton where they told one victim that they 'own the town and everything in it' (*New Zealand Herald*, 4 April 1996). During the trial of several Nomad members in 1996, a jury was told that the gang took property from people who owed them debts then sold the stolen goods back to their previous owners. Sometimes they took a cut of people's welfare benefit money as well (*New Zealand Herald*, 16 January 1996).

After uncovering an early taxing operation in Foxton during 1994, police said that the activity was 'quite blasé' and no attempts were made to conceal the offenders' identities or gang affiliations (*New Zealand Herald*, 7 May 1994). In fact, unlike many crimes, taxing was reliant on people knowing the offender – intimidation being an important component of successful taxing. Reflecting the nature of much taxing, the police explained, 'A lot of people on the fringe of criminal activity themselves are getting taxed and are too scared to complain' (*New Zealand Herald*, 7 May 1994).

In 1995, a number of Nomads members, including the gang's feared boss, Dennis 'Mossie' Hines, awoke a woman in Foxton and demanded her boyfriend's marijuana stash. After the drugs were retrieved, Hines threatened to kill the woman in an effort to scare her into silence. However, the threat did not work and the victim went to the police. At the depositions hearing in the case, the court was introduced to this hitherto publicly unfamiliar term of taxing – which was explained to them as a form of stealing property (*New Zealand Herald*, 5 April 1995). That same year, police seized four cars that had been taxed by the gang over a 6-month period (*New Zealand Herald*, 30 September 1995). In April 1996, nine Nomads members were convicted of various charges stemming from the taxing of drug dealers and others in the community, using what Justice Heron described as 'mafia tactics' (*New Zealand Herald*, 27 April 1996).

Another case of taxing in 1996 involved Mongrel Mob members raiding a 'tinnie house' in Palmerston North, and taking drugs and cash. Although the occupants were 'terrified', they complained to the police and those involved were prosecuted (*New Zealand Herald*, 6 March 1996). In 1997, another group of Mongrel Mob members stole a car from an Auckland man before contacting him and demanding $2000 for the car's return. It was reported that threats were made against his family to keep him quiet. Indeed, the man did remain quiet and ended up paying the gang $1500 (*Sunday Star-Times*, 13 May 1997). What relationship the man had with the gang is unclear, but it is unlikely, given the nature of taxing, that he had no connections at all.

Yet another gang that has gained a reputation for taxing is the Auckland-based Head Hunters (*New Zealand Herald*, 12 July 1999), a gang that in recent years has spread throughout much of the country. Few members of the Head Hunters have qualms about claiming cash or property from people who have slighted the gang in some way. Most often the victims accept their fate – either knowing they have breached a gang law, or simply because they have no choice. Without complaints being made, police are powerless to stop the practice. The former leader of Auckland's Outlaw Motorcycle Gang Unit, Detective Sergeant Cam Stokes (2003, pers. comm.) told me: 'Certainly a lot of people have been ordered to get up to the Head Hunters' clubhouse with their motorbikes and ownership papers and hand them over because of a comment they have made about one of the members. . . . This is unreported crime . . . [and] very common.'

Prominent Head Hunter leader Wayne Doyle, who along with several of his members was convicted of murdering King Cobra member Anthony Evalu in April 1985, is quite open about the practice. When asked about his gang's reputation for taxing in the 1990s he told me: 'That's a fair assessment for everybody. . . . Like everybody else there was a fair bit of that going on. . . . We couldn't deny that; everybody was doing it' (Wayne Doyle, 2008, pers. comm.). In speaking about taxing generally, Doyle told me that it usually involves those within the underworld or, as he put it, 'hood on hood', whereby those with strength take from those who show weakness, suggesting it is an easy way for a 'lazy man to make an earn'. It is, he said, 'the law of the jungle'.

Cam Stokes (2003, pers. comm.) described to me one incident involving the Head Hunters:

The central police did an electronic job [trace] on [a car thief] and during the course of the operation they found out that he was scoring his drugs from a gang member. So they did a spin-off operation and the drugs squad picked up and ran [an operation] on the gang member dealing drugs and caught him, and he got some jail for it. The gang member said to this car thief: 'The cops caught me 'cause of you, if it wasn't for you I'd never have been caught' – even though he was the one being loose on the phone, it was someone else's fault. So [the gang member] said you owe me for my lawyer's bills and some time in jail – and he was given a bill [believed to be $50,000].

Not all taxing operations go smoothly, however, even when they are confined to the underworld.

Violence, Taxing and Dispute Resolution

In August 2000, ex-Hells Angels President Petar Vitali, who was no longer affiliated with the gang, was targeted to be taxed for his aluminium runabout boat and his restored Mustang car by the Head Hunters. It is believed that Vitali's crime, in the eyes of the Head Hunters, was a boast he had made about stabbing a Head Hunters member some years previously when the Hells Angels were doing security work at a music concert. Certainly, the stabbing incident occurred, but the boast, the Head Hunters decided, was disrespectful and required that a tax be paid. In many ways, Vitali was a typical tax victim. He was a 'principled' villain and thus unlikely to violate gang code and lay a complaint with police, and he was also, by that stage, a lone operator and, as such, a vulnerable tax victim. However, although Vitali was no longer protected by the Hells Angels, he had a significant reputation as a hard man.

The taxing had not been officially sanctioned by the Head Hunters; the incident had been occasioned by a single member, on his own initiative, rounding up five of his comrades to take the action. The six men were in the process of removing Vitali's car and boat when Vitali arrived home. Vitali reacted immediately and drove his car straight into the Head Hunters' vehicle. He then drew a pistol and fired at the gang – although the official record has him picking up a gun that was dropped by one of the Head Hunters as the cars collided (see, e.g., *New Zealand Herald*, 24 August 2001, 27 July 2013). A number of shots were fired by Vitali, one of which hit a gang member in the stomach.

A member of the Henderson Criminal Investigation Branch (CIB) who investigated the incident told me:

> He got [Head Hunter] 'Choc' Te Awa in the gut, a couple of rounds went into his [Vitali's] car and at least one went through his [Vitali's] garage wall and we found it on the neighbour's lawn behind it. . . . We all thought Vitali was just the bees knees for that . . . he wouldn't have had to pay for a drink all night if he'd come to the Henderson Police Bar. (Anonymous, pers. comm., 2009)

Although some in the police found humour in one of New Zealand's toughest gangs having the tide turned on them, the Head Hunters had a man in hospital fighting for his life. Te Awa was – and remains – a staunch and highly respected member of the Head Hunters. If Vitali deserved to be taxed over a boast, it stands to reason that his latest escapade had him marked for far worse. Certainly, police expected the situation to escalate. Initially, Stokes had trouble locating Vitali. He told me:

> We couldn't find him and we were obviously keen to get it sorted out. And I found a telephone number and spoke to him on the phone and tried to get him to come in and get it sorted out, and he obviously didn't want to do that – be a sitting target. He said the only person who could sort it out for him would be one of the Head Hunters [leader Wayne Doyle] so we arranged for a conversation to take place between them. (Cam Stokes, 2003, pers. comm.)

Exactly what was said between Vitali and Doyle, who at that moment was serving time in Waikeria Prison, is unclear, but the two decided it would be settled between them and, unsurprisingly, would not involve police:

> I think what's happened is that they've decided that um whatever happened there'd be no complaints made to the cops about it, so they were going to sort it out in their own way. Because after Vitali spoke with Doyle, Doyle wanted to speak with Te Awa [the shot man] in hospital, and we made that phone call happen as well, and there was no complaints coming out of them at all. (Cam Stokes, 2003, pers. comm.)

In the end, the only conviction to come from the incident was against Vitali for recklessly discharging a firearm. The Head Hunters did not go after him, and it is believed that this is largely due to the forgiveness of the shot man. Exactly what deal – if any – was struck, is unknown. Stokes believes that the Head Hunters became ambivalent about retribution:

> We heard a little bit back that the Heads management wasn't that happy with what had gone on and they didn't think it was a cool sort of taxing to do. So, if they weren't comfortable with it there's a chance that it could have been, 'Well he was only doing the right thing looking after himself' and so [there was] no great come back from there. (Cam Stokes, 2003, pers. comm.)

Certainly no overt retribution against Vitali appears to have occurred. Vitali himself would not talk about the incident with me. Wayne Doyle (2009, pers.

comm.) told me that he intervened in the dispute from prison, but says that he cannot recall the details of what was worked out, saying the issue was put on the 'backburner' and that there remains significant ill feeling within his gang: 'He [Vitali] is not the most popular person around here.'

As Petar Vitali became unpopular with the Head Hunters, one person who initially ingratiated himself before also falling out with them was multi-millionaire property developer Mark Lyon (see Chapter 13). In the early 2000s, the maverick businessman became involved with the Head Hunters socially and, I have been told by numerous sources, with some aspects of their business. The exact nature of the problems that Lyon later had with the Head Hunters is unclear, but he was taxed heavily by the gang for goods estimated to be worth between $250,000 and $800,000 (*New Zealand Herald*, 10 January 2003). Although it is impossible to assess the accuracy of these figures, it seems likely that Lyon may have the dubious honour of being the most taxed individual in New Zealand gang history.

Taxing does not just occur to those outside the gang. Members who fall foul of their own gang are likely to find themselves taxed in particular, members who leave the gang in so-called bad standing are often forced to hand over cash or possessions. Taxing is used to regain any property or money owed to the gang, often with significant injuries added, and may also be used to enforce a sanction against a former member. An outlaw motorcycle club member who is kicked out of his club for misconduct is liable to be taxed of his motorcycle. The larger street gangs such as the Mongrel Mob and Black Power are equally disposed to seek redress from errant members in the form of taxing. Patched street gang members have offered numerous examples of this to me. In one incident, told to me by senior Mongrel Mob member Ngavii Pekapo (2004, pers. comm.), a member of his gang who had assaulted a female related to key Mob members was stripped of his patch and all of his possessions, and told to leave the Hawke's Bay area within 24 hours or face worse repercussions.

Indeed how quickly, and often viciously, gangs turn against their own members when protocols are broken is quite remarkable, and something I have witnessed numerous times. The high value placed on brotherhood means that any breach of trust is viewed, and treated, severely.

While violence has been synonymous with patched gangs for many years, taxing has become a profitable means by which to wield the power that a reputation for violence offers. But violence is not just used to benefit gangs through profit; it has also been used as a defensive mechanism to protect gang members from the law.

Intimidation, Violence and Justice

For many gang members, intimidation of others is a key aspect of gang life. Not only does a gang's imposing nature and reputation give members a feeling of power and status, it can also be used as a tool to protect gang interests. As with taxing, most people who are stood-over by gang members exist within the gang or criminal realms. However, during the latter half of the 1990s, a spate of incidents captured public attention which targeted people who were not by choice involved with gangs. Eventually, some high-profile gang members avoided justice altogether, resulting in a significant law change.

Concerns that gang members were intimidating witnesses of crimes in order to escape justice were raised as early as 1975 (New Zealand Police, 1975: 91–98). But it was not until the 1990s that such concerns became significant enough to prompt serious reaction. Police figures provided to the New Zealand Law Commission (1997:3) show that reported offences of obstruction or attempts to pervert justice increased from 112 in 1993 to 169 in 1997. Although cases specifically relating to gangs were not defined, a number of examples involving gangs brought the issue to public attention and, in turn, generated a political response.

A window into the world of victim intimidation was opened in 1993. After making a complaint to the police of multiple rapes by several Mongrel Mob members at the gang's Rotorua clubhouse, the female complainant was forced by a member of the gang, Gillies Jacobs, to recant her initial police statement implicating him. Jacobs beat the complainant with a baseball bat and forced her to pose as his girlfriend while a witness watched her sign an affidavit clearing those who had been charged with the offences. Once this intimidation became known, Jacobs was convicted of attempting to pervert the course of justice (*New Zealand Herald*, 22 July 1993). Charges against other members remained, however, and nine members of the gang were subsequently convicted on charges of rape and/or sexual violation, and sentenced to between 3 years, 9 months' and 12 years, 6 months' imprisonment (*New Zealand Herald*, 24 July 1993).

In 1995, the Mongrel Mob appears to have had more success in escaping justice after a 16-year-old hitchhiker was allegedly raped by two members of the gang's Hastings chapter. Although the victim had already testified once, a jury complication meant that the trial was aborted part way through. Immediately before the second trial, police said the woman was approached in the courthouse corridor and told not to give evidence against the members. The woman then refused to testify when put on the stand. Even after being placed in custody over the lunch

The Execution of Christopher Crean

One man who did choose to testify against a gang was Christopher Crean. In March 1996, a group of Black Power members had attacked a member of the Mongrel Mob outside Crean's house in the Taranaki region. The incident was brutal. The Mob member's face was slashed, and several of his fingers were severed with a tomahawk (*New Zealand Herald*, 17 October 1997). Crean witnessed the attack and opted to testify against the attackers. Black Power threatened Crean and suggested that a court appearance would not be in his interests. Police offered witness protection, but Crean refused it. His refusal, while brave, ultimately proved fatal.

Since 1988, Black Power members from the Taranaki region had twice beaten murder charges. Crown prosecutor Tim Brewer felt that these cases had helped convince the gang that they were invincible (*New Zealand Herald*, 17 October 1997). It is perhaps this feeling of invincibility that emboldened the gang in relation to Crean. They set about planning his murder. Christopher Crean, a street-preaching Christian, told his family that God would protect him. His family was less certain. His mother said, 'I told him he was dealing with the real world, not the spiritual world. But he didn't have any fear' (*New Zealand Herald*, 17 October 1997).

Twice, on the last two Sundays of September 1996, Black Power's hit on Crean was abandoned – on the second of those nights, Crean was carrying his child and the would-be hit man felt compassion for the youngster (*R v Manihera*, Unreported, Court of Appeal, Richardson P, March 1998). On October 6, however, it was deemed that that the hit would proceed regardless of circumstance. That night, a gunman carrying a 30-30 Winchester lever-action rifle approached Crean's house and knocked on the door. As Crean came to answer, a shot was fired. The bullet smashed through the glass panel in the door, entering Crean's stomach and exiting out of his back. He died in hospital the next day (*New Zealand Herald*, 17 October 1997). The use of a stomach shot was pre-planned as it was considered that a head shot through the door might miss (*R v Manihera*, Unreported, Court of Appeal, Richardson P, March 1998).

A Taranaki Black Power member said that the killing had sent a clear message to potential prosecution witnesses: 'Oh, well they know now. Who . . . wants to get in the stand now?' (*New Zealand Herald*, 23 July 1997). The implications that this killing had on the justice process are quite clear: if the gang escaped penalty, future testimony against gangs would certainly have been difficult to obtain. Given this, the police moved quickly to bring closure to the case. Despite the seeming confidence that the killing would deter further witnesses, it was from within the gang that crucial evidence was to come. The New Plymouth chapter's president and the gang prospect who drove the getaway car both gave evidence against their own comrades (*R v Manihera*, Unreported, Court of Appeal, Richardson P, March 1998). Four Black Power members were eventually convicted of murdering Crean and given mandatory life sentences. One of the men convicted, Dennis Luke, became the first person in New Zealand to be twice convicted of murder (the first coming in 1975 when he had been found guilty of kicking an old man to death in Wellington).

The fact that the Taranaki Black Power went after what in the gang scene is often referred to as a 'baldhead' or 'citizen' (meaning a person without gang or criminal associations), is highly unusual. Crown Prosecutor Tim Brewer told me:

> At the time I was unaware of a precedent, and I'm not aware of one [other example] now. This guy [Crean] wasn't in the gang milieu, he wasn't in a gang, he was a bona fide member of the public – and it was a very big line for them to cross. . . . They didn't see themselves as the enemy of everybody – they saw themselves as the enemy of the police and the enemy of other gangs. This was stepping outside their ethos. (Tim Brewer, 2009, pers. comm.)

Indeed, most gang members limit their violence to other gangs or gang-associated people. Despite rhetoric about the pressing danger of gangs, ordinary people have very little to fear from gang members. Indeed, this finding is supported – though not often publicly conveyed

– by people who have had dealings with the gangs. One caution to this general rule relates to 'white power' or racist skinhead gangs. Because they foster an ideology of contempt and hate that stretches beyond gang realms, outsiders are often targeted for violence. Members of the skinhead gang the Fourth Reich, for example, have murdered three outsiders on the South Island's West Coast – two, in 1991 and 2003, were racially motivated, and one, in 1999, occurred because the victim was homosexual.

Cam Stokes, a former Detective Sergeant in charge of the police unit investigating outlaw motorcycle clubs in Auckland, told me that 'indirectly they cause harm to many people [via the drug trade and associated problems], but in terms of direct things, no, not a great deal of risk, unless you are involved somehow with them' (Cam Stokes, 2003, pers. comm.). Similarly, an undercover police officer who infiltrated gangs during two operations in the North Island told me, 'The only people who I think have got anything to fear from gangs are people who are intimately connected to them in some manner. They don't give a toss about the other bal' heads and squares. . . . I mean, you know, who are they to the gang? Nobody' (Anonymous, 2006, pers. comm.). Another undercover police officer, who wants to remain nameless, when asked by me if gangs were a threat to the wider public, said:

> No, no I don't think so. But if you have a debt with them or you have done something to one of their family members or you are exceptionally wealthy [and in their circles] and you flaunt that and they see you as an easy target, then yes you do. But your 'average Joe' blue collar worker who goes to work in a factory and goes home at night, no. (Anonymous, 2005, pers. comm.)

This is in contrast to the fears that many people have of gangs, which are, undoubtedly, a construct of media representations. This is not to say people have nothing to fear, but rather that the high levels of fear are unwarranted.

break and told by Justice Ellis that she could be detained for 7 days, the young woman still refused to take the stand and say anything more than 'I have nothing to say' (*New Zealand Herald*, 27 June 1995). The judge finally abandoned the trial, discharged the two accused and told the jury, 'You have witnessed, I suppose, a disaster' (*New Zealand Herald*, 27 June 1995).

In extreme circumstances, those giving testimony against a gang have been invited to enter the witness protection programme. This programme usually requires witnesses to be relocated and to assume another identity. Police refuse to comment on the programme publicly for fear that even general disclosures may put people at risk. But in 1997, then Police Minister John Luxton told Parliament that 89 witnesses had received formal protection between 1993 and 1997 (New Zealand Parliamentary Debates [NZPD], vol. 562, 1997: 210). Nonetheless, the proportion that was specifically gang-related remains hazy. It is clear, however, that these figures could have been much higher. For many people, adherence to the criminal code of silence or the thought of living in fear of a gang may have outweighed their desire to testify. In other words, it is quite understandable that on considering the potential consequences to reputation or self, many people chose not testify in a gang trial.

The System Responds

As suggested by Huff (1990), it is often catalytic events that spur political action against gangs; and this was the case following the Crean murder outlined earlier. Then Police Minister Jack Elder believed the guilty verdicts in that case saved the judiciary from destruction: 'I can't stress enough the importance of this decision. If there weren't convictions for this, I think the long-term future of the justice system was under some considerable threat' (*New Zealand Herald*, 18 October 1997).

Despite the convictions for the murder of Crean, the fact remains that he had been killed for agreeing to testify in a gang trial, and the high publicity given to the killing meant others in a similar position were certainly feeling nervous. Aware of the fear felt by witnesses in the wake of the killing, police decided to counter the problem by keeping the identity of witnesses in gang trials secret. The test case for witness anonymity was the trial of Nomads boss Dennis Hines for beating and stabbing an opposition gang member at the Mountain Rock Music Festival in 1994 (Gilbert, 2013: 177). While Hines was initially convicted, on 15 August 1997 the Court of Appeal ruled that secret witnesses were unlawful and Hines's conviction was quashed and a retrial ordered (*R v Hines* [1997] 3 NZLR 529). The ruling had serious ramifications for other prosecutions where police were reliant on secret witnesses.

In Christchurch during the mid-1990s, it was well known that the Road Knights Motorcycle Club, with the Harris brothers at its core, had been intimidating people in an effort to indemnify the club's members from successful prosecution. Just 4 days after the Court of Appeal ruling in relation to Hines, the Crown was forced to withdraw a case against seven members of the Road Knights because nearly all of the 27 witnesses declined to testify if their identities could not be masked (*The Press*, 20 August 1997). Two months previously, three members of the same gang had been released after witnesses made it 'patently clear' to police that they did not want to testify in court (*The Press*, 13 July 1997). Christchurch-based opposition Labour MP Mike Moore, who became a leading anti-gang lobbyist in the latter half of the 1990s, said, 'It's anarchy, it's organised crime and the bad guys are winning' (*New Zealand Herald*, 20 August 1997).

In the same city in September 1997, Max Shannon, a Black Power member, laughed as he walked from the District Court after charges stemming from a clash with Highway 61 were withdrawn due to witnesses refusing to testify without anonymity (*The Press*, 4 September 1997). Following this, Labour MP Phil Goff informed Parliament that since the Court of Appeal ruling overturning the Hines conviction, fifteen gang members had charges against them withdrawn and that the police said more annulments were likely (NZPD, vol. 563, 1997: 4340). Again, Mike Moore went public, saying, 'I believe hundreds of cases do not get to court or are lost in court because of the terror and intimidation exerted by gangs' (*New Zealand Herald*, 8 October 1997). Later, however, Highway 61 exacted their own justice on Shannon, murdering him as he left Rugby League training in 2000 (Gilbert, 2013: 240).

Although the ruling on the use of anonymous witnesses against Hines appeared to be a failure for police, ultimately the situation was remedied. Immediately after the Court of Appeal gave judgment in *Hines*, the government said it would seek to change the law to overturn the decision (New Zealand Law Commission, 1997: 9). The Evidence (Witness Anonymity) Amendment Act 1997 was quickly drafted to allow in serious criminal cases the use of secret witnesses, meaning a person could give evidence in court without disclosing their identity, even to the accused. The police, after allowing anonymity in the Hines case, had lost the defence appeal, but now they had a powerful new legal weapon. The use of secret witnesses in the Hines case had drawn significant publicity and highlighted an important legal issue. A sharp public and political response resulted in a significant change to trial law (NZPD, vol. 564, 1997: 4957–77).

The issues behind the law change were not insignificant (for a discussion on these see New Zealand Law Commission, 1997a: 2). The right to know the identity of one's accuser has been a foundation principle of justice systems throughout the democratic world, an openness that allows an accused to prepare a proper defence. To be accused of a crime and not know who your accuser is is what one newspaper reporter described as 'the stuff of Kafkaesque nightmares' (*Sunday Star-Times*, 26 October 1997). However, to allow criminals to escape justice due to intimidation robs people of their right to the protections offered by the law. We may have expected a charged debate around the clash of these fundamental legal principles, but instead the law was fast-tracked through Parliament, despite the concerns expressed by numerous academics and members of the legal fraternity (*Sunday Star-Times*, 26 October 1997). The new law went from its conception, following the Court of Appeal case ruling in favour of Hines in August 1997, to its successful final reading on 9 December 1997, in less than 4 months. It appears that robust debate, and the ordinary parliamentary process, was superseded by the political desire to take swift action. Tampering with important elements of the criminal justice system should not ordinarily be done in haste, but in this instance it was seen as necessary.

Conclusion

Since the 1990s it has become clear that the unique rules of the underworld allow gangs to take advantage of their sophisticated organisation and strength. Without recourse to the criminal justice system, the strong are able to dominate the weak. This ability rarely moves past those who deliberately choose, or by circumstances are forced, to play outside conventional rules. Most gang members are aware that the majority of people will simply go to the police if they are threatened in any way, and gang power tends to vanish at that point. When it comes to the prosecution of gang members, however, gang power and the authority of the state has collided. The murder of Christopher Crean has highlighted the fact that gang activity which threatens the legitimacy of state justice will not be tolerated.

REFERENCES

Decker, S. H., and Van Winkle, B. 1996. *Life in the Gang: Family, Friends and Violence*. Cambridge: Cambridge University Press.
Gilbert, J. 2013. *Patched: The History of Gangs in New Zealand*. Auckland: Auckland University Press.
Huff, C. R. 1990. 'Denial, Overreaction, and Misidentification: A Postscript on Public Policy', in C. R. Huff (Ed.), *Gangs in America*. Newbury Park, CA: Sage, pp. 310–17.
Newbold, G. 1989. 'Criminal Subcultures in New Zealand', in D. Novitz and B. Willmott (Eds), *Culture and Identity in New Zealand*. Wellington: GP Books, pp. 260–76.
New Zealand Law Commission. 1997. *Evidence Law: Witness Anonymity*. Wellington: New Zealand Law Commission.
New Zealand Police. 1975. *The Gang War in Christchurch*. Unpublished.
Transparency International. 2016. 'Corruption Perceptions Index 2016'. Accessed 21 May 2017. https://www.transparency.org/news/feature/corruption_perceptions_index_2016

Contributors

Andrew Becroft was appointed the Children's Commissioner for New Zealand in June 2016. Prior to that he was the Principal Youth Court Judge of New Zealand from 2001 to 2016 and a District Court Judge from 1996 to 2001. After graduating from Auckland University in 1981 with a BA/LLB (Honours) degree, he practised in Auckland until 1986 when he assisted with the establishment of the Māngere Community Law Centre, working there until 1993. He then worked as a criminal barrister in South Auckland until his appointment in 1996 to the District Court in Whanganui. He is a former council member of the Auckland District Law Society and the New Zealand Law Society.

Trevor Bradley is a Senior Lecturer at the Institute of Criminology, Victoria University of Wellington. He teaches courses on introductory criminology, policing and crime prevention. Alongside an interest in criminological theory, he has written on a variety of topics including youth crime and justice, restorative justice, crime prevention and community safety and public perceptions of crime and policing. He is currently engaged in an ongoing programme of research focused on plural policing in New Zealand.

Simone Bull is a Principal Adviser to the New Zealand Police Executive. A relative newcomer to the police, she has worked in Policy, Strategy, and District Operations roles at Police National Headquarters over the past 8 years. Her particular area of expertise – combining her Ngāti Porou whakapapa with her training and experience – is Māori in the criminal justice system. Simone holds an undergraduate degree from the University of Canterbury and postgraduate degrees from Victoria University of Wellington, including a PhD in Criminology.

Sarah Beggs Christofferson is a Lecturer at the University of Canterbury. She is a Registered Clinical Psychologist who has previously worked in the justice sector in clinical, advisory and research positions, and is currently Chair of the Institute of Criminal Justice and Forensic Psychology. Her current research interests centre on the treatment of those who have sexually offended, the assessment of risk and change across treatment for this population, and the prevention of sexual abuse.

Jeremy Finn is a barrister and solicitor of the High Court of New Zealand and Professor Emeritus of Law at the University of Canterbury. His main interests are in criminal law, criminal justice and law and natural disasters. He is co-author of *Criminal Procedure in New Zealand* (2nd ed., 2015) and an updating author for *Adams on Criminal Law*. He has also published widely in legal history, disaster law, criminal law, the law of contract and in other fields.

David Fisher is a journalist at the *New Zealand Herald* who has previously worked at the *Herald on Sunday*, *NZ Listener* and *Sunday Star-Times*, among other titles in New Zealand and the United Kingdom. He has reported abroad from Afghanistan to Zimbabwe, written *The Secret Life of Kim Dotcom* (2013), twice won Reporter of the Year at the Canon Media Awards, and been named Press Fellow to Wolfson College, University of Cambridge.

Chris Gallavin is the Deputy Pro Vice-Chancellor of the College of Humanities and Social Sciences and Professor of Law at Massey University. Formerly the Dean of the Faculty of Law and Head of School at the School of Law, University of Canterbury, his research areas are criminal law and the law of evidence. He has published extensively in the areas of domestic and international criminal justice and is a well known media commentator on the New Zealand criminal justice system. In 2015 he co-founded the New Zealand Public Interest Project with seven other legal, investigative and scientific experts to look at miscarriage of justice cases in New Zealand.

Jarrod Gilbert is a Senior Lecturer at the University of Canterbury and the lead researcher at Independent Research Solutions. He undertook an extensive ethnographic study into gangs which led to *Patched: The History of Gangs in New Zealand* (2013), an award-winning and best-selling book. He is a columnist for the *New Zealand Herald* and in 2015 won the Canon Media Award for Best Blog. He is currently working on a new book, *Murder: A New Zealand History*.

Randolph C. Grace is Professor of Psychology at the University of Canterbury. He received his PhD from the University of New Hampshire in 1995 and has published over 120 articles and book chapters in a variety of basic and applied research areas including choice behaviour and decision making, behavioural economics, methodology, comparative cognition, conditioning and learning, clinical/forensic psychology, tobacco control and neuropsychology. He is past President of the Society for the Quantitative Analyses of Behavior, a Fellow of the American Psychological Association, and a board member of End Smoking NZ.

Anthony McLean studied Psychology at Victoria University of Wellington, completing his PhD in the Experimental Analysis of Behaviour in 1983. He has worked as a scientist-practitioner for the New Zealand corrections system, and subsequently as a consultant in several capacities including research and treatment evaluation. He joined the University of Canterbury in 1988, where he currently teaches and researches in the areas of behaviour analysis and correctional psychology.

Sacha McMeeking (Ngāi Tahu) is the Head of Aotahi, the School of Māori and Indigenous Studies, and Co-Director of the Māui Lab at the University of Canterbury. Before moving into academia, she held a range of senior roles within Te Ao Māori, with responsibilities for policy and legislative reform and more recently incubating kaupapa Māori transformative innovation. Her research is in the area of Māori and indigenous peoples' strategies, approaches and entrepreneurship to advance self-determination and social change.

Greg Newbold is a Professor of Sociology at the University of Canterbury. He has written or co-written nine books and around 100 academic articles. Regarded as one of New Zealand's leading criminologists, he is frequently cited in the media and has served on a number of high-powered government policy-making boards and committees. Since 1989 he has served on the Board of Trustees of the Salisbury Street Foundation, a government-funded residential community centre established to assist the reintegration of long-term violent and sexual recidivists.

Sacha Norrie (Ngāi Pākehā) graduated with a BA/LLB from the University of Auckland before working as the Research Counsel to the Principal Youth Court Judge. She is currently a criminal and youth lawyer in South Auckland.

> Nō Aerana me Kōtirana ngā tīpuna
> He uri nō Ngāi Pākehā
> I tipu ake i te rohe o Tainui waka
> Ko Whaingaroa te ūkaipō

I te Whare Wānanga o Tāmaki Makaurau i riro i a ia āna tohu mō te ture me te tuhinga auaha. Ka haere atu ai ki te tari o te Kaiwhakawā Matua o Te Kōti Taiohi hei kairangahau mōna. Ināianei, kei te mahi ia hei rōia ki Manukau ki te Kōti ā-Rohe me te Kōti Taiohi.

John Price has been a member of the New Zealand Police for 30 years and has worked in a variety of operational and leadership roles both in General Duties and Criminal Investigations throughout the country. In 2005 he was deployed to Thailand for Operation Phuket as part of the response team after the South Asian Tsunami and undertook a Disaster Victim Identification Ante-Mortem Commander role. He was also the Operations Commander managing the Rescue and Search Phase of the 22 February 2011 Christchurch Earthquake. He took up the role of National Manager: Training and Development at the Royal NZ Police College in December 2012 before taking up his current position of District Commander: Canterbury Police District in June 2015. John holds a Bachelor of Education and a Diploma in Teaching.

Tara Ross is a Senior Lecturer and Head of the Journalism programme at the University of Canterbury. She was an award-winning senior reporter for *The Press* and the *Sunday Star-Times* newspapers, and has worked as a freelance writer and editor, and for community news publications. Of Pākehā and Tuvaluan descent, her research centres on journalism, diversity issues, ethnic minorities and Pacific media. She is a research fellow with the Macmillan Brown Centre for Pacific Studies and a research associate of the Pacific Media Centre at AUT University.

Mike Webb is the National Manager of New Zealand Police's Assurance Group. He has served in various senior roles at Police National Headquarters over the past decade and a half, including National Manager: Organisational Performance, Chief Legal Adviser, General Manager: Planning, Policy and Partnerships, and periods relieving as Deputy Commissioner: Resource Management and Deputy Chief Executive: Strategy. He holds postgraduate degrees in Law and Political Science from the University of Canterbury, and in Criminal Justice Policy from the London School of Economics.

Debra Wilson is an Associate Professor in the University of Canterbury School of Law, where she teaches courses in criminal justice, criminal law, sentencing law, and genetics/neuroscience and the criminal law. The author of *Genetics, Crime and Justice* (2015), she has also published articles in the areas of criminal law and medico-criminal law.

Heather Wolffram is a Senior Lecturer in Modern European History at the University of Canterbury, where she teaches a course on the history of crime, criminology and policing in modern Europe. While over the last decade she has published numerous articles and a book on the history of parapsychology in Germany, her current research is focused on the history of forensic psychology and forensic medicine in European and colonial contexts. Her book *Forensic Psychology in Germany: Witnessing Crime, 1880–1939* is forthcoming from Palgrave Macmillan.

Index

Entries in *italics* denote figures; entries in **bold** denote tables.

AC (Armed Constabulary), 78, 148
ACC (Accident Compensation Corporation), 106
accused persons: past conduct of, 159; rights of, 147; young, *see* young defendants
ADHD (attention deficit hyperactivity disorder), 20, 269
adversarial system of criminal justice, 142–3, 147
African Americans, 27, 308–9
age structure: of offenders, 52–3, 61; of police, 99, 100; of prison population, 131
aggravating and mitigating factors, 15, 192, 198
alcohol: arrestees under influence of, 100; and criminality, 21; illegal sale of, 82–3; and violent crime, 55–6
alcohol-fuelled disorder, 75, 77, 82, 100, 104
alternative action, 255–6
Ancient Greece, crime theory in, 3, 5–8
anger management, 113, 116
anomie, 24–5, 27, 117
antisocial behaviour, 21, 30, 211, 252, 271, 273
AOS (Armed Offenders Squad), 84–5, 98
APF (Armed Police Force), 77
Aramoana massacre, 58–9, 298
Arms Act 1983, 93, 155
Arohata women's prison, 120, 130
arrestees and detainees, rights of, 147
ARWCF (Auckland Region Women's Corrections Facility), 130–2
ASD (autistic spectrum disorder), 253, 269
ASOTP (Adult Sex Offender Treatment Programme), 133
ASRS (Automated Sexual Recidivism Scale), 212–13
assaults, data on, 56, *57*
attachment, 30
attention deficit disorder, 253; *see also* ADHD
Auckland Prison, *see* Paremoremo prison
Auckland South Corrections Facility, 131–2
Authorised Officers, 92

baby boom, 52
badges of rank, *95–6*
Bain, David, 59, 146, 151–5, 289
balance of probabilities, 149
balancing test, 158
Ball Report, 84
Barnett, Sam, 93, 121–3
Beccaria, Cesare, 11, 13–15
behaviourism, 22
Bell, William, 126, 200
Bennett, Betty, 86
Bentham, Jeremy, 11, 185–6
beyond reasonable doubt, 149–50
Bill of Rights Act, *see* NZBORA
biological positivism, 7, 16–21, 36
Black Power gang, 203, 322, 324–5, 328

blocked opportunities, 25–6
bloody code, 12, 15
bodgies and widgies, 50–1
bodies corporate, offences by, 167–9
body types, *see* somatotypes
Booth, Pat, 282, 287
borstal detention, 120–1, 124–5
Bow Street Runners, 72–3, 75
brain dysfunction, 20–1
breaking news, 300
Bulger, James, 308
Burdett, Susan, 288–9
burglary, 49–50, 52–3, 65, 102, *103*, 308
business elites, 309
Byers, Mark, 129

cannabis, synthetic, 264
care and protection status, 259
Carter, Rubin 'Hurricane,' 280
CCRCs (Criminal Cases Review Commission), 280, 291–3
CCTV, 53, 61
character evidence, 148, 161
Chicago School, 27–8
children: as defendants, 179–81; as offenders, 254; *see also* sexual offenders
Chisholm, Donna, 287–8
Christchurch Men's Prison, 132, 136
Christchurch Women's Prison, 130
CIB (Criminal Investigation Branch), 78–9, 85, 87–8, 94, 98, 320
CID (Criminal Investigation Department), 76
civil policing, 70, 77–8
class, and criminality, 26–7, 37
Classicism, 6, 11–15, 17, 23–4, 42
closest-court principle, 174–5
cocaine, 66
cognitive theories of criminality, 23
Cohen, Albert, 26–7
colonisation, consequences of, 228, 230, 232–6, 241, 246
commitment, inadequate, 30
common law, 142, 144
Communications Centres, 91
Communist Party, 82
community alternatives, *see* community corrections
community care, 125–6, 134
community consent to policing, 70, 73–4, 76, 78–9, 82–3
community corrections, 116, 134–6, 196–8; and categories of offences, 165, 167, 169; history in NZ of, 124–5, 130; statistics on, 201–2; for youth offenders, 260, 275
community detention, 135, 167, 193, 197, 201

335

INDEX

Community Justice/Iwi panels, 110
Community Magistrates, 171, 175
Community Probation Service, 135
community service, 125–6, 134
community work, 116, 126, 135; sentencing to, 193, 197; statistics on, 201–2; Comte, Auguste, 17, 24
concluding stories, 303
confessions, 153; false, 283–4; torture to elicit, 10
confidentiality, in law of evidence, 143, 145
confirmation bias, 285–6
conformity, 26, 30, 33, 36–7
consequentialist theories, 186
conspiracy, 165–6, 170
conspiracy theory, 286, 302
constables: in modern NZP, 92, 98; native, 79, 87; in pre-modern England, 71
Constitution Act 1852, 117–18
content creators, 297
contracts, in Classicism, 13–14
contributors, 1–2, 331–4
control and custody of offenders, 115–16
convictions: statistics on, 200–1; unsafe or wrongful, 158, 279–85, 291, 293
corporal punishment, 12, 15, 120
corrections system, functions of, 115–17; *see also* Department of Corrections
corrective training, 121, 260
corruption, 12–13, 79, 170, 285, 317
Corruption Perceptions Index, 317
counter-culture, 31
CPA (Criminal Procedure Act 2011), 163–77, 179, 182
CPK (Core Police Knowledge), 98
Crean, Christopher, 316, 324–5, 327, 329
Crewe murders, 281; *see also* Thomas, Arthur Allan
crime data: and crime news, 304, 307, 309; sources of, 46–50; women in, 67
crime news: effects of, 312–13; forms of, 300–4; and news values, 304–7; production of, 296–8; quality of, 299; understanding, 307–12
crime prevention, situational, 42
crime rates: fluctuations in, 20, 25, 46, 50, 68; socio-economic factors in, 28, 49
Crimes Act 1961, 123, 149, 155, 165–6, 169–70, 198
crime statistics, *see* crime data
crime victims: in cities, 52; media reporting of, 298, 307–8; and neurodisability, 269; reparation for, 110
criminal behaviour: drivers of, 7, 20, 228–30; psychological factors in, 21–3; psychologists specialising in, 221; social factors in, 26, 29, 37
criminalisation: and labelling theory, 33; selective process of, 38; criminal justice process, 115–17, 183
criminal justice system: costs of, 201, 228; media understanding of, 298; tikanga Māori in, 237–9, 242–5; young people's contact with, 252
criminal liability, 165
criminal opportunities, 36, 42
criminal personalities, 23
criminal procedure, minimum standards of, 147
Criminal Proceeds Recovery Act 2009, 53
criminal records, 188

criminal trials: changing venue of, 174–5; correct venue for, 182; in early modern Europe, 12; modes of, 163–4, 171, 173, 179; multiple charges or defendants, 172–4; overview of process, 164; reporting restrictions in, 298, 303; as status degradation, 33
criminogenic deficits, 218–19
criminogenic needs, 129, 216–17
criminological theory, 3, 5–7, 9, 41–2
criminology, extending boundaries of, 31, 38
critical criminology, 30–8, 229
CRNs (crimogenic needs), 129–30
Cross-over List, 259
crucifixion, 8
cultural awareness training, 240
cultural co-option, 239
cultural dislocation, 229, 262
cultural diversity, 27, 29
cultural heritage, 218
cybercrime, 102
CYF (Child, Youth and Family), 213, 253, 265
CYPTFA (Children, Young Persons and Their Families Act 1989): enactment of, 257–8; foundational pillars of, 254–6; and institutionalisation, 259–60; principles of, 261, 266–7; young defendants under, 178–81

Dallard, Bert, 120–1
Darwin, Charles, 16
death penalty: in early modern Europe, 12–13; in New Zealand, 118, 120–3, 198; Plato on, 8; reduction in, 15
decarceration movement, 34–5
degeneracy, 18, 42
delinquency, 27–9, 209, 211, 216
demonic possession, 9–10
Department of Corrections: civil action against, 302; managing offenders outside prison, 136, 200; prisons of, 130; risk assessments by, 211–12; tikanga Māori in, 239–40; treatment programmes provided by, 210, 219–23
desiderium ad cognitionis, 13
desisters, 251–2, 275
detectives: in Metropolitan Police, 76; in NZPF, 79; *see also* CIB
detention centres, 124–5
determinate sentence, 198–200
deterrence: and corrections system, 116; Plato on, 8
deterrence theory, 8, 14, 42, 186, 189
developing news, 300
deviance: double, 36; primary and secondary, 33–4
deviancy amplification, 34
differential association theory, 22, 29–30
discharge, with or without conviction, 192, 194
dishonesty crime, 50–4, *51*, 66–7, 97, 169, 202
District Commanders, 94, 108
District Court: children and young persons in, 179–81; trials held in, 170–4
diversion, in youth justice system, 101, 250, 254–5, 257, 260
DNA evidence, 53, 61, 283–4, 288–9, 293, 301
dog squad, 85

INDEX

domestic violence: data on, 47; feminist campaigning around, 38; intergenerational aspect of, 55; and jury trials, 177; media coverage of, 308; pro-active police involvement in, 58, 100, 105–6; and risk of offending, 228; and sentencing, 189–90
Doone, Peter, 107, 229
double jeopardy, 147
Dougherty, David, 287–8, 300
Doyle, Wayne, 319, 321
DRAOR (Dynamic Risk Assessment for Offender Re-entry), 214
drug crime: category of offences, 170; data on, 47, 64–6, 65
drug dealing: and gangs, 317–18; profitability of, 54, 61; sentencing for, 170, 199
drug use: among arrestees, 100; and burglary, 102; in prisons, 128; recreational, 26, 31, 65; as retreatism, 26; stimulant, 20
drunkenness, public, *see* alcohol-fuelled disorder
DTUs (Drug Treatment Units), 133, 222
Dudley, Earl of, 74
due process, 15
Durie, Mason, 240–1
Durkheim, Emile, 24–5, 27–8

ecology of crime, 27–8
ecstasy (MDMA), 66
editors, specialist, 297
education: and community sentences, 119, 121, 197; lack of, 26–7, 30, 216, 232, 251, 253, 265, 267–8; moral, 8; of police recruits, 97; and socio-economic disadvantage, 229
Effective Interventions, 130
Eichelbaum, Thomas, 291
electronic monitoring, 126, 135, 197, 301
Ellis, Peter, 289–91
emotions, managing, 220, 222
English policing, 70–3; *see also* London, policing in
Enlightenment, 11, 13
environmental degradation, 31–2, 38–41
epistemic considerations, 143
ESOs (Extended Supervision Order), 127, 134–6, 213
Ethnic Liaison Officers, 111
evidence: admission and exclusion of, 141–4, 146, 151, 151–6, 158, 161; contaminated, 284–5, 290; false, 282–3, 290; falsified, 285; improperly obtained, 146, 156–8; probative value of, 143–6, 159–61; right to not provide, 147–9; of secret witnesses, 327–9
Evidence Act 2006, 141, 143–5, 147, 154, 156, 159
execution, *see* death penalty
Executive Leadership Board (ELB), 94
exorcisms, 10–11
expert evidence, 142, 146, 284
eyewitnesses, misidentification by, 282–3, 293

fair trial, right to, 175, 233, 298
families, in youth justice system, 261, 263, 273–4; *see also* whānau
Family Court, 254, 259–60, 298
family intervention, 274

family violence, *see* domestic violence
family wellbeing, 240
FASD (foetal alcohol spectrum disorder), 253, 265, 269, 288–9
fear of crime, 299, 309, 313
female crime, *see* gender differences in crime
feminism and criminology, 31, 35–8, 63, 67–8
FGCs (Family Group Conferences): family issues in, 274; and labelling theory, 34; and oral communication skills, 269–70; and tikanga Māori, 238; in youth justice system, 250, 254–6, 261, 275
Fielding, Henry and John, 72–3
filming, covert, 157
financial success, cultural goal of, 26
fines, 134, 193, 195–6
fingerprints, 79–80, 103, 284–5
Finlay, Martyn, 125
Fisher, David, 301–3, 305–6, 310–11
Fourth Reich gang, 326
free will, 11, 14–15, 17, 23, 42
FReMO (Framework for the Reduction of Māori Offending), 239

gangs: bikie, *see* outlaw motorcycle clubs; campaigns against, 104; and 'citizens,' 325–6; and girl offenders, 271; history of in NZ, 54–5, 316; intimidation of witnesses, 323–5, 327–9; juvenile, 26; in prisons, 132, 203–4; rivalry between, 175, 289; skinhead, 326; as sub-cultures, 26; tattoos associated with, 35; 'taxing' by, 316–23
gender, and convictions, 201
gender blindness, 35, 38
gender differences in crime, 35–7, 66–8
gender-informed interventions, 220
genetics, 18–20, 22, 42
'getting tough on crime,' 5–6
gold rushes, 70, 77–8
Good, Daniel, 75
'Good Lives Model,' 218–19
Gotingco, Blessie, 136, 301–3
Governor-General, and prerogative of mercy, 282, 291–2
GPS bracelets, 133
green criminology, 39–40
Grey, George, 76–7
Guildford Four, 280, 291
guilty intent, 15
gun control, 58
Guy, Scott, 146, 158

habitual criminals declaration, 121
Hanan, Ralph, 123, 125
Haora, Bradley, 48
hapū, 229, 234, 243, 258, 262–3, 265, 272, 276
hara, 243–4
hard labour, 77, 118, 121
Hawke's Bay Prison, 239
Head Hunters, 305, 319–22
He Ara Hou, 129
hearsay evidence, 144, 146

INDEX

Hells Angels, 320
heroin, 65–6
He Whaipānga Hou, 230
High Court: children and young persons in, 179–81; and PPOs, 136; trials held in, 171–4
Highway 61 gang, 289, 328
Hines, Dennis, 318, 327–9
hippies, 65
Hirschi, Travis, 30
Hobbes, Thomas, 13–14
Hobson, William, 87
home detention, 116, 126, 134–5, 193, 197–8; statistics on, 201–3
homicides: and category of offence, 170; children accused of, 180; data on, 47, 58; in prison, 128, 132; related to domestic violence, 38; *see also* manslaughter; murder
Hood, Lynley, 291
housing, overcrowded, 229, 265
human rights violations, 38
Hume, Arthur, 118–19, 136

imprisonment, *see* prison sentences
incapacitation theories, 187, 189
indeterminate sentences, 119, 121, 199–200, 204
individual rights, 13–14
infanticides, 58, 170, 243
informants, 104, 143, 283
infringement offences, 167–8, 180
inherited criminality, 19, 42
innocence, presumption of, 147–8, 150, 158, 279–80
Innocence Project, 293
innocent prisoner's dilemma, 284
innovation, 24, 26
insanity defence, 15, 185
Intensive Monitoring Group, 267
intensive supervision, 135, 167, 193, 197, 201–2
intergenerational issues, 55, 236, 240, 245, 273
international law, 170
international treaties and conventions, 171
interrogation, coercive, 286
Invercargill Prison, 131–2
investigative stories, 303
investigator bias, 285–6
IOM (Integrated Offender Management), 129–30
IPCA (Independent Police Conduct Authority), 107, 231
IQ (intelligence quotient), 22
Irish Constabulary, 76–7
ISR (Integrated Safety Response), 106
iwi, 229, 234, 237, 243, 258, 263, 265, 272, 276
Iwi Liaison Officers, 98, 111

Jacobs, Gillies, 323
Jacobs, Patricia, 19
jails, in colonial period, 118; *see also* prisons
journalists, *see* reporters
judge-alone trial, 163, 175–8
judges: and law of evidence, 141–3; symbolism of, 12
judicial oath, 117
Juries Act 1981, 174, 176

jury: intimidation or interference with, 177–8; majority needed in, 176; role of, 142–3
jury trial, 163; children and young people as defendants, 179–81; and multiple charges or defendants, 172–4; right to elect, 169, 171–2, 176–7, 179
justice: perverting, 323; right to, 147
Justices of the Peace, 71

Kant, Immanuel, 187
kaumātua, 54, 109, 238, 240, 262–3
Kia Mārama, 133, 215, 222
King Cobras, 319
Kowhiritanga, 220–1, 223
Kretschmer, Ernst, 18
kuia, 238, 240, 262

labelling theory, 32–5, 38–9, 252
Laurenson, Tyrone, 87
lawyers: confidential discussions with, 143; right to consult, 150
lay advocates, 262–3
lead poisoning, 7
learning disabilities, 253, 269
learning theories of criminality, 22, 29
legal representation, poor, 286–7
legitimacy of the state, 117
Lemert, Edwin, 33
LES (Law Enforcement System), 47
lex talionis, 10
liberty, right to, 147
life imprisonment, 199–200; for drug offences, 66; non-parole period for, 64, 131
lockup, hours of, 123, 130
Lombroso, Cesare, 17–18, 42
London, policing in, 71–6, 79–80
long service and good conduct medals, 98
LSD, 64–6
Lyon, Mark, 305–6, 322

Macdonald, Ewen, 146, 158–61
Mahuika, Apirana, 109
maleness, and crime, 19, 37; *see also* gender
mana, 243, 263
manslaughter: category of offence, 170; children and young people charged with, 179–81, 254, 256; life sentence for, 199; reducing charge to, 149
Māori Advisory Boards, 111
Māori communities: disintegration of, 234–5; policing in, 70, 76–7, 107–11, 231; pre-European social control in, 243; and youth justice system, 261
Māori Focus Forum, 237
Māori identity, 229–30, 239
Māori land, seizures of, 78, 233–5
Māori language, *see* te reo Māori
Māori leadership, 240–1
Māori people: in criminal justice system, 201–2, 225–9, 232, 235–6, 242, 245–6, *see also* Māori prisoners; drug use by, 65; government services for, 240–1; socio-economic disadvantage of,

228–32, 236, 245–6; urban population of, 51, 54; in youth justice system, 253, 257–8, 262, 272, 276
Māori police: first, 78–9; on leadership boards, 94; numbers of, 86–7, 235–7; problem-solving partnerships with community, 109; recruiting, 84, 88, 236, 245
Māori prisoners, 131, 133, 203–4, 226–7, 239–40
Māori Prisoners Act 1880, 233
Māori social movements, 31
Māori women, 86–7, 94, 226
marae: alternatives to court processes on, 178, 238–9; community corrections and, 126; Youth Court on, *see* Rangatahi Courts
marijuana, 33, 54, 64–6
marriage, rape within, 63
mass murder, 58–9
Matthews, Charles, 119–20
maximum penalty: and categories of offences, 165–7, 169, 173; and PCWs, 110; principles of imposing, 190; for rape, 63–4, 127; and right to jury trial, 176; and 'three strikes' rule, 199; and young defendants, 179
Mayne, Richard, 76
McCann, Madeleine, 307
McKinnel, Tim, 288–9
Media, *see* news media
mental capacity, diminished, 284
mental health incidents, 101, *102*
mercy, royal prerogative of, 292
Merton, Robert King, 25–6, 37
methamphetamine: in case studies, 264–5, 305–6; media coverage of, 307; profitability of, 54; substitutes for, 20; use of, 66
Metropolitan Police, *see* London, policing in
MFUs (Māori Focus Units), 133, 239
Middle Ages, crime theory in, 6, 9–10, 25
Milton Prison, 132
Minister of Police, 93
Ministry of Justice, data from, 48–9
MIRP (Medium Intensity Rehabilitation Programme), 220–1, 223
miscarriages of justice, 279–80; addressing, 291–4; common factors in, 282–7; NZ examples of, 281, 287–91
Mongrel Mob, 264, 288–9, 318–19, 322–4
moral entrepreneurs, 33
moral panics, 291, 309
moral responsibility, 191
morphine, 65
Mothers and Babies Units, 134
motivational interviewing, 221
Mt Eden Prison, 85, 119, 121, 123–4, 131–2, 288
murder: children and young persons accused of, 179–80; death penalty for, 121–3; incitement to commit, 170; non-parole period, 125, 127; in prisons, 128; rates of, 58–9; sentencing for, 64, 131, 191, 199–200; use of term, 184–5
muru, 243–4

name suppression, 298
National Land Transport Fund, 101, 112
Native Land Court, 233–4

NCAR (North Carolina Assessment of Juvenile Risk), 213
Neo-classical compromise, 15–16, 21
Neo-liberalism, 24
neurodisability, 253, 265, 269–70, 275–6
neurotransmitters, 20–1
news media: coverage of crime, 296–9, 301, 303–4, 307–9, *see also* crime news; preventing injustices, 280, 282, 287–8, 299–300; reception of, 313; reporting on gangs, 326; sources for, 298, 300, 309, 312; *see also* reporters
New South Wales, colonial policing in, 76
newsrooms, 296–9
news values, 304
New Zealand: contemporary policing in, 70, 91, 112–13, *see also* NZP; economy of, 52; environment degradation in, 40–1; history of corrections in, 117–30, *see also* Department of Corrections; history of policing in, 76–89; social movements in, 31; surveillance and intelligence in, 82
New Zealand prisons: current status of, 130–4; history of, 118–30
Ngawha Prison, 132
noa, 243
Nomads gang, 318, 327
non-epistemic considerations, 143
non-parole periods, 64, 123, 125–7, 131, 199–200
non-violent responses, 39
NPTs (Neighbourhood Policing Teams), 98, 104–5
NZ-ADUM (New Zealand Arrestee Drug Use Monitoring), 100
NZBORA (New Zealand Bill of Rights Act 1990), 141, 145–8, 150–1, 155–7, 177
NZCF (New Zealand Constabulary Force), 78
NZP (New Zealand Police): articles of, 109; as corruption-free, 317; daily activities of, 100–2, **101**; demography of, 84–9, 98–100, *99*, 236–7; expenses, **112**; foundation of, 83; media coverage of, 297; organisation of, 91–4; predecessors of, *see* NZCF; NZPF; ranks of, 94–6; recruiting to, 97–8; regional distribution of staff, **92**; specialist sections of, 84–5; uniform of, *95*
NZPF (New Zealand Police Force), 78–9, 81–3
NZPIP (New Zealand Public Interest Project), 293

O'Brien, Bill, 84
OC (oleoresin capsicum), *95*
offence process approach, 217, 219, 221–2
offences: categories of, 164–72; parties to, 165–6
OLC (oral language and communication difficulties), 269–70
operational independence, 93
Operation Austin, 108–9
opinion evidence, 146
ordeal, trial by, 10
order to come up for sentence, 195
organised criminal groups, 155, 177
outlaw motorcycle clubs, 50, 316, 319–22, 326, 328

Pacific Liaison Officers, 111
paramilitary policing, 70, 77–8

INDEX

Paremoremo prison, 124, 132–3
Parihaka, 233, 243–4
Park, Robert, 27–8
parole, eligibility for, 124–5, 127
parolees, 126, 131
party liability, 170
Pasifika Courts, 178, 262
Pasifika gangs, 55
Pasifika people: conviction rates, 201; sentencing of, 202; and violent crime, 54–5; in youth justice system, 258
Pasifika police, 84, 87–8
Pasifika prisoners, 133, 203–4
Patterson, Wayne, 310–11
PCWs (pre-charge warnings), 110, 231
PEACE interrogation method, 286
peacemaking criminology, 39
Peel, Robert, 73–4, 76
peer influence, 29, 213, 229, 251
penal code, 15
periodic detention, 124–6, 134
perjury, 283, 304
persisters, 252, 275
PFUs (Pacific Focus Units), 133
Phillipstown, 104
Plato, 7–8
plea bargaining, 284, 303–4
PNHQ (Police National Headquarters), 84, 92, 103, 107, 111
Police Commissioner, 93, 107, 111, 237
police data, 46–9
police helicopters, 61
police interviewing procedures, 286, 288
police unions, 94, 289
policing: community involvement in, 74; cost of, 112–13; levels of activity, 47; pillars of, 91, 105–7; systemic bias against Māori in, 230–1
Policing Act 2008, 71, 93–4, 97, 107
policing districts, 92
'Policing Excellence' package, 105, 107
politicised research agenda, 32
Pora, Teina, 158, 288–9, 292, 300
positivist criminology, 6, 16–17, 31–2
potentially overriding rules, 164, 172–8
poverty, and crime, 28, 37, 52, 60, 228–9, 272
power-control theory, 37
PPO (Public Protection Order), 136
predestined actor model, 17
prejudice, in law of evidence, 144–5, 154, 159–61
Pre-Sentence Report, 198
preventive detention, 200; history of, 121, 126–7; non-parole period for, 131; and violent crime, 64
primary offence, 49, 128, 131
prisoners: security classes of, 132–3; status and rights of, 120, 123–5, 127–8; transporting, 92
prison escapes, 80, 85, 116, 123, 128, 133
prison farms, 120, 132, 137
prison population: demographics of, 203, 226–7; size of, 5, 34–5, 64, 118, 125–8, 130–1, 137, 204
prisons, functions of, 115–16; *see also* New Zealand prisons

prison sentences: costs of, 201; imposing, 198–9; lengthening of, 64, 128, 137; replacing corporal punishment, 15; statistics on, 201, 203–4; for young offenders, 260
private prisons, 131–2
privilege, in law of evidence, 143
Privy Council (UK), 152, 289, 292
probation, 116, 119, 121, 134; in determinate sentences, 199; *see also* supervision
probation officers, 134, 196–8, 214
Proceeds of Crime Act 1991, 53
production journalists, 297
proof: burden of, 147–8, 279, 293; standard of, 149–50
propensity evidence, 144, 146, 159–60
property crimes: and Māori, 66; rates of, 49–50, 53, 55; reporting of, 308; *see also* burglary; robberies
proportionality, principle of, 11, 13
prostitution, 71, 82–3
protective custody, 128
provocation, defence of, 149
psychological positivism, 21–3
psychological treatment of offenders, 209–10; computerised, 129; intensity of, 210–11; measuring impact, 214–15; New Zealand programmes, 219–23; targets, 216–17
Pūao-Te-Ata-Tū report, 258, 276
public safety, 93, 219, 255, 260
public sector, and NZP, 93
punishment: consequences of, 188; contrary justifications of, 42; and corrections system, 116; in early modern Europe, 12; forms and justifications of, 8; as iatrogenic, 39; theories of, 14–15, 185–7, 204; *see also* corporal punishment
punishment diets, 125

racism, in crime reporting, 308–9
racist gangs, 326
racist language, 231
Rainbow Warrior, 86
Rangatahi Courts, 178, 238, 261–3, 267, 272, 276
Rangipo prison farm, 132
rape: data on, 62, 63; feminist campaigning around, 38, 61, 63; by gang members, 323; maximum penalty for, 64, 127; media reporting on, 287–8, 300; use of term, 61
rape culture, 297
Ratcliffe Highway murders, 73–4
Ratima, Raymond, 299
rational choice perspective, 6, 11–14, 17, 23, 42, 186
rationality, impaired, 15
reason and logic, and law of evidence, 142–3, 145
recidivism: programmes for reducing, 239–40; and punishment, 15, 127, 187; rates of, 125, 129–30; risk of, 198, 210–13, 215–16; of young offenders, 274
reconciliatory processes, 39
reform, Plato on, 8
reformative detention, 119–21
Reformative Recreation, 121–3
rehabilitation: and corrections system, 116; recent initiatives in, 129–30

INDEX

rehabilitation programmes, 42, 196–7, 271
rehabilitation theory, 187, 189
Reid Technique, 286
release-to-work schemes, 124
relevance, in law of evidence, 144–6, 154, 158, 160
remand prisoners, 124, 132
remission, 64, 125, 127, 131
reoffending, *see* recidivism
reparation, 110, 188, 193, 196–7, 201, 257
repeat offenders, 119, 166
reported crime, categories of, 47
reporters: access to courts, 299, 303; and confidentiality, 143; and crime news, 297–8, 300; investigative work by, 287, 291, 303–4; news values of, 304
Resource Management Act 1991, 168
responsiveness strategies, 237
responsivity, 217–19
restitution, 8, 31
restorative justice, 39, 130, 189–91, 238, 246
retreatism, 26
retribution, and corrections system, 116–17
retributionist theory, 187, 189–90
retroactive penalties, 147
Rewa, Malcolm, 289
Rimutaka Prison, 124, 133
risk assessments, 210, 213–15, 222, 331
risk factors: dynamic, 214–15, 220; static, 211, 213–16
risk-needs-responsivity (Andrews and Bonta) model, 210, 218–19, 223
Ritalin, 20
RNZPC (Royal New Zealand Police College), 84, 91–2, 97, 109
Road Knights Motorcycle Club, 328
road policing, 100; *see also* traffic offences
roads, unsafe, 111
road user levies, 112–13
robberies: as category, 47; data on, 60, 61; and poverty, 16, 52
Robertson, Tony, 136, 301–3
Robson, John, 123, 125
RoC*RoI, 211–12, 220
Rolleston Prison, 133
routine activities theory, 42

'Safer Communities Together,' 71, 109
schools, *see* education
SCUs (Self-Care Unit), 133–4
search warrants, 151, 155–6
secondary parties, 165
secret witnesses, 327–9
Security Intelligence Service, 82
security systems, 52–3, 60–1
sedition, 82
self-control, 209, 220, 251
self-esteem, low, 216–17, 262
self-identity, 262
self-incrimination, protection against, 146–7
self-reports: crime data, 49, 66; of criminal activity, 231–2; of offender risk, 215–16
Senior Leadership Team, 94
Sensible Sentencing Trust, 302

sentencing, 183; aggravating and mitigating factors, 192; costs of, 201; and gender, 66; principles of, 190–1; purposes of, 188–90, 204; starting point, 198; statistics on, 200–4; types of, 192–200; *see also* community corrections; prison sentences
Sentencing Act 2002, 188, 190, 192–3, 195–6, 199, 204
Sentencing Guidelines, 198
sex roles, 35–6
sexual abuse, and young female offenders, 271
sexual assault, data on, 56, 61–2
sexual offenders: against children, 121, 222; ESOs for, 127; police as, 108–9; risk assessment for, 212, 215; treatment of, 116, 133; young, 259
sexual violation: rates of, 271; use of term, 61–2
sexual violence, 38, 47, 309; *see also* rape
Shannon, Max, 328
Sheldon, William, 18
silence, right to, 147
sly-grogging, *see* alcohol, illegal sale of
Smith, Nick, 128
SMP (Short Motivational Programme), 221
social contract, 11, 13–14
social control theory, 30, 37
social disadvantage, 229, 241–2
social disorganisation, 27–9
social learning theory, 22, 217
social media, 298, 313
sociological positivism, 23–9
somatotypes, 18
SPA (Summary Proceedings Act 1957), 155, 157
Spring Hill Prison, 132
SRBA (stab-resistant body armour), 95
SRP (Short Rehabilitation Programme), 220–1
status degradation ceremonies, 33
status frustration, 27, 30
stigmata, biological, 17–18, 42
stigmatization, social, 33–5, 308
Stokes, Cam, 319, 321, 326
strengths-based approach, 218–19, 241
structural inequalities, 229, 232, 242, 245
STURP (Special Treatment Unit Rehabilitation Programme), 133
STUs (Special Treatment Units), 133, 221–2
sub-cultures, 26–7
sub judice, 303, 311
substance abuse, treatment for, 220; *see also* alcohol; drug use
suicides: assisted, 58; deaths from, 101; in prison, 128; threats and attempts, *102*
Summary Offences Act 1981, 167, 180
super male syndrome, 19
supervision: as community correction, 134–5, 193, 196; costs of, 201; *see also* intensive supervision
survival curves, 213, *214*
Sutherland, Edwin, 29
systemic bias, 228–30, 232, 236, 246

tapu, 243
tasers, 95, 112
tattoos, 35

INDEX

Taumaunu, Heemi, 261
'taxing', *see* gangs, 'taxing' by
TBI (traumatic brain injury), 253, 269
Te Awa, 'Choc,' 320–1
teenagers, *see* young persons
Te Kooti Rangatahi, *see* Rangatahi Courts
Te Piriti, 133, 222
te reo Māori, 234, 238–9, 246–7, 262, 276
theology, 9
theory, use of term, 6–7
therapeutic jurisprudence, 266
thief-takers, 72–3
thinking errors, 23
Thomas, Arthur Allan, 158, 281–2, 287, 292, 300
Thomson, David, 125
Thorp, Thomas, 291
'three strikes' law, 64, 127, 199
tikanga Māori, 226, 237–40, 243–5, 262, 272
traffic infringement notices, 113
traffic offences, 47, 100, 180, 202–3, 254, 256
trapped lifestyles, 227, 235
treason, 170, 198
Treaty of Waitangi, 31, 107–9
Trentham School, 84
Tunbridge, John, 79
tunnel vision, 285
Turning of the Tide Strategy, 237
twin studies, 19
Twitter, crime news on, 309

underworld justice, 316, 319–20, 329
unemployment: and crime, 37, 52–3; and robbery, 60; and violent crime, 55–6
unlawful sexual connection, 61–2
unreasonable search and seizure, 147, 150–1, 155, 157
urbanisation, and crime, 25, 27, 51–2
Urewera 11 case, 146, 155–7

victim empathy, 222, 253
Victim Impact Statement, 198
victimisation data, 49
victims, *see also* crime victims
violent crime, 55; and lead poisoning, 7; Māori imprisoned for, 131; media reporting of, 307; penalties for, 63–4; rates of, 54–63, 55, 126–8; sentencing for, 200, 202–3; and sexual abuse, 271; women as perpetrators, 67–8; and working-class boys, 37
Vitali, Petar, 320–2
vitric blue, 95
VPUs (Violence Prevention Unit), 133
VRS (Violence Risk Scale), 214–16

wages, of police, 94, 96–7
Waikeria Prison, 132, 321
Waikune prison farm, 120, 132
wartime, policing in, 81–4
watchmen, 71–3, 75
Watson, Cushla, 86
Weatherston, Clayton, 148–9

whakataukī, 109, *111*, 275
whānau: in Family Group Conferences, 238; relationship to offenders, 229, 240, 244–5; representation in Youth court, 263
whanaungatanga, 243
Whānau Ora, 240–2
wing patrons, 97
witness protection programme, 324, 327
women: as criminals, *see* gender differences in crime; women offenders; as police officers, 83–8, 94, 99; as victims of male violence, 35, 38; young, 68, 82, 253, 271
women offenders: sentencing of, 66, 202; theories of, 36; treatment programmes for, 220–1
women prisoners, 131, 134, 203, 226
Women's Christian Temperance Union, 83
women's liberation, 35–6
women's prisons, 120, 130
women's refuges, 58
work, for prisoners, 128, 130
work camps, 119
working class, 27, 37, 54
Workman, Kim, 129
wrongful convictions, 158, 279–80, 282–5, 293

YLS-CMI (Youth Level of Service – Case Management Inventory), 213
young defendants, 164, 178–82
young persons: brain development of, 20, 250–1, 269, 275; as defendants, 179–81; delinquency in, 209; risk of reoffending, 211, 213; socio-economically disadvantaged, 232; *see also* children; youth offenders
Youth Advocates, 261, 263
Youth Aid, 98, 107, 179, 260
Youth Court: case studies of, 264–5; crossover with Family Court, 259; diversion in, 255; education officers in, 267–8; and FGCs, 255–6; language skills and, 269–70; Māori at, 253, 272; specialist judges for, 260; as therapeutic model, 266–7; as venue for cases, 178–82
Youth Court orders, 181, 256–7
youth crime, Cohen on, 26
youth culture, 31, 50, 54, 64
Youth Drug Court, 267
youth forensic services, 270
youth justice, principles of, 255, 266
youth justice system, 250; challenges for, 267–76; FGCs in, 34; girls in, 271; marae-based processes in, 238; pre-CYPTFA, 257; *see also* Youth Court
youth offenders, 254; discharge without conviction, 194; female, 270–1; institutionalisation of, 257, 259–60; and labelling theory, 34, 251–3; sentencing, 202; thought processes of, 217–18; violent backgrounds of, 273–4
youth prison, 253, 257, 259, 272

zemiology, 38
zonal hypothesis, 28
zone of transition, 28–9